Other resources from O'Reilly

Related titles

VoIP Hacks

Network Security Hacks™

Windows XP Hacks™

Nokia Smartphone Hacks™

Palm and Treo Hacks™

Blackberry Hacks™

Skype Hacks™

Windows XP Unwired

Linux Unwired

802.11 Wireless Networks: The Definitive Guide

Hacks Series Home

hacks.oreilly.com is a community site for developers and power users of all stripes. Readers learn from each other as they share their favorite tips and tools for Mac OS X, Linux, Google, Windows XP, and more.

oreilly.com

oreilly.com is more than a complete catalog of O'Reilly books. You'll also find links to news, events, articles, weblogs, sample chapters, and code examples.

O'REILLY NETWORK

oreillynet.com is the essential portal for developers interested in open and emerging technologies, including new platforms, programming languages, and operating systems.

Conferences

O'Reilly brings diverse innovators together to nurture the ideas that spark revolutionary industries. We specialize in documenting the latest tools and systems, translating the innovator's knowledge into useful skills for those in the trenches. Visit *conferences.oreilly.com* for our upcoming events.

O'REILLY NETWORK Safari Bookshelf

Safari Bookshelf (*safari.oreilly.com*) is the premier online reference library for programmers and IT professionals. Conduct searches across more than 1,000 books. Subscribers can zero in on answers to time-critical questions in a matter of seconds. Read the books on your Bookshelf from cover to cover or simply flip to the page you need. Try it today for free.

SECOND EDITION

WIRELESS HACKS™

Rob Flickenger and Roger Weeks

O'REILLY®

Beijing · Cambridge · Farnham · Köln · Paris · Sebastopol · Taipei · Tokyo

Wireless Hacks™, Second Edition

by Rob Flickenger and Roger Weeks

Published by O'Reilly Media, Inc., 1005 Gravenstein Highway North, Sebastopol, CA 95472.

O'Reilly Media, Inc. books may be purchased for educational, business, or sales promotional use. Online editions are also available for most titles (*safari.oreilly.com*). For more information, contact our corporate/institutional sales department: (800) 998-9938 or *corporate@oreilly.com*.

Editor:	Brian Sawyer	**Production Editor:**	Philip Dangler
Series Editor:	Rael Dornfest	**Cover Designer:**	Ellie Volckhausen
Executive Editor:	Dale Dougherty	**Interior Designer:**	David Futato

Printing History:

September 2003:	First Edition.
November 2005:	Second Edition.

 This book uses RepKover,™ a durable and flexible lay-flat binding.

ISBN: 0-596-10144-9
ISBN13: 978-0-596-10144-2
[M]   [1/07]

Contents

Chapter 4. Hardware Hacks

Foreword

It's a pleasure to watch a book mature. The first edition of *Wireless Hacks* gave me a warm feeling inside, like holding my hands over the vacuum tube in a pre-transistor radio. The glow of this book illuminated Rob Flickenger's intense interest in spreading knowledge of cool stuff in order to spread more knowledge about the world in general.

This second edition, which brings the practical deployer (building networks is part of his day job) and fellow wireless hacker Roger Weeks onboard, feels more like a device constructed by the love child of The Professor from *Gilligan's Island* and Mr. Spock: it beeps, it twitters, there are coconut shreds, and then, surprisingly, it produces a glass of tea out of thin air or transports several people to geosynchronous orbit.

The book has grown up, just a little, which makes it no less charming or useful. *Wireless Hacks* isn't about breaking technology to serve your needs. Rather, it's about bending it. So much of today's wireless networking hardware, software, and firmware has been carefully tailored to suit what the manufacturer or service provider feels you are entitled to do with it. But we own the tech and, for unlicensed networks, we own the airwaves. *Wireless Hacks* stands up, raises its hand, and says, "Excuse me, I don't buy into your world view."

A great number of the tips and some of the lengthy *hacks* in the book should become standard operating procedure at companies that use wireless tech and want to increase its value for their use. Being able to more broadly use Bluetooth beyond limited, support purposes; extending range of equipment legally without using expensive proprietary or identically branded devices; or having the flexibility to crack open the hardware or software to fiddle with its innards and tweak to one's liking is less about hacking and more about just making things work.

Wireless Hacks could as easily have been titled *It's My Equipment, Damnit*, and perhaps those of you reading the foreword to find out whether this book is for you would find that title more comforting. While I was raised with a soldering iron in one hand and a diode in the other, self-modding my 1979-era OSI C1P 6502-based computer, I guarantee that while the spirit pervades this book, molten metal isn't a necessity—but it is an option—for carrying out most of the tasks in the book.

Rob and Roger and their legion of colleagues contributing tips are trying to make the world smaller by extending signals further. This book is another step in the right direction for a small, wireless world.

—*Glenn Fleishman*
August 28, 2005, Seattle, WA

Credits

About the Authors

Rob Flickenger has been a professional systems administrator for more than ten years, and an all-around hacker for as long as he can remember. Rob enjoys spreading the good word of open networks, open standards, and ubiquitous wireless networking. His current professional project is Metrix Communication LLC, which provides wireless hardware and software that embodies the same open source principles he rants about in his books. Rob also works with the U.N. and various international organizations to bring these ideas to places where communications infrastructure is badly needed. He hopes that all of this effort is contributing toward the ultimate goal of infinite bandwidth everywhere for free. He is the author of two other O'Reilly books: *Linux Server Hacks* and *Building Wireless Community Networks*, which is now in its second edition.

Roger Weeks has over a decade of experience in systems and network administration. He's been building Linux systems at home and in the enterprise since 1998, and recommends that you check out *http://freenetworks.org* if you're interested in community wireless. He is currently the senior network administrator for Mendocino Community Network, a small ISP in coastal northern California. MCN is owned by the local school district, and puts their profits back into the local schools. Roger is a coauthor of another O'Reilly book, *Linux Unwired*.

Contributors

The following people contributed their hacks, writing, and inspiration to this book:

- Richard Baguley is a freelance journalist who writes about computers, technology, and video for publications such as *PC World*, *Wired*, and camcorderinfo.com. He lives in the San Francisco Bay area with his wife Kath and a French Bulldog called Fester. His home is shared with an ever-changing variety of foster cats who like nothing better than to gnaw on any cables that he leaves lying around, which explains why he likes wireless networking so much.

- Marcel Bilal is a computer scientist, with a focus on Wireless LAN technologies. He lives in Berlin, Germany and works for an IT-service provider (IT-Dienstleistungszentrum Berlin) as a systems admin. You can find him at *http://aws.netzfund.de* or *marcel_bilal@web.de*.

- James Duncan Davidson is a freelance author, software developer, and consultant focusing on Mac OS X and related technologies. He is the author of *Running Mac OS X Panther*, coauthor (with Rael Dornfest) of *Mac OS X Panther Hacks*, coauthor (with Apple Computer, Inc) of *Learning Cocoa with Objective-C*, and coauthor (with Michael Beam) of *Cocoa in a Nutshell*, all published by O'Reilly Media. Duncan is also a contributor to the O'Reilly Network (*http://www.oreillynet.com*), as well as publisher of his own web site, x180 (*http://x180.net/*). In what sometimes seems like a previous life, Duncan created the widely used Apache Tomcat and Apache Ant and was instrumental in their donation to the Apache Software Foundation by Sun Microsystems. He was also the specification lead and author of two versions of the Java Servlet API and two versions of the Java API for XML Processing (JAXP).

- Schuyler Erle (*http://nocat.net*) hacks on free software and agitates for the cause of community networking. Schuyler is also chief architect of NoCatAuth, a leading open source captive portal application.

- Michael Erskine (*http://www.freeantennas.com*) works at kaballero.com.

- Preston Gralla is the author of more than 30 books about computers and the Internet, including *Windows XP Hacks*, *Internet Annoyances*, and *Windows XP Power Hound*. He's been writing about technology since the dawn of the PC, was a founding editor of both PC Week and PC/Computing, an executive editor of ZDNet and CNet, and has contributed to dozens of publications, including PC Magazine, The Los Angeles Times, USA Today, and Computerworld, among others.

- Bryan Hurley studies Computer Science at the University of Maryland, Baltimore County. He is working on wearable computing research dealing with location, audio, and mood sensing. In addition to cutting the cord on the PistolMouse, he has built augmented reality systems at the United States Naval Research Laboratory in Washington, D.C. He lives in Columbia, Maryland. Bryan can be contacted at *hurleymail@gmail.com*.

- Jeff Ishaq (*http://www.ishaq.biz*) is a software engineer and writer living in Santa Cruz, California. He is the author of *Treo Fan Book* for O'Reilly, and has been developing Palm software since 1996. In his spare time, he enjoys eating spicy food, trail running, playing guitar, and alpine snowboarding. He hopes someday to organize his office.

- Brian Jepson is an O'Reilly editor, programmer, and coauthor of *Mac OS X Tiger for Unix Geeks* and *Linux Unwired*. He's also a volunteer systems administrator and all-around geek for AS220 (*http://www.as220.org*), a nonprofit arts center in Providence, Rhode Island. AS220 gives Rhode Island artists uncensored and unjuried forums for their work. These forums include galleries, performance space, and publications. Brian sees to it that technology, especially free software, supports that mission.

- Scott MacHaffie (*http://www.nonvi.com/sm*) is a programmer. He learned to program in 1980 and has been getting paid for it since 1987. He has a B.S. and an M.S. in Computer Science, from University of Washington and Portland State University, respectively. He has studied Human-Computer Interactions and User Interface design for many years. Scott writes games for Palm OS devices as a hobby. He and his wife are learning to speak Irish Gaelic. Scott also teaches aikido when he can get a break from his twin boys, and he is knowledgeable about early Celtic, Irish, and Scottish history.

- Dr. Trevor Marshall (*http://www.trevormarshall.com*), based in the heart of Southern California's "Digital Coast," offers a full spectrum of consulting services in technologies ranging from Wi-Fi security and Internet infrastructure through RF, hardware, software, and audio/video to biomedical and prepress. Previous speaking engagements have included COMDEX, Microprocessor Forums, and WLAN/Wi-Fi Security conferences in Paris, Boston, and Santa Clara.

- Damon McCormick is a recent University of California, Berkeley, graduate with degrees in Electrical Engineering, Computer Science, and Philosophy. He enjoys the contradiction between an area of study that actively seeks an implementation of strong artificial intelligence and an area of study that claims strong artificial intelligence is practically impossible. Damon admits to computer security research and billiards addictions, and splits his spare time evenly between those activities and working on PlaceSite.

- Yasha Okshtein is an Interdisciplinary Engineering major at The Cooper Union for the Advancement of Science and Art. In his spare time, he tinkers with anything he can get his hands on, including Linux, RC

Cars, and various wireless devices. His web site is at *http://yasha.okshtein.net* and he can be reached at *flyashi@gmail.com*.

- Sean Savage is Project PlaceSite's Founder and Chief Instigator. Sean coined the term *zombie effect*, which describes feelings of alienation that occur when people in a semipublic place like a cafe or pub tune out the people and activities around them as they focus on laptops, mobile phones, or televisions. The zombie effect, and possibilities for countering it, is a driving force behind Project PlaceSite. Sean also coined the term *flash mob*, which is now listed in the Oxford English Dictionary and first appeared on his web site (*http://cheesebikini.com*). In 2005 Sean graduated with a Masters degree from U.C. Berkeley's School of Information Management & Systems. For two years he studied and designed location-based technology at Berkeley and, during the summer of 2004, at Intel Research Seattle. Sean is also a writer whose work has appeared in Wired, The Washington Post, The Miami Herald, and The Chicago Tribune.

- Terry Schmidt (*http://www.nycwireless.net*) is a leading expert on wireless networking technologies and applications. He has presented at major information technology conferences, including MacWorld, the O'Reilly Emerging Technologies Conference, and 802.11Planet.

- Cloyce D. Spradling is a full-time sysadmin and full-time developer of benchmarks and benchmark tools for one of SPEC's (*http://www.spec.org*) member companies. He likes monkeys, pirates, watching cartoons, and traveling with his wife and their rubber chicken. He can be reached at *cloyce+oreilly@headgear.org*.

- Jo Walsh is a freelance hacker and software artist who started out building web systems for the Guardian, the ICA, and state51 in London. Jo is trying to combine her interests in maps, spatial annotation on the semantic web, Wi-Fi geolocation, public transport planning, open geodata, and bots into something resembling coherence: *http://wirelesslondon.info*, a localized wireless captive portal service.

- Matt Westervelt is the founder of SeattleWireless (*http://seattlewireless.net*) and an evangelist for FreeNetworks worldwide. He left the corporate world to start Metrix Communication LLC, a company created to supply FreeNetworkers with high quality, standards-based wireless networking products. As a child, he watched a lot of Sesame Street, and has a firm (perhaps misguided) belief that cooperation can solve a lot of the world's problems.

- Ron Wickersham (*http://www.alembic.com*) is an inventor and the Chief Engineer at Alembic, Inc. where he designs guitar electronics. His hobbies involve everything interesting in the Universe including The Amateur Sky Survey and watering the flowers.
- Haihao Wu grew up in Shanghai and lives with his wife in Austin, Texas. He works for Freescale Semiconductor.
- Michael Juntao Yuan (*http://www.MichaelYuan.com*) is a mobile alpha geek and author of three mobile-technology–related books. Over the last couple of years, he has managed to accumulate more than a dozen smartphones; most of them are Nokia phones. He is the lead developer of Nokia's Series 40 Java Blueprint Application and is actively involved in various standards committees helping to define the next-generation Java platform on mobile phones. Michael currently works for JBoss Inc., the Professional Open Source software company, focusing on next-generation Java enterprise middleware. Michael has a Ph.D. from the University of Texas at Austin. When he is not working, writing, or playing with gadgets, he likes to travel and take pictures. Check out his picture albums at *http://www.jjcafe.net/photography*.

Acknowledgments

This book is really a cooperative venture, regardless of the two names on the cover. As Rob said when the second edition was proposed, writing a Hacks book is not only writing, but also project management.

Thanks to all of our contributors who provided such great and new material for the book, and to our editor, Brian Sawyer, who has been a great resource throughout the whole process.

Rob

I'd like to thank my family and friends for their continuing support by giving me the encouragement (and occasionally, solitude) needed to complete my various little projects.

Many hacks in this book were inspired by conversations with countless hackers who willingly share their ideas with anyone who will listen. A few came from the weekly "hack night" sessions that SeattleWireless hosts to foster such cross-pollination of ideas. Without the free and enthusiastic exchange of ideas, this book wouldn't have been possible. Thank you to all of the brilliant hackers around the planet who know that the value of sharing one's ideas can greatly exceed the value of keeping an idea to oneself.

Edd Dumbill, Casey Halverson, and Richard Lotz all provided technical review for the book. Ken Caruso and Matt Westervelt provided equipment, ideas, and valuable insight. Thank you, gentlemen!

And thanks everyone at O'Reilly who made this book a reality, and who continue to help relieve information pain in the world.

Roger

I wouldn't have dived deeply into things wireless if I hadn't met Rob at one of the early NoCat meetings he held at O'Reilly back in 2001. The next couple of years were full of long-distance network building, late-night hacking, and a real sense of community, not only for me but for everyone who was involved in actually building a community wireless network. I can't thank Rob enough.

I would also be amiss if I didn't thank personally all of the "Cats": Nate Boblitt, Adam Flaherty, Jim Rosenbaum, and Schuyler Erle. There isn't anything that can't get fixed, broken, and fixed even better when these guys are in the room.

During the entire time we've been married, my wife, Cynthia, has been totally understanding of the life of a geek. She puts up with long technical conversations, motherboards and computer pieces littering the floor, and even the long hours that come with working a network admin job. I love her more than words can express.

Preface

Wireless networking technology has shown an explosive growth worldwide over the past few years, bucking the general downward economic trend in the telecommunications industry. What is it about wireless networking that makes it so alluring on a grand scale? Why are there more than 75 million Wi-Fi devices worldwide, with some people projecting double that number by 2008? While marketing folks might tell you that the particular feature set and brand name of their product is driving demand, we believe the answer is much simpler: it's magic.

Right where you are sitting now, there could be dozens of wireless data networks slinging information to the far corners of the Earth. A neighbor orders food online while someone across the street is using voice chat to talk to relatives (for free!) in Hong Kong, all the while someone upstairs is downloading a new album from their favorite band's web site in San Francisco. The information flows all around you (and, indeed, even through you) without you seeing or hearing a thing. Make no mistake: wireless networking is probably the second most magical technology on the planet—just behind the Internet.

In hundreds of cities around the world, wireless networks are making ubiquitous connectivity more the rule than the exception, providing service (often free) to millions of users who suddenly need nothing more than a laptop and wireless card to get online. Wireless networking is getting people connected to each other more cheaply and easily than any other networking technology since the telephone.

Why Wireless Hacks?

The term *hacking* has a bad reputation in the popular press, where it is used to refer to someone who breaks into systems or wreaks havoc using computers as their weapon. Among enthusiasts, on the other hand, the term *hack* refers to a "quick-and-dirty" solution to a problem, or to a clever way to get something done. The term *hacker* is taken very much as a compliment, referring to someone as being *creative*, and having the technical chops to get things done. O'Reilly's Hacks series is an attempt to the reclaim the word, document the ways people are hacking (in a good way), and pass the hacker ethic of creative participation on to the uninitiated. Seeing how others approach systems and problems is often the quickest way to learn about a new technology.

Wireless Hacks is about getting the most out of your wireless networking hardware and software. In this book, you will find practical techniques for extending range, increasing throughput, managing wireless resources, and generally making your wireless networking vision a reality. Remember that reality is what you can get away with, and wireless hackers have found that they can get away with quite a lot using surprisingly little. This book will show you some of the best bits of their collected experience.

How to Use This Book

You can read this book from cover to cover if you like, but for the most part, each hack stands on its own. So feel free to browse, flipping around to whatever sections interest you most.

How This Book Is Organized

This book is divided into several subjects by chapter:

Chapter 1, *Bluetooth, Mobile Phones, and GPS*
> The last couple years have brought hundreds of millions of tiny battery-powered wireless devices to market. Some will get you an Internet connection just about anywhere with mobile phone service, while others keep your devices connected to the "last 10 feet," and some cover the whole globe. This chapter demonstrates some uses for these technologies, which will keep your devices (and yourself) connected, without wires.

Chapter 2, *Network Discovery and Monitoring*
> Wireless networking can be a lot of fun, but when it breaks, troubleshooting can be difficult without a good idea of what is really happening. This chapter will give you the tools you need to detect the presence of wireless networks, coordinate spectrum usage to avoid interference, and visualize network performance. It also covers a number of advanced data-monitoring techniques to pinpoint networking issues and even get an idea of your users' online habits.

Chapter 3, *Wireless Security*

There has been a lot of press over the last few years about the insecurity of wireless networks. In many cases, these alarmist reports are in fact absolutely true: the vast majority of wireless networks are either unintentionally left open, or worse, use unreliable security methods. This chapter explores the current standards for securing wireless networks and suggests several strong methods for protecting yourself and your wireless users from abuse.

Chapter 4, *Hardware Hacks*

If it weren't for the hardware, there would be no such thing as wireless networks. This extensive chapter tells you how to push wireless hardware to the limits, extending range and increasing performance and efficiency. It presents a large collection of components, along with sources and recommendations on how best to use them.

Chapter 5, *Software Hacks*

There also would be no such thing as wireless networks without the software, which ranges from the firmware that powers wireless cards and routers to the drivers required for those cards, up to general-purpose operating systems that can be used to build your own wireless access point, router, and firewall. This chapter covers all these topics and more.

Chapter 6, *Do-It-Yourself Antennas*

Since the first electrical spark was transmitted a few feet across a room more than 100 years ago, antenna design has been a fascination for wireless experimenters everywhere. This chapter presents several homebrew designs for wireless networking made by contributors from all over the world. These are practical, tested designs that can significantly extend the range of your wireless network.

Chapter 7, *Wireless Network Design*

Having the equipment in place is one thing, but being able to make a wireless segment stretch for miles requires real-world experience. This chapter is a collection of techniques to help simplify the job of building wireless networks that cover the area you require.

Appendix A, *Wireless Standards*

Wireless technology has not only produced impressive improvements to communications, but it has also produced an impressive list of acronyms. What is the difference between GPRS and GMRS? Which is fastest: 802.11, 802.11a, 802.11b, 802.11g, or 802.16? Exactly how do Wi-Fi and Bluetooth fit into all of this? This appendix will give you a good idea of what problems each technology is designed to solve, their relative strengths and weaknesses, and how to make the best possible use of each to fulfill your communication needs.

Appendix B, *Wireless Hardware Guide*

> Do you know the difference between a RP-TNC and a Reverse SMA connector? What about LMR versus Heliax antenna cabling? How do omni and sector antenna patterns differ, and why would you use one over the other? This appendix answers all of these questions and provides a comprehensive list of wireless equipment retailers.

Conventions Used in This Book

The following is a list of the typographical conventions used in this book:

Italic

Used to indicate new terms, URLs, filenames, file extensions, directories, and to highlight comments in examples. For example, a path in the filesystem will appear as */usr/local*. Also used for lowercased names of programs and tools, such as *tcpdump*.

`Constant width`

Used to show code examples, the contents of files, packages, modules, directives, commands, and the output from commands.

`Constant width bold`

Used in examples and tables to show commands or other text that should be typed literally.

`Constant width italic`

Used in examples and tables to show text that should be replaced with user-supplied values.

Gray type

Used to indicate a cross-reference within the text.

\

A backslash (\) at the end of a line of code is used to denote an unnatural line break; that is, you should not enter these as two lines of code, but as one continuous line. Multiple lines are used in these cases due to page width constraints.

Menu symbols

When looking at the menus for any application, you will see some symbols associated with keyboard shortcuts for a particular command. For example, to open a file, you would go to the File menu and select Open . . . (File → Open . . .).

You should pay special attention to notes set apart from the text with the following icons:

This is a tip, suggestion, or general note. It contains useful supplementary information about the topic at hand.

 This is a warning or note of caution.

The thermometer icons, found next to each hack, indicate the relative complexity of the hack:

 beginner   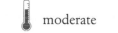 moderate   expert

Using Code Examples

This book is here to help you get your job done. In general, you may use the code in this book in your programs and documentation. You do not need to contact us for permission unless you're reproducing a significant portion of the code. For example, writing a program that uses several chunks of code from this book does not require permission. Selling or distributing a CD-ROM of examples from O'Reilly books *does* require permission. Answering a question by citing this book and quoting example code does not require permission. Incorporating a significant amount of example code from this book into your product's documentation *does* require permission.

We appreciate, but do not require, attribution. An attribution usually includes the title, author, publisher, and ISBN. For example: "*Wireless Hacks*, Second Edition, by Rob Flickenger and Roger Weeks. Copyright 2006 O'Reilly Media, Inc., 0-596-10144-9."

If you feel your use of code examples falls outside fair use or the permission given above, feel free to contact us at *permissions@oreilly.com*.

How to Contact Us

We have tested and verified the information in this book to the best of our ability, but you may find that features have changed (or even that we have made mistakes!). As a reader of this book, you can help us to improve future editions by sending us your feedback. Please let us know about any errors, inaccuracies, bugs, misleading or confusing statements, and typos that you find anywhere in this book.

Please also let us know what we can do to make this book more useful to you. We take your comments seriously and will try to incorporate reasonable suggestions into future editions. You can write to us at:

O'Reilly Media, Inc.
1005 Gravenstein Hwy N.
Sebastopol, CA 95472
(800) 998-9938 (in the U.S. or Canada)
(707) 829-0515 (international/local)
(707) 829-0104 (fax)

To ask technical questions or to comment on the book, send email to:

bookquestions@oreilly.com

The web site for *Wireless Hacks* lists examples, errata, and plans for future editions. You can find this page at:

http://www.oreilly.com/catalog/wirelesshks2/

For more information about this book and others, see the O'Reilly web site:

http://www.oreilly.com

Safari Enabled

 When you see a Safari® Enabled icon on the cover of your favorite technology book, that means the book is available online through the O'Reilly Network Safari Bookshelf.

Safari offers a solution that's better than e-books. It's a virtual library that lets you easily search thousands of top tech books, cut and paste code samples, download chapters, and find quick answers when you need the most accurate, current information. Try it for free at *http://safari.oreilly.com*.

Got a Hack?

To explore Hacks books online or to contribute a hack for future titles, visit:

http://hacks.oreilly.com

Bluetooth, Mobile Phones, and GPS

Hacks 1–22

There is much talk in the communications industry of providing *last-mile* connectivity. Think of Bluetooth as providing connectivity for the last 10 feet. Bluetooth excels as a handy cable-replacement technology, helping to eliminate the need for cumbersome wires that you might find on headsets, remote controls, PDAs, and other small devices. Bluetooth aims to end the days of needing to carry a three-foot piece of cable with obscure connectors on either end everywhere you go, just to interface to your laptop. You can use Bluetooth-enabled devices to talk to a laptop or a desktop, or even have them talk to each other to exchange data almost effortlessly. This chapter presents hacks on getting Bluetooth working with a wide range of devices and then doing some very interesting tricks.

If you can provide connectivity for the last 10 feet, how do you find yourself on this blue-green sphere we call Earth? The global positioning system (GPS) has migrated from being a military-only technology to something that is built into cars, phones, and a number of other devices. In this chapter, you can learn how to do some very unusual things with GPS that the designers probably never intended.

Mobile phones are everywhere. For many people, they have become the sole telephone of choice, enabling them to abandon land lines altogether. When you combine a mobile phone and Bluetooth, even more hacks become possible.

HACK #1 Set Up Bluetooth on Linux

Linux kernels from 2.6 onward have easy-to-use tools for Bluetooth.

Prior to the release of the 2.6 Linux kernel, getting Bluetooth support involved compiling your own kernel as well as the necessary utilities. There were also multiple Bluetooth stacks available, each with their own features, adapter support, and quirks. In 2.6, the BlueZ stack was crowned as the officially supported way to use Bluetooth in Linux, and that's the focus of this hack.

First, make sure you have a supported Bluetooth adapter. You used to be able to find a reasonably current list of BlueZ-supported hardware at *http://www.holtmann.org/linux/bluetooth/devices.html*. However, as of March 2005, this information has been removed because of threatened legal action from the Bluetooth SIG. What this basically means is that the association of companies who maintain the Bluetooth standard don't want anyone to advertise that their devices are *compliant* with Linux unless you pay the SIG a lot of money and fill out a bunch of paperwork. So, you're on your own here. Probably the best place to get advice is in the BlueZ Users mailing list, which can be found at *http://www.bluez.org/lists.html*.

Next, you'll need to make sure that your kernel has Bluetooth support enabled. All distributions shipping the 2.6 kernel have Bluetooth support. 2.4 kernels shipped with both the Red Hat 9.0 and Debian Sarge distributions already include Bluetooth support. You can test your kernel for Bluetooth support by running `modprobe rfcomm` as root. If the `modprobe` fails, you'll need to install the packages that support Bluetooth.

Red Hat and Fedora users should install these packages using *yum* or *rpm*. This assumes you're using GNOME as your window manager:

```
yum install bluez-utils gnome-bluetooth
```

Likewise, Debian and Ubuntu users should install using *apt*:

```
apt-get install bluez-utils gnome-bluetooth
```

This next bit is for UART-based (that is, non-USB) devices only, so if you're using a USB Bluetooth adapter, you can skip ahead. Serial-style USB devices, which include serial dongles and PCMCIA cards, need to be explicitly *attached* to the Bluetooth host controller interface, using the *hciattach* utility. When you connect the device, the appropriate kernel driver might be loaded automatically, leaving a log entry in */var/log/messages*.

If you're using a UART-based device, you may see a reference to a */dev/ttySn* serial device, where *n* is some integer. In any event, you can try attaching the device to the Bluetooth host controller device by running /sbin/hciattach /dev/ttySn any from the command line. Like any good Unix utility, you know that hciattach worked if it returns without printing anything. If it doesn't work, make sure you have the right device and check the manpage for other options.

Assuming that the hciattach command did work, you will want to add a reference to this device to your */etc/bluetooth/uart* file, so that the device can be appropriately attached to the Bluetooth host controller interface at boot time. If this file doesn't exist, create it. Add a single line to this file that reads /dev/ttySn any, replacing n with the appropriate serial device number.

Now that you have everything installed, plug in your Bluetooth adapter and try running /etc/init.d/bluetooth start as root. In Debian and Ubuntu, start Bluetooth with /etc/init.d/bluez-utils start. You should see some appropriate status messages in your */var/log/messages*. Assuming everything works, you might want to add the Bluetooth script to the appropriate *rc.d* directory for your default run level with the *chkconfig* utility or via a manual symlink. Chances are good your package install has already added this for you, but it's a good idea to check.

Now run hciconfig from the command line. You should see something like this:

```
hci0:   Type: USB
        BD Address: 00:11:22:33:44:55 ACL MTU: 192:8  SCO MTU: 64:8
        UP RUNNING PSCAN ISCAN
        RX bytes:99 acl:0 sco:0 events:13 errors:0
        TX bytes:296 acl:0 sco:0 commands:12 errors:0
```

If you don't see anything like this, make sure that *hcid* is running and that there aren't any error messages in */var/log/messages*. The BD Address shown is the unique Bluetooth identifier for your adapter, much like an Ethernet MAC address.

Now, bring another Bluetooth device within range of your computer, and make sure that the device is visible to Bluetooth scans. Then, run hcitool scan from the command line. It might take up to 15 or 20 seconds to complete its scan, and then it should display something like this:

```
$ hcitool scan

Scanning ...
        00:99:88:77:66:55       Nokia3650
```

You can now test the device to see which services it supports, using sdptool browse 00:99:88:77:66:55. You should see a lengthy list of supported services, providing information that can be used to configure access to those services.

—Schuyler Erle

Set Up Bluetooth on Windows XP

The Bluetooth wireless standard is a great way to get computers and gadgets talking to each other. Here's how to set it up on Windows XP.

Bluetooth wireless support is showing up in all sorts of devices these days, and the software is easy to use. Few consumers know about it or know how to use it, though. This hack will expose you to the basics of Bluetooth and how to set up some Bluetooth devices, and it will point you to some good sources of information about the ways you can use Bluetooth in your life.

Some people confuse Bluetooth with the 802.11x standards (Wi-Fi), since they are both wireless technologies. But Wi-Fi is intended primarily for Internet data and connecting computers, while Bluetooth is used to communicate between a wide variety of devices. Where WiFi needs to get into every corner of your world to be effective, Bluetooth is best at short ranges. In fact, the effective range of most Bluetooth communications is about 32 feet (10 meters).

Bluetooth can be used to connect all kinds of different devices—PCs, cell phones, cell phone headsets, PDAs, keyboards, portable game systems, audio headphones, GPS receivers, printers, digital cameras, barcode scanners, medical equipment, and even your car. Each device supports one or more profiles that dictate what types of devices it can communicate with and how that communication will take place. If two devices share a profile, they can communicate; otherwise, they will not even make the attempt.

Installing Bluetooth

My own initiation into Bluetooth was when I needed a new mouse for my laptop. I had avoided buying one of the infrared wireless mice because of the line-of-sight issues, but a Bluetooth mouse seemed like just the ticket. I purchased a Bluetooth wireless mouse and a Bluetooth dongle that plugs into my laptop's USB port. In addition to the dongle-type adapters, you can also get permanent Bluetooth cards that go into the PCI slot of your desktop computer. The installation procedure is mostly the same.

The Plug-and-Play mechanism in Windows XP works so well that I usually just attach any new piece of hardware without bothering to use the software CD unless I have to. But due to the way that Bluetooth works, it's best to install the software first so that you have an opportunity to configure Bluetooth prior to using it.

When you install the software, you'll find the usual assortment of wizard pages, asking you where you want to install the software and such. The installer might display a warning about Bluetooth devices and signed drivers. This is a security precaution and a convenience for you. If you click OK, the installer will temporarily disable the signed drivers messages while installing the Bluetooth adapter. Otherwise, you would end up with a lot of messages about unsigned drivers.

Once the installation is complete, attach your Bluetooth adapter. If you have a PCI Bluetooth adapter, install the card in an open slot and restart your PC. Windows XP will detect the adapter and associate the drivers with those that you installed earlier. You will probably see several messages show up in the system tray as it installs the drivers for the Bluetooth adapter.

Once Windows XP has finished loading the drivers, you can start configuring your Bluetooth adapter. The My Bluetooth Places icon, shown in Figure 1-1, will open a window that allows you to discover and browse nearby Bluetooth devices. There is also an icon in the system tray for Bluetooth; it's a blue circle with the runic B on it. The B in the system tray icon changes color depending on the status of the Bluetooth connection—red for when no Bluetooth adapter is connected, white for when an adapter is connected, and green for when a device is communicating with your PC.

Figure 1-1. The My Bluetooth Places desktop icon

Open the My Bluetooth Places window. If you have a Bluetooth device nearby and it is turned on, it might show up on this list. Ignore any devices for the moment while we go through the configuration process. In the upper-left corner of My Bluetooth Places, there is a list of links under the heading Bluetooth Tasks. Click the link labeled Bluetooth Setup Wizard. The choices you are presented with, shown in Figure 1-2, pertain to how you want to use your Bluetooth adapter. For now, choose the last option, the one that begins with "I want to change the name...."

If you want to set up service for a particular type of device, such as a mouse or a printer, choose the button labeled "I know the service I want to use...." If you want to connect to a specific device (in case more than one person is using a Bluetooth device in your proximity), choose the button labeled "I want to find a specific Bluetooth device..." and click the Next button. In this screen, you provide the name of your computer and the type of computer you are using (laptop or desktop). I use a generic name for the computer because this value is broadcast to the world. People who attempt to hack

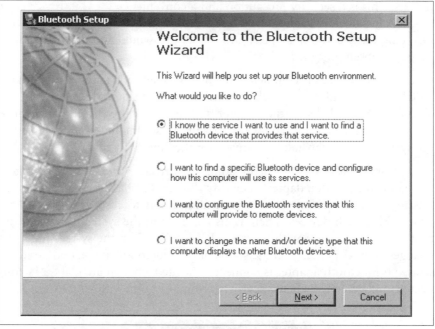

Figure 1-2. Bluetooth Setup Wizard

into Bluetooth-connected computers could use this information to their advantage. Click the Finish button to go back to My Bluetooth Places.

If you haven't already done so, now would be a good time to turn on your Bluetooth device and make sure it is running properly. Click the Bluetooth Setup Wizard link again. This time, when presented with the wizard screen of choices, choose "I know the service I want to use..." and click the Next button. The wizard will present you with a complete list of items that it knows how to communicate with. This is where you will go if you want to add a printer or a headset in the future. To set up the mouse, scroll the list to the bottom, select Human Interface Device, and click the Next button.

The next screen, shown in Figure 1-3, will cause Windows XP to search for all Bluetooth devices in range. If your device does not show up, make sure it is powered on and operating correctly. There might be a Connect or Pair button on the device that you must press to start the communication with the PC. If many devices are in the area, you can use the pop-up box beneath the list to show only certain types of devices. If the device you want to connect is in the list, choose it and click the Next button.

At this point, the Bluetooth wizard will attempt to connect with the device. If all went well, you should see the confirmation window shown in

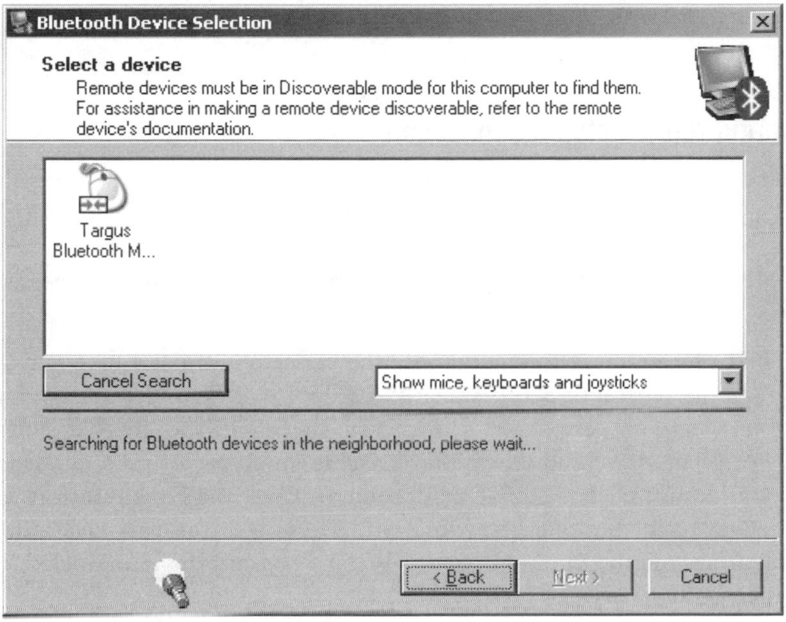

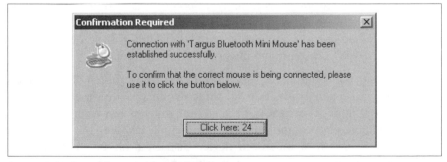

Figure 1-3. Bluetooth Device Selection screen

Figure 1-4. This is your way of knowing the device you are looking for is available and communicating with your computer. Once you click the confirmation button, your mouse and your PC are paired. If you ever see this window and you weren't expecting it, it could be a sign that someone nearby is attempting to communicate with your computer via the Bluetooth connection.

Figure 1-4. Bluetooth confirmation dialog

If you are planning to add multiple Bluetooth products to your computer, you add them by going to the Bluetooth Setup Wizard and choosing the "I know the service I want to use..." option for each device. Different devices will follow the same instructions as we've done with the mouse in this example, although there might be device-specific settings that you will have to configure once the connection is made.

Securing Your Bluetooth Connection

Bluetooth can make your computing experience more convenient by eliminating some of the need for cables. Unfortunately, because the signal is being broadcast on open frequencies, anyone is free to listen in or even participate in the discussion. That's why it's necessary for you to take precautions.

The first precaution is to enable only the services you need for your computer. In the Bluetooth Setup Wizard, the choice labeled "I want to configure the Bluetooth services..." allows you to enable and disable different types of Bluetooth communications. Disable any types of communications that you do not plan to use at that moment. Click the Finish button when you have made the changes you need. These services can be easily re-enabled through the Bluetooth Setup Wizard or from the link labeled View My Bluetooth Services.

The next precaution involves locking out other devices. Go to My Bluetooth Places and choose the link labeled "View or modify configuration." The Bluetooth Configuration screen, shown in Figure 1-5, allows you to choose how your Bluetooth connection communicates to the outside world.

Click the tab labeled Accessibility. Remove the check mark from the box labeled "Let Bluetooth devices discover this computer." This will prevent unwelcome intrusions by unknown devices. The Discovery tab allows you to configure which devices your connection can discover. This is useful if you are in an office environment with many different types of Bluetooth devices. The Local Services tab lets you configure how various types of devices interact with software services installed on your PC. This will be necessary for synchronizing a PDA, listening to music, or transferring files.

Two of the more publicized Bluetooth security problems are called *Bluejacking* and *Bluesnarfing*. Both of these exploits require the attacker to be within communication range of the victim, which is less than 32 feet (10 meters) for most phones and laptops. Bluejacking involves the unsolicited receipt of messages to a Bluetooth device, usually a phone. It's primarily used as a prank; your phone starts vibrating and you get a message criticizing your hairstyle or the brand of phone you are using. Your attacker will be close by, and chances are good that he is around 15 years old. Bluesnarfing is more dangerous because the attacker is out to retrieve datebook and contact information from your phone. In both cases, if you disable the

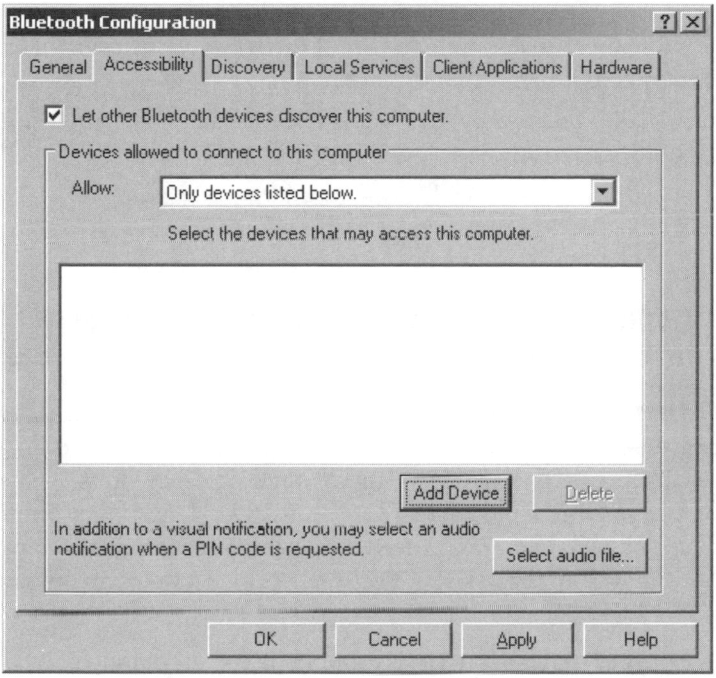

Figure 1-5. Bluetooth Configuration screen

Bluetooth features of your phone when you aren't using them, you won't have these problems.

Networking with Bluetooth

Bluetooth provides many of the same features Wi-Fi does. Bluetooth has a maximum data transmission rate of somewhere around 100,000 bytes per second, which is much lower than 802.11. Plus, its limited range means all the parties must be in very close proximity. For these reason, it's not an effective competitor to 802.11 for day-to-day wireless networking.

There are times, however, when an ad hoc wireless network using Bluetooth could be useful. If no network is present and no one has a floppy or flash drive handy, you can use a Bluetooth connection between the computers to share files. Keep in mind that the data rate for Bluetooth is miniscule compared to 802.11, so use it sparingly.

For details on how to pair your PC via Bluetooth with another device such as a cell phone to connect to the Internet, see "Connect Windows XP with a Bluetooth Phone" [Hack #5].

See Also

- The O'Reilly Wireless web site (*http://wireless.oreilly.com*) has a good deal of Bluetooth-related information.
- *Windows XP Unwired* by Wei-Meng Lee (O'Reilly) is a good source for Bluetooth-related advice.
- "Connect Windows XP with a Bluetooth Phone" [Hack #5]

—Eric Cloninger

HACK #3 Connect Mac OS X with a Bluetooth Phone

No hotspots nearby? Use your Mac and a Bluetooth phone to get online almost anywhere.

If your mobile phone plan [Hack #17] gives you some flavor of cellular data access—GPRS, EDGE, 1xRTT, or any of their acronym cousins—you can use that access with a Bluetooth phone and your Mac to get online. The benefits are obvious: you don't need a wireless access point in range, you don't have to pay for access to a hotspot, and a mobile signal is available (almost) everywhere.

Mac OS X makes cellular data access simple. If you are setting up your Bluetooth phone with your Mac for the first time, follow along and you'll be using your cellular data minutes in, well, minutes!

Requirements

Obviously, you're going to need a Mac with Bluetooth. Bluetooth has come standard with most PowerBooks for a couple years now or as an option on many other Mac models, including iBooks, PowerMacs, and iMacs. Third-party Bluetooth adapters are also available from vendors such as D-Link, for practically any Mac with a USB port.

Secondly, you'll need a Bluetooth-capable phone. Apple maintains a list of phones (*http://www.apple.com/macosx/features/isync/devices.html*) known to work with the iSync program that ships with Mac OS X 10.3 and later. There are also many Bluetooth phones not on this list that will happily pair with your Mac and which can be used to connect you to the Internet. Ross Barkman maintains a page (*http://www.taniwha.org.uk*) with updated modem scripts and information on Bluetooth mobile phones for use with Mac OS X.

Adding a Device

Mac OS X gives you a handy Bluetooth icon in the menubar. Click here to get a drop-down menu like the one shown in Figure 1-6. Choose "Set up Bluetooth Device..." to get started.

Figure 1-6. Bluetooth menubar

Make sure your mobile phone is turned on, you have Bluetooth enabled, and your phone is discoverable. You'll be prompted in a new window on your Mac to select a device type. Choose Mobile Phone, and click Continue. Mac OS X will search using Bluetooth to locate your phone, as shown in Figure 1-7.

Select your phone from the list, and click on Continue. Your Mac will now attempt to pair with your mobile phone. When this happens, an alert box on the Mac will give you a six-digit number that will also need to be entered on your mobile phone. This setup will vary from phone to phone, so consult your user's manual for directions. Once you've completed the pairing process, you'll be asked what services you want to use on your mobile phone, as shown in Figure 1-8.

Unless you plan on using your cell phone as an expensive but crappy analog modem, make sure you choose the last option on this screen: "Use a direct, higher speed connection to reach your Internet Service Provider."

Connection Setup

Now comes the fun part. There are hundreds of Bluetooth phones out there and many mobile providers, and each one is going to have a different setup. I'll present three different setups for larger U.S. providers. If you have a different provider, or live outside the United States, you'll want to either search online for details or contact your mobile provider for help.

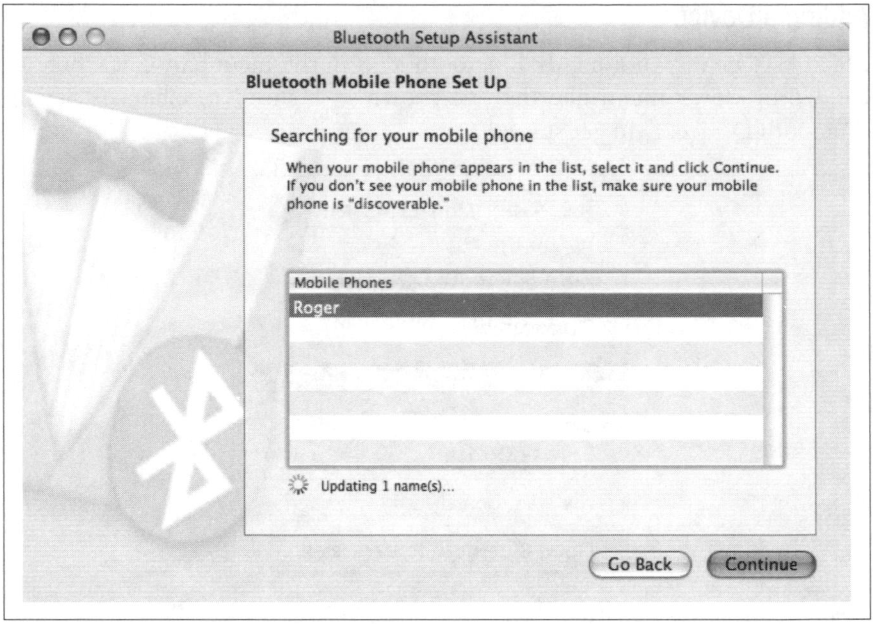

Figure 1-7. Locating your Bluetooth phone

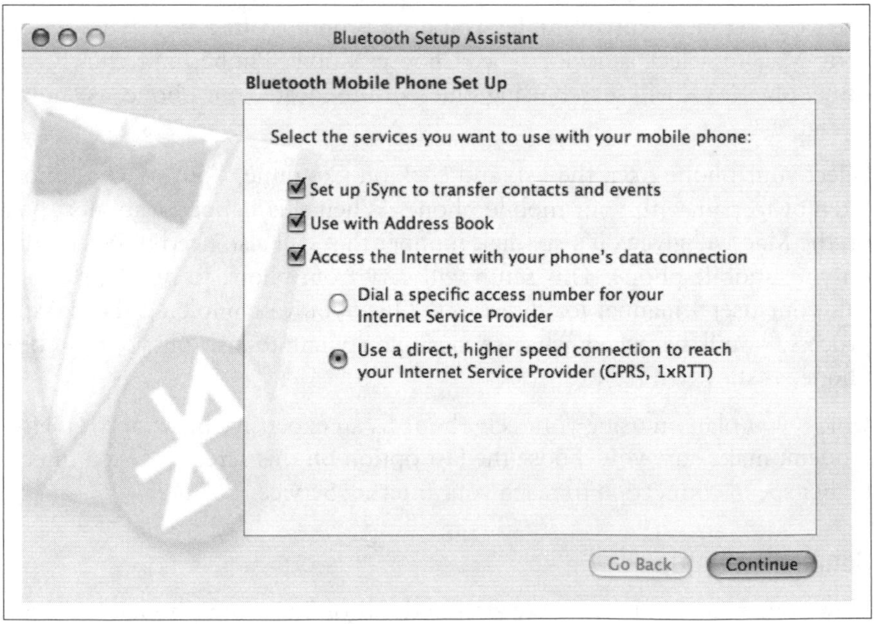

Figure 1-8. Bluetooth phone setup screen

Any connection setup is going to require a username, password, a CID string (also known as "APN" for GSM providers, and "phone number" for CDMA providers), and a modem script. Mac OS X ships with modem scripts for many popular mobile phone makers, but if you don't see your phone, check Ross Barkman's page.

Our example connection, shown in Figure 1-9, is for T-Mobile GPRS subscribers. Although the username and password are not used for this connection, you do need a specific APN string to enter in the CID field.

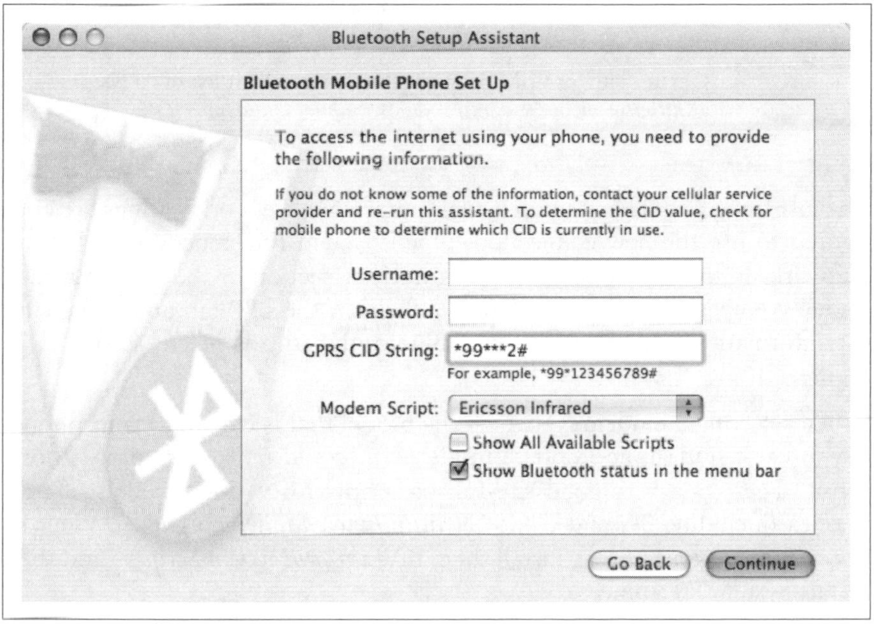

Figure 1-9. T-Mobile GPRS setup

Table 1-1 shows the usernames, passwords, and APN/phone numbers to use for popular U.S. carriers.

Table 1-1. Network settings for popular providers

Provider	Username	Password	APN/Telephone number
Cingular GPRS	ISP@CINGULARGPRS.COM	CINGULAR1	ISP.CINGULAR
Verizon 1xRTT	your.mobile.number@vzw3g.com	vzw	#777
AT&T	None	None	Proxy

Table 1-1. Network settings for popular providers (continued)

Provider	Username	Password	APN/Telephone number
T-Mobile	None	None	**WAP users** (`wap.voicestream.com`); **Internet Unlimited users** (`internet2.voicestream.com`); **Internet Unlimited users with VPN option** (`internet3.voicestream.com`)
Sprint	PCS Vision username	PCS Vision Password	#777

> Opera's site for GSM providers has an excellent list of APNs at *http://www.opera.com/products/mobile/docs/connect/*.

The last thing you'll need to do is make sure your Network settings are configured to use the new connection. Open System Preferences and click on Network. In the Network Port Configurations section, make sure your new phone connection is checked. Finally, click on the PPP tab and make sure the information you entered during Bluetooth setup is listed, as shown in Figure 1-10.

When selecting a modem type, pick the model that is closest to your phone. If you can't find an appropriate model, you could try a third-party phone script. There is a very good site full of scripts for various models of new phones (including 3G and GPRS) at *http://www.taniwha.org.uk*. Download the scripts for your phone, install them in */Library/Modem Scripts/*, and then restart System Preferences.

Finally, you may want to consider enabling dial-on-demand for your Bluetooth connection. In Network Preferences, select the Bluetooth modem, click PPP Options, then check the first checkbox, "Connect automatically when needed." Then show your Network Port Configurations, and drag the Bluetooth line somewhere near the bottom. Your Mac will try each connection in order from top to bottom when connecting to the Internet. On my laptop, I list them from fastest to slowest: FireWire first, then Ethernet, AirPort, Bluetooth, and finally Internal Modem.

Now, when you open any program that attempts to connect to the Internet, your Mac will automatically fall back to your Bluetooth phone when no other connection is available. Enjoy!

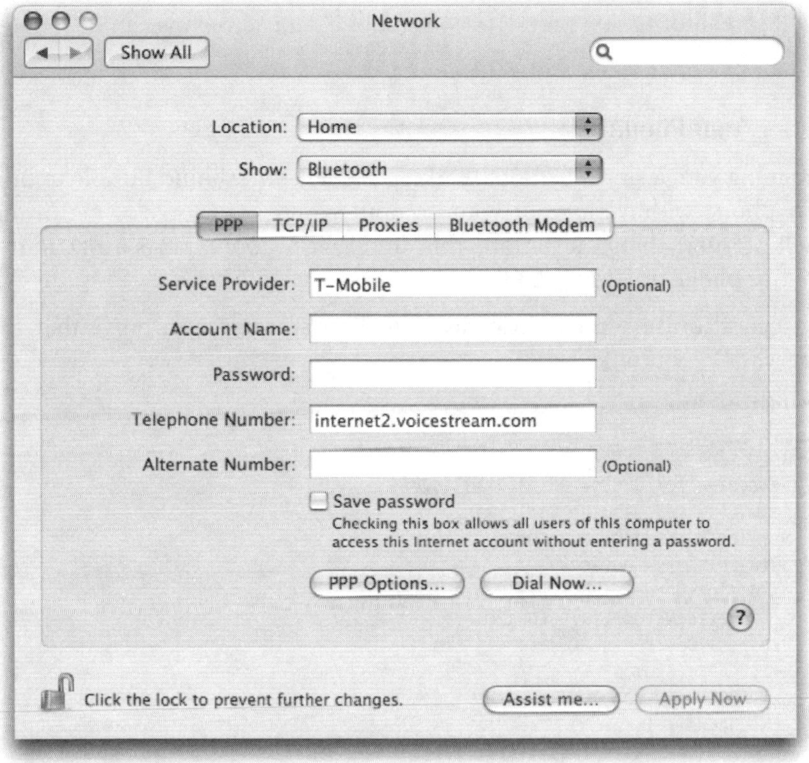

Figure 1-10. *T-Mobile Network settings*

HACK #4 — Connect Linux with a Bluetooth Phone

Use your Bluetooth phone as a modem when Wi-Fi isn't available.

No doubt the novelty of being able to scan for nearby Bluetooth devices from your Linux machine will wear off all too soon, and then you'll want to actually *do* things with your shiny new Bluetooth connection. Being able to use your cell phone as a modem from all those places you can't pull in a Wi-Fi signal would be pretty cool, wouldn't it?

Bluetooth supports a number of *profiles*, which define the way that Bluetooth devices can communicate with each other. In this case, we want to make use of the Dial-up Networking (DUN) profile, which relies on a protocol called RFCOMM to emulate a serial link between two devices. You can use RFCOMM to connect your Linux box to your phone, and then run pppd over the link to get access to the Internet. This should work using various mobile data protocols including CDPD, GPRS, EDGE, 1xRTT, and 1xEV-DO. More information on the various mobile data acronyms can be found in Appendix A.

Pairing Your Phone

Assuming you've got Bluetooth working [Hack #1], you should be able to bring your phone within range of your computer and scan for it using *hcitool*. We'll presume that you've done this, and that *hcitool* reports a BD address for your phone of *00:11:22:33:44:55*.

You can also use sdptool to verify that there's a device in range that supports the DUN profile:

```
sdptool search DUN

Inquiring ...
Searching for DUN on 00:11:22:33:44:55 ...
Service Name: Dial-up Networking
Service RecHandle: 0x10001
Service Class ID List:
  "Dialup Networking" (0x1103)
  "Generic Networking" (0x1201)
Protocol Descriptor List:
  "L2CAP" (0x0100)
  "RFCOMM" (0x0003)
    Channel: 1
```

Note this channel number, because you'll need it later. As you can see, *hcitool* and *sdptool* offer a lot of other useful Bluetooth diagnostic functions, which you can read more about on their respective manpages.

Before you can actually connect to the phone, however, you may need to set up what's referred to as *device pairing* between your Linux box and your phone, so that your phone knows to allow your computer access to its services, and possibly vice versa. Your computer's PIN can be found in */etc/bluetooth/pin*, and you will want to alter this to a unique value that only you know.

 It's important to note here that Bluetooth pairing is not a very secure process. Security researchers have found ways to hijack the pairing process and even force a re-pairing remotely. Until workarounds are found, the best thing you can do is change your PIN frequently, and use a PIN of the maximum length of 16 characters.

Most phones have a Bluetooth PIN that you can configure within the phone itself. The BlueZ stack comes with a little Python utility called *bluepin* that pops up a GTk+ dialog to ask for your phone's PIN as needed.

If you don't want to be bothered with pop-up windows, the following Perl script can be saved to */etc/bluetooth/pindb*, and you can use it store PINs for multiple Bluetooth devices:

```
#!/usr/bin/perl
while ( ) {
    print "PIN:$1\n" if /^$ARGV[1]\s+(\w+)/o;
}
__DATA__
# Your Bluetooth PINs can go here, in BD address / PIN pairs,
# one to a line, separated by whitespace.
#

00:11:22:33:44:55        11111
```

Make sure that */etc/bluetooth/pindb* is owned by root and is chmod 0700—you don't want other users being able to look up your PINs. The options section of your */etc/bluetooth/hcid.conf* should accordingly look something like this:

```
options {
        autoinit yes;
        security auto;
        pairing multi;
        pin_helper /etc/bluetooth/pindb;
}
```

This ensures that HCI devices are configured at boot, that pairing is allowed, and that *hcid* will check *pindb* for your PINs on a per-device basis. Be sure to restart *hcid* by running /etc/init.d/bluetooth restart if you made any changes to your */etc/bluetooth/hcid.conf*.

Now that your computer is set up for pairing, you'll have to set up your phone similarly, for which you'll need to refer to your user's manual. This set-up process often requires that the phone scan for your computer's Bluetooth adapter, so be sure that your computer is within range with a working Bluetooth adapter. The interface will probably come up as BlueZ (0) or something similar, unless you changed the name option in your *hcid.conf*. You probably want to set up the pairing on the phone as trusted, or the equivalent, so that the phone doesn't ask you to verify the connection each time you try to dial out from your Linux box.

Now that we have found a device in range that offers dial-up networking, and set up pairing with it, the next step is to bind an RFCOMM interface to that device. First, make sure that there are RFCOMM entries in your */dev* directory, using ls -l /dev/rfcomm*. If ls reports "No such file or directory," you can easily create 64 RFCOMM device entries by switching to the superuser and doing the following:

```
# for n in `seq 0 63`; do mknod -m660 /dev/rfcomm$n c 216 $n; done
# chown root:uucp /dev/rfcomm*
```

If you're running Debian or Ubuntu, you will want to *chown* your RFCOMM devices to group *dialout*, instead of *uucp*.

Now, as the superuser, bind */dev/rfcomm0* to your phone on the channel reported for DUN by *sdptool* earlier, using the *rfcomm* utility from bluez-utils:

```
# rfcomm bind /dev/rfcomm0 00:11:22:33:44:55:66 1
```

You'll know that the device was bound successfully if, like any good Unix utility, *rfcomm* just returns silently. You can demonstrate that it did actually work, however, by running `rfcomm` without any arguments:

```
# rfcomm

rfcomm0: 00:11:22:33:44:55 channel 1 clean
```

Configuring PPP Networking

Now you can just treat this serial device as if it were an ordinary modem. Just to prove it, try running `minicom` as root, and switch the serial device to */dev/rfcomm0*. When the terminal loads, type `AT` and press Enter. If the phone responds `OK`, then congratulations are in order—you're talking to your cell phone over a Bluetooth connection.

Before going any further, you might want to add the following to your */etc/bluetooth/rfcomm.conf* so that the RFCOMM device is configured by default when Bluetooth loads:

```
rfcomm0 {
        # Automatically bind the device at startup
        bind yes;
        device 00:11:22:33:44:55;
        channel 1;
        comment "My Phone";
}
```

From here, it's just a short hop to getting your computer on the Net. Put the following into */etc/ppp/peers/gprs*:

```
/dev/rfcomm0

connect '/usr/sbin/chat -v -f /etc/ppp/peers/gprs.chat'
noauth
defaultroute
usepeerdns
```

```
lcp-echo-interval 65535
debug
```

Then, save the following as */etc/ppp/peers/gprs.chat*:

```
TIMEOUT      15
ECHO         ON
HANGUP       ON
' '          AT
OK           ATZ
OK           ATD*99#
```

Alternately, if you prefer using *wvdial*, try adding the following to your */etc/wvdial.conf*:

```
[Dialer gprs]
Modem     = /dev/rfcomm0
Phone     - *99#
Username  - foo
Password  = bar
```

Note that while European providers give you a username and password, in the United States you still need to supply dummy values to satisfy *wvdial*. Consult your network provider's web site for details about what values you may need to use. Your GPRS is actually already authenticated by your very presence on the cellular network, so you don't have to re-authenticate just to use PPP. The phone number listed in the previous configuration files is the standard GPRS dial-up number, which may work for you right off the bat if your phone is configured properly.

Most GSM phones support multiple GPRS access points, so if the default for your phone doesn't work for you, try going into minicom and typing AT+CGDCONT? followed by a carriage return. Your phone should respond with a list of available Packet Data Protocol (PDP) contexts. Pick the one that seems the most appropriate, and then set your GPRS phone number in */etc/wvdial.conf* to *99***n#, replacing *n* with the number of the PDP profile you want to use. Failing that, try contacting your service provider for advice.

You can test this setup as root by running either pppd call gprs or wvdial gprs, depending on your setup, and watching */var/log/messages* in another window. The only hitch with this setup is that it doesn't set up your nameservers in */etc/resolv.conf* by default. The way around this on Red Hat and Fedora is to store the following in */etc/sysconfig/network-scripts/ifcfg-ppp0* (or *ppp1*, *ppp2*, etc., as you prefer):

```
# comment out CHATSCRIPT and uncomment WVDIALSECT if you're using wvdial
DEVICE=ppp0
MODEMPORT=/dev/rfcomm0
CHATSCRIPT=/etc/ppp/peers/gprs.chat
# WVDIALSECT=gprs
```

This way you can just use `ifup ppp0` and `ifdown ppp0` to bring the link up and down. To get the identical result on Debian, use the `pppd` configuration just shown and add the following to your */etc/network/interfaces*:

```
iface ppp0 inet ppp
    provider gprs
```

If you're not using a Red Hat- or Debian-like distribution, you can always just add the following additional lines to your */etc/ppp/peers/gprs* to make DNS work right, and use `pppd call gprs` and `killall pppd` to bring the link up and down:

```
welcome 'cp -b /etc/ppp/resolv.conf /etc/resolv.conf'
disconnect 'mv /etc/resolv.conf~ /etc/resolv.conf'
```

That's just about all you need to know to get online from anywhere you can get GSM service. Just don't expect blistering speeds from it: as of this writing, GPRS ranges in speed from under 5k/s to just over 20k/s, depending on your service—not exactly high speed by modern standards, but amazingly usable where you would otherwise have nothing at all.

Hacking the Hack

As a little bonus, here's a short *iptables* script to let you share that GPRS with anyone in Wi-Fi range, and which could be stored as or called from */etc/ppp/ip-up.local*:

```
# Enable IP forwarding and rp_filter (to kill IP spoof attempts).
echo "1" > /proc/sys/net/ipv4/ip_forward
echo "1" > /proc/sys/net/ipv4/conf/all/rp_filter

# Load relevant kernel modules, if necessary.
for i in ip_tables ipt_MASQUERADE iptable_nat
    ip_conntrack ip_conntrack_ftp ip_conntrack_irc \
    ip_nat_irc ip_nat_ftp; do
    modprobe $i 2>/dev/null;
done

# Masquerade anything that's not from a PPP interface
# (e.g. ethernet, Wi-Fi, etc.)
iptables -t nat -A POSTROUTING -o ppp+ -j MASQUERADE
```

But what, you ask, about regular dial-up connections? How about faxes? Well, it turns out that you're in luck: simply replace the GPRS access number with any regular phone number of your choice and (on most phones) you get a 9,600 baud data connection to that line. Configuring *efax* or *mgetty-sendfax* to use Bluetooth to fax from a GSM phone in this manner is therefore left as an exercise for the reader.

—*Schuyler Erle*

Connect Windows XP with a Bluetooth Phone

HACK
#5

Don't worry about normal phone dial-up connections, hotspots, or WiFi. No matter where you are, the Internet is with you, as long as you have a Bluetooth-enabled phone.

Lots of phones these days include Bluetooth connections, and if you have one, Internet access for your Windows XP laptop is only a phone call away. All you'll need to do is fire up your laptop and phone, connect them to one another, and make the Internet connection. To do this, you'll of course need a laptop with Bluetooth capabilities as well.

> If your laptop doesn't have Bluetooth capability, it's easy to add. You just need a USB Bluetooth adapter. Companies such as D-Link, Keyspan, Belkin, and many others sell them, often for around $30. Just plug the little device into your USB port, follow installation instructions, and you'll be set.

Don't expect broadband connection speeds when you do this—at least not yet. The exact connection speed you'll get varies according to the precise technology your cell phone uses and, of course, depending on the quality of your current cell phone connection. These days, though, expect 20 to 40kbps with a GSM/GPRS cell phone, 20 to 150kbps with EDGE, about 50 to 120kbps with CDMA 1xRTT, and from 300 to 500kbps with CDMA 1xEV-DO. If you don't know which technology your cell phone uses, check with your cell phone carrier, and they'll let you know.

The exact screens you'll see when you make the connection will vary somewhat from phone to phone, so for this hack I'll show you how to do it with the Sony Ericsson T68i Bluetooth-enabled phone. The steps with other Bluetooth-enabled cell phones should be very similar.

First, turn on your cell phone and laptop, and make sure they're within range of one another. Then turn on the phone's Bluetooth radio. To do this on the Sony Ericsson T68i, press the joystick button and select Connect → Bluetooth → Options → Operation Mode → On.

Next, you'll have to make the phone *discoverable* so that your laptop can find it. On the Sony Ericsson T68i, press the joystick button and then select Connect → Bluetooth → Discoverable.

Now you need to discover the phone in Windows XP. In Windows Explorer, go to My Bluetooth Places and select View Devices in Range. You should see the Sony Ericsson T68i icon; right-click it and select Discover Available Services. You'll get to a group of icons that show the list of available services. Now right-click the Dial-Up Networking service and select Connect Dial-up Networking, as shown in Figure 1-11.

Figure 1-11. Connecting to the Internet through Dial-Up Networking

You'll be asked whether you want to accept or decline the connection or "add to paired." It's a good idea to select the "add to paired" option. That way, the next time you want to connect to the Internet using your laptop and cell phone, they'll automatically discover one another and you won't have to go through the entire discovery process.

When you select "add to paired," the screen shown in Figure 1-12 will appear. The device name will already be filled in for you. Make up a PIN that you want to use for pairing the devices, and type it into the Bluetooth PIN code box.

Bluetooth PIN Code Request

Device Name: T68

Before a connection can be established, this computer and the device above must be "paired."

The Bluetooth pairing procedure creates a secret key that is used in all future connections between these two devices to establish identity and encrypt the data that these devices exchange.

To create the paired relationship, enter the PIN code and click OK.

Bluetooth PIN Code: •••••

OK   Cancel   Help

Figure 1-12. Pairing your phone and laptop

> It's a good idea to use only numbers for your PIN; other-wise, you might have problems with keying in alphabetic characters using your phone's PIN dialog box.

On your cell phone, you'll have to accept the pairing. A dialog box will appear asking if you want to accept the pairing. Select Add to Paired, and type in the same PIN you used on your laptop.

From now on, connecting to the Internet is the same as with any other dial-up connection. The familiar dial-up connection dialog box will appear in XP, asking for a username, password, and phone number. Enter the information you normally use to connect to your ISP, including your username, password, and phone number. Click the Dial button, and you'll dial in and connect.

—Preston Gralla

HACK #6 Use Your Treo as a Modem

Use your Palm Treo to connect your laptop to the Internet. You can also use your Treo as a backup Internet connection for your desktop machine.

If you've signed up for your carrier's wireless data plan, you can get the *entire* Internet on your Treo. It may not seem like it at times, because the small screen can really constrain your web-browsing experience when compared to, say, your laptop or your desktop computer, but it's all there— every last byte. Better still, it is possible to feed the Internet connection of your Treo through to your laptop computer. This is called *tethering*, and it allows your tethered laptop to work with the Internet as if it were connected via a normal dial-up, cable, or DSL modem—except that you are connected through your Treo. Anywhere your Treo has enough signal strength to connect to its wireless data service, you can tether it to supply a laptop with Internet.

Setting up tethering is specific to the model of your Treo and your cellular service provider, as summed up in Table 1-2. You use either your Treo 650's Bluetooth connectivity to use the Treo as a wireless modem for your laptop or desktop, or you need a third-party Windows application called PdaNet, which allows you to connect your Treo (as a modem) to your laptop or desktop via the USB sync cable.

> Tethering might be frowned upon by your carrier. Carriers will argue that tethering is abusing a network infrastructure that is set up in anticipation of the light bandwidth consumption of average smartphone users. Power users will argue that when paying $45 per month for "unlimited Internet," you are entitled to get that for which you've paid. So it's important that you become familiar with your service provider's policy on tethering if you plan to use it frequently—you may be surprised.

Table 1-2. *Wireless providers*

Device	Carrier	Tethering technique
Treo 650	Sprint	Built-in Bluetooth DUN is now supported, provided you apply the "Treo 650 Updater 1.12 for Sprint PCS," found at *http://www.palm.com/us/support/downloads/treo650updater/sprint.html*.
		You may also use PdaNet for tethering over your USB sync cable or wirelessly over Bluetooth.
	Verizon and other CDMA carriers (e.g., EarthLink)	Built-in Bluetooth DUN is *not* supported, and no firmware update is promised.
		Hack your device to enable Bluetooth DUN now, without waiting for Verizon's firmware update. The hack is fairly stable.
		You may also use PdaNet for tethering over your USB sync cable or wirelessly over Bluetooth.
	Cingular and other GSM carriers (e.g., AT&T Wireless, Rogers)	Built-in Bluetooth DUN is *not* supported. Cingular promises a firmware update "later this year," according to a Palm support page dated March 31, 2005.
		Hack your device to enable Bluetooth DUN now, without waiting for a firmware update. The hack is fairly stable.
		You may also use PdaNet for tethering over your USB sync cable or wirelessly over Bluetooth (no hack required).
Treo 600	All	This device does not support Bluetooth. Your only option is to use PdaNet for tethering over your USB sync cable.

Treo 650 Bluetooth DUN

To enable Bluetooth DUN on your Treo 650:

1. Run the Bluetooth application.
2. Enable the Dial-up Networking settings, as shown Figure 1-13. (If you don't see this setting, you need to check for a firmware update for your Treo 650, or apply the shadowmite patch; see the sidebar "The shadowmite Patch).

Figure 1-13. *Turning on the dial-up networking setting on a Treo 650*

The shadowmite Patch

The Treo 650 Bluetooth DUN hack, also called the *shadowmite* patch, after the handle of the developer who discovered it, exposes the Dial-up Networking setting in the Bluetooth preferences panel for those devices that don't already show it. For various reasons (some say political—remember, some carriers would rather you didn't know about tethering), Palm disabled this DUN setting at the last minute before shipping the Treo 650 device. That means that hacking this setting to appear and subsequently enabling it is certainly *not* going to be supported by the technical support departments of Palm or your carrier! The good news is that the shadowmite patch appears stable, it's totally reversible (to un-patch, simply delete the patch file), many people are using it without incident, and there's an online forum where you can post questions. *Before* you go this route, make sure that your carrier hasn't already released a firmware update that enables DUN support (as Sprint has)! For more information on the shadowmite patch, including the patch itself, visit *http://www.shadowmite.com/HowToDUN.html*.

The steps in getting Bluetooth DUN set up on your laptop (or desktop) varies with operating systems and Bluetooth hardware—please consult your manuals for help here. But in general, you want to do something like this:

1. Make sure your Treo is on and Bluetooth has been enabled!

2. Open the Bluetooth control panel/system preferences on your laptop (or desktop).

3. Your Treo 650 should be discovered; Mac users will need to set up a new Mobile Phone device.

4. Establish a connection between your laptop and your Treo 650.

5. Look for your Treo 650's Dial-Up Networking service on your laptop; if you only see its Object Exchange service, try performing a soft reset on your Treo 650.

6. Create a dial-up connection to your Treo 650's Dial-Up Networking service on your laptop. See Table 1-3 for the values that should work for you. A quick phone call to your carrier can get you going if these don't work.

Table 1-3. Carrier data connection information

Carrier	Username	Password	Phone number
Sprint	YourSprintPCSVisionUsername@ sprintpcs.com **(you might not need the @***sprintpcs.com*** part)**	YourSprintPCSVisionPassword	#777
Verizon	YourPhoneNumber **@***vzw3g.com***	vzw	#777
Cingular	WAP@CINGULARGPRS.COM	CINGULAR1	**99***1#
T-Mobile	none	none	*99#

PdaNet

You can download the PdaNet application from June Fabrics PDA Technology Group at *http://www.junefabrics.com*. It has a 15-day trial, after which the application costs $34 to register to your Treo device.

> For Treo 600 users with a Mac, the picture is grim. (Treo 650 users with a Mac should opt to use the Bluetooth technique described earlier). PdaNet suggests it can run under Virtual PC, though that only gives your emulated PC access to the Internet—and this usage is not supported. There is also WirelessModem, which you can download from *http://www.notifymail.com/palm/wmodem/*. It has a 14-day free trial; then it's $37.50 to register the application. Be very careful with this application: many users are unable to maintain an Internet connection to their Mac for more than five minutes, and there is no return policy.
>
> There is a great guide to connecting your Treo 650 to a Mac using Bluetooth at *http://vocaro.com/trevor/treo-dun/*.

Once you've downloaded and run the installer for your specific Treo model (check carefully!), you are prompted to select the appropriate cell phone service from the screen in Figure 1-14.

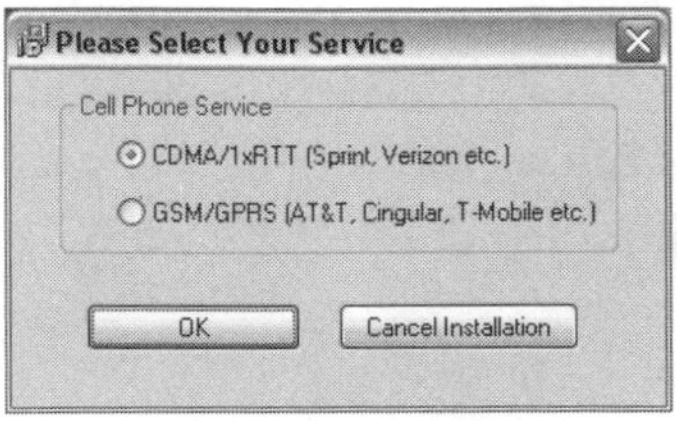

Figure 1-14. Selecting your carrier in PdaNet's installer

The Windows component is installed to your desktop, and then you are prompted to HotSync the Palm component onto your Treo (see Figure 1-15).

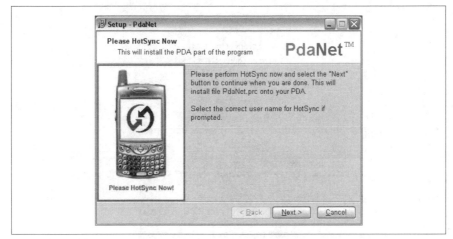

Figure 1-15. PdaNet's installer, queuing up a PRC to install onto your Treo

Once the installation is complete, you will notice a new PdaNet icon in your System Tray (the icons by your clock), which indicates your connection status, as shown in Figure 1-16.

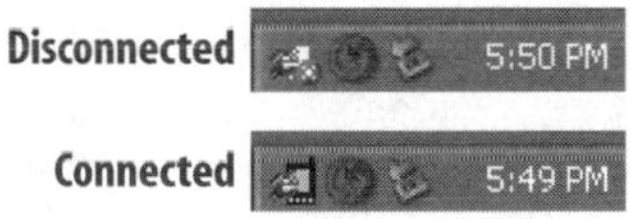

Figure 1-16. PdaNet's icon indicating a connected or disconnected state

The PdaNet icon indicates whether you have an active Internet connection through your Treo; right-click on it to get to the advanced PdaNet settings.

After you've installed the PdaNet application onto your Treo, make sure your device is connected to your laptop with a USB HotSync cable (serial HotSync cables will not work), and then simply launch the PdaNet application on your Treo. Figure 1-17 shows PdaNet running on a Treo.

Your Treo automatically attempts to establish a connection to its wireless Internet service; if successful, PdaNet will then tether that connection over your USB HotSync cable to your laptop. Figure 1-18 shows PdaNet's desktop component confirming its Internet connectivity.

Figure 1-17. PdaNet, ready to connect your laptop to the Internet

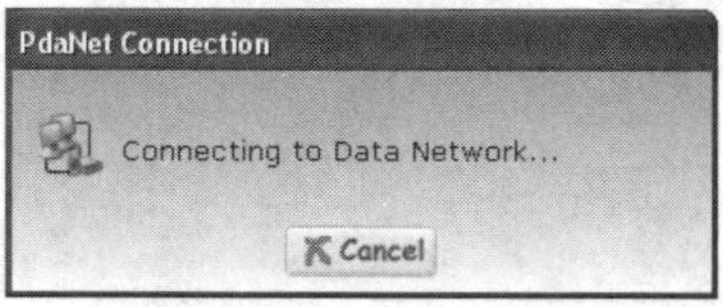

Figure 1-18. The Windows component tethering to your Treo's wireless data network

You should be able to use any Internet applications on your laptop, as long as your Treo is able to keep connected to its wireless Internet service. Be sure to disconnect it when you're done!

> Though some service providers' wireless data plans offer unlimited usage, most allot a certain number of kilobytes per month, and will charge you a fortune for overages. Check into this before you consume too many KB on your Treo.

—Jeff Ishaq

H A C K   Send SMS from a PowerBook
#7

Stop fiddling around with your phone's keypad and use a PowerBook for text messaging.

Short Message Service (SMS) is better known as text messaging for mobile devices. It has proven to be surprisingly popular in many parts of the world (particularly Japan, the Philippines, and much of Europe), but for one reason or another has been less than enthusiastically received in the United States. Part of the barrier to entry for many people is the sometimes painful text entry interface on most mobile phones.

The demand for tiny phones has squeezed out virtually all hope of a usable integrated keyboard. While predictive text technologies such as *T9* have helped make typing require fewer keystrokes, the interface is still far from intuitive. Many people find themselves obsessively hitting number keys in a feeble effort to express themselves, most times mistyping one or two letters along the way. And entering punctuation marks and symbols is so inconvenient that most people don't bother.

If you have a Bluetooth-enabled phone, there is a better way. Mac OS X provides some good integration with these devices and SMS.

> A complete list of phones supported by Mac OS X is available at *http://www.apple.com/macosx/features/isync/ devices.html*.

To get started, be sure that Bluetooth is enabled and that your phone is paired with your laptop. When you launch Address Book with Bluetooth enabled, you will notice an extra Bluetooth button at the top-left corner of the window, as shown in Figure 1-19. Click this button to enable Bluetooth integration in Address Book.

⊖ ⊖ ⊖	Address Book

Rob Flickenger

mobile 206-465-7523

work rob@nocat.net

Note:

Updated: 7/7/05

[+] [Edit]   37 cards   ◀ ▶

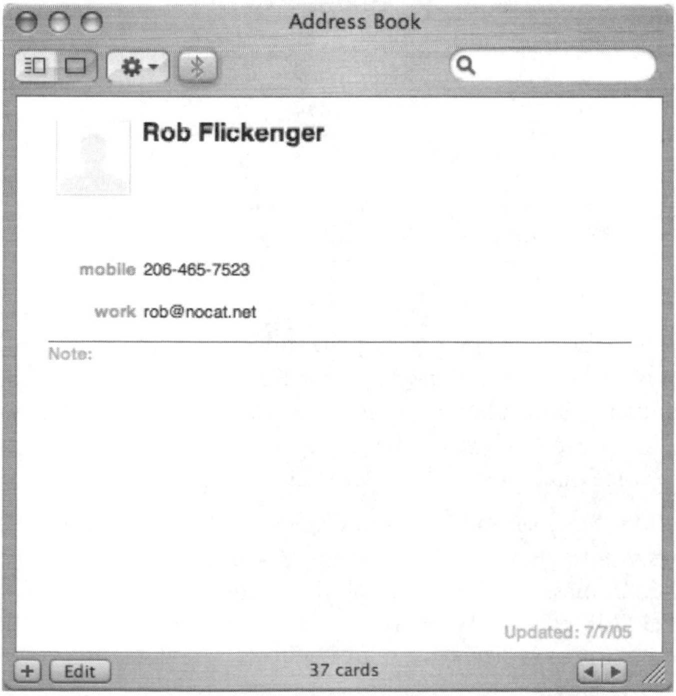

Figure 1-19. Bluetooth integration in Address Book

Having Bluetooth enabled turns on a number of useful features. In addition to being able to simply dial the number directly from an Address Book entry, you can also send an SMS message. Click the label to the left of the number you want to message (Figure 1-20) and select SMS Message. This opens a small textbox for you to type in your message. Lo and behold, you can use your standard keyboard to enter SMS messages!

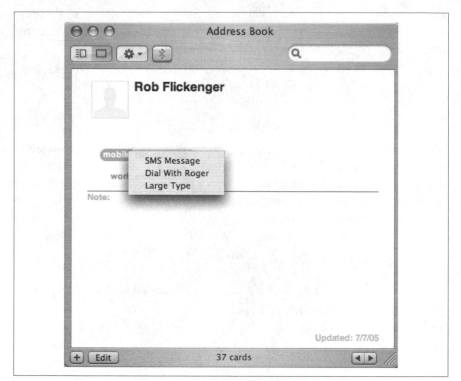

Figure 1-20. Sending SMS

Address Book also gives you possibly the most useful Caller ID implementation there is. When your phone rings, Address Book will pop up a window with the name and phone number of the person calling, shown in Figure 1-21. You can choose whether to answer the call, send the caller straight to voice mail, or send back an SMS message.

Clicking SMS Reply sends the call to voice mail, but it also opens a window that allows you to enter an SMS message. As long as Address Book is open, incoming SMS messages will be displayed automatically and will allow you to reply via SMS as well. While not nearly as portable as SMS on a mobile phone, using a regular keyboard with SMS can help you be more expressive much more quickly.

Figure 1-21. Caller ID from your phone

Incidentally, one good application for SMS messaging is in situations where mobile phone coverage is flaky on one side (or both sides) of the conversation. In areas where mobile voice calls drop out frequently or aren't even possible, SMS messages will automatically be retried until they get through. This can be ideal for squeezing in a quick message to a friend when you can't otherwise establish a phone call. A low bandwidth message that gets through no matter what can be infinitely more useful than a high bandwidth message that just never gets there.

Windows users who would like to have similar SMS functionality with their Bluetooth phones should check out [Hack #14] for an application that lets you do that and much more.

HACK #8 Remote Control Mac OS X with Bluetooth Phones and PDAs

Use your phone/PDA as a remote control for presentations or media players, and create new remote functions with AppleScript.

The Salling Clicker is one of the best applications available for Bluetooth. It turns a whole range of Bluetooth-capable mobile phones and PDAs into full-color, programmable remotes for Mac OS X. You can launch applications, control presentations in PowerPoint or Keynote, and use it as a general-purpose mouse. It plays media files in iTunes, DVD Player, and VideoLan Client and now supports the EyeTV and AlchemyTV digital video recorders (DVRs).

The software works with 21 models of Sony Ericsson phones, 12 Nokia phones, a couple models from Motorola, and it supports almost all PalmOS 4 or 5 devices with PalmSource Bluetooth. A complete list of supported devices is listed in the FAQ at *http://homepage.mac.com/jonassalling/ Shareware/Clicker/faq.html#supported_devices*.

Installing Clicker

You can download the software directly from the author's web site at *http://homepage.mac.com/jonassalling/Shareware/Clicker/*. The application is shareware and costs $19.95. A trial version, limited to 30 clicks from your remote, is also available.

The download package comes with a basic installer, which will install itself as a new control panel and automatically launch. In order for you to use Salling Clicker, your phone or PDA must be paired with your Mac. If you haven't done this already, run the Bluetooth Setup Assistant, found in /*Applications/Utilities*.

After software installation, Salling Clicker appears as a new item in System Preferences. When you open the new preferences item, a small circular icon will also appear in the menu bar, as shown in Figure 1-22. Click Select Phone, and ensure that your phone is on and somewhere near your computer and that you have Bluetooth enabled on your Mac.

Figure 1-22. The Clicker's menu bar icon

Select your phone from the list and save the changes. You can now use your phone to steer Mac OS X, as well as to publish custom menus to the phone itself. Under the Clicker Items tab, you can create custom menus of whatever you like and publish them to your phone. Control Mac OS X by navigating these menus on the phone and selecting what you want to do, such as launch an app or skip to the next track in iTunes. Some phones (such as the Sony Ericcson T630) even allow you to use the phone as a mouse, making it possible to control any application. Just select System → Control Mouse, and you can use the tiny control stick on the phone as a pointer.

If you have a Symbian-based smartphone, such as any of the Nokia Series 60 phones, or a Sony Ericsson P900, there's an additional installation step you'll need to take to get Salling Clicker working. In the downloaded Salling Clicker package, locate and launch the installer program for your particular phone. This will activate Bluetooth File Exchange to transfer some neces-sary Salling Clicker files to your phone. Depending on your phone and its particular security settings, you might either need to enable file transfers, or click Yes on the phone to allow the transfer. You'll also see a security warn-ing on the smartphone, which is normal, because the Clicker software hasn't been approved by the phone manufacturer.

Lastly, if you have a device that runs PalmOS Version 4 or 5, you also need to install a small software package on your PDA. Locate the PDA installa-tion for your Palm in the downloaded Salling Clicker package. You can choose to install it through Palm HotSync or Bluetooth File Exchange.

Connecting to Clicker

Now your smartphone or PDA is ready to connect to Salling Clicker, just as you connected a regular phone in the previous section. You'll need to open the Clicker application on the PDA or smartphone and select the Connect option. Also, make sure your Mac Bluetooth is configured for Discovery; otherwise, the phone will never find the Mac.

Since Bluetooth's range is limited to 30 feet or less, it is possible to signal Clicker to take action when your phone moves in and out of range. You can control this functionality by looking under the Phone Events tab, shown in Figure 1-23. For example, you might want Clicker to pause iTunes and turn on the screensaver whenever you leave your machine. The program comes with many default events, and you can click Show More to select other scripts to run at specified times.

If the built-in actions don't do everything you need, you can always create your own. The actions are just AppleScript snippets, so anything that you can do with AppleScript can be triggered with the phone. You can edit exist-ing actions or create your own by Control-clicking in the Scripts section under the Clicker Items tab in the Clicker control panel, as shown in Figure 1-24.

Clicker comes with handy actions for remotely controlling slideshows in PowerPoint or Keynote, and since it can simulate any keystroke, it can be used with just about any other application, too. It is particularly handy when making presentations, because you are virtually guaranteed to have your phone with you (and it is likely to be charged). The latest version of Salling Clicker, if used with Microsoft PowerPoint 2004, will preview the title of the upcoming slide on your phone. You're guaranteed not to lose a beat when you know what the next slide is!

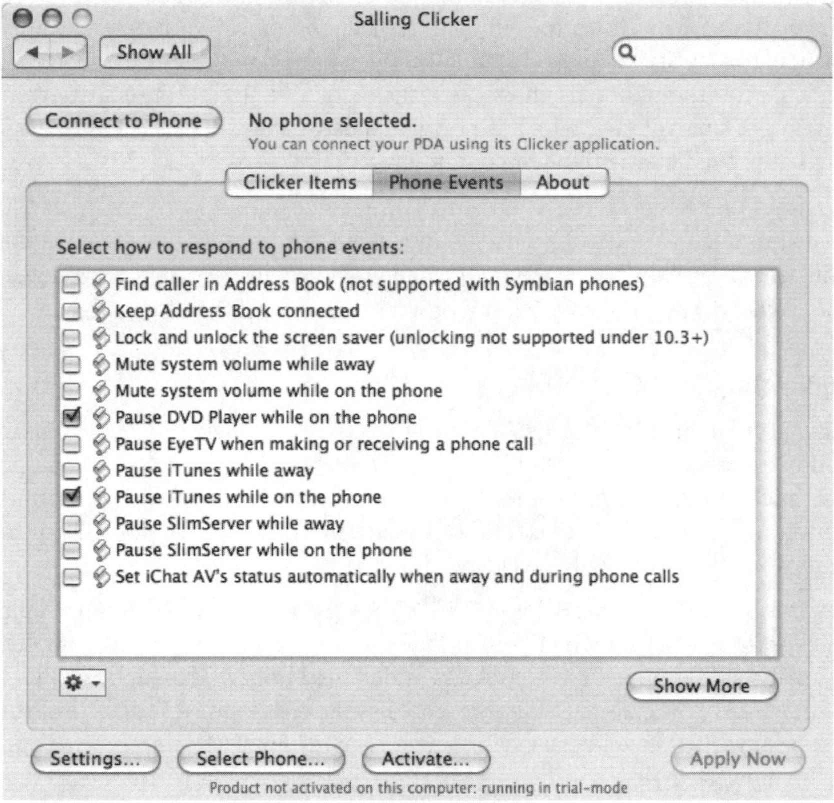

Figure 1-23. Assigning any action you like to the Proximity Sensor

Hacking the Hack

When most people think of Bluetooth, they think of voice or data applications, but Clicker is a clever app that transcends the traditional *cable replacement* idea. If you use Mac OS X and own any of the supported phones, smartphones, or PDAs, you will probably find all sorts of novel uses for this software. Particularly because it is easy to use and is fully scriptable, Clicker is an application that just screams "hack me!"

At the time of this writing, the author, Jon Salling, has responded to requests for support of Microsoft smartphones and PocketPC-based PDAs. Check back on the product web page for updates to the program, because this will be a major addition to device support for Salling Clicker.

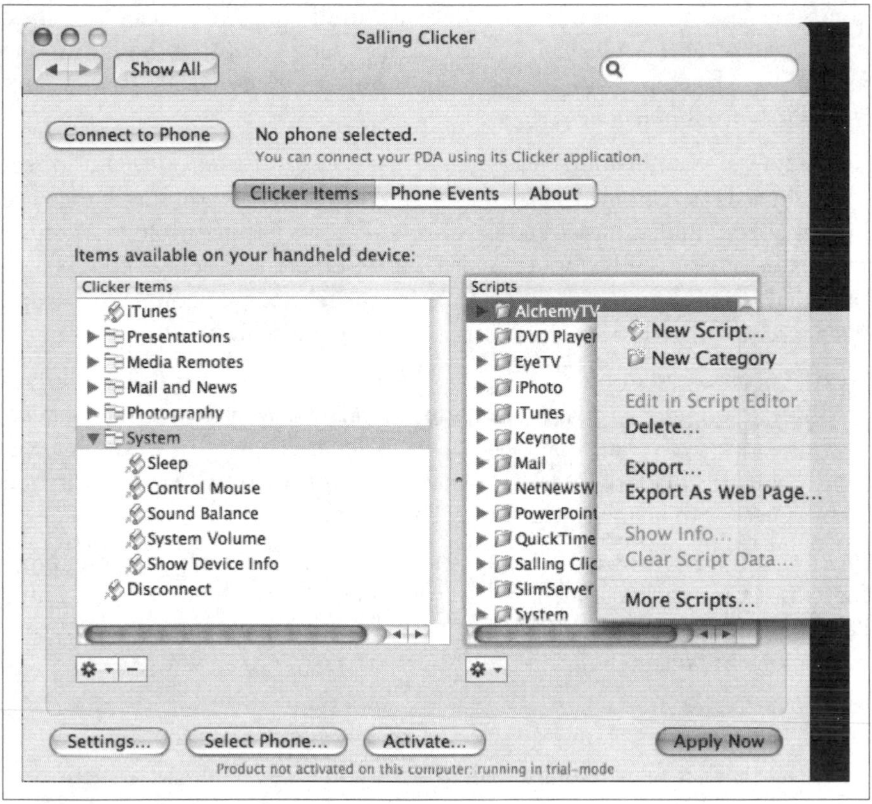

Figure 1-24. Writing your own Clicker actions

Remote Control Linux with a Bluetooth Phone

HACK #9

Never fear, Linux users! You too can control your machine with a Bluetooth phone.

Continuing with the remote control theme, here's an option for Linux users who would like to have functionality similar to Salling Clicker [Hack #8] or PuppetMaster [Hack #13].

Bluemote is a software package written specifically to take advantage of the capabilities of a Sony Ericsson phone. We tested it using a T630, but several other models from the same manufacturer should also work. Many of the steps in this hack are similar to the next hack [Hack #10]. In fact, Bluemote was inspired by the *bluexmms* application, extending this control to the operating system.

In order to get Bluemote working, you'll need a working Bluetooth stack and utilities [Hack #1] and a Sony Ericsson phone that is paired with your computer [Hack #4]. Download the software itself from *http://www.geocities. com/saravkrish/progs/bluemote*. You will also need a copy of the scripts the author has developed for the package, found at *http://www.geocities.com/ saravkrish/progs/bluemote/scripts.tar.gz*.

Uncompress the Bluemote package. In the newly created *bluemote* directory, there is a compiled *bluemote* binary file. The author states that the binary was compiled under Fedora Core 1, and we had no problem running it on later versions of Fedora Core or Ubuntu Linux. The source code is also provided, should you wish to compile it yourself. It's a good idea to copy *bluemote* to somewhere in your path, such as */usr/local/bin*.

Next, uncompress the scripts package. Bluemote looks for the newly created *scripts* directory in your user home directory, so if it isn't there now, you should move it appropriately. To take advantage of the scripts for volume control, you will need to install the *aumix* software. Ubuntu and Debian users can install it with apt-get install aumix.

Finally, you'll need to create a *.bluemote* directory inside your home directory. In the unpacked Bluemote source code package, you will find a file called *bluemote-example.cfg*. Copy this file to the new *.bluemote* directory and rename it *bluemote.cfg*:

```
mkdir ~/.bluemote
cp ~/scripts/bluemote-example.cfg ~/.bluemote/bluemote.cfg
```

Chances are that your phone is paired with your computer using channel 1. You can determine this by executing rfcomm without any parameters:

```
rfcomm
rfcomm0: 00:0F:DE:E5:2E:65 channel 1 clean
```

Bluemote requires your phone to use channel 4. This is easily accomplished by running the following command using *sudo* or as the root user:

```
rfcomm bind /dev/rfcomm0 00:0F:DE:E5:2E:65 4
```

You can confirm this was successful by executing rfcomm again with no parameters.

That's got all of the requirements out of the way! Now, you can run *bluemote* from the command line. If you wish, you can append --log to have the program save debug information in the *.bluemote* directory.

If everything has been done correctly, your phone should now prompt you to accept a new connection from your Linux machine. You'll need to enter a PIN on the phone, and if you have left the Bluetooth settings alone, a window should pop up on your Linux box, asking you to confirm the PIN.

Once the pairing is complete, after a few seconds your phone should say "Bluemote loaded" on the main screen. Navigate to the Connectivity → Accessories menu, and you'll be presented with a selection of items you can now use to control your Linux machine:

Mute/Unmute and Volume Control
> These options control system sound settings.

Rhythmbox
> This option conveniently shows what is currently playing in the GNOME media player.

Media
> This menu allows you to control the transport in either Rhythmbox or XMMS.

Lock Screen
> This option allows you to lock the GNOME screen remotely.

Mouse control
> This option seems to work only partially using the joystick, but you can use keys 5 and 9 to move side to side, and keys 6 and 8 to move up and down. Key 1 performs mouse clicks.

If you own a Sony Ericsson phone and use Linux as your primary operating system, you really should check out this free and convenient program.

HACK #10 Control XMMS with Bluetooth

Use your Bluetooth phone to control your music remotely under Linux.

If you have a mobile Bluetooth device that you'd like to use to control the XMMS media player in Linux, you might be in luck. There are actually a couple of applications out there that use a WAP-like serial interface to Sony Ericsson's T-series phones (including the T68i and the T39m) to configure them for use as XMMS remote controls.

The first of the two is a standalone Ruby-based application called *bluexmms*, which is available from *http://linuxbrit.co.uk/bluexmms*. Make sure your phone is paired [Hack #4] with the Bluetooth interface on your computer. Install *bluexmms*, and then use *rfcomm* to bind an RFCOMM device to channel 2 on the T68i, which is the T68's generic telephony service.

Next, run bluexmms /dev/rfcomm1 on your device, substituting the name of the RFCOMM device you just created. You should now be able to go to Accessories → XMMS Remote on your phone's menu, and voilà! You can now control XMMS directly from your phone.

A second, but similar approach, involves an XMMS plug-in called BTE (a.k.a. *btexmms*), which can be downloaded from *http://www.lyola.com/bte*. Build and install the plug-in, and create an RFCOMM device on channel 2, as just described. Then, go into the XMMS preferences menu and, under Effects → General Plugins, enable and configure the BTE Control plug-in. Set the device to whatever RFCOMM device you created for this purpose, and save your changes. Now you should be able to access the remote control from Accessories → XMMS Remote, as described previously.

If you don't have a Sony Ericsson T-series phone, you might try Bemused, which runs on SymbianOS devices, such as the Nokia 3650/7650 and the Sony Ericsson P800. Unlike the T68 apps just listed, which rely on the computer to establish a connection to the phone, Bemused instead uses a client that initiates the connection from your phone to a server running on your computer.

You can get the Bemused server and client from *http://www.compsoc.man.ac.uk/ ~ashley/bemused*. First, unpack *bemused.zip* and upload and install the *.sis* file on your phone. Then, download *bemusedlinuxserver.tar.gz*, and build and install it on your computer. You'll need to advertise Bluetooth serial port services on your laptop by running sdptool add --channel=10 SP, and then edit and configure */etc/bemused.conf* appropriately. The Bemused README suggests using Bluetooth channel 10 on your computer, but any unused channel will do. Start your X11 window manager of choice, if you haven't already. Run bemusedserverlinux from the command line. At this point, you should be able to fire up the Bemused application on your phone and have the full power of XMMS at your fingertips, from clear across the room.

If you don't have one of these devices, don't fret; nearly every Bluetooth device these days implements some kind of serial communications layer. Using examples from the projects just listed, you can probably create an XMMS remote control for your own phone or PDA. The hackability quotient of Bluetooth for this particular kind of application is pretty high.

Clearly, if you've made it this far, you're probably thinking that, with a wireless remote control for XMMS, you could plug a dedicated MP3 server running Linux into the hi-fi amplifier in your living room and never need a monitor or a keyboard for it. Or maybe you're considering plugging a low-power FM transmitter into your sound card, so you can listen to your music collection from any radio in the house.

You're absolutely right. Bluetooth can do this and much more. Read on for more hacks that show you just what you can do with a Bluetooth device and various computer operating systems.

—*Schuyler Erle*

Liven Up Parties with a Participatory Slideshow

With a laptop, a Bluetooth adapter, and an LCD projector, you can make slideshows of other people's photographs.

Since time immemorial, slideshows have been a dreaded tool of oppression and tedium. Heretofore constrained to only the slides that the presenter wished to show, the slideshow's audience was doomed to mind-numbing boredom, if it turned out that the slides failed to entertain.

Thanks to the ubiquity of mobile phones with both cameras and Bluetooth, the institution of photographic slideshows can now be thrown open, willy-nilly, to the viewing public as both a read and write medium! Allowing people to contribute photos from their phones to a participatory slideshow can offer interesting and often quite entertaining results.

The Slideshow

To set up a participatory slideshow, you'll need a laptop or a PC running Linux, a supported Bluetooth adapter, and an overhead projector. The concept of this hack can certainly be adapted to other operating systems, but the implementation shown here is specific to the Linux Bluetooth stack and to the X11 Window System used on most open source operating systems. The best Linux distros for this purpose are Debian or Ubuntu, because all of the pieces are already available through apt-get.

If you haven't got a Linux PC handy, Ubuntu (*http://www.ubuntulinux.org/download*) can be installed on an old leftover Pentium in about a half hour. If you use Ubuntu, you'll want to make sure you have the universe and multiverse repositories in your *etc/apt/sources.list*. If you're using another version of Linux, you should be able to find the source code and possibly even binary packages for all the software you'll need somewhere on the Net.

Once you've selected a suitable computer, install the BlueZ Bluetooth stack [Hack #1]. Next, plug in your Bluetooth adapter, and make sure the kernel can see it by running *dmesg* and checking for a suitable notification towards the bottom of the output. (If your Bluetooth adapter is built-in, dmesg | grep -i Bluetooth is your friend.) Next, as root, back up your *etc/bluetooth/hcid.conf* and then alter it so that it reads more or less as follows:

```
options {
    autoinit yes;
    security none;
    pairing none;
}
device {
    name "slideshow";
```

```
        class 0x100;
        iscan enable;
        pscan enable;
    }
```

These settings turn off Bluetooth security (thus allowing anyone to send files to the Bluetooth device), set the name of the device to slideshow, and allow anyone to scan for it. Naturally, once you no longer want anyone sending anything to your computer, you should copy your backup of *hcid.conf* back into place. Now, as root, run /etc/init.d/bluez-utils restart to restart your Bluetooth manager. On other Linux distros, *hcid.conf* lives in */etc*, rather than */etc/bluetooth*, and */etc/init.d/bluez-utils* might be called */etc/init.d/bluetooth*, instead.

Next, you'll need an OBEX server to receive files sent from people's phones. OBEX is a FTP-like file transfer protocol that runs on top of Bluetooth. A simple OBEX server, quite logically called ObexSERVER, is available using apt-get. The source code for ObexSERVER lives at *http://www.frasunek.com/sources/unix/obexserver.c*, but you'll need to have the OpenOBEX libraries from *http://openobex.sf.net* to build it.

You'll also need an image viewer for X11 that supports a slideshow mode. There are a ton of these out there, with the most popular possibly being GQview and *feh*. Of these two, I prefer GQview, but I'll show how to use *feh* also. Again, both of them are available using *apt-get*. If you decide to use GQview, you'll want to load it up, and then go to Edit → Options... to configure the slideshow options on the General tab. Check the Random and Repeat boxes, and set the delay to something short, like five seconds, as shown in Figure 1-25.

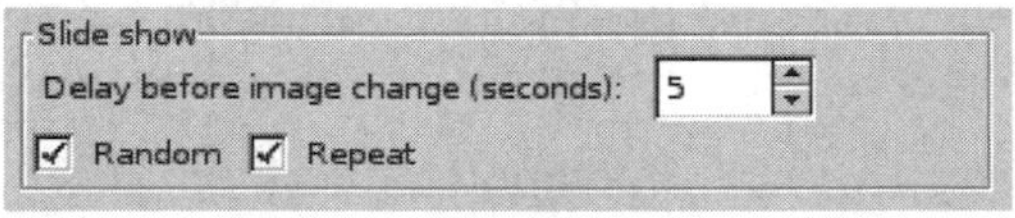

Figure 1-25. Setting the slideshow options in gqview

Also, over on the Image tab, you'll probably want to select "Fit image to window" and "Allow enlargement," as shown in Figure 1-26. If you'd rather use *feh*, we'll see later on that this configuration is done on the command line instead.

Last but not least, you'll need to create an empty directory to hold the contributed slideshow images. I used */home/sderle/slideshow*, but any directory you can write to is fine.

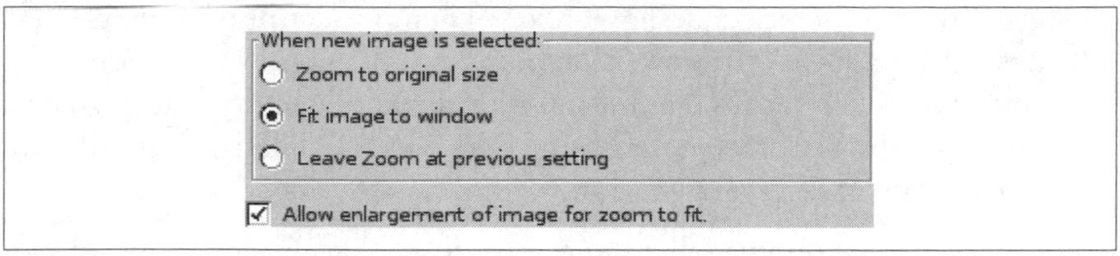

When new image is selected:
- ○ Zoom to original size
- ◉ Fit image to window
- ○ Leave Zoom at previous setting
- ☑ Allow enlargement of image for zoom to fit.

Figure 1-26. Setting the default image zoom options in GQview

Finally, seed the slideshow with a single file, which can be an image of anything. The best bet for the seed image is a plain slide that reads "Share your favorite photos by sending them via Bluetooth to 'slideshow'!" You can hack up a slide with some words to that effect using the GIMP in about three minutes. Once everything's configured, you're ready for the code that makes it all go.

The Code

The following shell script accepts images via Bluetooth and displays them in fullscreen mode using GQview:

```
#!/bin/bash

SLIDESHOW_PATH=/home/sderle/slideshow

xset s off
xset s noblank
sdptool add --channel=10 OPUSH

cd $SLIDESHOW_PATH
gqview --slideshow --fullscreen &
while true; do
    obexserver
    mv /tmp/*.{jpg,JPG} .
done
```

First, the calls to xset turn off the X11 screensaver functions, so that it doesn't load the screensaver after some period of inactivity or make the screen go blank. The call to sdptool sets up the Bluetooth channel to receive files via the OBEX PUSH profile.

 You might need to run this bit as root first, or change the script to use *sudo* for that line, and then type in your password when you start the script.

Next, the slideshow script switches to the slideshow image directory; don't forget to change SLIDESHOW_PATH to point to wherever you plan to keep the photos. Once in that directory, the script starts up *gqview* to run in the background, in fullscreen slideshow mode. Then, the script runs *obexserver*, which waits for a file to arrive via Bluetooth, and then puts the file into */tmp* and quits. Our script moves that file into the current directory, where *gqview* will automatically detect its presence and add it to the slideshow. Finally, we loop back to run obexserver again, and so on.

Once this script is running, all you need to do is plug the computer into an overhead projector, and you're set. To stop the slideshow, hit Ctrl-Q to get out of *gqview*, and then Ctrl-C in your terminal to kill the slideshow script.

The nice thing about using GQview, as mentioned earlier, is that it regularly scans the current directory for new files, unlike *feh*, which scans the directory contents once at startup. If you wanted to use *feh* instead, you could do the following in the slideshow script, which restarts *feh* every time a new file arrives:

```
cd $SLIDESHOW_PATH
while true; do
    feh -D5 -F -z -Z * &
    obexserver
    mv /tmp/*.{jpg,JPG} .
    killall feh
done
```

The principle is basically the same, however. The main advantage of this is that it saves you the trouble of having to configure (and possibly later reconfigure) the image viewer just to display a slideshow; the disadvantage is that it increases the likelihood that *feh* will display some photos with disproportionate frequency, because each time it reloads it loses its idea of which ones it's already shown.

Enjoy your new participatory slideshow! If you use this idea at a party or other gathering, please do let us know how it works out for you.

—*Schuyler Erle*

HACK #12   Send SMS from Linux

Tired of one letter typing on your phone keypad? Send complete SMS messages from Linux instead.

As shown in "Send SMS from a PowerBook" **[Hack #7]** and "Control Your Bluetooth Phone with FMA" **[Hack #14]**, it's relatively simple to set up your Bluetooth phone so that you can send Short Message Service (SMS) text messages using your computer. Fortunately, there's also a way to do this in Linux.

In order to make this work, you'll need to have your Bluetooth phone paired and configured as a dial-up networking device **[Hack #4]**. Once those tasks are done, your phone will be communicating with your Linux box using Bluetooth, and you will have a new serial device mapped to */dev/rfcomm0* that you can use.

What this means practically is that you can treat your Bluetooth phone as a modem, and send it standard AT commands, using any serial terminal program like *gkermit*, *minicom*, or *screen*.

To find out whether your phone lets you send SMS messages using AT commands, you'll need to connect to your phone with one of these programs, and execute the query AT+CSMS=0. Here is an example using the *screen* program:

```
screen /dev/rfcomm0
ATE1 #this won't be echoed to the screen, but it turns echo on
OK
AT+CSMS=0
+CSMS: 1,1,1

OK
```

The output after the AT+CSMS=0 command is listed in three columns, which indicate whether the device is capable of receiving messages, sending messages, or sending broadcast messages. In this case, the phone is capable of all three.

If your cell phone supports this capability, you can work with text messages using AT commands. You can list your text messages with AT+CMGL=4 (the 4 indicates all messages: use 0 for unread, 1 for read, 2 for unsent, and 3 for sent messages) and read a message with AT+CMGR=*MESSAGE_NUMBER*:

```
AT+CMGL=4
+CMGL: 1,1,,28
07919170389103F2040B91XXXXXXXXXXF100013011320211500A0AD3771D7E9A83DEEE10
+CMGL: 2,1,,25
07919170389103F2040B91XXXXXXXXXXF100013011329135610A06C8F79D9C0F01

OK
AT+CMGR=1
+CMGR: 1,,28
07919170389103F2040B91XXXXXXXXXXF100013011320211500A0AD3771D7E9A83DEEE10

OK
```

However, you'll want to put the phone into text mode, so the responses that you receive are human-readable. Use AT+CMGF=1 for this, and try reading the message again:

```
AT+CMGF=1
OK
AT+CMGR=1
```

```
+CMGR: "REC READ","+14015559000",,"03/11/23,20:11:05-20"
Soup's on!

OK
```

You can send a message with AT+CMGS="*PHONE_NUMBER*" (but make sure you've set responses to be human-readable with AT+CMGF=1). You'll be prompted for the message; type it and press Ctrl-Z when you are finished:

```
AT+CMGF=1
OK
AT+CMGS="4015559000"
> Hello, world!^Z
OK
```

You can also use the *gsmsendsms* utility from *gsmlib* (*http://www.pxh.de/fs/ gsmlib/index.html*) to send the *message*:

```
bjepson@debian:~$ gsmsendsms -d /dev/rfcomm0 4015559000 "Hello, World"
```

—Brian Jepson

HACK #13 Remote Control Windows with Bluetooth Phones and PDAs

Use your phone/PDA as a remote control for media, presentations, and other programs.

If you're a Windows user, you've probably skimmed "Remote Control Mac OS X with Bluetooth Phones and PDAs" [Hack #8] and thought, "Why can't I do that?" Well, you too can control your PC via Bluetooth, with a wide range of phones and PDAs.

Requirements

Most PCs, aside from some newer laptops, do not come with built-in Bluetooth. To take advantage of the programs in this hack, you'll need a Bluetooth adapter. USB-based adapters are available for as little as $20. Some of these devices are low-power Class 2 devices, transmitting up to 10 feet, while other Class 1 devices have extendable antennas and claim to cover upwards of 300 feet. If you're planning on using the device with software for presentations, the longer-range models are probably what you want.

Windows requires drivers to operate with your Bluetooth device. Windows XP comes with built-in Bluetooth driver support, and if your USB device is recognized when you insert it, we recommend that you use the Microsoft drivers [Hack #2].

In our examples, we were not able to get our USB Bluetooth adapter to work with the third-party drivers that shipped with the unit. Uninstalling those drivers and allowing the Microsoft drivers to detect the device resolved the issues.

Installing PuppetMaster

This hack uses PuppetMaster software, which is available from *http://www. lim.com.au/PuppetMaster*. If you are in doubt about the capabilities of your Bluetooth phone, check that site for more information on device support. While PuppetMaster supports a variety of phones and PDAs, we tested using a Sony Ericsson T630. Setup and capabilities in these programs vary from phone to phone, so be sure to check to see if your phone is supported.

In addition to a Bluetooth adapter, PuppetMaster requires Windows 2000 or XP and one of the following mobile devices with Bluetooth onboard:

- Symbian Series 60 phone (complete list at *http://www.series60.com/ products*)
- Symbian UIQ phone (complete list at *http://www.uiq.com/uiqphones*)
- Microsoft Smartphone
- Microsoft PocketPC 2003
- Java Phones with Bluetooth API support
- Sony Ericsson T68, T610, T630, K700i, or Z1010

Installation of the software is simple. Accept all of the defaults. Once PuppetMaster has been installed, run it from the Start Menu. A circular icon will appear in the taskbar, indicating the program has loaded, and you should see the status window shown in Figure 1-27.

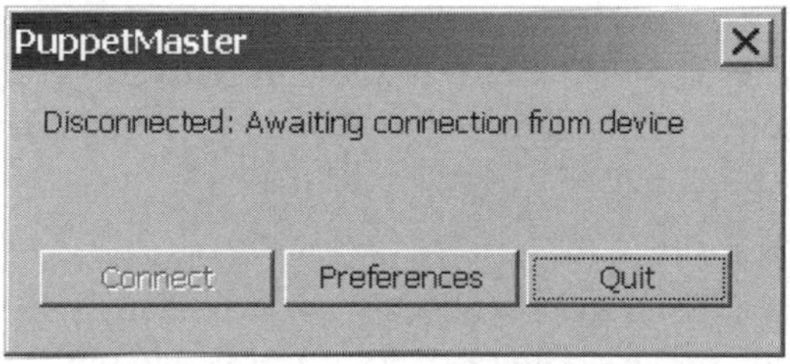

![PuppetMaster status window showing "Disconnected: Awaiting connection from device" with Connect, Preferences, and Quit buttons]

Figure 1-27. Initial PuppetMaster status

In our testing, we did not have the Sony Ericsson T630 phone paired with our test PC. If you are using non-Microsoft Bluetooth drivers, you might need to pair your phone with your PC ahead of time. Instead, we selected the Preferences button in the dialog to open the PuppetMaster Preferences window, as shown in Figure 1-28.

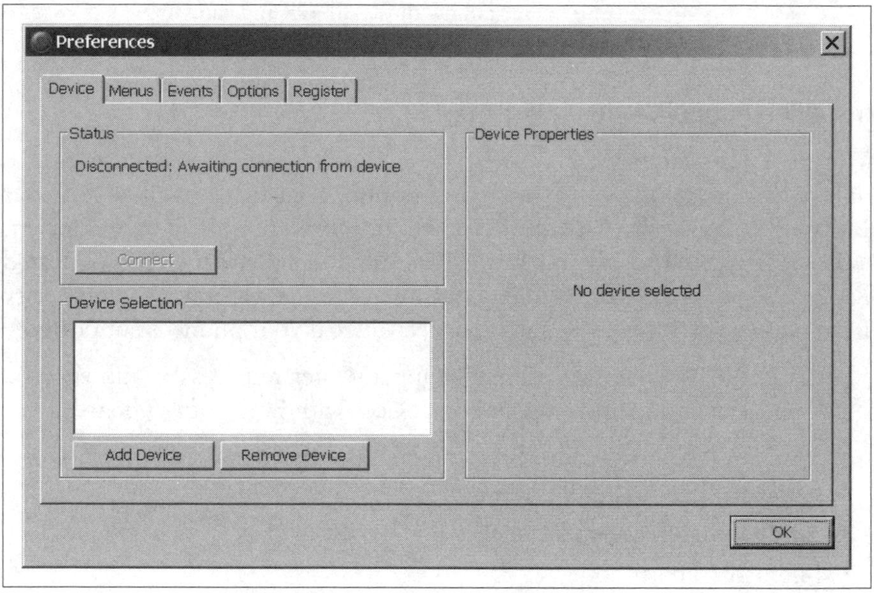

Figure 1-28. Adding your phone in the Preferences window

At this point, enable Bluetooth on your phone to make it discoverable. Click the Add Device button, and PuppetMaster will scan available Bluetooth devices, or virtual COM ports if your non-Microsoft drivers support this feature. In either case, you will be presented with a list of appropriate device connections that PuppetMaster found (Figure 1-29).

Choose your phone from the list and click Add. You'll be prompted on your phone to allow the connection and enter a numeric PIN. Once you've entered the PIN on the phone, a confirmation window will appear on the PC, asking for the same PIN. Confirm the choice to add your phone to PuppetMaster. To complete the setup, click Connect in the Preferences dialog.

Controlling Your PC

Now that you are connected, you can control many aspects of your PC directly from your phone. Using the Sony Ericsson T630, select Connectivity → Accessories from the phone menu to display a whole list of items that can be controlled from the phone. As shown in Figure 1-30, you can add menu categories in PuppetMaster, and then add items to those categories to expand your control options.

Figure 1-29. Available Bluetooth devices

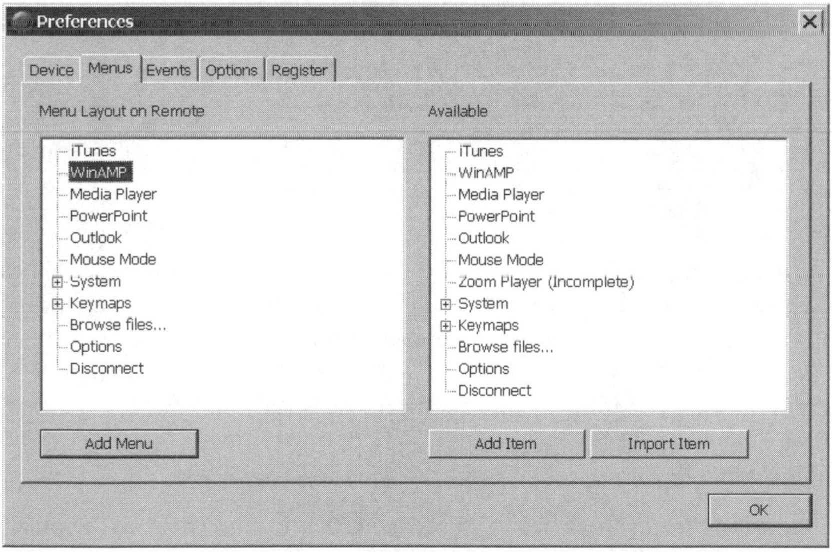

Figure 1-30. Customizing PuppetMaster menus

Out of the box, PuppetMaster supports controlling iTunes, WinAmp, and Windows Media Player. Most importantly for presentations is the ability to control PowerPoint. You can perform system commands such as shutting down, activating the screensaver, or browsing files. Another great function for presentations is Mouse Mode. On phones that have a directional control, such as the T630, you can direct the mouse cursor remotely.

One final set of abilities that PuppetMaster gives you is Events. As shown in Figure 1-31, you can set up special events to occur when the phone comes in range of the PC, when it leaves range, or when you get a call.

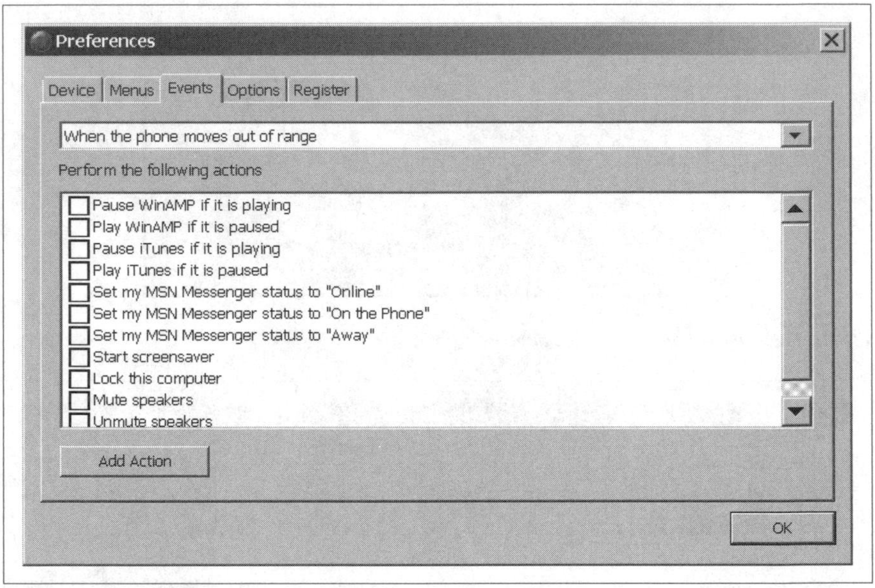

Figure 1-31. Adding custom events

Events are handy if you are using your phone as a media controller. You can have iTunes pause the currently playing track when your phone rings, so you can hear your caller. If your phone goes out of range of the PC, you can make it assume that you have left and activate your screensaver, set your status to Away in your IM program, and mute the speakers.

Hacking the Hack

PuppetMaster is an amazingly cool program that extends control of your PC to many types of Bluetooth phones and PDAs. If you use Linux, check out "Remote Control Linux with a Bluetooth Phone" **[Hack #9]** for a hack that lets you do the same thing. If you have a Sony Ericsson phone, definitely go on to "Control Your Bluetooth Phone with FMA" **[Hack #14]**, which shows even more great things you can do over Bluetooth with your phone.

Control Your Bluetooth Phone with FMA

HACK #14

flOat's Mobile Agent lets you take complete control of your Bluetooth phone.

flOat's Mobile Agent (FMA) is a whole different program design than PuppetMaster [Hack #13]. While it does allow you to control your PC remotely from your Bluetooth phone, it also is a complete synchronization utility, allowing you to edit your phone contacts; store, sort, and send text (SMS) messages; and much more.

You can get the binary installer or the source code from *http://fma.sourceforge.net*. This is an open source package licensed under the GPL, so if you're a Windows programmer, you can hack away at the source code all you like.

Requirements

FMA is designed around the capabilities of the Sony Ericsson T610/T630 phones. Many other phones have been tested, but there is no central list of known working phones. You will need to search for your phone by clicking the Tested Devices link on the FMA web site, which will take you to a SourceForge bug reports page.

The program is also somewhat different from PuppetMaster in that, in addition to Bluetooth, it also supports infrared and serial phone connections. For serial support, you can use Windows 98 or greater; infrared requires Windows 2000 or greater, and Bluetooth is supported on Windows XP only.

Bluetooth requirements are the same as for PuppetMaster. FMA supports both native (Microsoft) Bluetooth drivers and third-party drivers. Unlike PuppetMaster, we were required to pair our T630 phone with the test PC before FMA would communicate with the phone. FMA can talk to your phone in several ways. As shown in Figure 1-32, you can tell FMA which COM port has been mapped to the phone; you can specify the MAC address of your phone for the Native Bluetooth drivers; and you can also use infrared if your phone supports it.

Setup

While the FMA setup is similar to any other program you've installed in Windows, there are a couple sections that you should be familiar with prior to installation. The first is the selection of components, shown in Figure 1-33. If you opt to not install the Microsoft Components, FMA will not work correctly until it is reinstalled with the components.

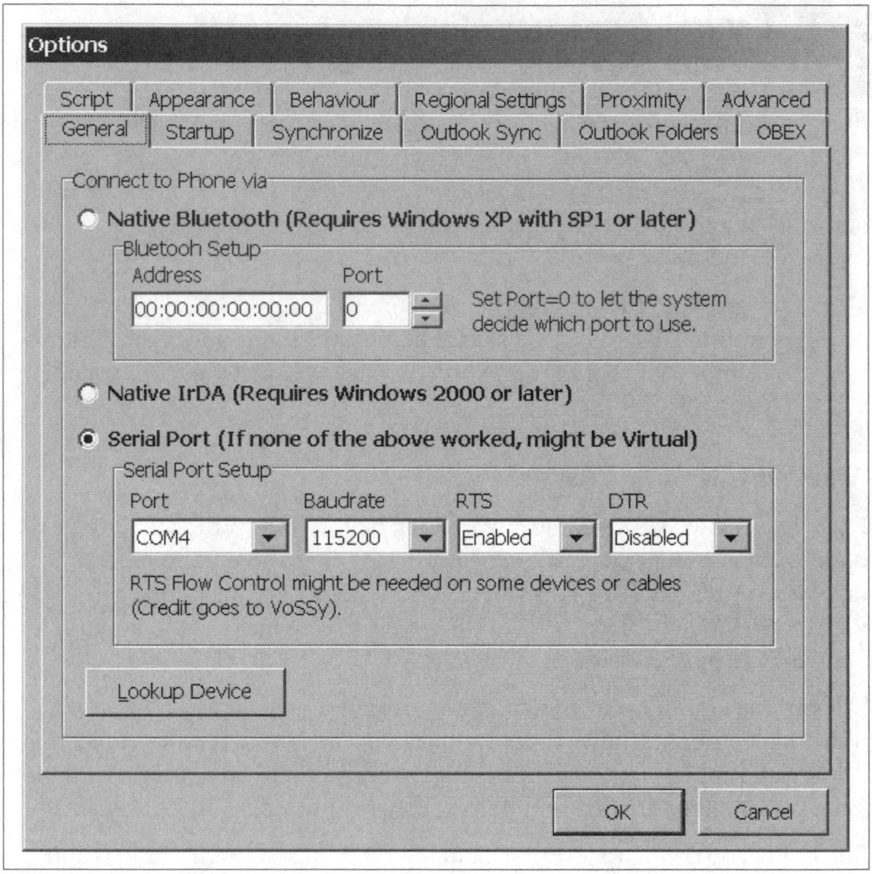

Figure 1-32. FMA Bluetooth connection types

Secondly, you can customize the installation as usual by choosing where icons are created, as shown in Figure 1-34. You need to make sure to include at least the two top Microsoft components; otherwise, FMA will not function. It would be nice if there were documentation to cover this with the package.

Once the program completes installation, it will launch automatically. A phone icon will appear in your taskbar, showing that the program is running. As covered in the next section, you might need to adjust the Bluetooth device settings using the Tools → Options menu to make sure FMA can communicate with your phone.

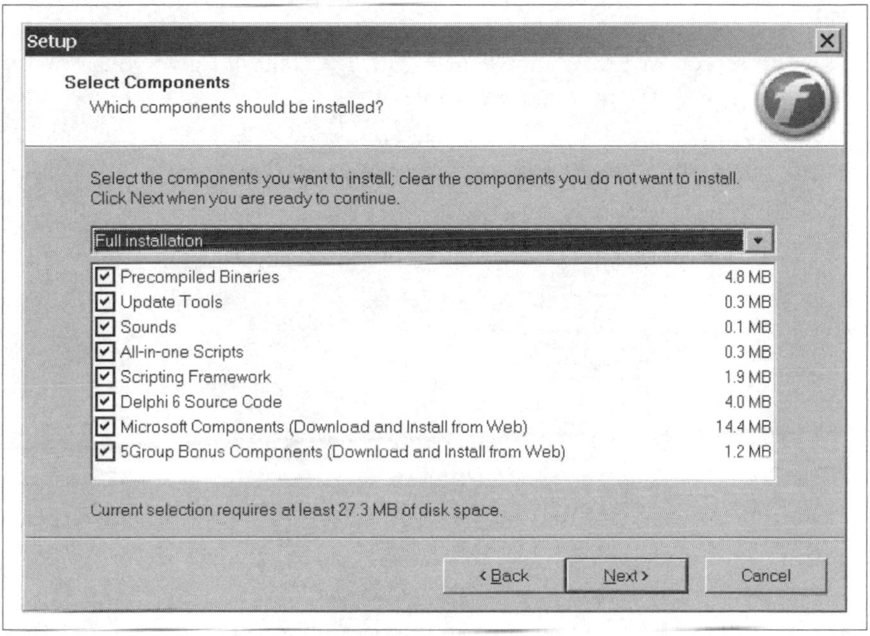

Figure 1-33. Choosing the components for installation

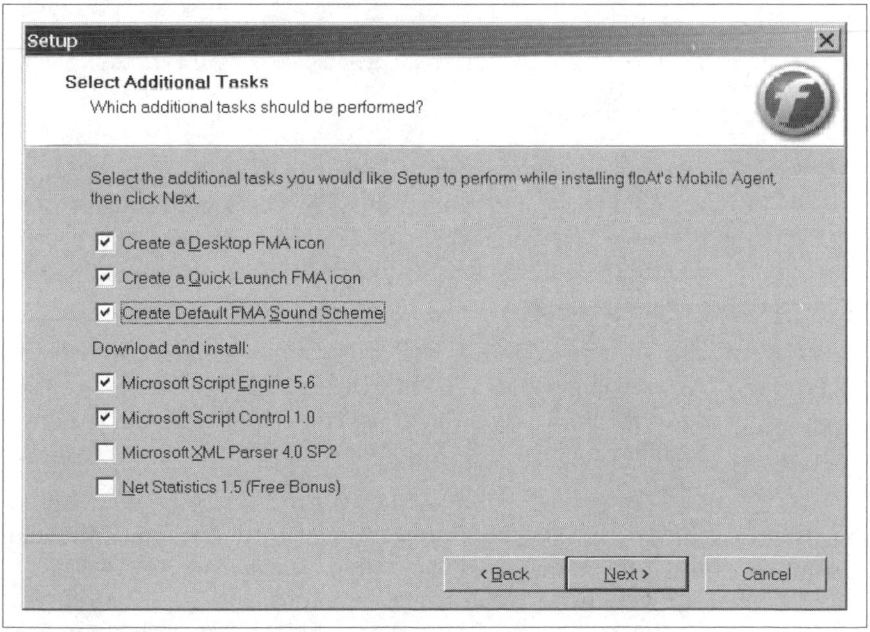

Figure 1-34. FMA additional installation tasks

FMA

The main screen of FMA, shown in Figure 1-35, should give you a pretty good idea of what the program is capable of.

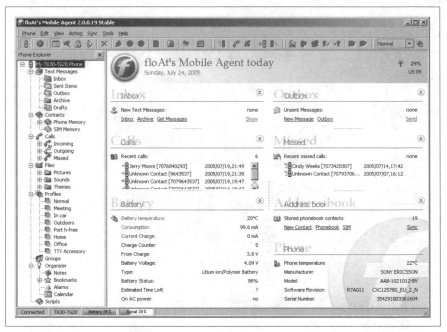

Figure 1-35. The main FMA screen

FMA gives you complete control over your text messaging. Choose Action → New Message to compose and send your SMS messages. The New Message window is shown in Figure 1-36. You can also view new messages in your Inbox, organize them in the default folders shown, or create new folders to categorize your messages.

The program also gives you control over your contacts, both in phone and SIM memory. As shown in Figure 1-37, FMA lets you assign custom icons to a contact, and give them a custom ringtone. You can also set the preferred number for the calling contact, as well as associate each contact with a specific contact in Outlook.

When FMA is loaded and communicating with your phone, you can make and answer calls from your PC. When a new call arrives, you will get a Caller ID pop-up window on your screen, as shown in Figure 1-38. If you have a headset connected to the PC, and the correct Bluetooth Audio settings turned on, you can use your headset to answer and receive calls.

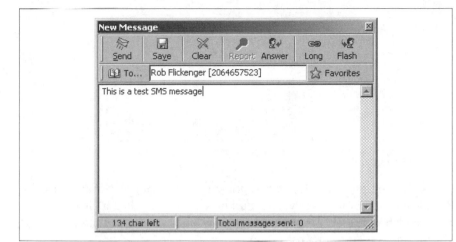

Figure 1-36. Sending an SMS message

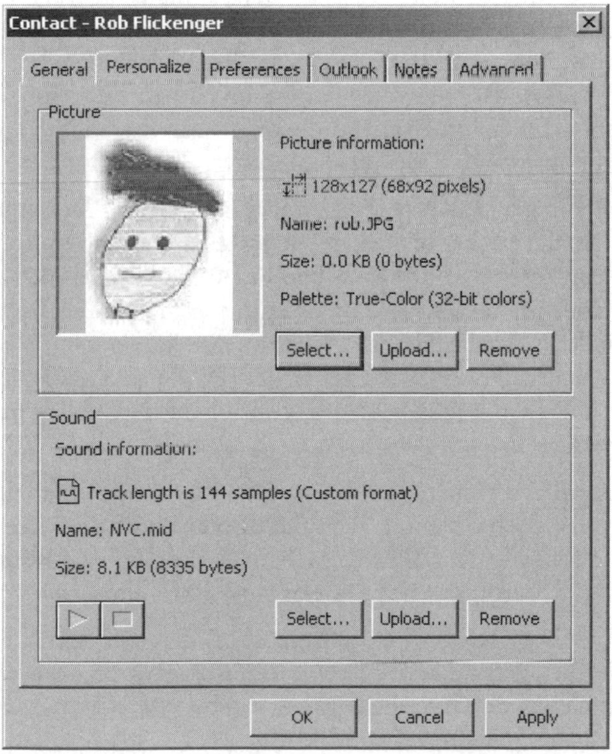

Figure 1-37. Personalizing your contacts

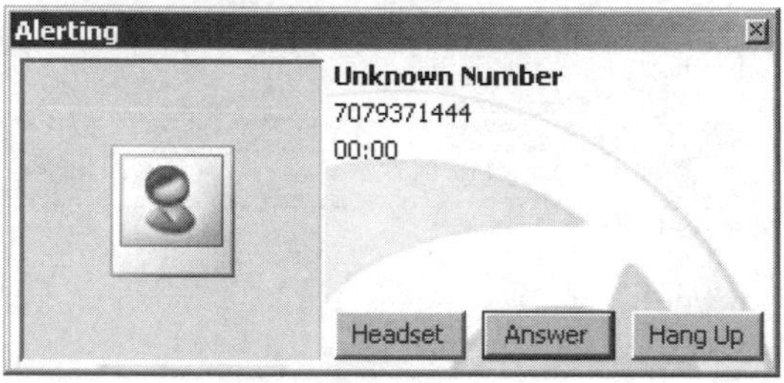

Figure 1-38. Caller ID integration

You have complete call logs of all incoming, outgoing, and missed calls. This can be a real lifesaver when you know that you called a client 37 days ago and left a message, but they tell you no one ever called them. Print out the log and send it to them as proof!

You can also browse the files on your phone. Tired of those hideous background pictures that come by default? Delete them. Sick of those horrible MIDI files that you get for ringtones? Delete them! Even better, replace them with custom pictures and MIDI files. From the FMA menu, choose Action → Upload and choose the file you want to upload to the phone. Supported image types are JPEG and GIF, and the only supported audio type is MIDI. There are millions of MIDI files available for free online.

You can really manage all aspects of your phone from FMA. It will even let you power off the phone or lock the keypad of the phone from your PC. Lastly, you can control your PC. When FMA is loaded, a menu of options appears on your phone's screen. By default, the menu includes controls for iTunes, Windows Media Player, Windows Media Center, Winamp, VLC (VideoLan Client), PowerDVD and WinDVD. There are also controls for PowerPoint and two mouse modes to control the PC mouse from the joystick or keypad.

FMA also provides a General Tools menu on your phone that allows you to turn the PC display on and off, lock the display, start the screensaver, and log off the current user, as well as hibernate, shutdown, and restart. You can even disconnect FMA from the phone or close FMA altogether!

FMA does have scripting support from the Microsoft Script tools that it downloaded during installation. You'll need to have a decent scripting background to make your own scripts and menus, but it is possible.

In short, FMA is probably the coolest Bluetooth application out there for certain Bluetooth phones and Windows users.

Control Your Computer from Your Palm

Have you ever wanted to do something on your computer from across the
room? How about from the other side of the world?

It can be useful to be able to access your desktop machine remotely. You
could check server logs, restart failed services, or even post to your weblog.
If you have a home network, you can set up all of your computers so that
they are accessible remotely.

Virtual Network Computing (VNC) is an open source application that is
designed to allow one machine to control another machine over a network.
It was originally developed at Bell Labs. VNC is also useful for collabora-
tion. Multiple viewers (clients) can connect to the same server. Each viewer
has its own cursor. You can use these cursors to point to content on the
remote machine. The viewers display the cursors for all of the other viewers
as well. Each cursor is displayed differently from the others so you can tell
them apart.

The server side comes in Windows, Mac, and Linux flavors. You can download these versions and get more information from the main VNC web site
(*http://www.realvnc.com*). There are other versions of VNC available as well.
For Windows and Linux machines, there is TightVNC (*http://www.tightvnc.
com*). For Windows, there is also UltraVNC (*http://www.ultravnc.com*),
which supports server-side scaling. For Macs, you will need OSXvnc (*http://
www.redstonesoftware.com/vnc.html*). The built-in VNC on Macs doesn't
work with PalmVNC.

You will also need an application to access the server. In typical computer-
speak, this application would be called the *client*, but VNC uses the term
viewer instead. The Palm viewer is called PalmVNC (*http://palmvnc2.free.fr*).
You can also download UltraVNC for Windows with PalmVNC.

> For a different kind of remote control experience, check out
> the Pebbles Project (*http://www.pebbles.hcii.cmu.edu/*), which
> makes a variety of remote control products for Palm devices.
> For example, their SlideShow Commander is a specialized
> application for remotely controlling PowerPoint Presenta-
> tions. If you're on a Mac, check out Salling Clicker [Hack #8],
> a general-purpose remote control package that can be
> extended with a little bit of AppleScript programming.

Set up VNC on Your Desktop

To access your desktop remotely, you need to know its external IP address.
If you have a single computer that is directly connected to the Internet and

has a static IP address, that's easy. All you have to do is look up your IP address in the appropriate place and write it down for use in setting up PalmVNC.

If you have a dynamic IP address (e.g., your home computer is sitting behind a router), the situation is a little more complicated. You need to consider using an IP publishing service (see the "IP Addresses" sidebar). An IP publishing service will typically let you choose a hostname within their domain. You end up with a name like *hostname.domainname.com*. Keep this symbolic address handy for setting up PalmVNC.

IP Addresses

All computers on the Internet have an Internet Protocol (IP) address. An IP address uniquely identifies any computer on the Internet. It is used for routing sessions to the appropriate machines.

An IP address is a four-part number. Each part is a number in the range 0–255. The numbers are separated by decimal points. Thus, an IP address can look like 192.168.0.1 (a typical home network address) or 127.0.0.1 (a reference to the local machine). IP addresses can be static, which means that the addresses don't change. Internet Service Providers (ISPs) usually charge a bit more for static addresses. Most people (at least at home) have dynamic addresses. A dynamic address is assigned by the ISP on a periodic basis. Thus, a dynamic address won't necessarily be the same from day to day. To connect to a computer over the Internet, you either need to know its IP address, or you need to have a name for it (e.g., *www.google.com*). The name is then mapped via a Domain Name System (DNS) server into the actual IP address.

If you have a dynamic IP address, you can hook up with a free service to publish the address. The service acts as a DNS server for a name you select (a hostname within their top-level domain) and maps that name to your computer's current dynamic IP address. You download a small program that runs on your PC and that updates the IP address for your computer in the service's DNS. You get to choose a hostname for your computer within the domain names offered by your service. Then you can refer to your computer via *hostname.domainname.com*. Some service providers are No-IP.com (*http://www.no-ip.com*), Dynu (*http://www.dynu.com*), and DynDNS.org (*http://www.dyndns.org*).

Download and install the appropriate version of VNC on your desktop machine. After VNC has finished installing, run the configuration part of it. You will be able to choose a password for VNC, as shown in Figure 1-39.

Choose a good password (at least eight characters and a mixture of upper- and lowercase characters, numbers, and punctuation). This password is all that is needed to access your machine over the Internet, so choose carefully. Either write it down or remember it; you will need the password when configuring PalmVNC.

Figure 1-39. VNC server configuration under Windows

Setting up OSXvnc on a Mac. When you run OSXvnc, you will see a screen similar to Figure 1-40. Select a display number (usually 1) and port (usually 5901). Set a password; this is the password you will use when you log in from PalmVNC.

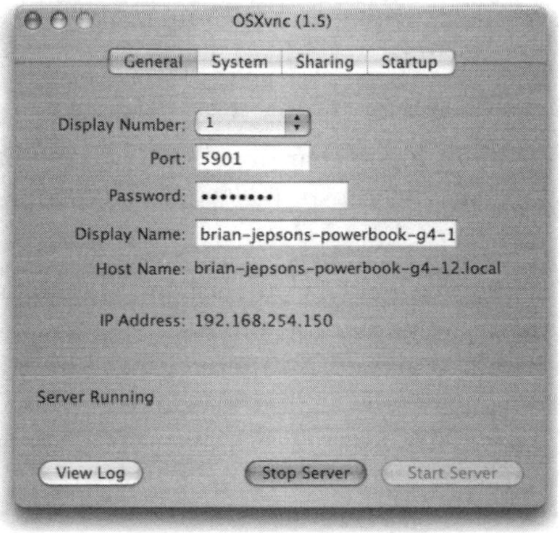

Figure 1-40. OSXvnc general setup screen

When your Mac is set up, then you can proceed to setting up PalmVNC. When everything is working and you are connected, you should see a screen on your Palm device that looks like Figure 1-41.

Figure 1-41. Viewing a Mac desktop with PalmVNC

Securing the connection. You will need to open some ports in your firewall for VNC, and VNC itself needs access to ports 5900-5902 on your computer. By default, VNC sends information (including passwords) as plaintext. You can use SSH (a secure protocol that can encapsulate other types of connections such as VNC; see *http://www.openssh.org* for more information) instead for more security. You will need to open port 22 in your firewall for SSH, if you have not already done so.

Some of the servers (notably TightVNC) have SSH set up by default. For other VNC servers, the process is fairly simple. From the client side of a desktop machine, you want to run something similar to the following:

```
ssh -L 5902:localhost:5901 remotehost -l username
```

PalmVNC comes with a plug-in that does RSA-40 encryption. If you want more security than that, you can tunnel your VNC connection through a VPN.

Whenever VNC is running, it will look for incoming connections. If you have a personal firewall (e.g., Norton Internet Security, ZoneAlarm), you'll need to set the firewall to allow VNC to access the Internet. If you have a port-based firewall, you'll need to allow access to the ports that VNC uses. By default, VNC uses ports 5900 and 5800 (port 5800 is only used for a Java-based viewer), but you can change those ports under the Connections tab.

Setting up VPN. There is a Palm VPN client called Mergic VPN (*http://www. mergic.com*). To set up a VPN, you need to have an externally visible IP address for your desktop machine. Enter that IP address into Mergic VPN in the area titled VPN Server Name or Address, as shown in Figure 1-42.

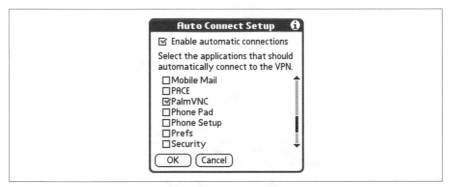

Figure 1-42. Setting up Mergic VPN

You can create multiple VPN accounts for connecting to different machines. Set the account name in the Account edit box. Note that this name is only used to distinguish between different setups in Mergic. The actual username for logging into VNC goes into the User Name field. You can also choose to have Mergic VPN autoconnect to the server when specific applications are run.

You can run PalmVNC using the VPN from Mergic. You can see Mergic VPN being set to run automatically whenever PalmVNC runs in Figure 1-43.

Figure 1-43. Setting up MergicVPN to autoconnect whenever PalmVNC is run

You also need to configure a VPN service on your desktop machine.

Setting up VPN on Windows XP. Windows XP comes with VPN available by default. Start by creating a new network connection (from the Network Connections section of the Control Panel). Select an Advanced Connection, as shown in Figure 1-44.

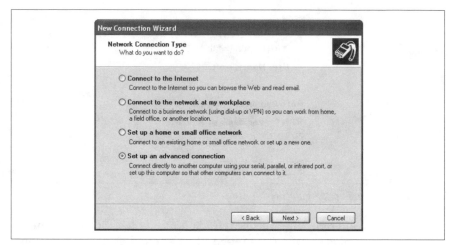

Figure 1-44. Selecting an advanced connection to set up VPN in Windows XP

The next dialog box lets you select the advanced connection options. Select Accept incoming connections, as shown in Figure 1-45. Next, choose the device that you want to allow VPN connections from.

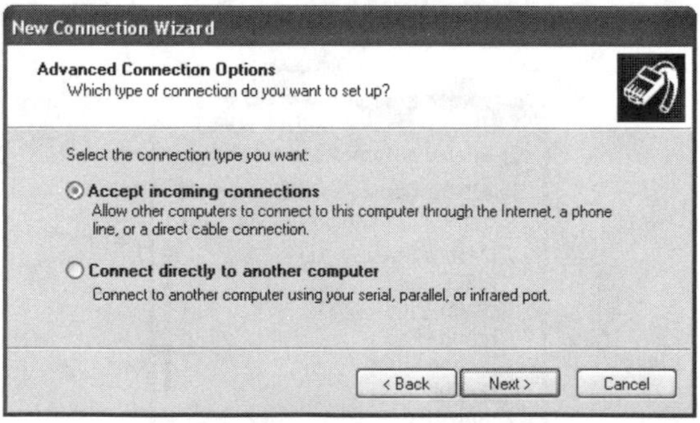

Figure 1-45. Selecting Accept incoming connections from the Advanced Connection Options dialog box

Then, you will need to allow VPN connections in the dialog box shown in Figure 1-46.

After that, select the users that you want to allow to use VPN. You will need one of these usernames (and the corresponding password) when you set up

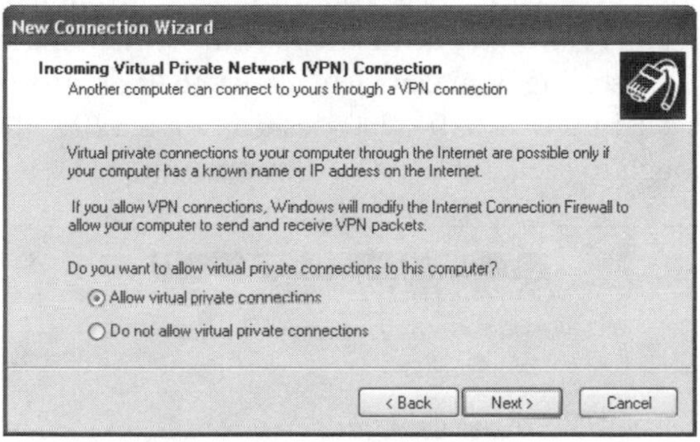

Figure 1-46. Allowing incoming VPN connections in Windows XP

Mergic VPN. The final steps are to allow access to different types of services (at a minimum you need TCP/IP; others are at your choice) and to set up the IP address for your computer.

Set up PalmVNC

Download PalmVNC from *http://palmvnc2.free.fr*. Unzip it and install *palmvnc.prc* onto your Palm device.

Connect your Palm device to the Internet and run PalmVNC. Set up a new connection to your desktop machine, as shown in Figure 1-47. Enter the IP address for your desktop machine and the password you used when setting up the VNC server, and then tap OK and Connect from the next form. If everything is working, you should now see your desktop on your Palm device.

Figure 1-47. Setting up a PalmVNC connection

You can move around the desktop by using the narrow scrollbars on the right and bottom of the screen. If you set up server-side scaling when you were configuring the server, then you can take advantage of scaling by selecting from PalmVNC's menus or the Advanced dialog box, as shown in Figure 1-48. At 1:2 scaling, you can view a 640×640 desktop on a 320×320 Palm device or even up to a 640×960 desktop on a 320×480 Palm device. That's large enough to see (and do) a decent amount.

Advanced Properties ⓘ

Begin at: X: 0   ,Y: 0

Scale: 1: 1

NT user name: username

NT password: ‐Prompt‐

Base port: 5900

☑ Enable desktop sharing

(OK) (Cancel)

Figure 1-48. Advanced connection properties in PalmVNC

No matter which operating system your desktop is running, you can still control it with PalmVNC and an appropriate server. Make sure that you use an appropriate level of security for the environment you are in (running over a local network or running over the Internet).

—Scott McHaffie

HACK #16 Control Your Home Theater from Your Palm

You know that stack of infrared (IR) remotes that's always spilling onto the floor? Your Palm can take the place of all of them.

You need software to convert your Palm into an infrared (IR) remote. Two choices are OmniRemote (*http://www.pacificneotek.com*) and NoviiRemote (*http://www.novii.tv*). You should look at the home theater devices that these two programs support and pick the one that is compatible with your gear.

If neither program covers all of your devices, then you have a couple of choices. If you have the remotes for your devices, and you are looking at simplifying down to just your PDA, then you can switch the applications into learning mode. Line up the remote and your Palm device on a flat surface with the IR end of the remote pointed at the IR port on your PDA and run through all of the important buttons on the remote. Save the buttons for each device under a unique name.

If you are missing some of the remotes, then you can try to find an IR code library on the Web. One good source is RemoteCentral (*http://www.remotecentral.com*), which has IR files under the Files tab on the home page. The files for the Philips Pronto can be used with OmniRemote by using a converter from the OmniRemote web site. If you can't find your specific device, then try to find a similar device by the same manufacturer.

Once you have all the codes for the devices you want to control, it is time to create button layouts. There are a variety of interesting button layouts on the Web. The web sites for the IR software have some button layouts, as does RemoteCentral. You can look at these for inspiration.

You should keep in mind what you want to do with each button layout that you create. For example, a common layout is *watching DVDs*. To do this, you may need to turn on the TV, DVD, and home theater systems. You could combine these actions into a macro, then have a single Power button that turns everything on. You might also need volume, play, pause, stop, fast forward, rewind, menu, and arrow keys. A button layout for watching TV might include a number pad, and channel-up and channel-down buttons.

Hardware

One of the big problems with using a Palm as an IR remote is the limited range of the Palm's IR port.

Fortunately both companies also provide hardware versions of their products. Pacific Neo-Tek (*http://www.pacificneotek.com*) sells a Springboard module for the Handspring Visor and Handspring Prism. You will need to find a used Visor. The Visors have a Springboard slot in the top that can take plug-in modules. All you have to do is stick the OmniRemote module into the Visor. The software is pre-loaded on the module.

NoviiRemote makes a product called the NoviiRemote Blaster. This is an SD card that functions similarly to the OmniRemote product, except that it works with SD-compatible devices such as recent Palm-branded devices.

At the time of this writing, I was unable to locate a similar product for the Sony Clié.

Detailed Instructions

The first part of these instructions apply to using both OmniRemote and NoviiRemote:

1. Make sure that the software (or hardware) that you want to use is compatible with your PDA. If not, consider buying a cheap Palm to use as a dedicated remote control.

2. Even if you plan on buying a hardware device to install in your PDA, start by downloading the corresponding trial software—you need the software to check that it can control your device.

Using NoviiRemote. NoviiRemote provides standard button layouts for a number of different devices, such as TVs, VCRs, etc. You can easily switch between different devices, as shown in Figure 1-49.

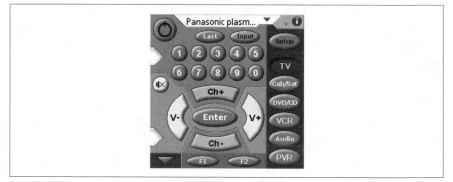

Figure 1-49. NoviiRemote

Here are some tips for using NoviiRemote:

- Use the trial version of NoviiRemote to make sure that the controls work. Start with the default *codebases* (collections of remote control codes) that came with the software. For each device you want to control, try out the included codes to see if the functions you want to use work.

- If the included codebases don't work, then check the company's web site for additional (sometimes user-supplied) codebases. Download these and try again.

- If the downloaded codebases don't work, then you can try using OmniRemote instead, if it supports your PDA.

- If none of that works and you have the remote controls for the devices that don't have codebases, then you can put the program into "learn" mode and teach it all of the buttons. If you are successful with this, then you can help other users by uploading the results back to the company's web site.

Using OmniRemote. OmniRemote, shown in Figure 1-50, provides macros in addition to the standard buttons. A macro can combine multiple actions (e.g., turn on the TV and turn on the VCR). OmniRemote supports a different set of devices natively than NoviiRemote.

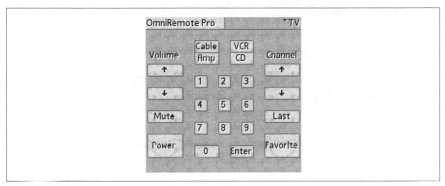

Figure 1-50. OmniRemote Pro

Here are some tips for getting the most out of OmniRemote:

- Use the trial version of OmniRemote to make sure that it can control your devices. You need to either program all of the buttons yourself (if you have the corresponding remote controls), or you can try to find codes on the Web.

- If you want to find codes on the Web, start by downloading *CCFCnvt. zip* from the OmniRemote web site, unzipping it, and installing it. This program is called CCF Converter, and it converts remote control libraries from *.CCF* format to the internal format that OmniRemote uses.

- Go to RemoteCentral (*http://www.remotecentral.com*) and look under Files for code databases for the Philips Pronto device, a popular remote that can control just about anything. These databases are the *.CCF* files that you can convert. If you find files that seem to match your home theater devices, then download them. You will need to unzip the files as well.

- Run *CCFCnvt.exe*. You will see a screen similar to Figure 1-51. In this program, you will click Read CCF to load each of the CCF files that you downloaded in the previous step. For each file, look for the device that you want (many of the CCFs are for a set of devices so you may need to experiment to figure out which file corresponds to the device you want).

When you find the appropriate device in CCF Converter:

1. Use the arrow button to add it to your selected list. Repeat this for each device.

2. When you have collected all of your devices, then select Create PDB File to generate a new database with your devices in it.

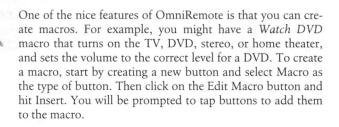

Figure 1-51. CCF Converter

3. Go to your Palm Desktop and press Install or Quick Install.

4. Click Add and choose the PDB file that you created in the previous step.

5. HotSync your PDA to download the configurations.

6. Test to make sure that you can correctly control your devices now.

> One of the nice features of OmniRemote is that you can create macros. For example, you might have a *Watch DVD* macro that turns on the TV, DVD, stereo, or home theater, and sets the volume to the correct level for a DVD. To create a macro, start by creating a new button and select Macro as the type of button. Then click on the Edit Macro button and hit Insert. You will be prompted to tap buttons to add them to the macro.

Either of these devices can simplify your remote controls. You will end up with a single Palm device instead of a stack of remotes. You also have the ability to create sophisticated macros to handle multiple common chores at once. You can see an example of creating a macro to turn on the TV, increase the volume, and switch to channel 25 in Figure 1-52.

Macros can give you a lot of power in a single button. With a few macro buttons on a single page, you can easily perform a number of functions.

—*Scott McHaffie*

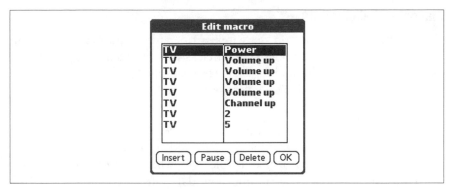

Figure 1-52. TV macro in OmniRemote

 Choose a Cellular Data Plan

If you're going to use your phone to connect to the Internet, make sure you've got the right data plan.

Your cellular phone can connect you to the Internet in a lot of ways, but it's going to cost you. Before you commit to a costly data plan, you need to consider what you'll do with the phone. Will you send and receive email on the phone? Do you plan to send a lot of camera phone pictures or video clips? How about posting to your weblog [Hack #18]? And most important, will you use your phone to connect (*tether*) your laptop to the Internet [Hack #4]?

It's possible for you to use your phone for a lot of what your computer can do, and yes, there are plenty of hotspots around for that data fix when you need it. But I think you'll give in and tether eventually—just wait until the first time you open up your laptop and find no WiFi signal while your phone is showing five bars!

 We will use the word *tether* even when referring to wireless methods of using your handset, such as the Bluetooth connection.

Data plans come in two flavors: metered and unlimited. With a metered plan, you get anywhere between 1 and 20 MB per month as a base allotment, and if you go over, you pay by the kilobyte. There are two types of unlimited plans: handset plans and really, honest, we-mean-it unlimited plans that let you use your phone as a wireless modem for your laptop or PDA.

Flavors of Cellular Data

The phone typically relies on the wireless operator's data network to connect to the Internet. The underlying wireless network technology is known as the *data bearer* of the mobile data. Here's a quick overview of the data bearers available from today's wireless service plans.

GSM

> The GSM network provides data access over the phone (data calls). It works in the same way as the dial-up modem on a PC. The benefit of this technology is that it is available everywhere you can get coverage. However, the drawbacks are the slow data rate (between 9.6 and 13.2 Kbps) and the dedicated phone call for the connection. Since the call must be connected for the entire data session, it counts against your airtime minutes. If you want to make a voice call, you must first disconnect the data call. GSM data is known as 2G (second generation).

GPRS

> The GPRS network allows the phone to have direct access to the packet-switched data from the network. The phone does not need to dial any calls. This feature allows the phone to have always-on access to data without using up airtime minutes. GPRS is known as 2.5G (halfway between second and third generation). The data speed of 2.5G data bearers (between 20 and 40 Kbps) is also faster than that of the 2G data bearers.

EDGE

> The EDGE network works much like the GPRS network, except that EDGE has a much faster data rate (up to 230 Kbps). The EDGE network coverage is still limited. In the United States, only AT&T Wireless (now part of Cingular Wireless) has national EDGE coverage. Only a handful of devices released since 2004 support the EDGE data bearer.

UMTS

> The UMTS network is what's known as third-generation (3G) wireless networking technology. It offers broadband data speeds of around 384 Kbps. However, UMTS coverage is very limited. In the States, it is currently available in only a few selected cities. In addition, UMTS service plans can be very expensive. New phones such as the Nokia 6630 support UMTS.

1xRTT and 1xEV-DO

> CDMA-based networks have two kinds of data bearers: Single Carrier Radio Transmission Technology (1xRTT) and Single Carrier Evolution Data-Only (1xEV-DO). 1xRTT has typical rates of 70–120 Kbps, and 1xEV-DO has typical downstream speeds of 300–500 Kbps (with

upstream speeds the same as those of 1xRTT). In the States, 1xRTT is available nationwide from Verizon Wireless, but only selected cities have 1xEV-DO.

Which data bearer is available to you depends on your wireless operator, your location, and your service plan. GPRS service should be available from all GSM operators wherever you have voice coverage. Likewise, 1xRTT should also be available from most CDMA operators. If your current service plan does not include any data service, you can call up your wireless operator and add it for an extra monthly fee. The data service is typically metered by the bandwidth you use in a billing period. In the United States, most operators also offer flat-fee subscriptions for unlimited data use; for example, T-Mobile charges $20–$30 per month for its GPRS-only network and Cingular charges $80 per month for its EDGE and GPRS networks.

Figure Out What You'll Need

This could be the hard part, but the good news is that you can just take a best guess. If the plan you select doesn't work out, most providers will let you change data plans midstream. Here are some considerations.

Web browsing

> If you're going to browse the Web using your built-in browser, chances are good that you won't use a lot of data, simply because that browser doesn't offer the rich graphical and multimedia content you get with a desktop browser—in this case, it might be OK to go with a metered plan. However, if you use a third-party browser, it's possible you could end up using a lot of data, especially if you find yourself turning to your phone for web surfing more than you do your laptop.

Email

> If you plan to use your phone for sending and receiving email, this won't take up a huge amount of data (but see the next item). For the most part, email is text, and unless you're likely to use your phone to work with office documents, you probably won't move a lot of data with email. As such, you could get away with a metered data plan. If you're going to be sending and receiving lots of photos and video, get yourself an unlimited plan.

Tethering

> If you plan to connect your laptop to your cell phone to get online, welcome to what some folks think is a gray area. Here's the problem: most of the low-priced unlimited data plans are intended for use with your phone only. However, it's technically possible to connect your laptop to your phone and get online. You will probably get away with this if you

don't use a lot of data. However, anecdotes abound concerning people who claim to have received nastygrams from their cellular operator after using large amounts of data in this way. It's insanely simple for a cell provider to distinguish between traffic that originates from a phone and traffic that originates from a laptop. For example, every web browser transmits a User-Agent identifier every time you load a page; this is a dead giveaway.

Some providers will bill you differently based on your usage. AT&T Wireless (which was being absorbed into Cingular at the time of this writing) had a $24.99 monthly handset data plan, but vowed it would charge $1 per megabyte to users who tethered a laptop or PDA to their mobile phone. Furthermore, cell providers routinely, and sometimes temporarily, block access to certain ports (there have been reports of SSH, secure IMAP, and POP for email, and even secure HTTP being blocked), with the (misguided) rationale that most handset users don't need those ports.

If you plan to use your cell phone as your laptop or PDA's lifeline to the Internet and you don't want to risk unexpected overages or a service disconnection, go with an unlimited plan that explicitly supports tethering.

SMS and MMS
  In theory, SMS and MMS come out of a different billing bucket than does Internet data, so the number of messages you send and receive shouldn't affect your choice of a data plan.

All those guidelines aside, the best thing to do is choose an unlimited data plan, if one is available (otherwise, pick the most generous metered plan). That way, if you don't use a lot of data, you can progressively downgrade each month. If you do use a lot of data, at least you won't get whacked with per-kilobyte charges.

Compare the Plans

Although wireless data might seem as though it's brand-new, its pricing is settled, for the most part. Usually you'll pay around $5 to $10 per month for something that lets you do basic web surfing and email, and around $20 to $30 for more capabilities. So, if you're planning to use a lot of third-party network applications, such as instant messaging and RSS readers, you should go for the plan that gives you more. If you plan to use your phone as a wireless modem for your laptop, you should definitely choose an unlimited plan that supports tethering. Table 1-4 shows a few unlimited data plans that were current as of this writing.

Table 1-4. Unlimited data plans by provider

Provider	Handset	With tethering
Cingular	$24.99; MEdia Net Unlimited	$79.99; Data Connect Unlimited
Nextel	$19.99; Enhanced Data Service Plan	$54.99; Unlimited Wireless PC Access Plan
Orange UK	£88.13; (if you exceed 1000MB per month, you will probably get a nastygram)	Same as handset
Sprint	$15; Unlimited Vision	None
T-Mobile	$4.99; Unlimited t-zones (email and web only) $9.99; Unlimited t-zones Pro	$29.99; T-Mobile Internet ($19.99 with a qualifying voice plan)
Verizon Wireless	$15; VCAST $4.99; Mobile Web (uses up plan minutes)	$79.99; BroadbandAccess or NationalAccess Unlimited

If you think Table 1-4 looks very U.S.-centric, you're right. Although the United States lags behind in terms of the latest gizmos, it's a feeding frenzy for those who are determined to get all-you-can-eat data. In other parts of the world, metered data plans are more common. And the States has its share of those as well. Table 1-5 shows some of these plans, from the low-end to the high-end offerings, and includes the range of charges you can expect if you go over the metered limit.

Table 1-5. Metered data plans by provider

Provider	Low-end metered	High-end metered	Overage
Cingular	512KB for $2.99	60MB for $59.99	Varies with plan: $0.005/KB to $0.01/KB
Nextel	1MB for $9.99	100MB for $99.99	Varies with plan: $0.003/KB to $0.01/KB
Orange France	5MB for €5	20MB for €20	Varies with plan: €0.10/KB to €0.15/KB
Orange UK	4MB for £4	400MB for £52.88	Varies with plan: £0.59/MB to £1/MB
Rogers (Canada)	256KB for CAN$3	100MB for CAN$100	Varies with plan: CAN$1.02 to CAN$10/MB
Sprint	Unlimited plans only	N/A	N/A
Telcel Mexico	1000KB for MEX$100	50,000KB for MEX$500	Varies with plan: MEX $0.10/KB to MEX$0.02/KB
T-Mobile	Unlimited plans only	N/A	N/A
T-Mobile Germany	5MB for €5	500MB for €110	Varies with plan: €0.80/MB to €3.90/MB

Table 1-5. Metered data plans by provider (continued)

Provider	Low-end metered	High-end metered	Overage
Verizon Wireless	20MB for $39.99	60MB for $59.99	Varies with plan: $0.002/KB to $0.004/KB
Vodafone UK	2.6MB for £2.55	51.1MB for £34.04	£2/MB

In most cases, you'll choose the data plan when you sign up for your voice service. However, most providers will let you add or change your data plan at any time. But before you make a change, ask the all-important questions: will this require me to agree to a contract extension, and will I be charged a termination or activation fee to make this kind of change? If you don't like the answer to either question, you should reconsider adding a data plan until it's time to renew your contract, or look into setting up a data plan on a separate line of service.

> One problem you might run into is a customer service rep that is unfamiliar with the plan you want. The best thing you can do is make sure you know the name of the service. To find this out, visit the provider's web site. If you can't find the name of their data plan in 5 minutes, go through this simple exercise: add a phone to your shopping cart and then choose a voice plan—preferably, the same one you are signed up for. The data plans available to you might depend on what level of voice service you have. For example, the price for T-Mobile's unlimited Internet plan is $19.99 with most voice plans, and $29.99 without a voice plan (or if you have a cheap plan).
>
> At this point, the provider's web ordering system should offer you a data plan (you might need to click around for an optional services or features link), and you should write down the name of the service, call customer service, and ask them to add it to your plan.

Once you've selected a data plan, log into your provider's web site every day or so and keep an eye on your data usage as you go—if you accidentally configure your email client to check mail every 30 seconds, you could be in for a surprise. The data total that shows up on the web site will probably be behind by 24 hours, perhaps more if you've used your data plan while roaming.

If you're on a metered plan and see yourself getting dangerously close to the limit, change plans right away. Although most providers will prorate the new plan after you change it, make sure you understand what exceptions are in place between the date you change the plan and the date your billing cycle resets. For example, suppose your billing cycle ends on the 28th of each month, and you are just shy of the 20MB limit on a metered plan when you switch to an unlimited plan on the 23rd of the month. You might think that you can use as much data as you want between the 23rd and 28th, but be sure to ask—when it comes to cellular billing, nothing is as simple as it appears.

—*Brian Jepson*

HACK #18 Blog from Your Mobile Phone

Use a mobile blogging service to post blog entries with pictures from your mobile phone.

Not long ago, bloggers could only update their blogs using a computer. Inspiration, however, does not always coincide with the presence of a bulky computer. At the turn of the century, some adventurous and creative bloggers started blogging from their mobile devices. The word *moblog* was thus coined, referring to blogging from a mobile device (mobile phones, PDAs, etc.).

If blogging without a computer is convenient, moblogging with a camera phone is exciting. In just a few clicks you can snap a quick shot and add a few punch lines, and minutes later the neatly formatted post on your personal blog can be shared with the entire world! Figure 1-53 shows a snapshot of O'Reilly editor Brian Jepson's moblog. You can see Brian's world through pictures taken from his phone camera and comments that captured his instantaneous thoughts. (The dry spell between November and March? That's when Brian used a phone without a camera for a few months before switching back to his Nokia 3650.)

There are two major approaches to moblogging, regardless of the myriad phone models and their different capabilities: SMS moblogging and email moblogging. This hack introduces and compares these two methods, with an emphasis on the latter.

> Instead of email, you can also use MMS to post blog entries from your camera phone. The MMS message is sent to an email address, and hence, MMS moblogging is essentially the same as email moblogging.

SMS Moblogging

SMS moblogging works on any handset that can send SMS, which is virtually every mobile phone nowadays. You write the blog entry on the mobile phone and send it via SMS to a service phone number provided by a moblog

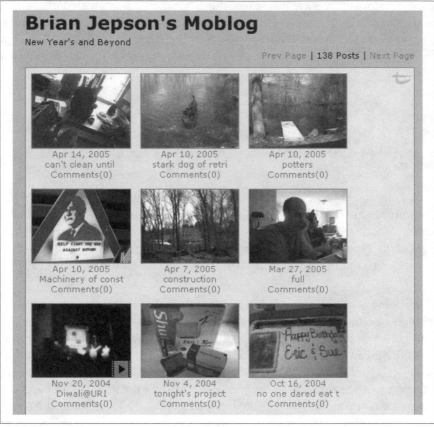

Figure 1-53. An example photo moblog from Brian Jepson

service. The moblog service interprets the received SMS message and posts it to your blog. You can be identified by the caller ID or an ID code embedded in the SMS message. A good example of such an SMS moblog service is Txt-solutions (*http://blog.txtsolutions.com*). Txtsolutions can host your blog on its own site, or post your blog entries to your account in a list of supported third-party blog hosts.

 If the SMS moblog service posts the blog entries to a third-party blog host on your behalf, it needs to know your login information on that third-party site.

Despite the meager prerequisite of the handset, SMS moblogging has some major drawbacks. First is the nagging 160-character limitation for SMS. Second, even if you are laconic enough to squeeze each of your posts into fewer than 160 characters (not words), SMS moblogging is text-only. Third, you need to pay extra to the SMS moblog service provider. For example, Txtsolutions charges £0.10 for each message. This charge is in addition to your regular SMS fee (from your wireless operator) and cost for the blog hosting service if it applies.

Email Moblogging

If your mobile phone supports sending email or MMS, email moblogging doesn't have any of the drawbacks of SMS moblogging:

- There is no practical length limitation, as long as your thumbs don't complain.
- You can post photos from a camera phone, adding richness to your post.
- There is no extra charge besides what you pay for the wireless data and regular blog hosting service.

Email moblogging works in much the same way as its SMS counterpart, except that you send email from the phone to a (hopefully) secret email address. The email Inbox is polled by the moblog service at regular intervals (e.g., every five minutes). When a new message is detected, the moblog service retrieves the message and parses the content. If the moblog service supports picture attachments (most do), you can even have a mobile photo blog!

 It is important that you keep the email address private. Any message sent to that email address will be automatically posted on your blog.

The easiest way to set up an email-based moblog is to use a blog hosting service that supports email posting. It typically takes only a few minutes. After you open a regular blog account at the hosting service, there is usually a field under the user preferences screen where you can set the private email address. All emails sent to this address will be posted to the blog you just opened.

Most popular blog hosting providers now support email posting from mobile phones, either free of charge (e.g., Blogger) or with a premium paid account (e.g., LiveJournal). Table 1-6 compares several providers that emphasize moblog support.

Table 1-6. Moblog support in popular blog hosting services

Name and URL	Cost (USD/yr)	Photo attachment	Notes
Blogger; http://www.blogger.com	Free	N	Free email posting feature. No photo attachment support.
LiveJournal; http://www.livejournal.com	$25	Y	Email posting option available for paid account only. Photo attachments are supported.
TypePad; http://www.typepad.com	$60	Y	Moblogging feature available for all account types; 50MB storage and 1GB per month bandwidth for basic subscription.
Radio UserLand; http://radio.userland.com	$40	Y	Cost includes desktop blog software and one year of hosting. Email attachment posting requires additional software; 40MB storage.

Besides the major blog providers, some new providers specialize in moblog hosting. Among them are Textamerica (*http://www.textamerica.com*) and Fotolog (*http://www.fotolog.net*). Both of them offer free accounts for users to blog directly from their mobile phones.

> The free accounts often come with the condition that the service provider can display advertisements on your blog pages.

Photo Moblogging to Any Blog Service

The aforementioned photo moblogging solutions tie you into specific blog hosting services. But in many cases, you do not want this tie-in:

- You could be running your own blog server and do not use any of the blog hosting services.
- Your favorite blog host might not provide photo moblogging features.
- You might not want to pay the extra money to add photo moblogging support.

Is there a service that is free and independent of your blog server? As it turns out there is, and it's called Flickr.

Flickr (*http://www.flickr.com*) started out as a photo storage provider. The one feature that makes Flickr really interesting from a moblog point of view is that it allows you to upload photos (to Flickr) by email and create a blog entry at your designated blog site. The blog site can be any of the blog hosts mentioned in the previous section, or even your own web site running popular blog server software.

The post includes the email content as its main body and an inline thumbnail, which is linked to the picture stored on Flickr. The thumbnail posting feature in Flickr is really cool and sets it apart from other services, especially if you have a camera phone that produces megapixel pictures. Without resizing to thumbnails, megapixel pictures would clutter up your blog and mess up the web page layout (e.g., sidebars, etc.).

The free account at Flickr allows you to upload up to 20MB of photos per month. A subscription fee of $24.95 per year will push the quota to 2GB per month. Considering most (mobile phone) moblog attachments are smaller than 100KB, the free Flickr account is more than sufficient for even the most aggressive mobloggers. Combining the Flickr email posting service with a free blog hosting service (or your own blog server), you can set up a powerful and free moblog with photo posting in no time!

Figure 1-54 shows the information Flickr needs to post to your blog site on your behalf. Obviously, it needs to know your site address and account credentials.

Add a weblog

Confirm your details

Service: Blogger

Username: mymobloghack

Password: ********
☑ Store your password?

Weblog: My Moblog (#11282344)

URL: http://mymobloghack.blogspot.com

Label: My Moblog

ALL DONE

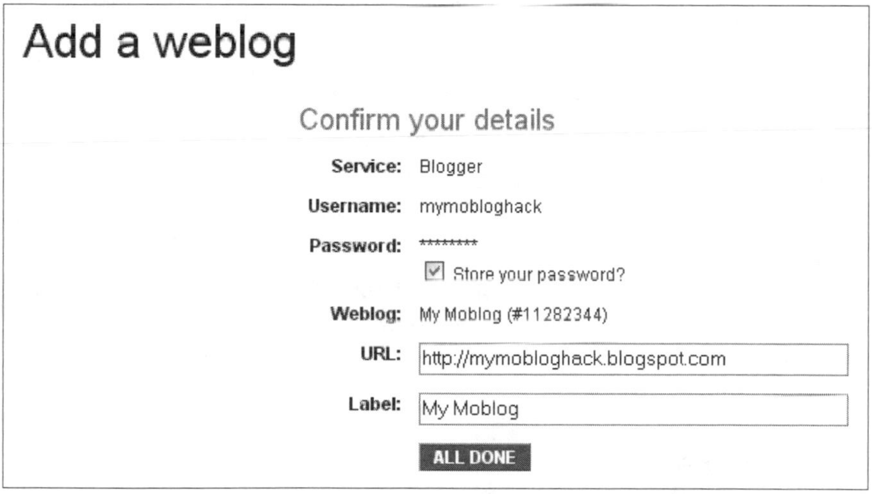

Figure 1-54. Confirming URL and account credentials of your blog site

Figure 1-55 shows the private posting email addresses Flickr provides to you when you open an account. One address is for adding pictures to your Flickr account, and the other is for adding the pictures and then posting thumbnails to the designated blog.

Smart client for Flickr. The default email application on many phones restricts the size of an attachment to a maximum of 100KB. To get around this limitation and to provide a more integrated user experience, you can use

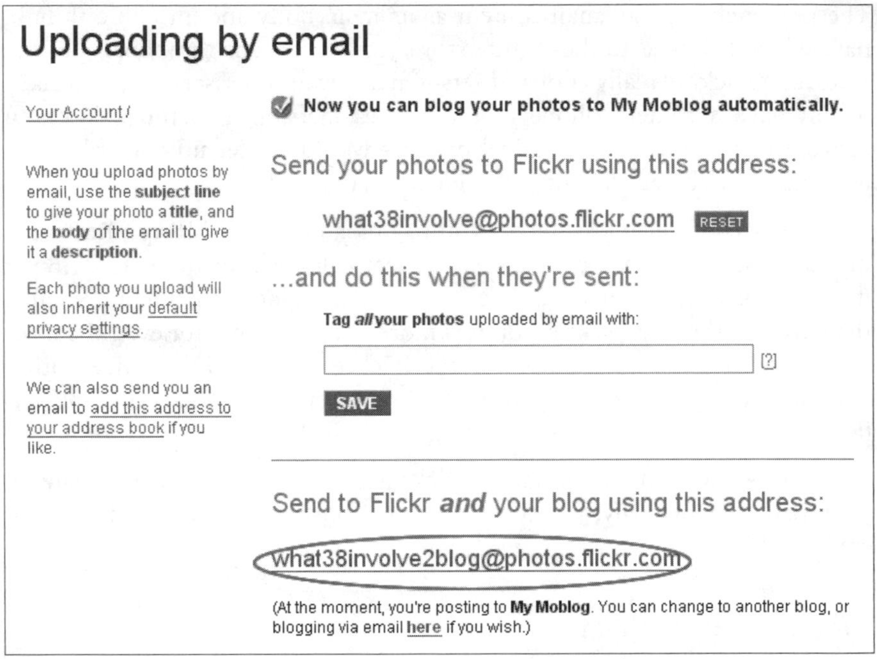

Uploading by email

Your Account /

When you upload photos by email, use the **subject line** to give your photo a **title**, and the **body** of the email to give it a **description**.

Each photo you upload will also inherit your default privacy settings.

We can also send you an email to add this address to your address book if you like.

✅ **Now you can blog your photos to My Moblog automatically.**

Send your photos to Flickr using this address:

what38involve@photos.flickr.com   RESET

...and do this when they're sent:

Tag *all* your photos uploaded by email with:

[ ] [?]

SAVE

Send to Flickr *and* your blog using this address:

what38involve2blog@photos.flickr.com

(At the moment, you're posting to **My Moblog**. You can change to another blog, or blogging via email here if you wish.)

Figure 1-55. The free email address Flickr provides for each account to post blog entries and pictures

a phone application that takes pictures and then automatically posts them to Flickr without having to switch applications and enter email addresses.

Manoj TK wrote a little open source J2ME (Java 2 Mobile Edition) program that does just that. You can download it from *http://sourceforge.net/projects/moblogger2/*. To learn how the program works, please refer to *http://manojtk.blogspot.com/2005/01/smtp-email-attachments-from-nokia-6600.html*.

Hacking the Hack

Many power bloggers run their own blogging server so that they can have complete control over the content and presentation of their blog. While Flickr can interoperate with many popular blog systems, it is still a hosted service that is beyond the blogger's control. For instance, there is no guarantee that the free Flickr service won't be replaced by a for-pay service in the future. If you want complete end-to-end control over your moblog, you can customize existing blog server software to make it support email posting with photo attachments from a mobile phone. In this hack, you will learn how to set up the popular WordPress blog server to support photo moblog postings.

Running your own server also gives you complete access to web site visitor statistics, the ability to back up the web site, and many other features.

Setting up WordPress. WordPress (*http://www.wordpress.org/*) is an open source blog server based on PHP and MySQL. It is available free of charge from the WordPress web site. You can run it on your own server or on any ISP server account that supports PHP 4.1 and MySQL 3.23.23 or greater. As a PHP and MySQL application, WordPress runs on almost any modern operating system, including Linux, Unix, BSD, Windows, and Mac OS X.

By following the installation instructions (see *http://wordpress.org/docs/installation/5-minute/*) you can install WordPress in five minutes. After creating a user account, you can start to post and publish blogs on your very own blog server now! Out of the box, you can use Flickr to post photos to your freshly installed WordPress server. In the rest of this hack, I will discuss how to set up WordPress so that you can moblog with it without needing a third-party service.

Email posting with WordPress. WordPress supports email posting, albeit with two main drawbacks. First, it does not support email attachments. And second, it does not filter the sender's email address. Anyone can send email to the email address and have their messages appear on your blog. Without sender-address filtering, your moblog can be easily flooded with spam messages.

A patch by "lansmash" fixed both drawbacks. Applying the patch is straightforward. First, download the file *wp-mail-0.2.zip* from the web address *http://blade.lansmash.com/index.php?cat=5*. Unzip the archive to the WordPress root directory. This adds the files *PEAR.php* and *mimedecode.php* to the directory, and replaces the original *wp-mail.php* file. Now, create two directories, *wp-photos* and *wp-filez*, under the WordPress root directory to store images and other attachments, respectively. You can choose other directory names as long as you remember to modify the corresponding settings in the new *wp-mail.php* file.

If you want automatic picture resizing (an important feature for megapixel camera phones), you need to install an additional hack provided by Hugo. Simply replace the default *wp-mail.php* file in your WordPress installation with a new file download from *http://www.vienna360.net/files/wp-mail.phps*.

Now, you can test your setup by sending an email message with a picture attachment to the email address specified in the Options → Writing section of the WordPress configuration page. Make sure you enter the correct server and login information. Nothing appears on your blog just yet. That is because the *wp-mail.php* script needs to be manually loaded to poll the email server for the new message. Do this by pointing your browser to *http://your-domain-name/MyMoblog/wp-mail.php*.

Of course, if you need to open a browser and load the *wp-mail.php* script manually every time you post a moblog entry, it defeats the whole point of moblogging. So, let's discuss how to automate the email polling process in WordPress.

Setting up email automatic polling. To automate the email polling and blog posting process in WordPress, you need to schedule a recurring task that loads the *wp-mail.php* script at fixed intervals (e.g., every five minutes). You need two tools for this: a lightweight URL loader called cURL to load the PHP script, and the open source *cron* daemon to schedule the recurring URL loading tasks. Both *cron* and cURL are installed by default on Linux, Unix, and Mac OS X computers. For Windows, you can install the Cygwin toolkit (*http://www.cygwin.com/*) to get a common set of Unix utilities including *cron* and cURL.

You can use a fully featured web browser, such as Firefox, to load the *wp-mail.php* script every five minutes. But that is a huge waste of server resources.

Next, log into your server and type the following on the command line:

```
crontab -e
```

This opens the *cron* control file, which contains all scheduled tasks, in the system's default text editor. You should append one line to the bottom of the file, save it, and exit the editor. *cron* automatically reloads the control file.

```
*/5 * * * * /usr/local/bin/curl http://yourdomain/wp-mail.php > /dev/null
```

The preceding line in the *cron* control file schedules the system to run the curl command every five minutes in every year, month, week, and day. That's it! You now have a fully functional photo moblog server.

If you do not want to use the default editor, you can always export the *cron* control file to a text file, edit it externally, and then import the edited file back to *crontab*. See the *crontab* manual for more information.

—Haihao Wu

Get Google Maps on Your Mobile Phone

#19 Turn your Java-enabled cell phone into a portable mapping appliance.

If you have a GSM phone from the last three years or so, you (probably) have a powerful mobile mapping appliance in your pocket.

Mobile GMaps is a free program that lets you view Google Maps on your cell phone. It is limited to J2ME (Java 2 Mobile Edition) enabled phones, such as the Symbian Series 60 and Series 80 phones. The program is available at *http://www.mgmaps.com*. Read the instructions on the download page at *http://www.mgmaps.com/download.php*.

The easiest way to install the app is to use your phone's browser to go to *http://wap.mgmaps.com*. Then click on the Download link, and agree when it asks if you want to download and install the application.

When the program completes installation, you'll get a *completed* message and then be returned to the *http://wap.mgmaps.com* page. You can now exit from your phone's web browser. On my Nokia 3650 the program *MGMaps* installed into the *Apps* folder. Click on the application, and then select Start from the Options menu.

By default you will see a map of the United States fully zoomed out. You can navigate with the 2, 4, 6, and 8 keys. Zoom in with 5 or # and zoom out with 7 or *. Figure 1-56 shows Mobile GMaps on a Nokia 3650.

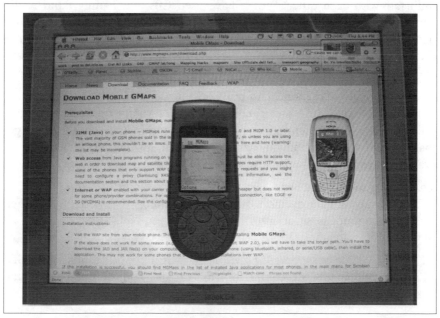

Figure 1-56. Mobile Gmaps on a Nokia 3650

Selecting Options gives you a menu of Satellite, Zoom, Location, Search, Settings, About, and Exit. Satellite flips you to Satellite imagery. Zoom brings up a menu that lets you zoom in, zoom out, or select a zoom level from 0–14. Locations are like waypoints on a GPS. You can set latitude, longitude, zoom level, and map or satellite view, and then return to that view from the Location menu. Search brings up a search screen that calls the Google search system.

There are a number of tricks and hints on the GMaps web site. Mobile GMaps was written by Cristian Streng. It is released under the Attribution/NonCommercial/NoDerivs Creative Commons license. This means that you can use and distribute the program for free, but you can't make derivative works or use it for commercial purposes.

And as Cristian says, "If you like Mobile GMaps and find it useful in your daily life, if it saves you time and money, please show that you value my time, my expenses, my effort and my knowledge and consider a donation to me."

—Rich Gibson

HACK #20 Share Your GPS

Caravanning with friends, but only one person has a GPS? Play nice and share.

Road trip caravans are more fun when the people in the two cars can communicate with each other. People have used CBs and Family Band Radio Service (FRS) radios for years just for this purpose. If you want to exchange data instead of voice over radio, you can set up a roving Wi-Fi network and then share a GPS between vehicles.

Connect a GPS to one computer and then set up a wireless network. Clients in other vehicles can connect to the GPS on the host machine. Normally, only one program at a time can access a serial port–connected GPS. This can quickly become a problem. You probably want to run gpsmap **[Hack #22]** to get maps, and then a program to log your position, and perhaps another program to let you create spatial annotations of your travels.

That is way too many connections for a single-user serial port! Fortunately, GPSd is available as a daemon that connects directly to the GPS and then acts as a server for position information. Once you have GPSd installed, all of your GPS aware applications can share a single GPS.

GPSd is available at *http://gpsd.berlios.de/*. It runs under Linux, FreeBSD, Mac OSX, and any POSIX compliant Unix variant. You can build and install

GPSd in the standard way, as shown here, but do follow any current instructions from the web site (replace *x.xx* with the current version):

```
$ tar xvfz gpsd-x.xx.tar.gz
$ cd gpsd-x.xx
$ ./configure
$ make
$ make install
```

Connecting the GPS

Most GPS units have a serial port and can be configured to output the current position using a standard protocol called NMEA. GPSD expects your GPS to send NMEA formatted data, but can also accept data in different formats. Check the GPSd site for how to enable other formats if you have a GPS that does not output standard NMEA sentences.

Once it is installed you can run it with this command:

```
$ gpsd -p /dev/ttyS0 -s 4800
```

If you have problems getting GPSd to start, consult the documentation. Once you've got it running you can connect to it with *telnet* to see what it is reporting:

```
$ telnet localhost 2947
Trying 127.0.0.1...
Connected to localhost.
Escape character is '^]'.
```

Now you are connected to GPSD. The commands are single characters, and you can chain them together. So if you want your Position, Altitude, and GPS Status, issue this command:

```
PADS
```

You will get the full GPS position, with your latitude and longitude, altitude, current date and time, and GPS status. The status is the last section: S=0 or S=1, where 1 means the GPS is connected and sending data and 0 means there is no data coming from the GPS.

You can now run Kismet, GPSDrive, and any other GPS-aware applications at the same time, and your friends in the other car can connect to your GPS over the Wi-Fi network. The Perl code in Example 1-1 will connect to GPSd and print the current position and time.

Example 1-1. Connecting to GPSd with dump_gps.pl

```perl
#!/usr/bin/perl

# /usr/local/sbin/gpsd -p /dev/ttyS0
use 5.6.1;
use IO::Socket;
use Term::ReadKey;
use strict;

BEGIN { $|++ }; # autoflush STDOUT.

# Set parameters based on command line options, with defaults.
my $GPSD     = shift( @ARGV ) || "localhost:2947";

# Connect to gpsd.
warn "connecting to gpsd \n";
my $gps = IO::Socket::INET->new($GPSD)
    or die "Can't connect to gpsd at $GPSD: $!\n";

while (1) {
    # Tell gpsd we want position, altitude, date, and status.
    $gps->print("pads\n");

    # Parse out the response. If the date is blank, gpsd needs
    # a second to catch up.
    my $location = <$gps>;
    my ($lat, $long, $alt, $date, $status) =
        ($location =~ /P=(.+?) (.+?),A=(.+?),D=(.+?),S=(.+?)/gos);

    next unless $status;

    # Print a line of data to both STDOUT and STDERR, and wait.
    print $_ join("|", $lat, $long, $alt, $date || "" ), "\n"
        for ( \*STDOUT, \*STDERR );

    sleep( 1 );
}
```

Save this into a file called *dump_gps.pl* and run it with this command:

```
$ ./dump_gps.pl
```

You will get coordinates, the altitude, and current date at one-second intervals. We use this trick further in "Broadcast Your GPS Position" [Hack #21].

See Also

- Casey West's O'Reilly Network article on his cross-car road trip network: *http://www.oreillynet.com/pub/a/wireless/2002/08/01/highway_lan.html*

—*Rich Gibson*

Broadcast Your GPS Position

HACK #21

Entertain yourself and passing wardrivers by abusing the beacon frame (and MAC address).

Have you ever wanted a lightweight protocol that would allow you to broadcast your current position? Many times you can see a wireless network, but you can't connect to it. In the NoCat community network (*http://nocat.net*) we would often do sight surveys that showed lots of networks, but we could not associate with them. Perhaps the access point has a more powerful network card, or a better antenna, and is able to blast a signal out, but you are not able to get your signal back to the access point.

What to do? With a complete abuse of the 802.11 beacon frame you can share your position with anyone around you!

802.11 wireless networks in both Ad Hoc and Infrastructure mode [Appendix A] send periodic beacon frames. These are about 50 bytes long and contain information that a client needs in order to associate with a wireless network. The beacon frame includes the Service Set Identifier (SSID), which is the name of the network.

Wireless discovery programs such as NetStumbler [Hack #24], iStumbler [Hack #27], and Kismet [Hack #29] get all of their information from sniffing for these beacon frames. So what happens if we change the SSID on the access point? What happens if we change it whenever we get a new GPS fix?

For our purposes the SSID, at 32 bytes, provides enough room to encode the latitude and longitude of our current position to 5 digits of precision (about 1 meter). We can also separate the coordinates with readable delimiters and still have 11 characters for a unique station ID.

To run this hack, you need to have a DIY Linux access point [Hack #63]. Then, set up the GPSd daemon and connect a GPS [Hack #20].

Once you have your access point and GPSd functional, use the Perl script in Example 1-2 to broadcast your current position by using the beacon frame.

Example 1-2. Broadcasting your position through GPSd using beacon_abuse.pl

```
#!/usr/bin/perl

# /usr/local/sbin/gpsd -p /dev/ttyS0
use 5.6.1;
use IO::Socket;
use Term::ReadKey;
use strict;

BEGIN { $|++ }; # autoflush STDOUT.
```

Example 1-2. Broadcasting your position through GPSd using beacon_abuse.pl (continued)

```perl
my $station_id = shift( @ARGV ) || 'myid';
my $GPSD       = shift( @ARGV ) || "localhost:2947";
my $delay      = 3; # number of seconds to sleep
my $ssid       = 'gpsd not initialized';;

# Connect to gpsd.
warn "connecting to gpsd \n";
my $gps = IO::Socket::INET->new($GPSD)
    or die "Can't connect to gpsd at $GPSD: $!\n";

while (1) {
    # Tell gpsd we want position, altitude, date, and status.
    $gps->print("pads\n");

    # Parse out the response. If the date is blank, gpsd needs
    # a second to catch up.
    my $location = <$gps>;
    my ($lat, $long, $alt, $date, $status) =
        ($location =~ /P=(.+?) (.+?),A=(.+?),D=(.+?),S=(.+?)/gos);
    # create new SSID
    $lat = sprintf("%9.5f",  $lat);
    $long = sprintf("%10.5f", $long);
    $ssid = "$station_id:$lat:$long";
    print "$ssid\n";
    `iwconfig wlan0 essid "$ssid" mode "Master" channel 1 rate "Auto"`;
    sleep( $delay );
}
```

Copy the code into a file called *beacon_abuse.pl* and run it from the command line:

```
$ ./beacon_abuse.pl myid
```

In this example, `myid` is the unique station ID that will preface the latitude and longitude in the SSID generated by the code. The code enters a loop where it connects to GPSd to get the current position, then changes the SSID of the network card and prints out the new SSID. You will know it is working if you get a series of new SSID's that consist of your station ID and the latitude and longitude; for example:

```
myid: 38.40254:-122.182889
```

Depending on your platform you can use MacStumbler, NetStumbler, or Kismet to watch the SSID change, as shown in Figure 1-57.

If your machine isn't moving too quickly, or you stop *beacon_abuse.pl*, you can connect to the machine as a normal access point, as shown in Figure 1-58.

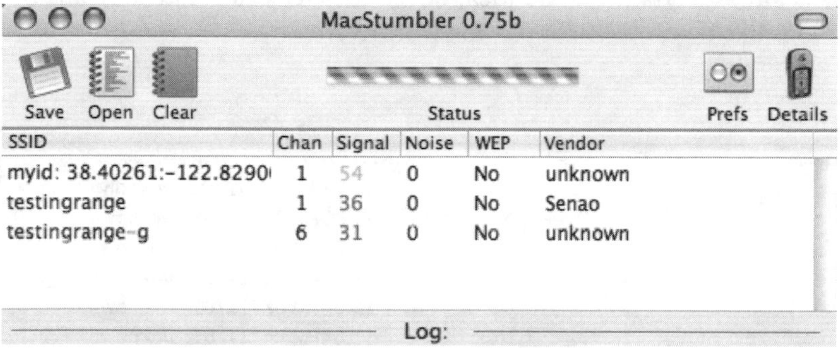

Figure 1-57. Watching the moving SSID in MacStumbler

Figure 1-58. A geolocated access point

One disadvantage of the script in Example 1-2 is that your Stumbler program probably shows only the most recent SSID. This is because the programs use the MAC address of the wireless card to uniquely identify the
access point. By design, this is the *right* thing to do, because MAC addresses
are not supposed to change. Unless we want them to change.

This code flips the MAC address, and sets the SSID as well:

```perl
#!/usr/bin/perl
$cnt=0;
while (1) {
    `ifconfig wlan0 hw ether 0000000000$cnt`;
    `iwconfig wlan0 essid "foo:$cnt" mode "Master" channel 1 rate "Auto"`;
    print "new essid foo:$cnt\n";
    sleep 1;
    $cnt++;
}
```

Copy the code into a file called *bad_plan.pl* and run it from the command
line:

```
$ ./bad_plan.pl
```

This is almost certainly a Bad Idea, but it does let you create amusing Stumbler logs like Figure 1-59 for passing wardrivers.

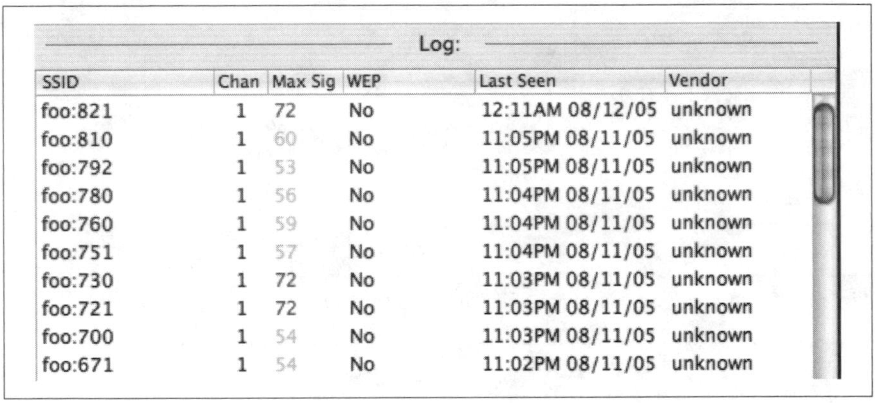

SSID	Chan	Max Sig	WEP	Last Seen	Vendor
foo:821	1	72	No	12:11AM 08/12/05	unknown
foo:810	1	60	No	11:05PM 08/11/05	unknown
foo:792	1	53	No	11:05PM 08/11/05	unknown
foo:780	1	56	No	11:04PM 08/11/05	unknown
foo:760	1	59	No	11:04PM 08/11/05	unknown
foo:751	1	57	No	11:04PM 08/11/05	unknown
foo:730	1	72	No	11:03PM 08/11/05	unknown
foo:721	1	72	No	11:03PM 08/11/05	unknown
foo:700	1	54	No	11:03PM 08/11/05	unknown
foo:671	1	54	No	11:02PM 08/11/05	unknown

Figure 1-59. How to confuse a wardriver

Changing your SSID on a whim is almost certainly a bad idea, but imagine an event such as Burning Man (*http://www.burningman.com*), where the action happens in a wireless-friendly flat plane. You could add a wireless card to the computer to serve MP3s in your art car and broadcast your position with GPS. Since the beacon frame drops down to 1MB and is sent relatively infrequently, you could have quite a few location-aware vehicles sharing a single Wi-Fi radio channel.

This hack lets you communicate your position (or anything else you can convey 32-bytes at a time) to a client and there is no way for the server, or anyone listening in, to identify which clients are getting the position information. This technique has lots of disadvantages, not least of which is that it destroys all normal use of the link, but that's what makes it a hack.

See Also

- More on 802.11 beacons: *http://www.wi-fiplanet.com/tutorials/article. php/1492071*

—*Rich Gibson*

Map Wi-Fi Networks with Kismet and GPSd

Use these two powerful Linux tools to map out the locations of Wi-Fi networks.

GPSd [Hack #20] is a great tool to get data from your GPS receiver. You can make it even more powerful by combining it with Kismet [Hack #29], allowing you to physically map locations of wireless networks.

In order to make this work, you will need to have both GPSd and Kismet installed and functioning with your Linux system. Consult the hacks on both pieces of software if you have setup questions.

If you plan to do some network mapping with Kismet, keep the following in mind:

- Put the computer somewhere safe and out of the way. Don't put it someplace where a sudden stop will send it into your lap or through a window.

- Forget that the computer is there while you are driving. If you have to fiddle with it, pull over first. If you can have a friend ride with you who can operate the computer, all the better. Do not let the computer distract you while you are driving.

- Make sure that the GPS gets a fix before you start driving. It's a lot harder for it to get a fix while you are in motion.

- Put the GPS somewhere that it can easily pick up the satellite signals. Your best bet is to get a magnetized external antenna that can attach to your roof. Be sure that there are no loose wires sticking out of your window. Don't slam the wires in the door!

Above all, when you are driving a car, your first responsibility is to drive safely. Pay attention to the road and drive carefully.

To begin mapping networks with Kismet and GPSd, take the following steps:

1. Load any modules needed for the serial port you're using for the GPS (optional):

   ```
   $ sudo modprobe pl2303
   $ dmesg | grep tty

   ttyS00 at 0x03f8 (irq = 4) is a 16550A
   ttyS02 at 0x03e8 (irq = 4) is a 16550A
   usbserial.c:PL-2303converternowattachedtottyUSB0(orusb/tts/0for
   devfs)
   ```

2. Start GPSd, specifying the serial port with -p and the speed with -s:

```
$ sudo gpsd -D9 -p /dev/ttyUSB0 -s 4800
  Telnet to GPSd and use p until you have a reliable fix, then
disconnect when you are done:
$telnet localhost 2947
Trying 127.0.0.1...
Connected to debian.
Escape character is '^]'.
p
GPSD,P=0.000000 0.000000
p
GPSD,P=41.485882 -71.524841
^]
telnet>q
Connection closed.
```

3. Launch Kismet with the -g (GPS) switch, and specify the hostname and port that GPSd is listening on:

```
$ sudo kismet -g localhost:2947
```

4. Go for a drive. Press Shift-Q when you are done with the drive to terminate Kismet.

When you shut Kismet down, it writes out logfiles. Check the logtemplate setting in *kismet.conf* to see where it puts its log files; for example:

```
logtemplate=/var/log/kismet/%n-%d-%i.%l
```

Kismet writes several logfiles in the logtemplate directory (in the following filenames, *I* starts at 1 and increments each time you run Kismet on a given day):

Kismet-MMM-DD-YYYY-I.csv
    Kismet log in semicolon-separated fields, one line per entry. The first entry contains the field names.

Kismet-MMM-DD-YYYY-I.dump
    Kismet log in a *pcap(3)* format suitable for loading under Ethereal (*http://www.ethereal.com*).

Kismet-MMM-DD-YYYY-I.gps
    Kismet log in a format designed to be read by the *gpsmap* utility, which is included with the Kismet distribution.

Kismet-MMM-DD-YYYY-I.network
    A human-readable dump of the networks that Kismet encountered.

Kismet-MMM-DD-YYYY-I.xml
    Kismet log in an XML format.

To generate a map, run *gpsmap* on the *.gpslog* file. See the *gpsmap* manpage for all the drawing and mapping options. If you choose to use a down-loaded map (the default), you must be online. Figure 1-60 shows a map generated by the following command:

```
$ gpsmap -S3 -p /var/log/kismet/Kismet-Feb-16-2004-5.gps
```

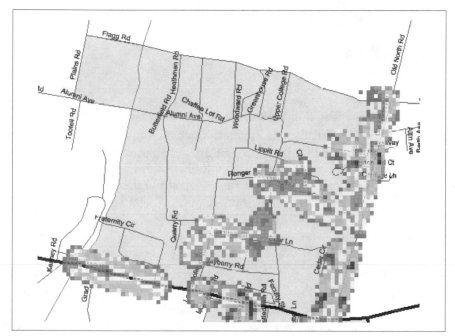

Figure 1-60. Wi-Fi power levels in the Kingston, Rhode Island area

The -S option specifies which map server to use:

```
(0=MapBlast;1=Map-Point;2=Terraserver;3=Tiger Census)
```

If you have trouble with one of these map servers, try another (Tiger is loosely maintained by the Census Bureau and is not up 100% of the time). Use -p to show power levels or -e to simply plot the locations of the hotspots on the map (see the *gpsmap* manpage for more options).

See Also

- For even more mapping goodness, check out "Analyze Elevation Profiles for Better Long-Range Wireless Networking" [Hack #94].

—*Brian Jepson*

## CHAPTER TWO

Network Discovery and Monitoring

Hacks 23–39

Perhaps the most difficult task in wireless networking is trying to visualize what is really going on. Radio waves are invisible and undetectable to humans without the aid of sophisticated tools, such as a spectrum analyzer. Such devices aren't cheap, ranging from several hundreds to tens of thousands of dollars, depending on their capabilities. Obviously, such devices are well beyond the reach of the average networking aficionado. And even if they weren't, a spectrum analyzer only gives you a visualization of what is going on at the physical radio layer; it doesn't give you any indication of what is happening with the actual network data.

Fortunately, every 802.11 networking device can not only transmit data, but can listen as well. Combined with sophisticated (and generally free) software, this can turn an average laptop or handheld into a powerful monitoring tool. This chapter shows how to use standard hardware to detect wireless networks and clients, generate statistics on their usage, and gather valuable insight into how your network is being used by sifting through the deluge of available radio information. Using these tools can help you coordinate networking efforts with people in your local vicinity to make the most efficient possible use of the available radio spectrum.

HACK #23 **Find All Available Wireless Networks**

Locate all wireless networks in range without installing any additional software.

So, you've got a laptop. You've got a wireless card. The card might even be built into your laptop. You know there are wireless networks in your area. How do you find them? You might even have an external antenna connected to your wireless card, hoping to establish a longer distance connection. How do you find that network a half-mile away?

If you are connected to a wireless network, you could download a tool such as NetStumbler [Hack #24], but this requires a network connection and you don't have one yet.

All of the major operating systems have integrated software that allows you to discover wireless networks and obtain some status information about the currently connected network.

Windows XP

Service Pack 2 (SP2) introduced some new behavior to Windows XP for wireless networks. Since SP2 has been available for over a year now, we will assume you have upgraded your installation. This section applies to SP2 only.

If any wireless access points are detected by your wireless card, Windows XP will inform you using a pop-up above the task bar, which says, "Wireless networks detected." Clicking the pop-up or the network icon opens a window titled Wireless Network Connection, as shown in Figure 2-1.

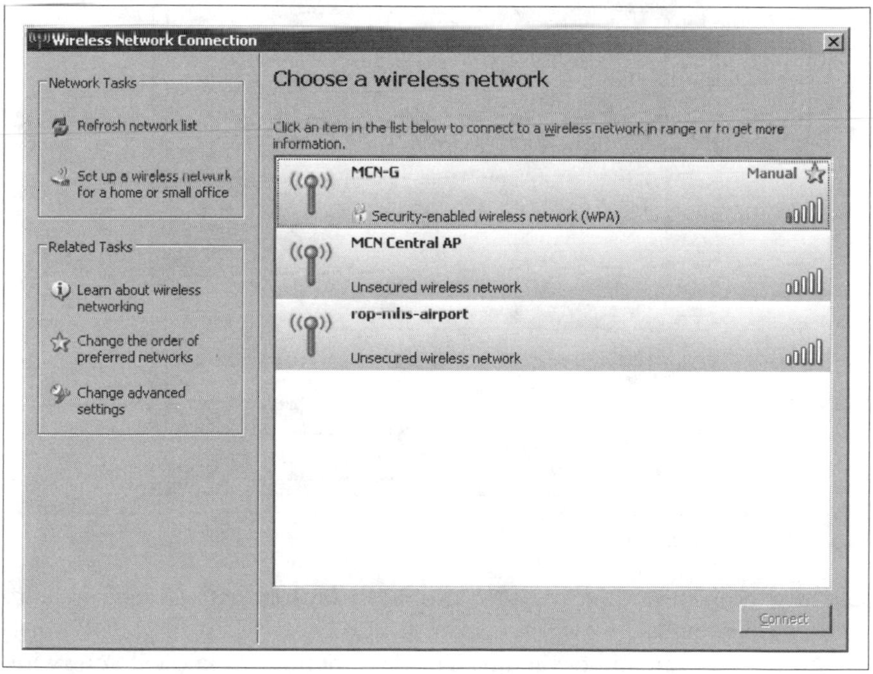

Figure 2-1. Available wireless networks

This window lists any wireless networks that are in range. In this example, there are three networks available. The window also shows you that the first wireless network requires the use of a WPA key.

To join a network, select one from the list and click Connect. If the network is unsecured, you will be asked to allow the unsecure connection. If security is enabled, you will be prompted for a WPA or WEP key and to confirm the key by retyping.

If you have difficulty connecting to any of the listed networks, click the "Change advanced settings" button to open the Wireless Networks Connection Properties window shown in Figure 2-2.

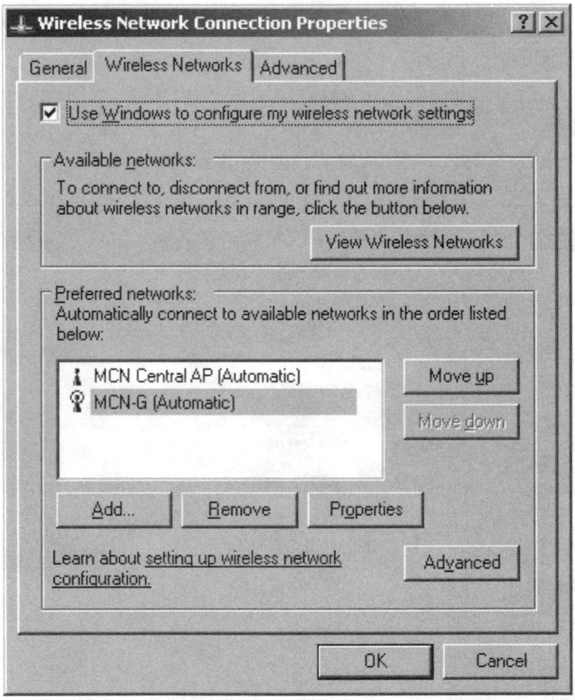

Figure 2-2. Advanced wireless network options

Clicking the Wireless Networks tab displays a button that will return you to the available wireless networks screen. It also shows a list of *preferred networks* that you can add or modify. This is important to know if your wireless access point does not broadcast the ESSID, because it saves you from repeatedly having to type in the name of the otherwise-invisible network and needing to remember its name in the first place.

At the top of this window, if the "Use Windows to configure my wireless network settings" checkbox is checked, Windows will automatically attempt to connect to any wireless networks listed in your preferred networks. If no preferred networks are available, it will provide you with a list of available wireless networks, as shown earlier in Figure 2-1.

To get status on the wireless network to which you are currently connected, right-click the network icon in the task bar and select Status. Figure 2-3 shows a typical status screen.

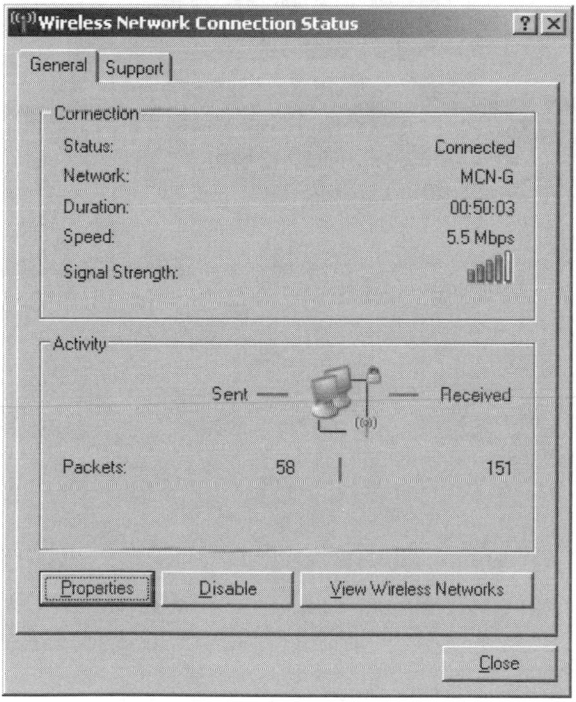

Figure 2-3. Wireless network status

While this gives you some basic connection information, it doesn't show you actual signal strength in dB, which would be very useful for testing wireless connections. You also do not get any information on signal-to-noise ratio. Clicking on the Support tab gives you IP addressing information for this wireless card.

Mac OS X

For Apple notebooks with a built-in AirPort card, all wireless configuration is handled through the System Preferences (System Preferences → Network), as shown in Figure 2-4.

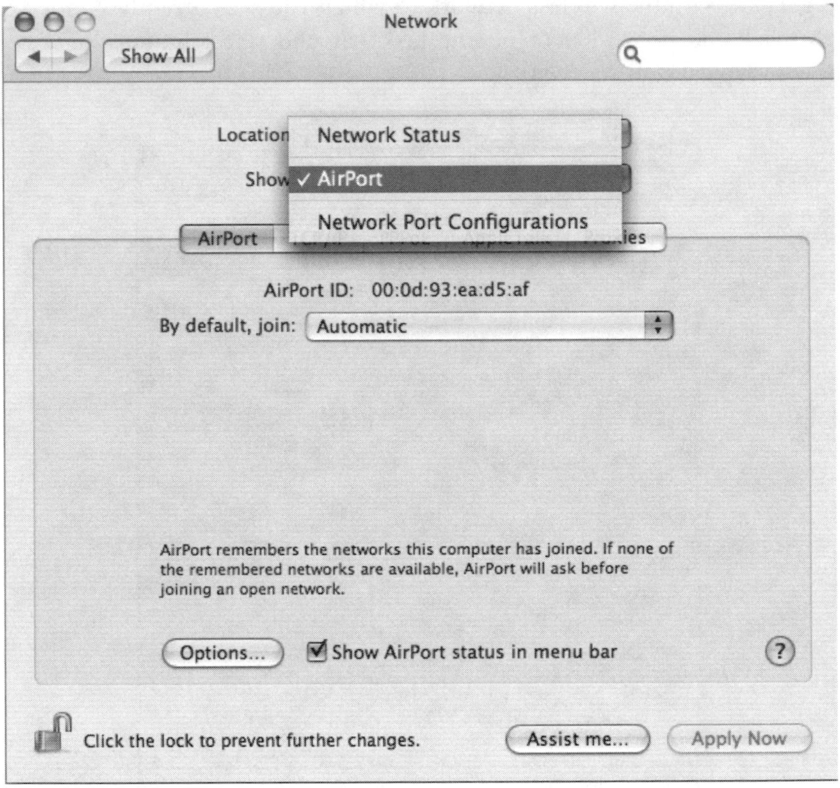

Figure 2-4. AirPort configuration

By default, you will have at least two available network cards. Click the Show pull-down menu for a choice of adapters, including Built-in Ethernet and AirPort. Select AirPort. To get to the wireless network settings, select the AirPort tab.

We'll come back to details of this screen later. Right now, you should be concerned with the "Show AirPort status in menu bar" setting, which should be checked. Once you check this box and close the configuration window, you'll see a new icon in the menu bar, as shown in Figure 2-5. The first thing you'll want to do is click the menu bar icon and select the option to turn on the AirPort card.

Figure 2-5. AirPort menu bar

Once the AirPort card is on, you'll be able to see a list of available networks; you can select any of these. If a password is required for the selected network, you'll be prompted for it.

To connect to a network that is not listed, choose Other.... You will be presented with the Closed Network box shown in Figure 2-6. This is how you can join networks that do not broadcast their ESSID.

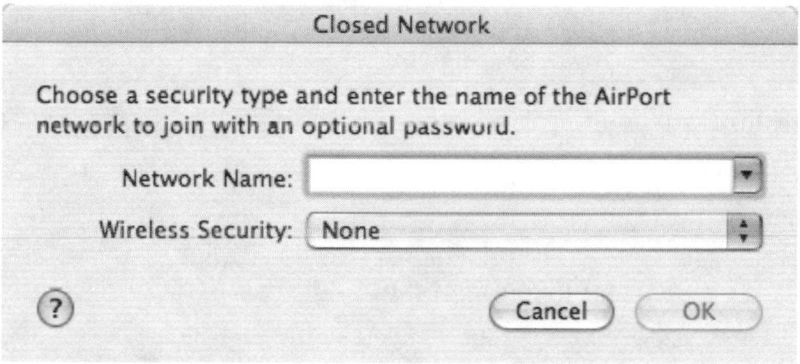

Figure 2-6. Specifying the ESSID for a closed network

Here, you can enter the network name (ESSID) of the wireless network you want to join and the password if one is required. Mac OS X supports WEP, LEAP, WPA, and 802.1x authentication types. You can select these from the drop-down menu labeled Wireless Security.

Once you've either selected an available network or entered information for another network not listed, you'll see which network is currently connected by using the AirPort menu bar, as shown in Figure 2-7.

The AirPort software offers a signal strength meter, though it is rather limited in its granularity. Click the AirPort icon in the menu bar and select Open Internet Connect; you'll see a window similar to Figure 2-8.

Combined with the lack of a connector for external antennas, this limits the AirPort wireless card as a useful tool for testing wireless network connections. For more advanced signal measurement on Mac OS X, you might want to take a look at iStumbler [Hack #27] or KisMAC [Hack #20].

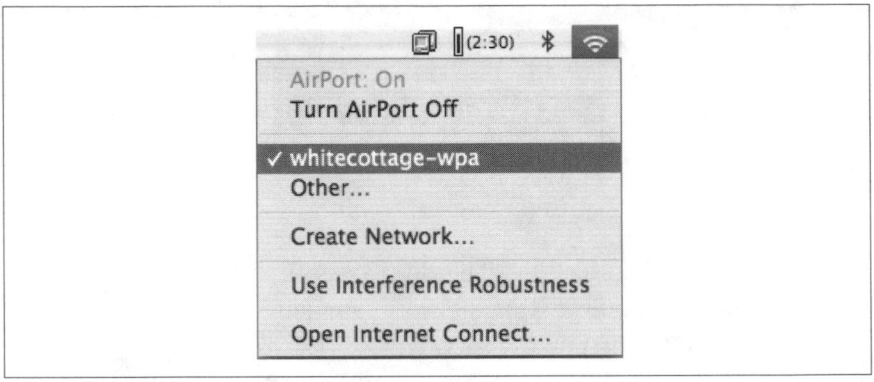

Figure 2-7. AirPort menu bar connections

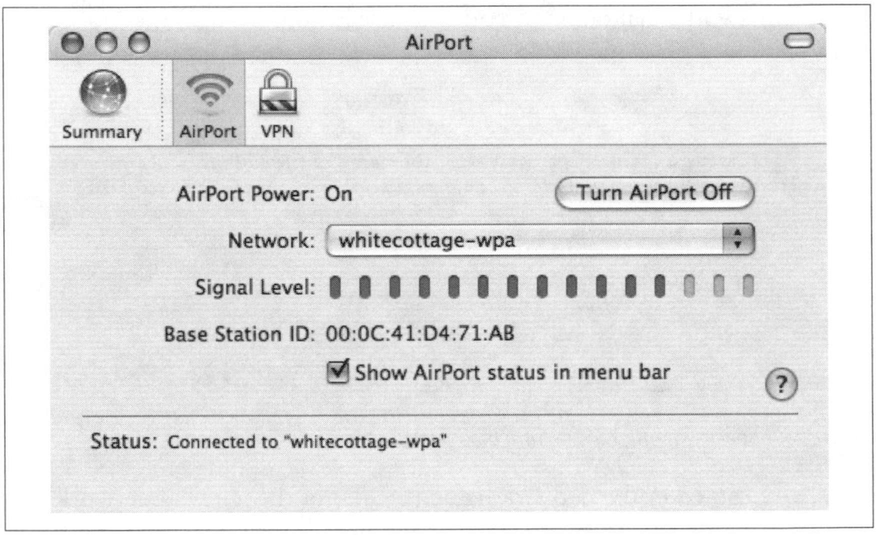

Figure 2-8. Apple's basic AirPort status

Linux

Using wireless networking cards in Linux can require a good deal of work, depending on your particular Linux distribution, your specific wireless card, and your hardware platform. I'm not going to cover that here. I assume here that you have PCMCIA support for your wireless card, the Wireless Extensions in your kernel, and the Wireless Tools package installed.

Not too long ago, these requirements involved compiling your own Linux kernel, compiling and installing a driver for your wireless card, and configuring the Wireless Tools by editing a number of configuration files. Along with other changes in the desktop distributions of Linux, built-in wireless

support is standard with all of the major 2.6 kernel distributions. Examples
in this section use Ubuntu Linux.

While wireless support has made many strides in current Linux distributions, one thing not readily available in default installations is any sort of
GUI for detecting wireless networks. There are several great packages that
do this, but from a fresh install, none of them are available. The best tools
for the job are still the basic Wireless Tools run from the command line.
These come installed by default if wireless drivers are present.

The Wireless Tools package provides four command-line tools:

iwconfig
  Allows you to manipulate the basic wireless parameters

iwlist
  Allows you to list addresses, frequencies, bit rates, and more

iwspy
  Allows you to get per-node link quality

iwpriv
  Allows you to manipulate the Wireless Extensions specific to a driver

iwlist is the tool you need at the command line to show you available wireless networks. To enable scanning, use the following command:

    $ **iwlist ath0 scanning**

This gives you detailed information about all detected networks and is supported in the newer versions of the Wireless Extensions/Tools. You'll see
output similar to this:

```
ath0      Scan completed :
          Cell 01 - Address: 00:02:2D:08:82:DA
                    ESSID:"foo"
                    Mode:Master
                    Frequency:2.442 GHz (Channel 7)
                    Quality=0/94  Signal level=-95 dBm  Noise level=-95 dBm
                    Encryption key:off
                    Bit Rate:1 Mb/s
                    Bit Rate:2 Mb/s
                    Bit Rate:5 Mb/s
                    Bit Rate:11 Mb/s
                    Extra:bcn_int=100
          Cell 02 - Address: 00:02:6F:20:B6:49
                    ESSID:"foo-a"
                    Mode:Master
                    Frequency:5.26 GHz (Channel 52)
                    Quality=0/94  Signal level=-95 dBm  Noise level=-95 dBm
                    Encryption key:off
                    Bit Rate:6 Mb/s
                    Bit Rate:9 Mb/s
```

```
                        Bit Rate:12 Mb/s
                        Bit Rate:18 Mb/s
                        Bit Rate:24 Mb/s
                        Bit Rate:36 Mb/s
                        Bit Rate:48 Mb/s
                        Bit Rate:54 Mb/s
                        Extra:bcn_int=100
          Cell 03 - Address: 00:02:6F:20:B6:4A
                        ESSID:"foo-g"
                        Mode:Master
                        Frequency:2.462 GHz (Channel 11)
                        Quality=0/94  Signal level=-95 dBm  Noise level=-95 dBm
                        Encryption key:on
                        Bit Rate:1 Mb/s
                        Bit Rate:2 Mb/s
                        Bit Rate:5 Mb/s
                        Bit Rate:6 Mb/s
                        Bit Rate:9 Mb/s
                        Bit Rate:11 Mb/s
                        Bit Rate:12 Mb/s
                        Bit Rate:18 Mb/s
                        Bit Rate:24 Mb/s
                        Bit Rate:36 Mb/s
                        Bit Rate:48 Mb/s
                        Bit Rate:54 Mb/s
                        Extra:bcn_int=100
```

If there are multiple access points visible from your machine, you'll receive detailed information on each one. Once you've found the access point you need to connect to, you can use *iwconfig* to tell your card about it.

> Wireless Tools functionality depends entirely on the capability of the specific driver for your wireless card. Some drivers do not support a mode necessary for scanning to function. Other drivers report erroneous signal level information, as shown in the previous output.

Anyone who works with wireless networks in Linux will likely be looking for a more powerful link-state monitoring tool. Be sure to take a look at AP Radar [Hack #26] or Wavemon [Hack #30] if you need more functionality than the simple command-line tools provide.

Discover Networks with NetStumbler
Find all available wireless networks with the NetStumbler monitoring tool.

Once you've tried using the wireless client software included with Windows XP, you'll quickly realize the major shortcomings of this utility. You won't get a detailed measurement of signal strength and you won't know when multiple networks are using the same channel.

NetStumbler (*http://stumbler.net*) is an excellent utility that will give you a great deal of detail about all of the wireless networks in range, including their ESSID, whether they use WEP, the channels they use, and more. At the time of this writing, the current version is 0.4.0. Installation is easy and quick, and for everything that NetStumbler does, the software package is remarkably small. Windows 2000 or better is required for the package to install.

NetStumbler does not support all wireless network cards, but support has improved markedly since earlier versions. You'll want to check the *README* file before installing to make sure you've got a compatible wireless card. Supported cards include all cards using the Hermes chipset (Lucent/Orinoco/Avaya/Agere/Proxim 802.11b). Most 802.11b cards using the Prism or Prism2 chipsets—including cards D-Link, Linksys, Compaq, Dell, and others—also work. Version 0.4.0 supports nearly any Wi-Fi card in Windows XP, including 802.11a/b/g cards using Atheros, Atmel, Broadcom, Cisco, and Centrino chipsets.

Options

When you launch NetStumbler, you're going to want to set some options. Click View and select Options. You'll see the Options dialog shown in Figure 2-9.

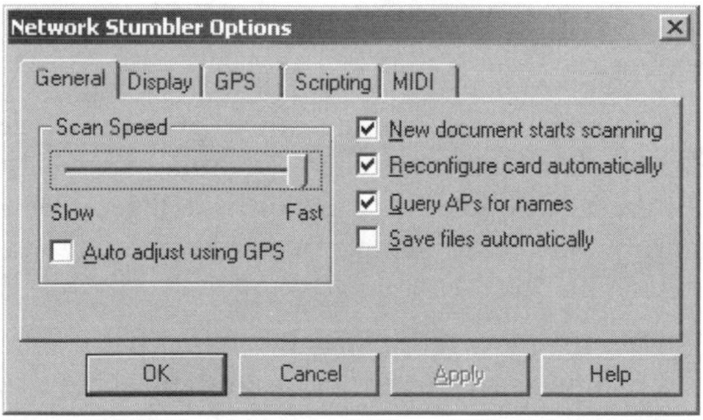

Figure 2-9. NetStumbler options

There are a couple important options here that you must select to get the best performance out of NetStumbler. You will want to set the scan speed to Fast, because you'll get more frequent and more accurate updates of wireless networks with that setting. Also, definitely check the "Reconfigure card automatically" option. If you don't check this, NetStumbler will find whatever wireless network your card is currently associated with, but it won't find any other networks.

One of NetStumbler's coolest features is the ability to give you MIDI feedback for signal strength. This is great for finding the best possible signal between two points, such as when you are trying to align antennas on a long-distance shot [Hack #98]. When the signal strength rises, so does the pitch of the tone that NetStumbler plays. This makes tuning an antenna similar to pointing a satellite dish; just move the antenna around until you hear the highest pitched tone. Choose a MIDI channel and patch sounds under the MIDI tab of the Options screen, as shown in Figure 2-10. You'll need a MIDI-capable sound card to use this option.

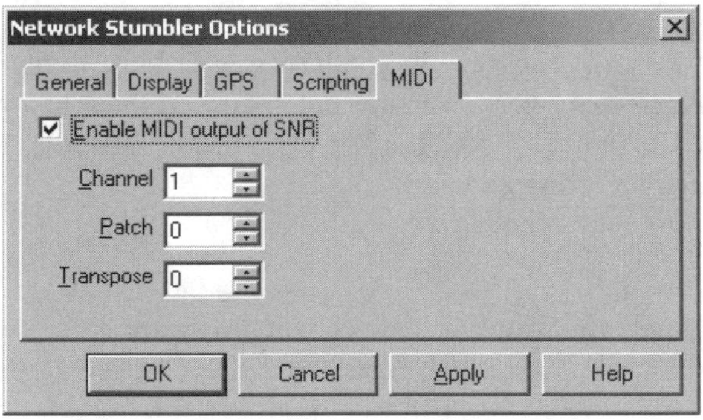

Figure 2-10. NetStumbler MIDI options

Network Discovery

With your options properly set, you're ready to discover wireless networks. Assuming your wireless card is installed, NetStumbler will start scanning immediately. If the MIDI option is turned on, you'll get *a lot* of audio feedback, particularly if you have multiple networks in your area. Figure 2-11 shows a typical NetStumbler session.

NetStumbler shows the most active links by color. Green indicates a strong signal, yellow is marginal, and red is almost unusable. Grey means the wireless network is not in reach. The lock symbol shown in the link buttons indicates that the network is using WEP or WPA.

You can see at a glance all of the wireless networks that NetStumbler has found, along with their signal strength, SNR, and noise. You can also see which vendor chipset the wireless network is using. This can be particularly handy when you are looking for a specific network in a populated area.

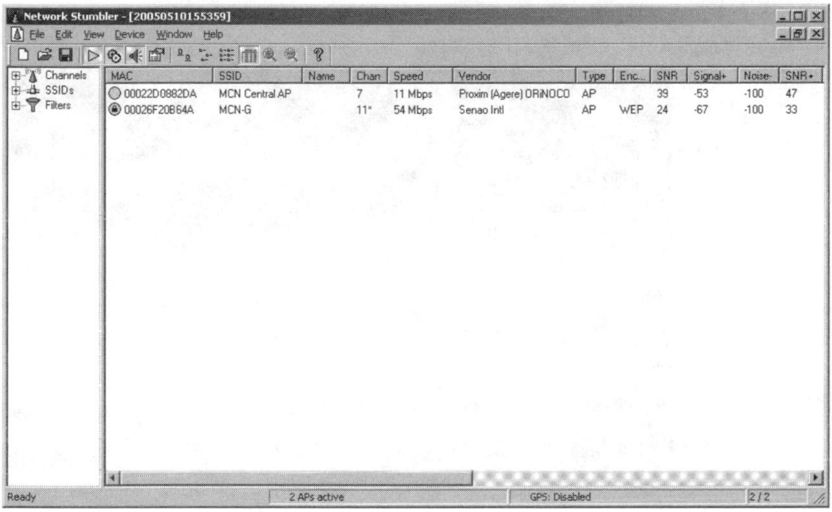

Figure 2-11. Detected networks

To use NetStumbler for fine tuning a wireless link, start up NetStumbler and make sure that it has found the network on the other end of the point-to-point link. Once it has done so, you'll start hearing the MIDI tones as it reports signal strength. A higher tone indicates better signal strength. Turn up your speaker volume, and then concentrate on pointing the antenna. You'll know it's pointed as accurately as possible when NetStumbler is generating the highest MIDI tone.

Another signal strength visualization method is available by drilling down through the navigational menus on the left side of the NetStumbler screen. Click on the plus sign next to SSIDs. If you then click a plus sign next to an SSID, you'll see every MAC address associated with that SSID. Click on the MAC address to see a graphical representation of signal strength to that wireless network.

As shown in Figure 2-12, this is a handy visual tool. You can use this to tell you when a directional antenna is placed properly, and you can also use it in a corporate environment to determine the best placement location for an access point.

NetStumbler will also interface with a GPS system connected to your PC. You can choose your GPS system type from a list in the View → Options dialog. Once you have told NetStumbler about your GPS unit, the main screen not only shows details of the wireless network, but it also shows the latitude and longitude of the wireless network.

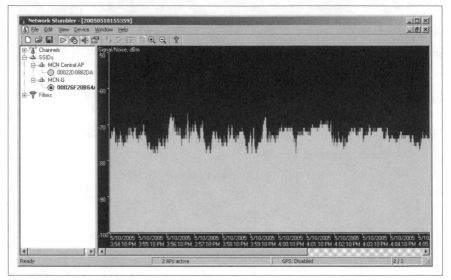

Figure 2-12. Visualizing your signal strength

Caveats

As mentioned at the beginning of the hack, NetStumbler includes NDIS 5.1 driver support for many types of wireless cards if you are running Windows XP. In order to make this work, you'll need to click on the Device menu. There will be two drivers listed. You must select the driver labeled NDIS 5.1 in order to make NetStumbler work with 802.11a/b/g cards. We've tested this successfully with cards based on Cisco, Atheros, and Prism 2 chipsets.

You will also find that NetStumbler makes no distinction between WEP and WPA. If it sees an encrypted network, it notes that as WEP and moves on. Whether this is because the program has not been updated recently is unclear.

NetStumbler is an active network scanner that sends out probe requests and watches for responses to those probes; as such, it won't detect so-called *closed* networks. To accomplish this, you need a passive monitoring tool such as Kismet **[Hack #29]** or KisMAC **[Hack #28]**. But for many situations, NetStumbler is a small, powerful tool for detecting and monitoring the majority of wireless networks.

Although NetStumbler is free to download and use, you should help the author out, particularly if you use it in a commercial enterprise. Donations can be made online at *http://www.stumbler.net/donate*.

Detect Networks with Handheld PCs
Easily monitor wireless networks while walking around.

If you have a handheld PC, you know how convenient it is. What you might not realize is that it makes an excellent wireless testing device. If your handheld has a Compact Flash or PC Card slot, you can use a wireless card in these slots. You might even have a newer model with built-in Wi-Fi and Bluetooth.

Two programs are available to detect wireless networks on Windows-based handhelds. For Pocket PC 3.0, Handheld PC 2000, and Pocket PC 2002, the author of NetStumbler, Marius Milner, has written a miniature version just for Pocket PCs: MiniStumbler. Windows Mobile 2003 support is not reliable in MiniStumbler, and the author is working on an update. You might be able to get it working, but it is not officially supported.

Windows Mobile 2003 users have the option of installing WiFiFoFum, which is designed expressly for this version of PocketPC software and indeed does not run on any earlier versions of the operating system. This hack covers both programs.

MiniStumbler

MiniStumbler is available for download at *http://stumbler.net*. At the time of this writing, the current version is 0.40. MiniStumbler supports Hermes chipset cards (Lucent/Orinoco/Agere/Avaya/Proxim). Many Prism 2 cards are also known to work. Check *http://stumbler.net/compat* for updated reports of cards that work.

To install MiniStumbler, download the executable file to your PC, which must have the Microsoft ActiveSync software. Make sure your PocketPC is in its dock or otherwise associated with ActiveSync. Double-click the file and follow the prompts. The installer will figure out which type of processor your PocketPC runs and install the proper binary. You can then run MiniStumbler from the Programs folder of your PocketPC.

As with NetStumbler [Hack #24], you'll want to set some options the first time you launch it. Select View → Options and make sure that "Reconfigure card automatically" and "Query APs for names" are both checked, as shown in Figure 2-13. On this screen, you can also set the scanning speed, which you'll want to set to Fast.

With MiniStumbler's options properly configured, you're ready to discover wireless networks. If your wireless card is installed and enabled, MiniStumbler will immediately start scanning for networks. A typical scanning session looks something like Figure 2-14.

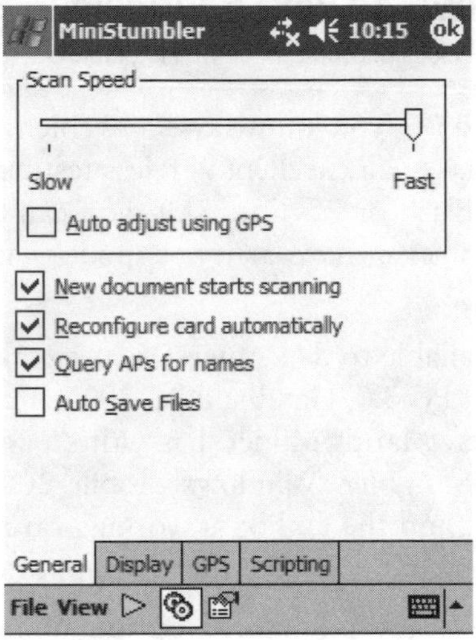

Figure 2-13. Setting your options

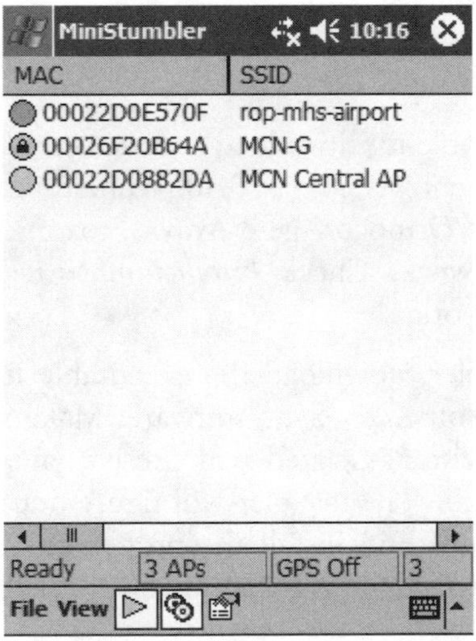

Figure 2-14. MiniStumbler in action

If you've ever used NetStumbler, you should be right at home. The data is displayed in exactly the same way, using the same color scheme for the networks it has detected (green, yellow, or red to indicate signal strength, grey for networks out of range, and a tiny lock icon for networks using WPA/WEP). If you need to pause the scanning process, simply click on the green triangle in the bottom menu.

While the tiny screen of a Pocket PC is wonderfully portable, it makes viewing large amounts of data painful. In order to see all of the data in MiniStumbler, you will have to scroll to the right. This rest of the data revealed includes signal strength, SNR, and noise levels.

MiniStumbler does not support any of the visualization views in NetStumbler, so you can't get a graph of wireless signal over time. However, there is support for location logging using a GPS. Choose View → Options, select the GPS tab (Figure 2-15), and then select the COM port and data type of your GPS. MiniStumbler will then show latitude and longitude locations for all of your wireless networks as it finds them.

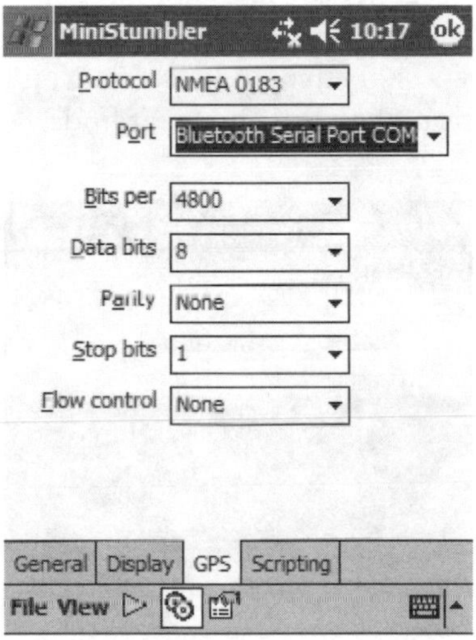

Figure 2-15. GPS configuration

Obviously, a GPS can effectively be used only for outdoor network detection, but the extreme portability of Pocket PCs makes them ideal for performing informal site surveys, checking for unauthorized access points, or establishing the coverage area of your wireless network. MiniStumbler might be missing many of the handy features of NetStumbler and Kismet, but it is simple to use and far better than the PocketPC system client for finding networks.

WiFiFoFum

At the time of this writing, this uniquely named program is the better option if your PocketPC runs Windows Mobile 2003. You can download the software from *http://www.aspecto-software.com/WiFiFoFum*.

> There is a list of supported devices and a FAQ if you run into
> problems. For the purposes of this hack, we have tested Ver-
> sion 0.3.3 on a Dell Axim X30.

There is no installer for WiFiFoFum, so you'll need to download the zip file,
uncompress it, and copy the three DLL files and one EXE file over to your
PocketPC via ActiveSync, or Bluetooth File Exchange if you have that
option. Once the files are copied over, you can start WiFiFoFum directly
from the location where you copied it.

As shown in Figure 2-16, the main screen of WiFiFoFum looks much like
other wireless network scanners. It does not have all of the details that MiniStumbler provides; there is no SNR, no noise level, and it does not graphi-
cally show you relative signal strength by color. You'll have to scroll to the
right to see the channels of the access points it finds.

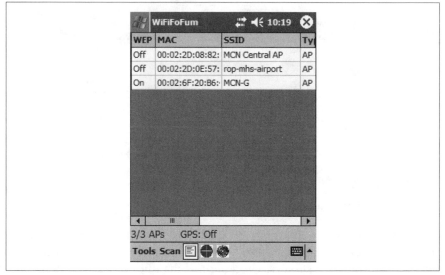

Figure 2-16. WiFiFoFum in action

Depending on your model of PocketPC and the wireless card driver, you will
need to change the selected type by clicking on Tools → Device. The default
choice is the WLAGS46B1 driver for Orinoco chipsets. In our case, the Dell
Axim X30 required us to choose the ODIM\WLAGS46B1 driver for WiFiFo-
Fum to begin scanning correctly.

There are some interesting options that you can set, as shown in
Figure 2-17. Scan time is adjustable from 100 to 5000 milliseconds. The
order of the fields in the scan is customizable. You can choose a location

where WiFiFoFum keeps scan logs and pick a WAV file that it plays when new access points are detected. As with MiniStumbler, there is no audio feedback for signal strength. GPS support is also available in the GPS options tab. Pick a serial port and baud rate, and new scans will begin to show latitude and longitude information.

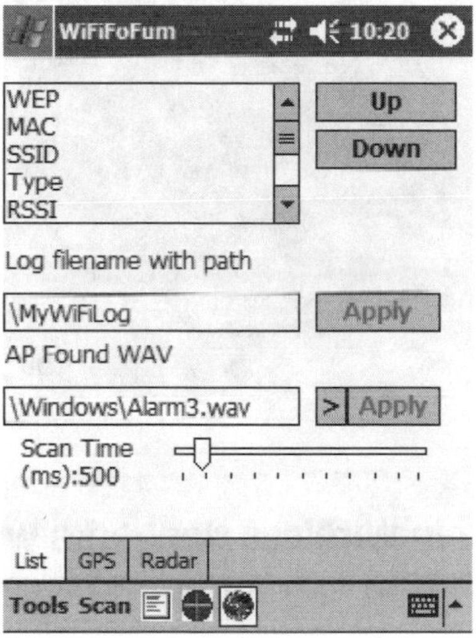

Figure 2-17. Setting your options

A unique feature of the program is the Radar display, which shows the relative locations of access points to your handheld based on their signal strength, as shown in Figure 2-18. Radar does not appear to be geographically accurate, but it does give you a picture of relative distance to access points.

WiFiFoFum is a great little scanning application. While it does not have all the features of MiniStumbler, it comes close, and it is your best choice if you have the most recent PocketPC operating system.

Other Handhelds

If you have a Sharp Zaurus or Compaq iPAQ running Linux, then you're in luck. Kismet [Hack #29] runs well on these machines, giving you the most powerful and tiny network monitoring tool there is. Zaurus users can find a complete HOWTO on installing Kismet at *http://aurach.ewu.edu/ield/ield_course/lectures/ield_appC*. iPAQ owners should go to *http://grox.net/misc/ipaq/kismet* for instructions using Familiar Linux.

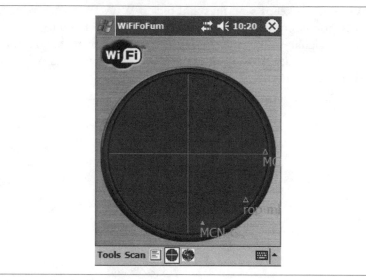

Figure 2-18. Radar display

Find and Join Wireless Networks with AP Radar

Use this handy GNOME application to find and join wireless networks.

From a purely functional perspective, the Wireless Tools included with Linux distributions are all you need to locate wireless networks. But as far as ease of use goes, they leave something to be desired. Unfortunately, most distributions do not install any other wireless tools.

AP Radar is an application designed to make wireless network detection and connection easier and more manageable. It is both a graphical network discovery tool and a wireless profile manager. Using the Wireless Extensions, it has the ability to watch for new networks while maintaining an association with your existing network. It automates connection tasks, so that when you come in range of your home network you are immediately associated.

Prerequisites

The program is the work of Don Park, and you can obtain source code from the project's development site at *http://apradar.sourceforge.net*. To compile successfully, you'll need to be running GNOME Version 2 or greater, and at least a 2.4.20 kernel. A 2.6 kernel is recommended.

AP Radar requires a wireless driver that is capable of running in Monitor mode. Most drivers support this mode, but there is an easy way to determine your driver's capabilities. Open a terminal and execute this command:

```
iwlist ath0 scanning
```

You should see the following output:

```
ath0      Scan completed :
          Cell 01 - Address: 00:02:2D:08:82:DA
                    ESSID:"foo"
                    Mode:Master
                    Frequency:2.442 GHz (Channel 7)
                    Quality=0/94  Signal level=-95 dBm  Noise level=-95 dBm
                    Encryption key:off
                    Bit Rate:1 Mb/s
                    Bit Rate:2 Mb/s
                    Bit Rate:5 Mb/s
                    Bit Rate:11 Mb/s
                    Extra:bcn_int=100
```

If you see any other output, the chances are good that AP Radar will not function with your wireless driver.

There are also a number of packages that AP Radar requires to compile. Here are the Ubuntu or Debian packages that you can install with *apt-get*:

- `libgtk-2.0`
- `libgtkmm-2.4.1`
- `libgtkmm-2.4-devel`
- `libiw-devel`
- `automake`
- `autoconf`

RPM users can consult the *README* file in the source code for required RPM packages. The first two packages, `libgtk` and `libgtkmm`, should come installed by default in Ubuntu Linux.

Building and Using AP Radar

Once you have the necessary packages installed, you'll want to get the AP Radar source code from CVS:

```
cvs -d:pserver:anonymous@cvs.sourceforge.net:/cvsroot/apradar login
cvs -z3 -d:pserver:anonymous@cvs.sourceforge.net:/cvsroot/apradar co -P
apradar
```

If prompted for a password during the CVS login, press Enter.

Once you're done, you'll have created an *apradar* directory. Change into the newly created directory, and execute these commands to configure and compile the source code:

```
sh autogen.sh
./configure
make
make install
```

Assuming that you received no errors during compilation, this will place the
AP Radar executable in */usr/local/bin/apradar*. The program needs root privileges to run, and the best way to do that is with *sudo*:

```
sudo apradar
```

If you experience problems starting AP Radar, they might be due to oddities
in your wireless card driver and how it writes status to */proc/net/wireless*. To
avoid this problem, you can start the program by specifying the interface
name:

```
sudo apradar -i ath0
```

The program screen appears, as shown in Figure 2-19.

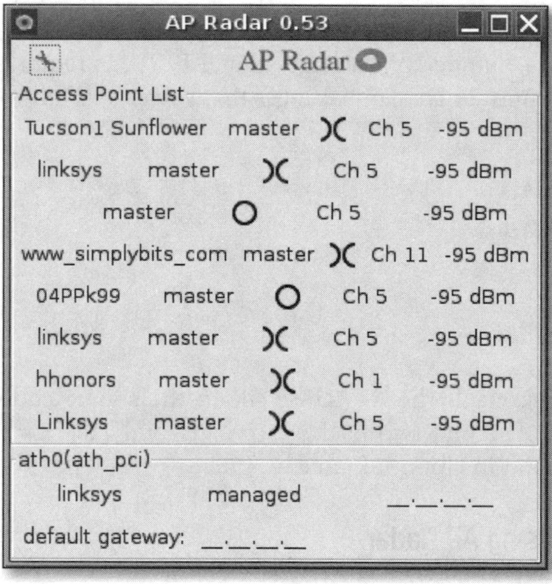

Figure 2-19. AP Radar

You should immediately see a list of all access points in range. Almost every
field on the screen either is clickable or provides you with information when
you hover the cursor over it.

To associate with any of the access points shown under Access Point List,
click on the name of the network. By default, AP Radar associates your wireless card with the selected access point, but it also runs *dhclient* to obtain an
IP address via DHCP.

DHCP and default gateway commands are accessed by clicking on the red symbol at the top left of the AP Radar screen:

Ping default gateway
> This monitors the gateway set in the Linux route table. When AP Radar does not receive pings from this gateway, it assumes that the gateway is out of range.

Run dhclient -1 *on associate*
> This allows you to specify whether you want AP Radar to obtain a DHCP address after it associates with an access point. Turn this off if you want static addressing.

Final Thoughts

AP Radar is an extremely handy little program that lets you simply join the wireless networks you need. It allows you to generally forget the Wireless Tools, unless you need to set specific wireless card parameters. What it doesn't do is provide anything in the way of diagnostic information on your wireless connection—no signal-to-noise information or any graphical display of network strength. Take a look at Kismet [Hack #29] or Waveiiion [Hack #30] if you need more detailed wireless network information.

H A C K   Detect Networks on Mac OS X
#27
Find out everything you ever wanted to know about the networks available in your area.

If you are simply looking for any available network, you can usually get by with the built-in AirPort software. However, if you are building your own network or troubleshooting wireless connections, you need much more detail than the standard tools provide. In particular, knowing which networks are in range and which channels they are using can be invaluable when determining where to put your own equipment. Here are two easy-to-use survey tools for Mac OS X that give you a far better idea of what's really going on.

MacStumbler

Sharing nothing but a name with the popular NetStumbler [Hack #24], MacStumbler (*http://www.macstumbler.com*) is the original network scanner for Mac OS X. It is simple to use, and it provides the details that you are most likely interested in: available networks, the channels they use, and their received signal strength. It also displays received noise, whether WEP is enabled, and a bunch of other useful details, as shown in Figure 2-20.

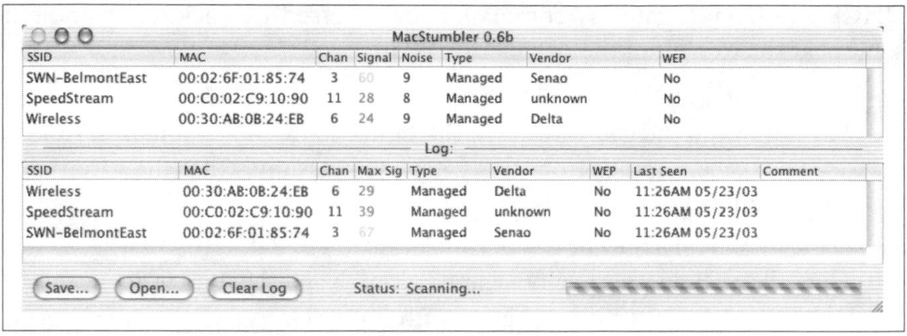

Figure 2-20. MacStumbler's main screen

Like many Mac OS X apps, MacStumbler is capable of text-to-speech, so it will speak the ESSIDs of networks that it finds as they appear. You can set the preferences to play different sounds when it detects an open network or a WEP network. MacStumbler also has GPS support, and can use GPS devices connected via serial or Bluetooth. With GPS support you can record the latitude and longitude of any access points. This feature is not only for wardriving; it is also very useful when mapping your outdoor wireless network.

Unfortunately, MacStumbler is three years old—the last update was July 2003—and it is showing its age. It supports only the Apple AirPort card, and no external PC Card or USB wireless devices. It also doesn't recognize WPA encrypted networks. Lastly, while MacStumbler does work on the latest 10.4 release of Mac OS X, there is no guarantee of future support, because development seems to have stopped.

iStumbler

A more up-to-date tool is iStumbler (*http://istumbler.net*). Just fire it up and it will find all available networks for you, complete with a real-time signal and noise meter. It scans Bluetooth and Bonjour networks and reports detailed information on both. It also works with both serial and Bluetooth-connected GPS units. Like MacStumbler, iStumbler supports scanning only when using the built-in AirPort card.

As shown in Figure 2-21, iStumbler's main window packs a lot of information into a small window. The menu on the left offers several monitoring options, including AirPort, Bluetooth, Bonjour, and GPS connections.

The connection monitor, which appears when you join a network listed in the AirPort section of iStumbler, is a nice feature. Figure 2-22 shows a sample window that you can make stay on top of other programs. You can adjust the transparency to your liking, so the monitor is always visible even if you are working on something else.

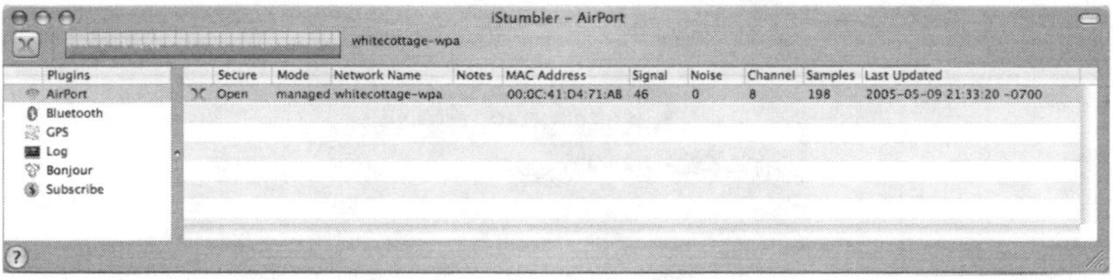

Figure 2-21. iStumbler's compact display

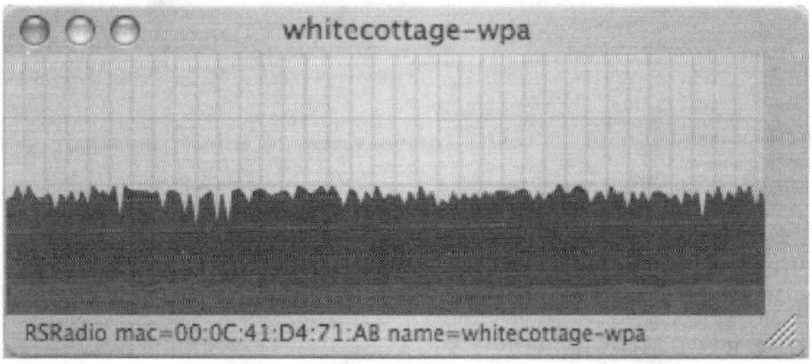

Figure 2-22. The handy connection monitor

iStumbler lets you join any listed AirPort network directly, without involving the AirPort configuration tools. Likewise, if you are monitoring Bluetooth, you can set up, pair with, or browse available Bluetooth devices. For Bonjour connections, there are options to connect to listed items.

A more powerful item is the Inspector, found in the Edit menu or by pressing Command-I. This is available for all modes in iStumbler, and it provides detailed information on the network or share that is highlighted in the main window. Figure 2-23 shows the detail taken by each sample of an 802.11g network.

Final Thoughts

Both of these tools will find all available Wi-Fi networks quickly and keep historical logs if you need to monitor wireless networks over time. If you need to find all available networks in range, either of these tools is ideal. iStumbler supports newer features of Mac OS X and is the better choice, particularly if you want to examine Bluetooth or Bonjour networks.

MacStumbler and iStumbler work by actively sending out probe requests to all available access points. The access points respond to the probes (as they would for any legitimate wireless client), and this information is then collected, sorted, and displayed by the scanners. Unfortunately, neither of these tools will find "closed" networks, because they don't respond to probe requests.

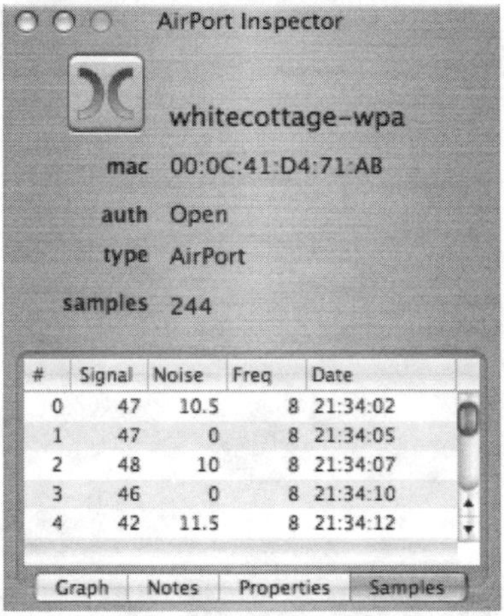

Figure 2-23. iStumbler Inspector

There is an unfortunate side effect caused by people who choose to hide their networks. Since it isn't easy to tell what channel they are using, it is likely that someone nearby will choose to use the same (or an adjacent) channel for their own network. This causes undesirable interference for everybody. To detect closed networks, you need a passive scanner, such as KisMAC [Hack #28].

HACK #28   Scan Passively with KisMAC

Glean detailed network information with KisMAC, a passive scanner for Mac OS X.

KisMAC (*http://www.binaervarianz.de/projekte/programmieren/KisMAC*) is a Mac OS X tool that shares part of its name with the popular monitoring tool Kismet [Hack #29]. This is a much more advanced network discovery and monitoring tool than either MacStumbler or iStumbler [Hack #27]. It requires Mac OS X 10.3 or above.

As covered in previous hacks, *active* scanners work by sending out probe requests to all available access points. Since these scanners rely on responses to active probing, it is possible for network administrators to detect the presence of tools such as MacStumbler and iStumbler, or any other tool that makes use of active network probes.

KisMAC is a *passive* network scanner. Rather than send out active probe requests, it instructs the wireless card to tune to a channel, listen for a short time, then tune to the next channel, listen for a while, and so on. In this way, it is possible not only to detect networks without announcing your presence, but also to find networks that don't respond to probe requests—namely, *closed* networks (i.e., access points that have beaconing disabled). But that's not all. Passive monitors have access to every frame that the radio can hear while tuned to a particular channel. This means that you can detect not only access points, but also the wireless clients of those access points.

Newer Macs with Airport Extreme cards are a problem for KisMAC. The Airport Extreme is an 802.11g radio based on a chipset from Broadcom. Broadcom does not publish details on their chipsets, so it is impossible for open source projects to write supporting drivers. This is a bigger problem than just network monitors for Mac OS X. It affects anyone wanting to run Linux or BSD on laptops with Broadcom-based wireless hardware.

For older Macs with 802.11b AirPort cards, there is better news. The standard AirPort driver doesn't provide the facility for passive monitoring, but KisMAC uses the open source Viha AirPort driver (*http://www.dopesquad. net/security*). It swaps the Viha driver for your existing AirPort driver when the program starts and automatically reinstalls the standard driver on exit. To accomplish this driver switcheroo, you have to provide your administrative password when you start KisMAC.

While KisMAC is running, your regular wireless connection is unavailable.

KisMAC also supplies an alternate driver called MacJack for Orinoco/Avaya/Proxim cards, as well as Prism II-based wireless cards. Prism II-based USB dongles are particularly handy for passive scanning on a new Mac laptop. Support for Atheros and PrismGT 802.11a/b/g cards, as well Cisco 802. 11b equipment, is new to the latest R64 release of KisMAC for Mac OS X 10.4.

To use any of the non-Apple wireless hardware, you'll have to add support for the specific type of card in the KisMAC Preferences pane. Click on the Driver icon to bring up the screen shown in Figure 2-24. Select the type of card you need and click Add. You can set a number of options for each card, but for the purposes of this hack, just accept the defaults.

Once you've set any other options, close the Preferences pane and click Start Scan. If you have any of the cards loaded that require alternate drivers, you'll again be asked for your administrative password to load the required driver.

KisMAC's main screen provides much of the same information as MacStumbler or iStumbler: SSID, signal strength, and so on. Double-clicking any available network shows a wealth of new information, as shown in Figure 2-25.

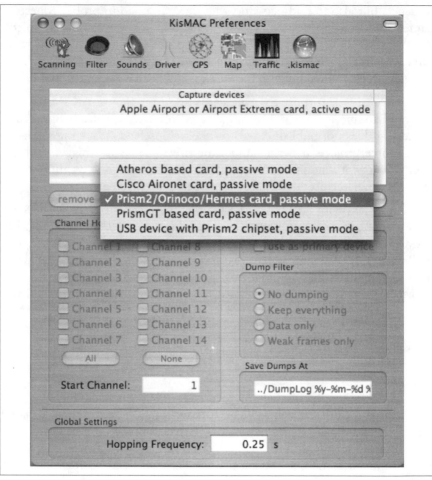

Figure 2-24. Adding a network card type

One interesting side effect of passive scanning is that channel detection isn't 100 percent reliable. Since 802.11b channels overlap, it is sometimes difficult for a passive scanner to know for certain which channel an access point is tuned to, and it can be off by one from time to time.

Now, let's go back to the Options page. As shown in Figure 2-26, KisMAC allows you to specify which channels you would like to scan on. This can help if you are trying to find access points that are using the same channel as your own.

KisMAC has a slew of nifty features, including GPS support with user-defined maps, raw frame injection (for Prism II and Orinoco cards), and even a real-time relative traffic graph (Figure 2-27). If it detects a WEP

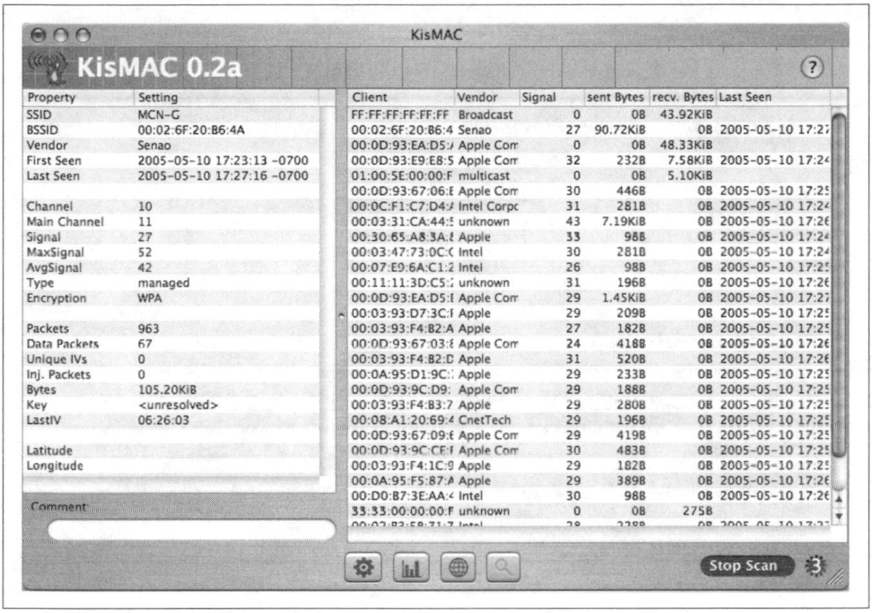

Figure 2-25. Detailed network information

network, it can use a number of advanced techniques to try to guess the password. And yes, it can read discovered ESSIDs aloud using Apple Text-to-Speech.

Perhaps the most powerful feature of all is KisMAC's ability to log raw 802. 11 frames to a standard *pcap* dump. Check the Keep Everything or the Data Only option in the Driver tab of KisMAC Preferences to save a dump file that can be read by tools such as Ethereal [Hack #31].

KisMAC is probably the most advanced wireless network monitor available for Mac OS X, although it is still quite beta. Keep iStumbler handy, because it is more stable and can operate without mucking about with replacement drivers. If you are simply looking for available networks, KisMAC is probably overkill. Sometimes you need as much detail as you can get to troubleshoot difficult network problems, and when you do, KisMAC is the right tool for the job.

HACK #29 Detect Networks with Kismet

Troubleshoot network problems with one of the most advanced wireless monitoring tools available.

Unlike simple beacon scanners such as NetStumbler [Hack #24] and MacStumbler [Hack #27], Kismet is one of the most advanced diagnostic tools available

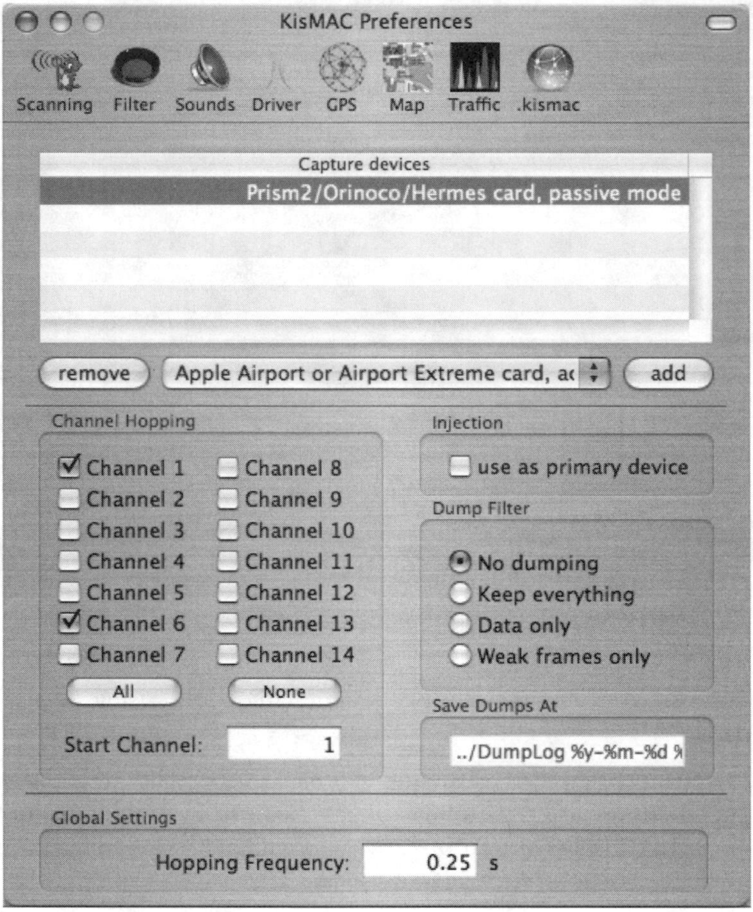

Figure 2-26. KisMAC channel selection

for wireless networking. It will run on Linux, Mac OS X, and the various BSDs. There is a port for running Kismet on the Linksys WRT54G, and you can even use it to collect data from remote sources on Windows.

Kismet is a completely passive network scanner, capable of detecting traffic from access points and wireless clients alike (including NetStumbler clients). It finds *closed* networks by monitoring the traffic sent from network users and logs all raw 802.11 frames in a standard format for later use with specialized diagnostic and analysis tools, as discussed in "Analyze Traffic with Ethereal" [Hack #31].

If you have a machine with multiple wireless cards, Kismet even splits the work of network scanning across all of them, making a scanner capable of

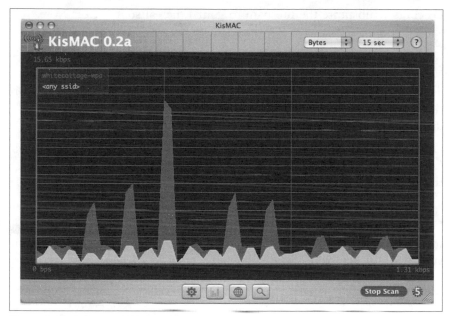

Figure 2-27. Relative traffic graph

simultaneously tracking all 802.11 traffic in range. These are just a few of the features of this amazing piece of free software.

Of course, with all of this power comes a fair amount of complexity. For starters, you need an 802.11a/b/g card driver capable of entering Monitor mode. Some of these drivers include Prism-based cards using the HostAP or wlan-ng drivers, Atheros-based cards using the Madwifi or ath(4) drivers, Prism54-based cards using the Prism54 drivers, and the Cisco Aironet cards using Cisco or airo-linux drivers.

Installation

If you don't need to compile any additional options into Kismet, all of the major Linux distributions provide a package. Ubuntu and Debian users can do an apt-get install kismet, Fedora and Red Hat users can use yum install kismet. Users of other distributions should check their package manager for kismet.

This hack also covers compiling Kismet from source. Download Kismet from *http://www.kismetwireless.net*. Unpack the source tree and navigate into the newly created folder. If you want to use Kismet's dump files with Ethereal (highly recommended), you need a copy of the Ethereal source tree. Configure Kismet with a line like this:

```
./configure --with-ethereal=../ethereal-0.9.12/
```

Of course, substitute the full path to your Ethereal source tree. Now, you should be able to build Kismet with a standard:

```
make; make dep; make install
```

Next, create a user that Kismet will assume when it isn't running as root. You can also use your own UID if you wish. Kismet needs to run as root initially, but it will drop its privileges to this UID as soon as it begins capturing data.

Edit */usr/local/etc/kismet.conf* (if you compiled from source) or */etc/kismet/kismet.conf* (if you installed a package) to suit your system. Here, you'll set the user ID that Kismet will use:

```
suiduser=yourusername
```

You'll also need to set the source= line to match your hardware. The format for this line is *driver,device,description*. See the comments in the file for supported drivers. Here's what I entered for my test Atheros card using the Madwifi driver:

```
source=madwifi_ag,ath0,madwifi
```

If you want Kismet to be able to read the SSID of detected networks aloud, download and install the Festival text-to-speech software. Fedora, RedHat, Debian, and Ubuntu users can all install the festival package. Kismet will play sound effects if you wish; by default, it expects */usr/bin/play* to be installed (part of the SoX sound utility), but any command-line audio player will work. All of the audio and other display parameters are configured in *kismet_ui.conf*.

Running Kismet

By default, Kismet will attempt to write logs and keep a *.pid* file in */var*. If your user does not have access to */var*, you'll need to start *kismet* as root or by using *sudo*. Note that once Kismet is in Monitor mode, your card can no longer associate with a wireless network, so you should use Ethernet (or another wireless card) if you need a network connection. Running Kismet will present you with a screen that looks something like Figure 2-28.

Once Kismet is up and running, you should see the main screen spring to life with all sorts of information. By default, Kismet initially sorts the network list based on the last time it saw traffic from each network. This list constantly changes, making it impossible to select one network for more detailed operations. Change the sort order by pressing S at any time, followed by the desired sort order (e.g., to sort on SSID, press SS). You can now use the arrow keys to select a particular network for further inspection.

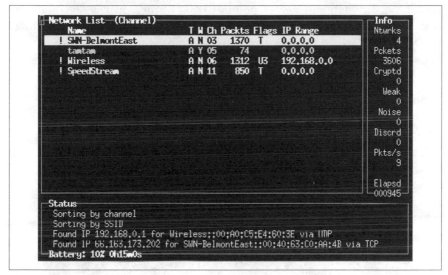

```
┌─Network List──(Channel)──────────────────────────────┐ ┌─Info──┐
│      Name              T W Ch Packts Flags IP Range   │ │Ntwrks │
│   ! SWN-BelmontEast    A N 03  1370  T    0.0.0.0      │ │     4 │
│     tamtam             A Y 05    74       0.0.0.0      │ │Pckets │
│   ! Wireless           A N 06  1312  U3   192.168.0.0  │ │  3606 │
│   ! SpeedStream        A N 11   850  T    0.0.0.0      │ │Cryptd │
│                                                       │ │     0 │
│                                                       │ │Weak   │
│                                                       │ │     0 │
│                                                       │ │Noise  │
│                                                       │ │     0 │
│                                                       │ │Discrd │
│                                                       │ │     0 │
│                                                       │ │Pkts/s │
│                                                       │ │     9 │
│                                                       │ │       │
│                                                       │ │Elapsd │
│                                                       │ │─000945│
├─Status────────────────────────────────────────────────┤
│ Sorting by channel                                    │
│ Sorting by SSID                                       │
│ Found IP 192.168.0.1 for Wireless::00:A0:C5:E4:60:3E via UDP│
│ Found IP 66.163.173.202 for SWN-BelmontEast::00:40:63:C0:AA:4B via TCP│
└─Battery: 10% 0h15m0s──────────────────────────────────┘
```

Figure 2-28. Kismet's main screen

Press H at any time to see the keystroke help, and press Q to close any pop-up window.

Now that networks are sorted, you can get more information on any one of them by selecting it and pressing I. Figure 2-29 shows the network information screen.

```
┌─Network List──(Channel)──────────────────────────────┐ ┌─Info──┐
│      Name              T W Ch Packts Flags IP Range   │ │Ntwrks │
│ ┌─Network Details─────────────────────────────────────┐
│ │ Name    : SWN-BelmontEast                           │
│ │                                                     │
│ │ SSID    : SWN-BelmontEast                           │
│ │ Server  : localhost:2501                            │
│ │ BSSID   : 00:02:6F:01:85:74                         │
│ │ Carrier : IEEE 802.11b                              │
│ │ Manuf   : Senao                                     │
│ │ Model   : Unknown                                   │
│ │ Matched : 00:02:6F:00:00:00                         │
│ │ Max Rate: 11.0                                      │
│ │ First   : Thu Jun  5 22:08:13 2003                  │
│ │ Latest  : Thu Jun  5 22:18:01 2003                  │
│ │ Clients : 3                                         │
│ │ Type    : Access Point (infrastructure)             │
│ │ Info    :                                           │
│ │ Channel : 3                                         │
│ │ WEP     : No                                        │
│ │ Beacon  : 100 (0.102400 sec)                        │
│ │ Packets : 1501                                      │
│ │                                        (+) Down─────┘
│ └─Battery: 10% 0h14m0s────────────────────────────────┘
```

Figure 2-29. Detailed network information

In addition to standard access points (APs), Kismet displays ad hoc networks, as well as *closed* networks (i.e., ones that do not broadcast their SSID). If there are no clients actively using a closed network, it displays the network information with a name of <no ssid>. Once a client associates with the closed network, this information is updated with the proper SSID.

Kismet also tracks a great deal of information about wireless clients. For example, to see the associated clients of a particular AP, as shown in Figure 2-30, press C from the main screen.

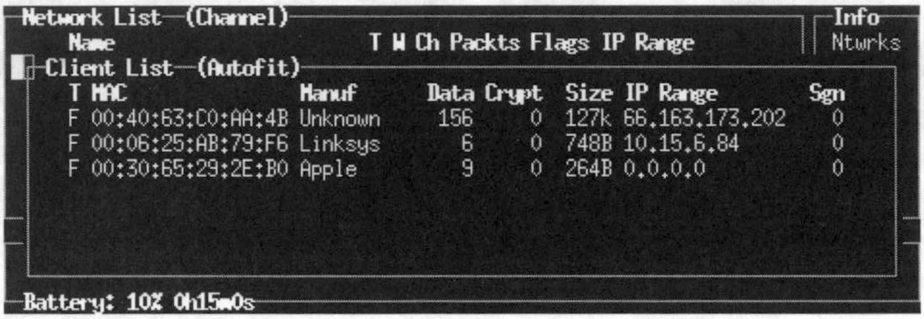

```
┌Network List—(Channel)──────────────────────────────────┐┌Info─┐
│ Name                        T W Ch Packts Flags IP Range ││Ntwrks│
│┌Client List—(Autofit)─────────────────────────────────┐ ││     │
▐│ T MAC              Manuf      Data Crypt Size IP Range    Sgn │
 │ F 00:40:63:C0:AA:4B Unknown    156   0  127k 66.163.173.202  0 │
 │ F 00:06:25:AB:79:F6 Linksys      6   0  748B 10.15.6.84       0 │
 │ F 00:30:65:29:2E:B0 Apple        9   0  264B 0.0.0.0          0 │
 │                                                              │
 │                                                              │
 │                                                              │
 │                                                              │
└Battery: 10% 0h15m0s─────────────────────────────────────────┘
```

Figure 2-30. Viewing associated clients for a particular wireless network

Kismet attempts to guess the IP network in use based on the traffic it sees. It also keeps statistics about how much traffic each client is generating, making it easy to discover who is hogging all of the bandwidth.

If you find that you are missing packets while monitoring a particular wireless network, this is probably because you are still scanning for networks. To focus on a specific channel, press L to lock channel hopping to the current 802.11 channel.

When tuned to one channel, Kismet captures much more data, because it doesn't have to divide its time between multiple channels. Consult the documentation if you would like to add more radio cards to completely cover the entire available spectrum.

Cleaning Up

When you are finished using Kismet, press Shift-Q to quit. This takes your wireless card back out of Monitor mode, but does not always reset its original network parameters. You might need to either eject the card and reinsert it or configure your SSID and other settings manually to start using wireless normally.

These are just a few of the insanely useful features that Kismet has to offer. On top of everything else, Kismet saves all recorded frames to a standard format, so you can use tools such as Ethereal [Hack #31] or AirSnort to pour over your captured data for later analysis. Getting Kismet running can be daunting at first, but it is worth the effort when serious network analysis is called for.

See Also

- Tons of information on RF Monitoring drivers (*http://airsnort.shmoo. com*)
- AirSnort on the iBook (*http://www.macunix.net:443/ibook.html*)
- Passive RF Monitoring on the iBook (*http://www.swieskowski.net/code/ wifi.php*)

HACK #30 Monitor Wireless Links in Linux with Wavemon

Monitor radio parameters in real time using Wavemon, a text-based tool for Linux.

When using Linux, the Wireless Tools provide a wealth of status information. These tools get their information from the standard kernel interface */proc/net/wireless*. While ideal for providing accuracy in measuring signal strength and noise data, these tools are not designed to give an indication of performance over time.

Wavemon (*http://freshmeat.net/projects/wavemon*) is a terrific little tool that does precisely this. It polls */proc/net/wireless* many times each second to give you a rolling report of how your wireless connection is performing. Its simple curses interface keeps the code quite small and is ideal for including in embedded distributions (such as Pebble [Hack #70]) to get real-time link data from remote access points.

Ubuntu users can install the package with an apt-get install wavemon command. Contributed RPM packages appear to be available at *http://rpm.phone. net* for distributions such as Fedora and RedHat. Alternatively, compiling from source is straightforward. Unpack the source code, and use standard compile commands:

```
./configure
make
make install
```

The main interface provides a nice graphical representation of the current link state, as shown in Figure 2-31.

All of the statistics are updated in real time, making it ideal for monitoring point-to-point links and fine-tuning antennas on long distance shots. For an even easier to read display, press F2 to bring up the Level Histogram shown in Figure 2-32.

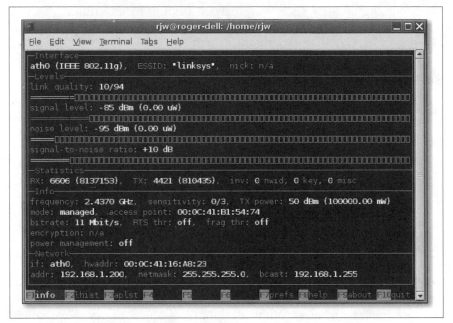

Figure 2-31. Wavemon in action

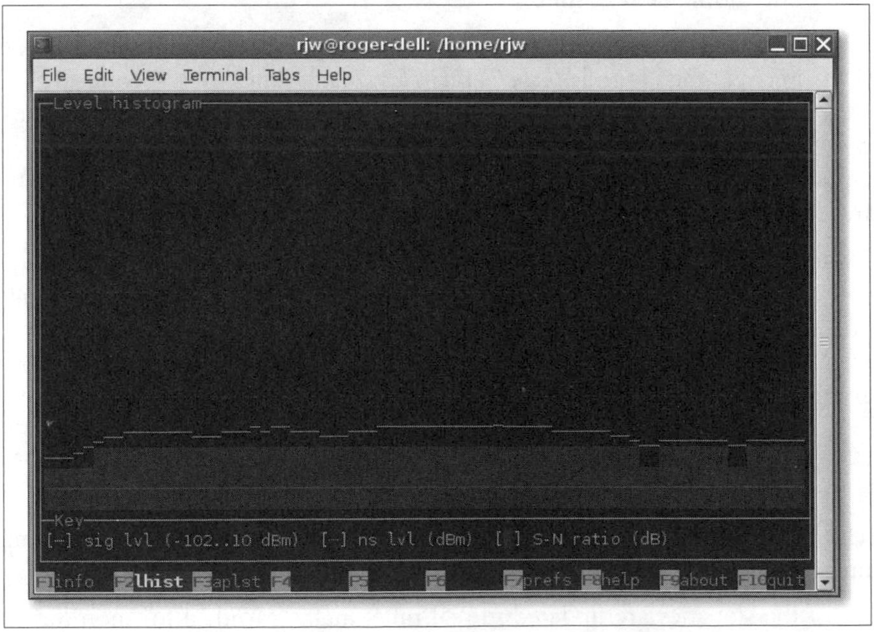

Figure 2-32. Scrolling histogram

This display is easy to read on a laptop, even in bright sunshine, making it an ideal tool for outdoor work. The histogram sweeps to the left, giving you a history of the last few moments of wireless connectivity. Since Wavemon runs in a terminal, you can easily run more than one instance to monitor multiple radio links simultaneously.

When you need a high-performance signal and noise meter for Linux, Wavemon is hard to beat.

HACK #31 Analyze Traffic with Ethereal

Sift through network data with one of the most advanced protocol analyzers available.

Ethereal is one of the most popular protocol analyzers on the planet. It runs on all major platforms, including Linux, BSD, Mac OS X, and Windows. Like *tcpdump* [Hack #33], it can capture packets directly from a network interface, or analyze data from a previously saved file.

Linux users can install the ethereal and ethereal-gnome packages using your distribution's package manager. BSD users can get ethereal from the *packages* or *ports* repositories depending on your BSD flavor. The Ethereal web pages at *http://www.ethereal.com/download.html* provide installers for Windows and Solaris, pointers to binary installers for many other operating systems, as well as the source code should you feel inclined to do some compiling.

While capturing data, Ethereal can give you real-time statistics about which protocols are actively in use (Figure 2-33). Start capturing by selecting Capture → Start…, select the interface you want to capture from, and click OK. Note that you need proper permissions (typically root privileges) to actually capture data.

If you would like to see these statistics again, with even more detail, after you have finished capturing packets, go to Tools → Protocol Hierarchy Statistics. You can use this on previously captured dump files as well. If you already have some captured data you can simply click File → Open… and select the file you'd like to analyze.

Ethereal displays the data it has collected in three ways. The top part of the window shows a summary of the data, with one packet per line. This lists the sequence, time, IP data, protocol, and general description of the packet. The data can be sorted on any of these fields by clicking the field name at the top. Selecting one packet displays more information in the other two window areas. The middle part of the window shows a hierarchical dissection of the packet, including the Ethernet, IP, TCP, and other layers. This

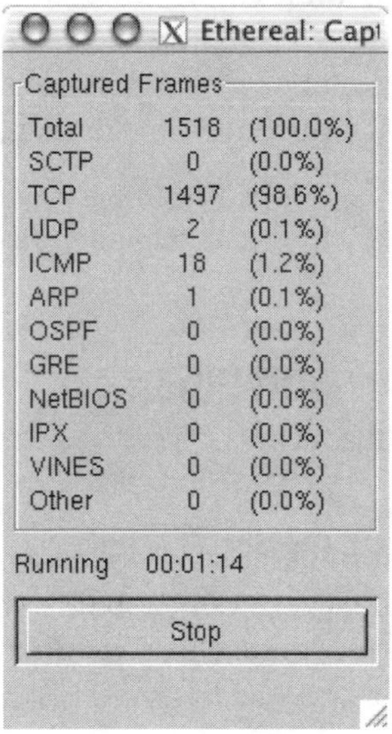

Figure 2-33. Ethereal providing statistics while capturing

allows you to quickly "drill down" into the particular piece of the packet that you are interested in. The bottom portion of the window shows a hex dump of the actual packet. Bits of the packet are automatically highlighted by selecting parts of the packet in the middle section. For example, selecting the IP source address in the middle section highlights the corresponding 4 bytes in the hex dump at the bottom.

Figure 2-34 shows Ethereal's ability to dissect high-level protocols such as HTTP. Select an HTTP packet at the top, and open the Hypertext Transfer Protocol drop-down in the middle section. This shows the contents of the packet in plain ASCII.

Of course, most TCP conversations are spread across several packets. Ethereal reassembles the entire stream for you by selecting one packet and clicking Tools → Follow TCP Stream. Figure 2-35 shows the results of following the previous HTTP stream.

It is difficult to tell in black and white, but the two conversations are actually displayed in different colors, making it simple to tell at a glance which side is speaking.

Speaking of colors, Ethereal can even display its packet data with color coding, defined by a rich pattern-matching language. This can make any data you are searching for leap out in bold red while showing everything else in pale gray, for example. It uses the same pattern-matching language to

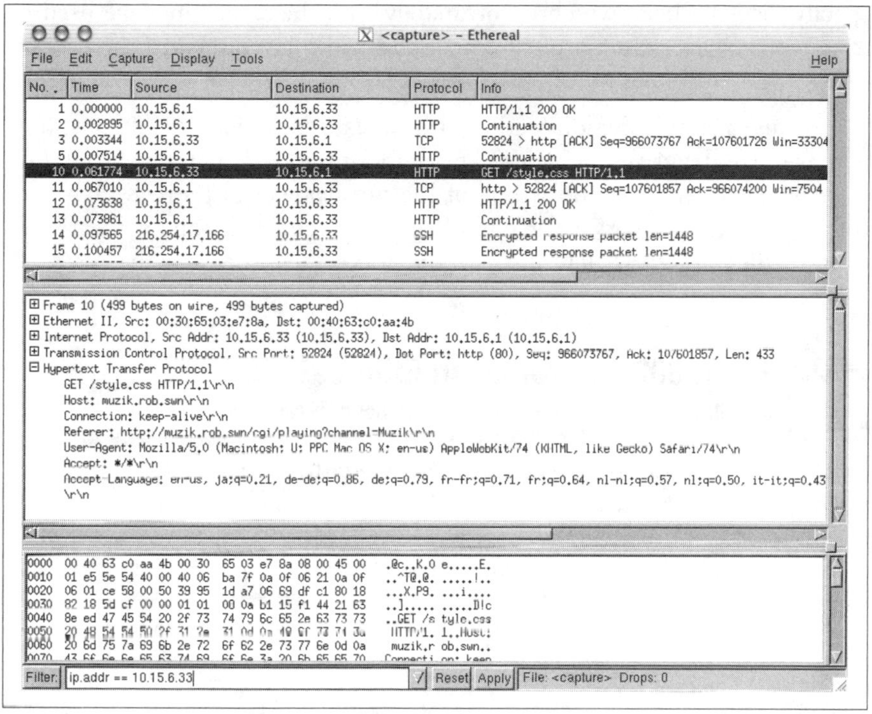

Figure 2-34. Ethereal decoding of an HTTP packet

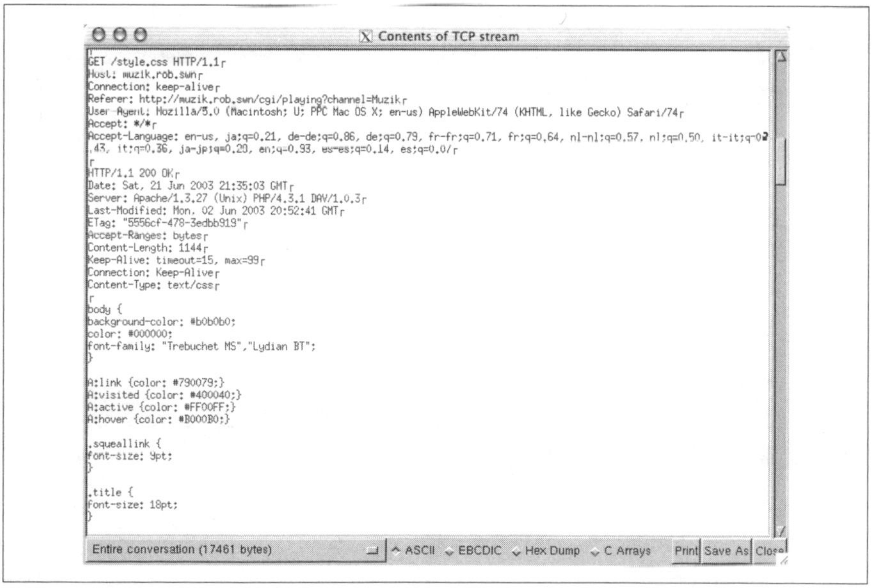

Figure 2-35. Ethereal reassembling a TCP stream

specify display filters, which unfortunately isn't the same language used by *tcpdump*. For an example of how to build a display filter in Ethereal, see "Track 802.11 Frames in Ethereal" **[Hack #32]**.

This is just a simple demonstration of Ethereal's basic features. It can show you as much detail as you care to know about the packets flying around on your wireless network, and is one of the most powerful tools available for tracking down network problems. See the documentation and example capture files at *http://www.ethereal.com* for some other creative uses for Ethereal.

HACK #32   Track 802.11 Frames in Ethereal
Use Ethereal to track wireless frame data it normally can't capture.

In addition to capturing Layer 2 and higher traffic on its own, Ethereal can open dump files saved by other tools that incorporate additional data, such as Kismet **[Hack #29]** or KisMAC **[Hack #28]**. Recent versions of Ethereal will happily display all 802.11 frame data that these passive monitoring tools can capture, as shown in Figure 2-36.

```
◯◯◯                    ⊠ DumpLog 03-06-21 14:50.dump - Ethereal
 File   Edit   Capture   Display   Tools                                                          Help

 No.    Time .    Source              Destination         Protocol     Info
 344 19.099107    00:02:6f:01:85:74   00:06:25:12:cf:c6   IEEE 802.11  Probe Response
 345 19.100770    00:02:6f:01:85:74   00:06:25:12:cf:c6   IEEE 802.11  Probe Response
 346 19.129647    00:02:6f:01:85:74   00:06:25:12:cf:c6   IEEE 802.11  Probe Response
 347 19.130652    00:02:6f:01:85:74   00:06:25:12:cf:c6   IEEE 802.11  Probe Response
 348 19.132844    00:02:6f:01:85:74   00:06:25:12:cf:c6   IEEE 802.11  Probe Response
 351 19.149973    00:02:6f:01:85:74   ff:ff:ff:ff:ff:ff   IEEE 802.11  Beacon frame
 352 19.252298    00:02:6f:01:85:74   ff:ff:ff:ff:ff:ff   IEEE 802.11  Beacon frame
 357 20.174012    00:02:6f:01:85:74   ff:ff:ff:ff:ff:ff   IEEE 802.11  Beacon frame
 358 20.276660    00:02:6f:01:85:74   ff:ff:ff:ff:ff:ff   IEEE 802.11  Beacon frame
 428 21.198078    00:02:6f:01:85:74   ff:ff:ff:ff:ff:ff   IEEE 802.11  Beacon frame
 429 21.300603    00:02:6f:01:85:74   ff:ff:ff:ff:ff:ff   IEEE 802.11  Beacon frame
 470 21.402410    00:02:6f:01:85:74   ff:ff:ff:ff:ff:ff   IEEE 802.11  Beacon frame

 ⊟ IEEE 802.11 wireless LAN management frame
   ⊟ Fixed parameters (12 bytes)
       Timestamp: 0x00000012FB3A8219
       Beacon Interval: 0.102400 [Seconds]
     ⊞ Capability Information: 0x0001
   ⊟ Tagged parameters (32 bytes)
       Tag Number: 0 (SSID parameter set)
       Tag length: 15
       Tag interpretation: SWN-BelmontEast
       Tag Number: 1 (Supported Rates)
       Tag length: 4
       Tag interpretation: Supported rates: 1.0(B) 2.0(B) 5.5 11.0 [Mbit/sec]
       Tag Number: 3 (DS Parameter set)
       Tag length: 1

 0000  80 00 00 00 ff ff ff ff  ff ff 00 02 6f 01 85 74   ........ ....o..t
 0010  00 02 6f 01 85 74 d0 66  19 82 3a fb 12 00 00 00   ..o..t.f ..:....
 0020  64 00 01 00 00 0f 53 57  4e 2d 42 65 6c 6d 6f 6e   d.....SW N-Belmon
 0030  74 45 61 73 74 01 04 82  84 0b 16 03 01 03 05 04   tEast... ........
 0040  00 01 00 04                                        ....

 Filter: wlan.bssid == 00:02:6f:01:85:74    / Reset Apply  File: DumpLog 03-06-21 14:50.dump
```

Figure 2-36. Ethereal displaying 802.11 frames

This allows you to watch the behavior of devices at the 802.11 protocol layer, which can give you valuable insight into what is actually happening on your wireless network. Keep in mind that Kismet and KisMAC will capture *all* 802.11 data they hear, including data for networks you might not be interested in. This is especially true if you capture data while the tools are scanning all available channels.

To focus on a particular access point, use a display filter on your data in Ethereal. The simplest way to create a filter from scratch is to build it interactively using the filter editor. At the bottom of the screen, click the Filter: button. Next, click Add Expression, which opens the filter editor. Select the information you want to see in the "Field name" pane. Since we are after the ESSID of an access point, select IEEE 802.11 → BSS Id. Click == as the Relation, and enter the MAC address of your access point in the Value field, as shown in Figure 2-37.

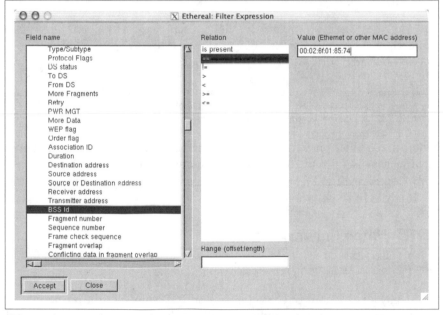

Figure 2-37. Creating a filter to focus on a particular access point

Click Accept and then OK. Ethereal then filters your data based on the expression you provided. This language is different than the *libpcap* filter expression language that *tcpdump* uses. The resulting expression is shown at the bottom of the main screen, next to the Filter: button. You can build more complex expressions by joining filters together with and and or. To see the effect the change has on your data, click Apply each time you change your filter.

If you need to analyze a WEP-encrypted packet dump, you need to provide the WEP key for Ethereal; otherwise, you will only be able to see encrypted packets. Under Edit → Preferences, select Protocols → IEEE 802.11. Enter your WEP key data here, and Ethereal automatically decrypts it for you, as shown in Figure 2-38.

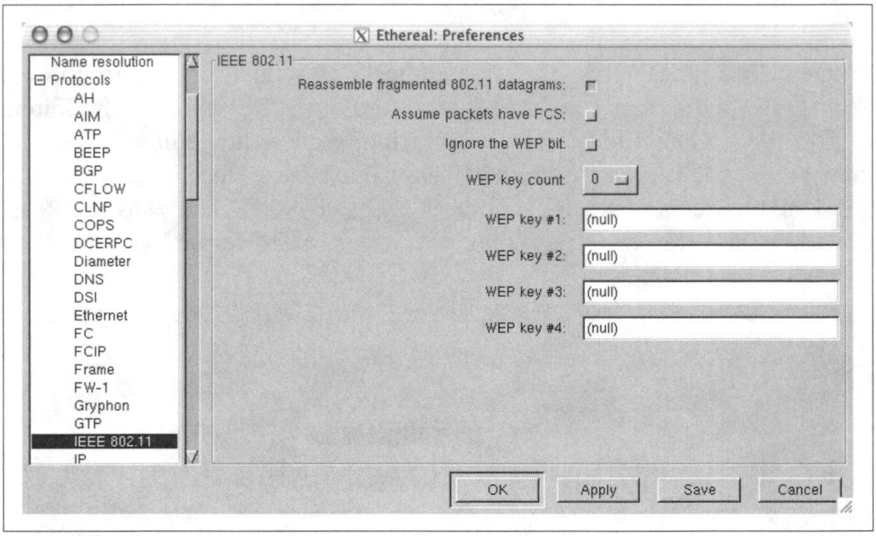

Figure 2-38. Supplying your own WEP key for decoding

Ethereal can filter on virtually every bit in an 802.11 management frame, making it a useful tool for analyzing a wireless link. Combining Ethereal with Kismet or KisMAC makes one of the most flexible and powerful wireless analysis packages available.

HACK #33 Watch Network Traffic

The tcpdump command-line packet-capture tool is invaluable for troubleshooting thorny network problems.

Practically all variations of Unix, Linux, and BSD ship with the *tcpdump* utility. Its deceptively simple interface hides a powerful and complex tool designed to capture data from a network interface, filter it, and print it out, so you can get a better grasp of what is really happening on your network.

Note that you need to be root to capture packets with *tcpdump*. The simplest way to start it is to run it while specifying the network device you would like to listen to:

```
# tcpdump -i eth0
```

If you are logged into a remote machine while doing this, you will see a flood of traffic fly by, even on an unloaded machine. This is because *tcpdump* is capturing your SSH session traffic and displaying it to your terminal, which generates more traffic, which is again displayed, in an endless loop of wasted bits. This is easily avoided by using a simple filter. For example, you could just ignore all SSH traffic, which uses port 22:

```
# tcpdump -i eth0 -n 'port | 22'
```

That command specifies the -n switch, which tells *tcpdump* to skip DNS lookups for every host it encounters. When capturing network data, the name of the game is speed. If your machine is tied up with some other network function (such as looking up DNS names), it could miss packets as they fly past, particularly on a busy network. Skipping lookups speeds up capturing, but it means that you will be looking at IP addresses and port numbers instead of names and services.

One common use for *tcpdump* is to look for ping traffic when troubleshooting connectivity problems. To see ICMP traffic only, specify the protocol in a filter. Don't forget the backslash when specifying protocol names:

```
# tcpdump -i wlan0 'proto \icmp'

tcpdump: listening on eth0
16:34:33.842093 10.15.6.33 > www.google.com: icmp: echo request
16:34:33.873784 www.google.com > 10.15.6.33: icmp: echo reply
16:34:34.893981 10.15.6.33 > www.google.com: icmp: echo request
16:34:34.940997 www.google.com > 10.15.6.33: icmp: echo reply
```

Here, you can see a user sending echo requests (*pings*) to *www.google.com*, which then sends echo replies. If you see echo requests with no associated echo reply, this indicates problems somewhere further up the network. If you are sending pings and you don't even see the echo request on your router, you know that the problem is somewhere between your client and your router. Making educated guesses at where the problem might be, combined with judicious *tcpdump* filters, can quickly find the source of the trouble.

You can also capture all data from a particular host using *tcpdump* with the host directive:

```
# tcpdump -i wlan0 'host 10.15.6.88'

tcpdump: listening on eth0
16:47:16.494447 10.15.6.88.1674 > florian.1900: udp 132 [ttl 1]
16:47:16.494524 florian > 10.15.6.88: icmp: florian udp port 1900
unreachable [tos 0xc0]
16:47:16.495831 10.15.6.88.1674 > florian.1900: udp 133 [ttl 1]
16:47:16.495926 florian > 10.15.6.88: icmp: florian udp port 1900
unreachable [tos 0xc0]
```

```
16:47:21.488711 arp who-has 10.15.6.88 tell florian
16:47:21.491861 arp reply 10.15.6.88 is-at 0:40:96:41:80:2c
16:47:28.293719 baym-cs197.msgr.hotmail.com.1863 > 10.15.6.88.1046: . ack 5
win 17128
```

This person is obviously using MSN Messenger, as evidenced by their connection to *baym-cs197.msgr.hotmail.com* port 1863, and by the UDP broadcasts to port 1900 as well. You can also see an ARP response that shows the user's MAC address starting with 0:40:96, indicating a Cisco card [Hack #39]. Without even resorting to Nmap [Hack #50] or another active scan, we could make a fair guess that this user is using a PC laptop running Windows. This information is revealed in just a few seconds, by observing a mere five or six packets.

Mac OS X is even chattier than Windows, revealing the user's name (and occasionally even their photo) in the form of iChat multicast broadcasts. Decoding this data is left as an exercise for the reader, but capturing it is simple enough:

```
# tcpdump -i wlan0 -X -s 0 -n -l 'port 5353'
```

This will show you a full dump of packets, both in hex and in ASCII, on only port 5353, which is used by iChat.

If you need to analyze large amounts of data, it is usually easier to use a graphical tool such as Ethereal [Hack #31] to pore over it. Since your access point probably isn't running Xwindows, you can use *tcpdump* to capture the actual data. Specifying the -w switch writes all packets to a file in *pcap* format, which many tools (such as Ethereal) will read:

```
# tcpdump -i wlan0 -n -w captured.pcap 'port 5353'
```

Now, just transfer the *captured.pcap* file to your local machine, and open it up in Ethereal.

For a command-line utility, *tcpdump* is a surprisingly complete packet-capture tool. It has a complex and powerful filter-expression language, and you can use it to capture precisely the data you are after. Be sure to read man tcpdump for many more details on what *tcpdump* can do for you.

grep Your Network
#34   See who's doing what, with a grep for your network interface.

The *ngrep* utility is an interesting packet-capture tool, similar to *tcpdump* [Hack #33] and Ethereal [Hack #31]. It is unique in that it attempts to make it as easy as possible to match which captured packets to print, by using a *grep*-compatible format (complete with regular expressions and a bunch of GNU *grep*'s switches). It also converts the packets to ASCII (or hex) before printing. The package is available from *http://www.packetfactory.net/Projects/ngrep*.

For example, to see the contents of all HTTP GET requests that pass through your wireless router, try this command as root:

```
# ngrep -q GET
```

If you're interested only in a particular host, protocol, or port (or other packet matching criteria), you can specify a *bpf* filter as well as a data pattern. It uses syntax similar to *tcpdump*:

```
# ngrep -qi rob@nocat.net port 25

T 10.42.4.7:65174 -> 209.204.146.26:25 [AP]
  RCPT TO:..

T 209.204.146.26:25 -> 10.42.4.7:65174 [AP]
  250 2.1.5 ... Recipient ok..

T 10.42.4.7:65174 -> 209.204.146.26:25 [AP]
  Date: Sun, 8 Sep 2002 23:55:18 -0700..Mime-Version: 1.0 (Apple Message fram
  ework v543)..Content-Type: text/plain; charset=US-ASCII; format=flowed..Sub
  ject: Greetings.....From: John Doe ..To: rob@nocal.net..Content-Transfer-En
  coding: 7bit..Message-Id: ..X-Mailer: Apple Mail v2)....What does t
  hat pgp command you mentioned do again?....Thanks,....--A Friend....
```

Since *ngrep* prints to STDOUT, you can do post-processing on the output to make a nice printing filter. If you process the output yourself, add the -l switch to make the output line buffered.

The Code

If you're interested in what people on the local wireless network are searching for online, try something like the Perl script in Example 2-1.

Example 2-1. go-ogle.pl uses ngrep to show you what people are searching for

```perl
#!/usr/bin/perl
use Socket;
$|++;

open(NG,"ngrep -d en1 -lqi '(GET|POST).*/(search|find)' |");
print "Go ogle online.\n";
my ($go,$i) = 0;
my %host = ( );

while( ) {

 if(/^T (\d+\.\d+.\d+\.\d+):\d+ -> (\d+\.\d+\.\d+\.\d+):80/) {
  $i = inet_aton($1);
  $host{$1} ||= gethostbyaddr($i, AF_INET) || $1;
```

Example 2-1. go-ogle.pl uses ngrep to show you what people are searching for (continued)

```
$i = inet_aton($2);
$host{$2} ||= gethostbyaddr($i, AF_INET) || $2;
print "$host{$1} -> $host{$2} : ";
$go = 1;
next;
}
if(/(q|p|query|for)=(.*)?(&|HTTP)/) {
next unless $go;
my $q = $2;
$q =~ s/(\+|&.*)/ /g;
$q =~ s/%(\w+)/chr(hex($1))/ge;
print "$q\n";
$go = 0;
}
else {
next unless $go;
$go = 0;
print "\n";
}
}
```

Running the Hack

I call the script *go-ogle.pl*. This runs an *ngrep* looking for any GET or POST request that includes *search* or *find* somewhere in the URL. Save the code to a file called *go-ogle.pl* and invoke it on the command line. The results look something like this:

```
# perl go-ogle.pl

Go ogle online.
caligula.nocat.net -> www.google.com : o'reilly mac os x conference
caligula.nocat.net -> s1.search.vip.scd.yahoo.com : junk mail $$$
tiberius.nocat.net -> altavista.com : babel fish
caligula.nocat.net -> 166-140.amazon.com : Brazil
livia.nocat.net -> 66.161.12.119 : lart
```

It will lazily unescape encoded strings in the query (note the ' in the Google query, and the $$$ from Yahoo!). It will also convert IP addresses to hostnames for you, because *ngrep* doesn't seem to have this feature, probably so it can optimize capturing for speed. The last two results are interesting: the Brazil query was actually run on *http://www.imdb.com* looking for a movie, and the last one was to *http://www.dictionary.com*. Evidently, IMDB is now in a partnership with Amazon.com, and Dictionary.com's search machine doesn't have a PTR record. It's amazing how much you can learn about the world by watching other people's packets.

Note that you must be root to run *ngrep*; for best results, it should be run from the router at the edge of your network or from any wireless client associated with a busy access point.

Check Wi-Fi Network Performance with Qcheck

Windows XP can't tell you the true throughput on your wired or wireless network. For that, you'll need free, third-party software that can help you improve throughput.

When you buy network hardware, including a hub/router and network cards, you're told that hardware's rated speed—for example, 100Mbps for an Ethernet network, or 11Mpbs for an 802.11b Wi-Fi network.

But those numbers only tell you how your network might perform in ideal conditions; as the saying goes, "your mileage may vary," and it usually does. Wi-Fi networks are particularly finicky and are especially prone to being affected by interference and other factors. Where you place your wireless access point and PCs and how you position their antennas can make a dramatic difference in the actual speed of your network. So, you'll want to know the true connection speed of your network, Wi-Fi networks in particular, so that you can optimize their performance when you troubleshoot them.

But how can you find out your true network performance? If you have a Wi-Fi card, you can find information about your connection by clicking the small network icon in the Notification Area (also called the system tray). When you do that, the Wireless Network Connection Status screen appears, as shown in Figure 2-39.

There's only one problem with that screen: it's highly inaccurate. True, its little green bars and Signal Strength indication give you a broad picture of the relative strength of your network connection. But the Speed indication isn't an actual measurement as far as I can tell; it appears to tell you only your maximum theoretical connection speed, given the nature of your hardware, and doesn't reflect your true current connection speed. When I use my Wi-Fi network, it always tells me the speed is 11Mbps, even when actual, real-time measurement shows my true throughput is less than half of that.

So, how do you measure the true speed of a network in your real-world conditions? Get the free program Qcheck (*http://www.ixiacom.com/products/ performance_applications/pa_display.php?skey=pa_q_check*). It performs a series of tests, including throughput and response time, and gives you a good snapshot of your network's real performance. When trying to optimize a Wi-Fi network, run Qcheck on each PC on the network to get baseline

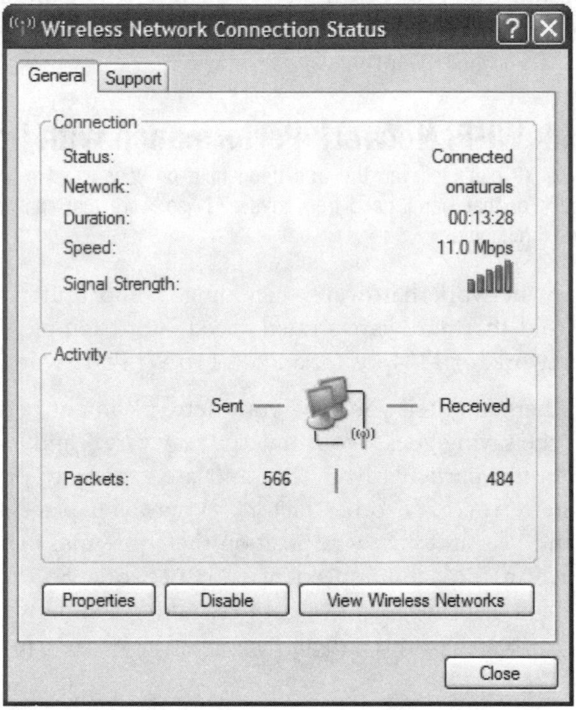

Figure 2-39. The Wireless Network Connection Status screen

performance results for each. Then run the test for each PC after you move the base station and PCs, change the positioning of the antennas, or make any other adjustments. That way, you'll be able to fine-tune your network for optimum efficiency.

Once installed on every machine in your network, Qcheck measures the performance of the network between any two of your PCs. Qcheck is made up of two components: the console where you run your tests, shown in Figure 2-40, and an endpoint program, which runs invisibly in the background on each PC on which you've installed Qcheck. While the exact metrics vary from test to test, the program works by sending data from one PC to another on your network. The data is then sent from the receiving PC back to the originating PC, at which point Qcheck measures the round-trip time, calculates throughput, and displays the results.

Note the throughput in Figure 2-40; it's 5.128Mbps. I was measuring the speed of my Wi-Fi network while seated on my back porch, which is about 30 feet and a wall away from my access point. Just to show you how much more accurate Qcheck is, the Wireless Network Connection Status screen

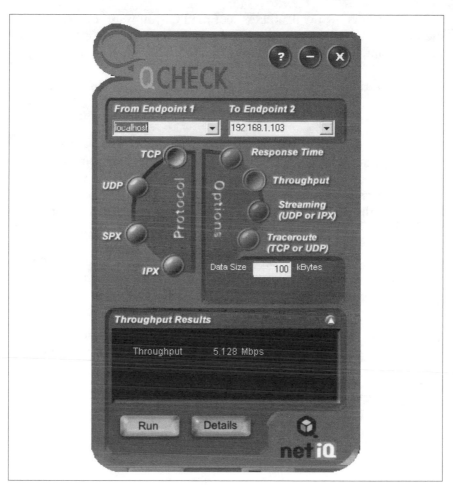

Figure 2-40. The Qcheck console

reported my speed as 11Mbps—the exact connection speed my laptop would have if I were inches away from the wireless access point. (And in actuality, protocol overhead accounts for more than half of the available bandwidth on a Wi-Fi network, even when devices are next to one another. My test run of about 5Mbps is therefore about as good as it gets for 802.11b. On an 802.11a or 802.11g network, expect somewhere around 22Mbps on that "54Mbps" connection.)

To run the Qcheck tests, run the console and then choose the two PCs between which you want to measure speed on your network. Only one must be the PC with the console on it, but each PC does have to have Qcheck on it. You don't need to run the console on each machine because the endpoints are running on them invisibly in the background; during Qcheck's installation, the endpoints are configured to launch on startup.

You'll need to know the IP addresses of the PCs you want to test. If one of the PCs you're testing is the one running the console, choose *localhost* for that endpoint. To find the IP address of another PC on your network, first go to that PC, right-click My Network Places, then double-click your network connection (it might read Local Area Connection, for example, or Wireless Network Connection). Click the Support tab, and you'll see the IP address.

Once you choose the PCs you want to test, choose the specific test to run. The best overall benchmark will be the Throughput test using either the TCP or UDP protocols. If you happen to use IPX or SPX on your network (some people still use these older protocols rather than TCP/IP), you can do benchmark throughput tests using them as well, though few home networks use those protocols. If you run any kind of streaming media across your network—for example, if you use your network to play MP3 files or other digital music on a PC and then stream it to another location in your house—choose the UDP streaming test. Streaming media use the UDP protocol, so the only way to test how they will perform on your network is to use the test for that protocol.

Make sure to run your test multiple times, and to be safe, run them a half hour or more apart. Because of the fickle nature of wireless transmissions, you can find dramatic differences in throughput from one moment to the next. For example, a few minutes after running the throughput test shown in Figure 2-40, I ran it again and was shown a throughput of 1.602Mbps. That one test was an anomaly, and subsequent tests were more in keeping with my initial one.

—*Preston Gralla*

H A C K
Estimate Network Performance
#36   Just how quickly can you squeeze data through your access point?

Many people use online tools such as DSL Reports' Speed test (*http:// speedtest.dslreports.com*) to estimate the performance of their Internet connection. When run from a machine directly connected to the Internet, this can give you a fairly good indication of your upload and download capacity.

This tool becomes less useful when trying to estimate the available bandwidth on other networks. For example, on a large wireless network, it is useful to measure the actual capacity of a network link regardless of the speed of the Internet connection. One useful utility for measuring performance is *iperf*, a simple, freely available tool that will run on Linux, BSD, Mac OS X, and even Windows. You can download it online at *http://dast.nlanr.net/ Projects/Iperf*.

In order to measure performance, it needs to be used in pairs, with one instance at either end of a link. On one end of the link to be measured, start up *iperf* in server mode:

```
server:$ iperf -s
```

Note that it doesn't matter which end is used as the server, as both upload and download speeds will be tested. On the other end of the link, run *iperf* in client mode, specifying the server to be tested:

```
testmachine:$ iperf -c testmachine -r


------------------------------------------------------------
Server listening on TCP port 5001
TCP window size: 32.0 KByte (default)
------------------------------------------------------------
------------------------------------------------------------
Client connecting to testmachine, TCP port 5001
TCP window size: 32.5 KByte (default)
------------------------------------------------------------
[  4] local 10.15.6.33 port 50421 connected with 10.15.6.4 port 5001
[ ID] Interval       Transfer     Bandwidth
[  4]  0.0-10.2 sec  2.95 MBytes  2.43 Mbits/sec
[  4] local 10.15.6.33 port 5001 connected with 10.15.6.4 port 60977
[ ID] Interval       Transfer     Bandwidth
[  4]  0.0-10.0 sec  3.09 MBytes  2.60 Mbits/sec
```

By default, `iperf` uses port 5001 for its communications. If this port is in use, you can specify a different one with the -p switch on both sides:

```
server:$ iperf -s -p 30000
testmachine:$ iperf -c livia -r -p 30000


------------------------------------------------------------
Server listening on TCP port 30000
TCP window size: 32.0 KByte (default)
...
```

If you don't want just anyone connecting to your *iperf* server, don't forget to kill the server side with a Ctrl-C when you are finished making your measurements.

In addition to simple TCP testing, it can also manipulate various TCP parameters, test UDP streams, use multicast or IPv6, and even use a custom defined data stream for testing. Running with the defaults should give you a good basic idea of how much data you can cram through your connection, particularly if it is not being used by any other clients. For more complete details on some of the testing this flexible tool can do, see the online documentation at *http://dast.nlanr.net/Projects/Iperf/iperfdocs_1.7.0.html*.

Get Real-Time Network Stats

#37   Get a picture of utilization on your network over time with ntop.

If you're looking for real-time network statistics, you should check out the terrific *ntop* tool. It is a full-featured protocol analyzer with a web frontend, complete with SSL and graphing support. Although *ntop* isn't exactly light-weight, it does give you a nice picture of who's talking to whom on your network. Get it at *http://www.ntop.org*.

ntop needs to run initially as root in order to throw your interfaces into promiscuous mode and start capturing packets, but then releases its privileges to a user that you specify. If you need to run *ntop* for long periods of time or you have a large network, you'll probably be happiest running it on a dedicated monitoring box.

Here's a quick reference on how to get *ntop* up and running quickly in Linux. It should be trivial to do this also on BSD, Mac OS X, Solaris, and other Unix-like creatures. First, create an *ntop* user and group:

```
# groupadd ntop
# useradd -c "ntop user" -d /usr/local/etc/ntop -s /bin/true -g ntop ntop
```

Then unpack and build *ntop* per the instructions in *docs/BUILD-NTOP.txt*. I assume that you have the source tree unpacked in */usr/local/src/ntop/*.

Create a directory for *ntop* to keep its capture database in:

```
# mkdir /usr/local/etc/ntop
# chown root /usr/local/etc/ntop
```

The capture database should be owned by root, and *not* by the *ntop* user.

If you'd like to use SSL for HTTPS, copy the default SSL key to */usr/local/etc/ntop*:

```
# cp /usr/local/src/ntop-2.1.3/ntop/*pem /usr/local/etc/ntop
```

Note that the default SSL key will not be built with the correct hostname for your server. Now we need to initialize the *ntop* databases and set an administrative password:

```
# ntop -A -u ntop -P /usr/local/etc/ntop

21/Sep/2002 20:30:23 Initializing GDBM...
21/Sep/2002 20:30:23 Started thread (1026) for network packet analyser.
21/Sep/2002 20:30:23 Started thread (2051) for idle hosts detection.
21/Sep/2002 20:30:23 Started thread (3076) for DNS address resolution.
21/Sep/2002 20:30:23 Started thread (4101) for address purge.

Please enter the password for the admin user:
Please enter the password again:
21/Sep/2002 20:30:29 Admin user password has been set.
```

Finally, run *ntop* as a daemon and start the SSL server on your favorite port (4242, for example):

```
# ntop -u ntop -P /usr/local/etc/ntop -W4242 -d
```

By default, *ntop* also runs a standard HTTP server on port 3000. You should strongly consider locking down access to these ports at your firewall, or by using command-line iptables rules on your Linux machine.

Let *ntop* run for a while, and then connect to *https://your.server.here:4242*. You can find out all sorts of details about what traffic has been seen on your network, as shown in Figure 2-41.

Info about host nocat.net

IP Address	206.201.239.5 ■ [unicast]
First/Last Seen	09/21/02 21:27:16 - 09/21/02 21:35:20 [8:04]
Domain	net
Last MAC Address/Router	00:01:30:B8:23:D0
Host Location	Remote (outside specified/local subnet)
IP TTL (Time to Live)	54:54 [~10 hop(s)]
Total Data Sent	110.8 KB/1,159 Pkts/0 Retran. Pkts [0%]
Broadcast Pkts Sent	0 Pkts
Data Sent Stats	Local (100 %)
IP vs. Non-IP Sent	IP (100 %)
Total Data Rcvd	384.4 KB/1,372 Pkts/0 Retran. Pkts [0%]
Data Rcvd Stats	Local (100 %)
IP vs. Non-IP Rcvd	IP (100 %)
Sent vs. Rcvd Pkts	Sent (45.8 %) Rcvd (54.2 %)
Sent vs. Rcvd Data	Sent (22.4 %) Rcvd (77.6 %)
Further Host Information	[Whois]

Host Traffic Stats

Time	Tot. Traffic Sent	% Traffic Sent	Tot. Traffic Rcvd	% Traffic Rcvd
Midnight - 1AM	0	0.0 %	0	0.0 %
1AM - 2AM	0	0.0 %	0	0.0 %
2AM - 3AM	0	0.0 %	0	0.0 %
3AM - 4AM	0	0.0 %	0	0.0 %
4AM - 5AM	0	0.0 %	0	0.0 %
5AM - 6AM	0	0.0 %	0	0.0 %
6AM - 7AM	0	0.0 %	0	0.0 %

Figure 2-41. Showing lots of real-time network information with ntop

While tools such as *tcpdump* [Hack #33] and Ethereal [Hack #31] give you detailed, interactive analysis of network traffic, *ntop* delivers a wealth of statistical information in a slick and easy-to-use web interface. When properly installed and locked down, it will likely become a favorite tool in your network-analysis tool chest.

Graph Your Wireless Performance

#38   Comprehensively track the performance of your wireless links over time.

The monitoring tools mentioned so far give you a good instantaneous reading of received signal and noise levels for a given radio link. While useful for proving a link and installing your gear, remember that radio conditions change over time. Doing the occasional spot check doesn't really give you the full picture of what is going on.

For example, take a look at Figure 2-42. This displays radio data for a one-mile link, averaged over several days. You can see that in the middle of each day, the signal drops by as much as 6 dB, while the noise remains steady. Remember that these are really negative numbers, so in this graph, a smaller number is better for signal. The repeating pattern we see indicates the effect of *thermal fade*.

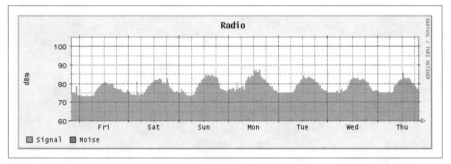

Figure 2-42. Thermal fade in the middle of the day

This particular link is a simple waveguide antenna mounted in the middle of a low, sloping roof. As the roof and the rest of the environment heats up, the perceived signal is apparently less. At night, when things cool down, the perceived signal increases. The effect of thermal fade in this installation was later mitigated (by about 2 or 3 dB) by relocating the antenna, placing it closer to the edge of the roof. With less hot roof in the path, the effect of the day's heat was reduced. Nothing can completely eliminate the effects of the sun on a long distance path, but without a historical graph, it would be difficult to account for the effect at all.

Figure 2-43 shows another interesting artifact, this time averaged over several weeks. This link is about a mile-and-a-half long, and still shows some of the effects of thermal fade. But look at the noise readings. They are all over the map, reading as high as -89 and jumping to well below -100. This most likely indicates the presence of other 2.4 GHz devices somewhere in the path between the two points. Since the noise remains steady for some time and then changes rapidly to another level, it is probably a device that uses channels rather than a frequency-hopping device. Given the wide variety of perceived noise, I would guess that the most likely culprit is a high-powered 2.4 GHz phone somewhere nearby. It is probably impossible to ever know for sure, but this data might warrant changing the radio to a different channel.

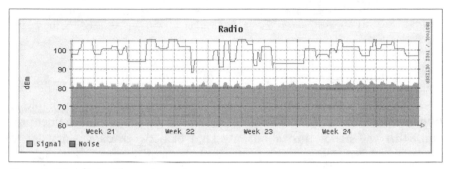

Figure 2-43. A link with a noisy environment

These graphs were generated using Linux and some freely available tools. A modest Linux server can monitor a large number of radio devices, and the requirements on each of the access points (APs) is quite small. I will assume that you are using a DIY AP running Linux **[Hack #63]**, although similar techniques can be used for just about any kind of radio device.

You can monitor signal strength using any available TCP port above 1024 on the access points. We'll use port 10000 here, but you should choose your own port based on your setup. On each of the APs to be monitored, as well as on the machine doing the monitoring, add lines like these to */etc/services*:

```
mon0    10000/tcp
mon1    10001/tcp
mon2    10002/tcp
```

Then, add a line like this to the */etc/inetd.conf* on the monitored machines:

```
mon0 stream tcp    nowait nobody /usr/local/bin/iwconfig iwconfig eth1
```

Be sure to use the path to *iwconfig* for your system, and specify the device to be monitored at the end. You can add as many lines as you like, using a different port each time:

```
mon1 stream tcp    nowait nobody /usr/local/bin/iwconfig iwconfig wlan0
```

If you need more ports, add more lines to your */etc/services*. When all of your radio cards are set up, restart *inetd*. You can verify that the changes have taken effect by using telnet:

```
# telnet localhost mon0

Trying 127.0.0.1...
Connected to localhost.
```

```
Escape character is '^]'.
eth1      IEEE 802.11-DS  ESSID:"NoCat"  Nickname:"pebble"
          Mode:Managed  Frequency:2.457GHz  Access Point: 00:02:2D:1C:BC:CF
          Bit Rate:11Mb/s   Tx-Power=15 dBm   Sensitivity:1/3
          Retry limit:4   RTS thr:off   Fragment thr:off
          Power Management:off
          Link Quality:14/92  Signal level:-83 dBm  Noise level:-96 dBm
          Rx invalid nwid:0  Rx invalid crypt:0  Rx invalid frag:6176330
          Tx excessive retries:7880  Invalid misc:0   Missed beacon:0

Connection closed by foreign host.
#
```

To collect the radio data, you need Netcat installed on the machine that does the collection. Netcat is a free and insanely useful utility available at *http://www.securityfocus.com/tools/137*. Think of it as a scriptable telnet program that will handle just about any kind of network data you want to throw at it. I use Netcat to connect to each of the machines, and scrape the results with a Perl script.

With the Netcat binary (*nc*) installed on your system, use the wrapper script in Example 2-2 to collect the data.

Example 2-2. radio.pl, a wrapper script that collects Netcat data

```perl
#!/usr/bin/perl  -w
use strict;

my $ip = shift;
my $port = shift;
($ip && $port) || die "Usage: $0 ip port\n";

open(NC, "nc $ip $port |") || die "Couldn't spawn nc: $!\n";

while(<NC>) {
  if(/Signal level:-?(\d+).*Noise level:-?(\d+)/) {
    print "$1 $2\n";
    exit;
  }
}

die "Warning: couldn't find signal and noise!\n";
```

I put this script in */usr/local/sbin/* and invoke it with the IP address and port number on the command line. It simply returns two unsigned numbers representing the current signal and noise readings:

```
$ radio.pl 10.15.6.1 mono0

83 96
$
```

In case you haven't recognized it already from the graphs, the tool that actually stores the data and draws the pretty graphs is Tobi Oetiker's excellent Round Robin Database Tool (RRDtool); *http://people.ee.ethz.ch/~oetiker/*). Like many powerful tools, RRDtool can be imposing at first, sometimes to the point of frustration. Efficient data collection and accurate visual presentation isn't as simple as you might think. Of course, RRDtool will handle just about any data type you track, but getting it working can be tricky the first time.

Personally, I prefer to use a tool like Cacti (*http://www.cacti.net*) to manage my RRDtool graphs for me. It is fairly simple to install, has an easy to use web interface, and does the dirty work of managing your RRDtool databases. With Cacti installed, simply set up *radio.pl* (Example 2-2) as a data input script, and create a data source for each radio to be monitored. See the Cacti documentation for more details. Tutorials on how to set up and use Cacti are available at *http://www.cacti.net/documentation.php*. The Cacti pages also have an excellent web-based forum where you can get questions answered by developers and active users.

When properly configured, Cacti automatically generates Daily, Weekly, Monthly, and Yearly averages for all of your data sources.

If you prefer to roll your own RRDtool, use a command such as this to create your database:

```
/usr/local/rrdtool/bin/rrdtool create \
/home/rob/radio/radio.rrd \
--step 300 \
DS:signal:GAUGE:600:0:150 \
DS:noise:GAUGE:600:0:150 \
RRA:AVERAGE:0.5:1:600 \
RRA:AVERAGE:0.5:6:700 \
RRA:AVERAGE:0.5:24:775 \
RRA:AVERAGE:0.5:288:797 \
RRA:MAX:0.5:1:600 \
RRA:MAX:0.5:6:700 \
RRA:MAX:0.5:24:775 \
RRA:MAX:0.5:288:797
```

Be sure that the *rrdtool* binary is in your PATH, and change the print "$1 $2\n"; line in *radio.pl* to something like the following:

```
`rrdtool update /home/rob/radio/radio.rrd --template signal:noise N:$1:$2`;
```

Add *radio.pl* to a *cron* job that runs every five minutes or so to regularly collect the data:

```
*/5 * * * *          /usr/local/sbin/radio.pl 10.15.6.1 mon0
```

Finally, once you have collected some data, you can generate a graph like the one shown in Figure 2-43 with this command:

```
/usr/local/rrdtool/bin/rrdtool graph - \
  --imgformat=PNG \
  --start="-604800" \
  --title=" Radio" \
  --rigid \
  --base=1000 \
  --height=120 \
  --width=500 \
  --upper-limit=105 \
  --lower-limit=60 \
  --vertical-label="dBm" \
DEF:a="/home/rob/radio/ radio.rrd":signal:AVERAGE \
DEF:b="/home/rob/radio/ radio.rrd":noise:AVERAGE \
AREA:a#74C366:"Signal" \
LINE1:b#FF0000:"Noise" \
> graph.png
```

While the other tools mentioned in this chapter will give you a good instantaneous estimate of how well your link is doing, RRDtool, Netcat, and the script in Example 2-2 will give you impressive historical data that can be invaluable for troubleshooting your network. In addition to signal and noise, RRDtool can also track uptime, network traffic, associated clients, transmission errors, and any other data you can think of. The reward of having clear historical graphs is well worth learning to deal with the complexity of RRDtool.

Find Radio Manufacturers by MAC

HACK #39

Discover what sort of radio cards and laptops are in use on your local network.

If you've got a wireless network, you might be wondering about who is using your wireless network. Sure, you have their IP addresses [Hack #49], and their MAC addresses are easily found with a simple arp -an. But what kind of computers or network cards are they using?

The IEEE maintains the database of *organizationally unique identifiers* (OUI). These are the first 24 bits of the MAC address, parceled out to vendors who manufacture Ethernet devices. If you know the first three bytes of a MAC address, you can look up the device's manufacturer directly from the IEEE. There is a searchable database on the Web at *http://standards.ieee.org/ regauth/oui/index.shtml*. Note that to use this service, you need to specify the OUI separated by hyphens, not colons (e.g., 00-02-2d, not 00:02:2d.).

The Code

Of course, this is handy for the occasional query, but what if you want to instantly see the manufacturer of all devices on your local subnet? Just after performing a broadcast ping [Hack #49], try the Perl script in Example 2-3.

Example 2-3. machine.pl, which uses arp and the IEEE database to identify network cards

```perl
#!/usr/bin/perl

my %cards;
my %ips;

open(ARP,"arp -an|") || die "Couldn't open arp table: $!\n";

print "Looking up OUIs.";
while(<ARP>) {
 chomp;
 my $addr = $_;
 my $ip = $_;
 $addr =~ s/.* ([\d\w]+:[\d\w]+:[\d\w]+):.*/$1/;
 $addr =~ s/\b([\d\w])\b/0$1/g;
 $addr =~ s/:/-/g;
 next unless $addr =~ /..-..-..-/;

 $ip =~ s/.*?(\d+\.\d+\.\d+\.\d+).*/$1/;
 print ".";
 $cards{$addr}||=`curl -sd 'x=$addr' http://standards.ieee.org/cgi-bin/
ouisearch`;
 ($cards{$addr} =~ /Sorry!/) && ($cards{$addr} = "Unknown OUI: $addr");
 $ips{$ip} = $addr;
}
print "\n";
for(keys(%ips)) {
 $cards{$ips{$_}} =~ s/.*.hex.\s+([\w\s\,\.]+)\n.*/$1/s;
 print "$_ -> $cards{$ips{$_}}\n";
}
```

This script works well on Linux, Mac OS X, and BSD. It requires only Perl and the cURL network utility (*http://curl.sourceforge.net*), and it assumes that the *arp* utility is in your path. For efficiency's sake, it queries the IEEE only once for each OUI it encounters.

Running the Hack

Save the code to a file called *machines.pl* and invoke it from the command line, where it will produce output somewhat like this:

```
$ perl machines.pl

Looking up OUIs.........
10.15.6.98 -> Compaq Computer Corporation
```

```
10.15.6.44 -> Aironet Wireless Communication
10.15.6.64 -> Aironet Wireless Communication
10.15.6.49 -> APPLE COMPUTER, INC.
10.15.6.75 -> Netgear, Inc.
10.15.6.87 -> APPLE COMPUTER, INC.
10.15.6.62 -> Senao International Co., Ltd.
```

This node has a Compaq card, two Cisco Aironet cards, two Apple Air-Ports, a Netgear card, and a Senao card associated with it. This quickly gives you some idea of the demographic of your wireless users; plotted over time, it might show some interesting trends.

Some vendors are not listed in the OUI database, but the vast majority are. Some vendors are listed under the name of a subsidiary company (frequently from Taiwan), which can be misleading. But for an informal poll of who is using your wireless network, this script can be quite illuminating.

## CHAPTER THREE

Wireless Security
Hacks 40–51

When it comes to wireless networking, there is no such thing as physical security. You might be able to lock down the physical network infrastructure of a business or other facility, but radio waves pass through walls, carrying your network data with them. Don't delude yourself by thinking that a low-powered access point (AP) won't reach much further than your parking lot. Remember that although you might not see your network while using a laptop outside your building, someone with a large enough antenna can likely read your network traffic from a mile or more away.

I have personally seen a simple 24 dBi dish detect hundreds of wireless networks from the top of Queen Anne hill in Seattle. These were networks with SSIDs like *Linksys* and *default*, which obviously were coming from low-end, consumer-grade access points without any external antennas. I certainly couldn't have made a reliable network link to them, but I could have passively logged their traffic from miles away quite easily. Short of wrapping your entire building with a metal screen to build an effective Faraday cage, you should expect the signal of your APs to leak out well beyond your immediate vicinity.

This chapter is devoted to workable methods for controlling access to your wireless network. A control mechanism could be something as simple as a WPA key, or as complex as a captive web portal with a RADIUS backend. We will also look at several ways you can protect your own data when using other wireless networks, even if those networks are completely public and open.

HACK #40   Stop Moochers from Stealing Your Wi-Fi Bandwidth

If you have a Wi-Fi network at home or at work and you are worried that passersby might be connecting to it and stealing your bandwidth, here's what you can do.

If you have a Wi-Fi network, it's a breeze for anyone passing by to detect it. And if you haven't protected yourself properly—or if someone is dedicated enough to stealing your bandwidth—moochers can get in and suck up all your bandwidth by doing things such as downloading movies and MP3s. That means there's less bandwidth for you.

There's an easy way to find out if someone is leeching your bandwidth and then to send them alerts telling them you know they're using your bandwidth and you'd like them to get off your network. Download AirSnare, a free program for Windows XP which monitors your network for wireless intruders, reports on who they are, shows you their activity, and sends them warnings.

Before you install AirSnare, you need to download and install a library of tools called WinPcap, an architecture that captures and analyzes network packets. Get it from *http://winpcap.polito.it/install/default.htm* and follow the installation instructions.

Next, download and install AirSnare from *http://home.comcast.net/~jay. deboer/airsnare.*

> Strictly speaking, AirSnare isn't precisely freeware. Its author calls it *beggarware*. That is, he lets you use it for free, but he asks that you make a donation to him to help him develop the program further.

Before you use AirSnare, you need to know the MAC address of any network card that will be using your wireless network. The MAC address is a number that uniquely identifies a network card or other piece of communications hardware. You're going to tell AirSnare that these MAC addresses are trusted ones and shouldn't be treated as intruders.

You can find out the MAC address for your PCs in several ways. One simple way is to go to a command prompt in Windows, type `ipconfig /all`, and press Enter. In the results you get, look for the numbers next to `Physical Address`, such as `00-08-A1-00-9F-32`. That's the MAC address.

Write down the MAC address of every PC on your network. Include the addresses for all your PCs, even if they connect to the network via Ethernet rather than wirelessly. For example, if you have a laptop that you some-times connect to your network wirelessly and sometimes via Ethernet, when you issue the `ipconfig /all` command and press Enter you'll see two sets of entries, each of which has its MAC address. Copy down both of them.

Next, go to *C:\Program Files\AirSnare*, open *trustedMAC.txt* with a text edi-tor, and add each MAC address (such as `00-08-A1-00-9F-32`) on a new line in the file. Follow it by a space, and then type in a description of the com-puter; for example, `00-08-A1-00-9F-32 Preston's New Laptop`.

Now go to *C:\Program Files\AirSnare* and run the file *AirSnare.exe*. You have to run the file from this location because the program doesn't install an icon on the desktop or show up as an entry in Windows' All Programs menu.

 Not all Wi-Fi adapters will work with AirSnare. If you get the error message `runtime error '-2147220982 (8004020a)' procedure packetsethwfilter failed. error code= 0`, it means your Wi-Fi adapter won't work with it. Try installing the software on another computer on your network.

Choose your network adapter from the list that appears, and AirSnare will spring into action. Whenever it finds a MAC address on the network that you haven't told it is a friendly one, it sounds an alert and changes its screen color to red. Then it starts logging any traffic between the MAC address and the network in its Unfriendly MAC Watch Window. It gives details about all the traffic, including the port being used and the destination IP address. It also identifies common ports such as FTP, Telnet, email, web, DHCP, and other popular ports so that you have more information than just a port number.

You can save all the information to a log file by clicking the Stop button and clicking "Write to log file." All the information will be saved in a text file. Filenames start with *ASlog* and are followed by the date and time; for exam-ple, *ASlog043024_2305.txt* indicates the log was saved on March 16, 2005, at 23:05 (that's 11:05 p.m.).

Once you know someone is using your network, you want to warn them away, which you can do with the program's AirHorn module. Choose Win-dow → AirHorn Window. In the Server box type in your computer's host-name or its IP address. If you're not sure what those are for your PC, use the `ipconfig /all` command from earlier in this hack, and get the information from there.

In the Send To box, enter the IP address of the computer to which you're sending a warning, which you'll find in the Unfriendly MAC Watch Window. Then, in the Send From box, type your name or how you want to be identified and type the message you want to send, as shown in Figure 3-1. Click Send Message, and the warning will be sent on its merry way.

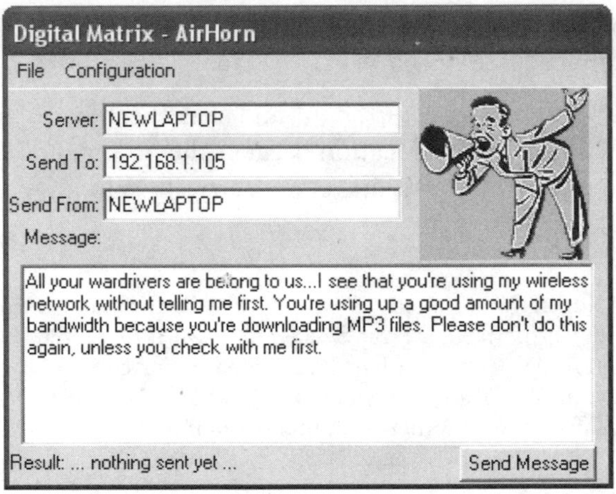

Figure 3-1. Sending a message to intruders

There's only one problem with this warning module: it works only if both you and the person on the other end have the Windows Messenger service turned on. The Windows Messenger *service* isn't the Windows Messenger *chat program*. Rather, it's used to send notifications over local area networks—for example, when a network administrator warns users that a server is about to be taken down. Because the Windows Messenger service has frequently been used to send spam, though, many people have turned it off. And Windows XP SP2 turns it off by default. So, don't count on this part of the program working.

Hacking the Hack

Knowing that you have a bandwidth moocher is one thing, but kicking him off your network is another thing entirely. Sometimes a warning will suffice, but if one of you isn't using the Windows Messenger service, you won't even be able to warn him. So, what to do if you can't get through, or you can get through and the moocher ignores you?

You can kick him off your network, using your wireless router's built-in capabilities. How you do this varies from router to router, but here's how to do it using the Linksys BEFW11S4. Go to the administrator's screen by going to *http://192.168.1.1*. Leave the username blank, type **admin** for the password, and press Enter. (If you've changed the username and password from the default, use those instead.)

Next, click Status, and from the screen that appears, click Local Network. A page will appear with basic information about your router. Click DHCP Client Table, and you'll see a list of all the devices on the network, with their IP addresses and MAC addresses, as shown in Figure 3-2. Check the box next to the intruder and click Delete, and he'll be kicked off your network.

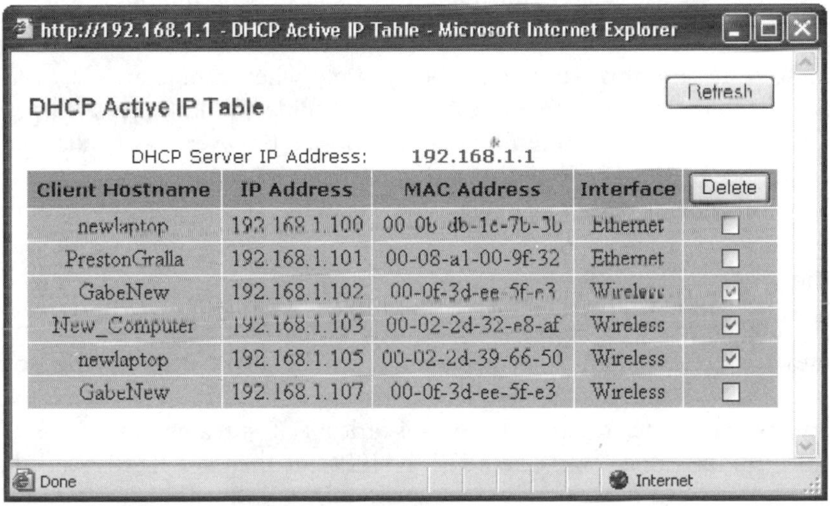

Figure 3-2. Kicking Wi-Fi bandwidth moochers off your network by deleting them from the IP table

To make sure he can't get on again, you can tell your wireless router not to allow him onto your network. In my example of a Linksys router, log on to the administrator's screen and click Security. From the page that appears, click Edit MAC Filter Setting. On the Filtered MAC Address page that appears, you'll be able to ban devices with specific MAC addresses from getting onto your network. Type in the MAC address in an empty box, and click Apply. From now on the intruder will be barred.

There are even better ways to keep intruders off of your wireless network. Chief among these is the use of WPA encryption. If you really want to share your wireless network, consider using WPA Enterprise **[Hack #44]**. However, that level of authentication is not for everyone. To let public users into your wireless network, but still allow control over their usage, set up a captive portal **[Hack #71]**.

—*Preston Gralla*

Visualize a Network

HACK #41

Get a compelling visual representation of what people are looking at on your network with EtherPEG and DriftNet.

While tools such as *tcpdump* [Hack #33] or Ethereal [Hack #31] give you detailed information about what people are doing on your network, the information they provide just isn't interesting to most people. They might understand that their wireless data is vulnerable to eavesdroppers, but somehow they still have an attitude of, "It's hard to do, so it won't happen to me."

For some reason, this attitude is quickly cured when people are shown the following tools. While they are really simple utilities, I think they are as revolutionary to network monitoring as the Mosaic browser was to the Internet. Rather than make logs for later analysis, they simply show you what people are looking at online, in real time.

EtherPEG

EtherPEG (*http://www.etherpeg.org*) is a clever hack for Mac OS X that combines all of the modern conveniences of a packet sniffer with the good old-fashioned friendliness of a graphics-rendering library. It watches the local network for traffic, reassembles out-of-order TCP streams, and scans the results for data that looks like a GIF or JPEG. It then simply displays that data in a random fashion in a large window. As shown in Figure 3-3, it's a real-time metabrowser that dynamically builds a view of images from other people's browsers, built up as other people look around online.

The source code and a couple compiled binaries are freely available; make sure you download the right version, at the bottom of the EtherPEG web page.

The compiled binaries for Mac OS X assume interface names of *en0* or *en1*. If you are using other numbered interfaces, you will need to have the Xcode Tools installed and compile the source directly.

EtherPEG is decidedly not a commercial app designed for extensive eavesdropping. It is a simple but effective hack that indiscriminately shows all image data that it can assemble. It makes no attempt to display where the images have been downloaded from, or who requested them. It doesn't even save a local copy for later perusal; once you quit the app, all collected data is lost.

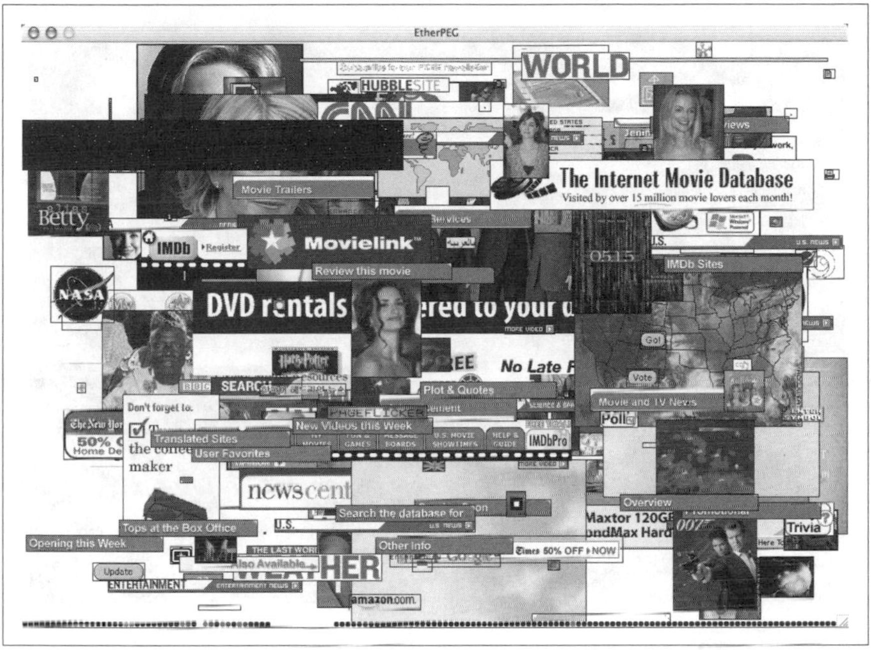

Figure 3-3. EtherPEG in action

It you are looking for a similar (and even more functional) application that will run on an OS other than Mac OS X, read on.

DriftNet

Inspired by EtherPEG, DriftNet (*http://www.ex-parrot.com/~chris/driftnet*) is a network image grabber for X11. In addition to decoding image files from sniffed network data, it has a couple other features. It can save all decoded images for later processing (say, by a screensaver app) and has experimental support for decoding an MPEG audio stream.

Ubuntu users can install DriftNet with an apt-get install driftnet command. Contributed RPMs are available for Fedora and Red Hat, as well as other Linux distributions. Ports are also available for FreeBSD users. The code has been tested to compile on Linux and Solaris.

As shown in Figure 3-4, DriftNet's interface is just as simple as EtherPEG. You can click on individual images to save them to disk or, if you want to save all grabbed images, start up driftnet with the -a switch. This starts DriftNet in *adjunct* mode, which doesn't open a window, but simply saves all image data to a temporary directory (which can also be specified with the -d switch). Other applications can then use this ever-growing collection of images as a data source for their own ends.

Figure 3-4. DriftNet in action

DriftNet has received a surprising amount of bad press as being the worst sort of *spyware* utility and is sometimes billed as usable only for invading other people's privacy. This is a rather specious way of looking at the capabilities of DriftNet or EtherPEG, since neither program can give you any indication where the images you grab have come from or their end user destination.

On the contrary, tools like this are tremendously useful. Not only can a systems administrator use such a tool to discourage inappropriate use of a corporate network (by simply leaving it running on a monitor in a public place), but it can also provide an amazing insight into the mood of a crowd of wireless users.

What better way to find out what is going on in the minds of wireless users than to see what they are looking at on their screens?

> For the results of an experiment in sampling the group sub-conscious, see the original weblog on the subject at *http://www.oreillynet.com/pub/wlg/1414*.

If nothing else, tools such as DriftNet and EtherPEG help to remind people of the importance of good wireless security practices and of the use of discretion when using wireless networks in general.

This sort of eavesdropping is possible only because people use insecure protocols and unknowingly broadcast their network traffic in the clear for all to hear. If you are using strong application layer encryption such as SSH or IPSec, or the modern wireless layer encryption of WPA/802.11i, this sort of tool is completely useless.

As a friend of mine says, "Running EtherPEG or DriftNet while sitting at a public wireless hotspot is analogous to looking at the covers of books and magazines people are reading."

HACK #42 Secure Your Linux Network with WPA

Take advantage of a strong wireless authorization and encryption protocol in Linux.

Linux might best be described as a *modular* operating system. Since all of the underlying architecture, down to the last code byte, is freely available for anyone to read and modify, there are lots of little programs that provide useful functions, but which are not necessarily part of a Linux distribution.

Wi-Fi Protected Access (WPA) support is one good example. While wireless cards that support WPA have been available since 2003, not one of the major Linux distributions installs all the necessary pieces to support WPA-enabled wireless cards. Some distributions do at least include packages that can be installed, while others require you to compile your own. Lastly, WPA on Linux requires you to have some knowledge of how your wireless card and networking stack function in order for things to work properly.

What is WPA? The original version of WPA was devised by the Wi-Fi Alliance and was based on a draft version of the IEEE 802.11i protocol. WPA defined a subset of the draft 802.11i and was designed to be implemented on existing Wi-Fi hardware. WPA is an intermediate solution to improve the hopeless security quagmire of Wired Equivalent Privacy (WEP) while waiting for the full 802.11i standard to be ratified. WPA uses the Temporal Key Integrity Protocol (TKIP) to generate per-packet encryption keys, supports both external and pre-shared key authentication, and implements new key handshakes.

The IEEE working group approved the full 802.11i specifications in June 2004. The Wi-Fi Alliance has based their new WPA2 standard on the completed 802.11i. WPA2 supports more robust encryption algorithms to replace TKIP. At the time of this writing, access points, wireless cards, and drivers that support WPA2 are just becoming available.

If you have a wireless card and access point that supports WPA, you should run, not walk to your Linux notebook and follow this hack through. The bad old days of WEP cracking are far behind us.

Requirements

You'll need a Linux kernel in the 2.4.x or 2.6.x series with the Wireless Extensions v15 or newer. Practically any installation you've done on a notebook during the last two years will fit those requirements. In addition, you'll need a full development environment, including GCC, if you want to compile wpa_supplicant from source.

Drivers. The key piece of software you need is a wireless driver that supports WPA/WPA2. The following drivers are known to work:

HostAP
> Prism 2/2.5/3 radio chipsets (*http://hostap.epitest.fi*)

Madwifi
> Atheros 802.11a/b/g radio chipets (*http://madwifi.sourceforge.net*)

Atmel
> Atmel USB/PC Card chipsets (*http://atmelwlandriver.sourceforge.net*)

Driverloader
> Windows NDIS drivers (*http://www.linuxant.com/driverloader*)

Ndiswrapper
> Windows NDIS drivers (*http://ndiswrapper.sourceforge.net*)

IPW2100
> Intel ipw2100 chipsets (*http://ipw2100.sourceforge.net*)

IPW2200
> Intel ipw2200 chipsets (*http://ipw2200.sourceforge.net*)

Broadcom
> wl.o embedded driver (*http://www.linksys.com/support/gpl.asp*)

While this book doesn't cover all of these drivers, see [Hack #63] for details on installing HostAP, Madwifi, and Agere drivers. [Hack #81] covers Driverloader and Ndiswrapper.

The final piece of software you will need is *wpa_supplicant*, available at *http://hostap.epitest.fi/wpa_supplicant* from Jouni Malinen, the author of the HostAP driver. Several Linux distributions have packages available, including Ubuntu, RedHat Enterprise, Fedora Core, Mandrake, and SuSE.

WPA types. There are three main types of authentication supported within *wpa_supplicant*:

WPA-PSK
> Also called "WPA-Personal" in many consumer models of access points, WPA-PSK relies on a pre-shared key (PSK) for authentication, similar to WEP.

WPA with EAP

Also called "WPA-Enterprise" in some access points, WPA with EAP uses 802.1x to authenticate users against an authentication server such as RADIUS. (See later in this chapter **[Hack #44]** for details on setting up your own WPA authentication server.)

> EAP stands for Extensible Authentication Protocol, and coverage of its many flavors is beyond the scope of this book. A few of the main EAP protocols include EAP-TLS, EAP-PEAP, and EAP-TTLS.

WPA2

Implementations are still fuzzy at the time of this writing, but WPA2 is supposed to have support for both Personal and Enterprise types of authentication.

One other primary difference between WPA and WPA2 is important to note: the required encryption level. WPA allows the use of RC4 encryption with TKIP. WPA2 mandates AES encryption for all connections. Many older radio cards and access points will not be capable of the demanding computation required for AES encryption.

Installing wpa_supplicant

In order for the install to proceed, you will need to have installed one of the wireless drivers that are listed in the previous section. This hack covers the install of *wpa_supplicant* from an Ubuntu package and compiles *wpa_supplicant* from source on Fedora Core 3.

Ubuntu package. To install *wpa_supplicant* on Ubuntu Linux, you'll need to configure *apt*. Edit */etc/apt/sources.list* and uncomment the following lines:

```
deb http://us.archive.ubuntu.com/ubuntu hoary universe
deb-src http://us.archive.ubuntu.com/ubuntu hoary universe
deb http://security.ubuntu.com/ubuntu hoary-security universe
deb-src http://security.ubuntu.com/ubuntu hoary-security universe
```

The universe repository contains packages that are not developed or supported by the Ubuntu release crew. This is where you'll find the necessary package.

To update your *apt* index, issue the following command:

```
sudo apt-get update
```

Once *apt* has finished updating the indexes, go ahead and install the package:

```
sudo apt-get install wpasupplicant
```

After the package is installed, you're ready for configuration, as discussed later in the "Configuration" section of this hack.

Fedora Core 3 compile. If you need support for EAP-TLS, EAP-TTLS, or EAP-PEAP, make sure that you have OpenSSL installed. Most distributions have openssl available as a package, or you can get the source from *http://www. openssl.org*.

You'll also need a working compiler. If you included the Development Tools during the initial Fedora Core installation, you should have all the necessary pieces.

Download the source code from *http://hostap.epitest.fi/wpa_supplicant*. Extract the compressed tar file, and change to the newly created directory:

```
tar xzvf wpa_supplicant-0.3.8.tar.gz
cd wpa_supplicant-0.3.8
```

The code doesn't use the standard *./configure* script you might be used to in other open source code. Instead, you'll need to generate your own *.config* file based on the specific options you need. Fortunately, this is pretty straightforward. You need to include a line that specifies your wireless driver, and specify any EAP types that are required for your installation. WPA-PSK is supported by default, so no option is required.

Here is a *.config* file for an Atheros radio card that uses the Madwifi driver, and which needs only WPA-PSK authentication:

```
CONFIG_DRIVER_MADWIFI=y
CONFIG_WIRELESS_EXTENSION=y
```

If you don't know which EAP method you need, or if you want to use multiple wireless cards, you can easily specify all of the possible options:

```
CONFIG_DRIVER_HOSTAP=y
CONFIG_DRIVER_PRISM54=y
CONFIG_DRIVER_HERMES=y
CONFIG_DRIVER_MADWIFI=y
CONFIG_DRIVER_ATMEL=y
CONFIG_DRIVER_WEXT=y
CONFIG_DRIVER_NDISWRAPPER=y
CONFIG_DRIVER_BROADCOM=y
CONFIG_DRIVER_IPW=y
CONFIG_WIRELESS_EXTENSION=y
CONFIG_EAP_MD5=y
CONFIG_EAP_MSCHAPV2=y
CONFIG_EAP_TLS=y
CONFIG_EAP_PEAP=y
CONFIG_EAP_TTLS=y
CONFIG_EAP_GTC=y
CONFIG_EAP_OTP=y
```

```
CONFIG_EAP_SIM=y
CONFIG_EAP_AKA=y
CONFIG_EAP_PSK=y
CONFIG_EAP_PAX=y
CONFIG_EAP_LEAP=y
```

This will give you all of the possible driver and EAP combinations available.

Once you've created a *.config* file, compile the software with a simple make command. There is no make install, so once the compile finishes, you will need to copy the binaries to an appropriate directory; for example:

```
cp wpa_cli wpa_supplicant wpa_passphrase /usr/local/bin
```

Configuration

Once you've installed *wpa_supplicant*, you need to write a configuration file to use with network configuration specific to your connections. The author recommends using a path of */etc/wpa_supplicant.conf* but the file can live anywhere you like, as long as it is readable by the system during boot.

If your network uses WPA-PSK, the included binary *wpa_passphrase* will be useful when you're making the necessary fields for a configuration file. Since the WPA-PSK passphrase is necessary to join your network, you must include it in the configuration file. *wpa_passphrase* allows you to generate a hash of the passphrase so that your clear text is not included in any readable file.

Simply call *wpa_passphrase* with your ESSID and passphrase:

```
wpa_passphrase MyNetwork testing123
```

The program will give you output that looks like this:

```
network={
        ssid="MyNetwork"
        #psk="testing123"
        psk=c170778beb697d9b97fd415845bf8117e2803dc3e1581e3de22d8539116b0fbd
}
```

Copy and paste this into your configuration file, or for an easy shortcut, call *wpa_passphrase* and redirect the output to a file:

```
wpa_passphrase MyNetwork testing123 > /etc/wpa_supplicant.conf
```

This file is all you'll need for a basic WPA-PSK connection. Once you've tested the connection and verified everything is working, remove the commented line with your clear-text passphrase from */etc/wpa_supplicant.conf*.

A more elaborate configuration file, with connections for a home WPA-PSK network and EAP-TLS for a work connection, might look like this:

```
#my home network
network={
```

```
        ssid="MyNetwork"
        key_mgmt=WPA-PSK
        psk=c170778beb697d9b97fd415845bf8117e2803dc3e1581e3de22d8539116b0fbd
}
#my work network
network={
    ssid="MyWork"
    scan_ssid=1
    key_mgmt=WPA-EAP
    pairwise=CCMP TKIP
    group=CCMP TKIP
    eap=TLS
    identity="joe@WORK.com"
    ca_cert="/etc/cert/ca.pem"
    client_cert="/etc/cert/user.pem"
    private_key="/etc/cert/user.prv"
    private_key_passwd="password"
}
```

For more example configurations, consult the *README* file that comes with the source code. The most up-to-date *README* can also be found online through a web-based CVS checkout at *http://hostap.epitest.fi/cgi-bin/viewcvs. cgi/*checkout*/hostap/wpa_supplicant/README?rev=HEAD&content-type=text/plain*.

Testing and Usage

To test the configuration, make sure your radio card is active and set to the correct ESSID. Then, call wpa_supplicant with the radio card interface, the location of the configuration file, and the debug option:

```
wpa_supplicant -iath0 -c/etc/wpa_supplicant.conf -d
```

You will see quite a bit of debug output, more than we can reproduce here. You can verify a successful connection by using *iwconfig* to ensure that you can see the MAC address of your access point and then executing a ping to see if you have TCP/IP connectivity.

Once you've established a successful WPA session, you can call wpa_supplicant without debugging and place it background (daemon) mode:

```
wpa_supplicant -iath0 -c/etc/wpa_supplicant.conf -B
```

These examples assume you have specified a single driver to be included in the compiled *wpa_supplicant*. If your *.config* file specifies multiple drivers during the compile, you must call wpa_supplicant with the appropriate driver; for example:

```
wpa_supplicant -iath0 -c/etc/wpa_supplicant.conf -B -Dmadwifi
```

Here's a list of driver names you can specify:

```
hostap = HostAP driver (Prism2/2.5/3; also used with Linuxant DriverLoader)
prism54 = Prism54.org driver (Intersil Prism GT/Duette/Indigo)
hermes = Agere Systems Inc. driver (Hermes-I/Hermes-II)
madwifi = MADWIFI 802.11 support (Atheros, etc.)
atmel = ATMEL AT76C5XXx (USB, PCMCIA)
wext = Linux wireless extensions (generic)
ndiswrapper - Linux ndiswrapper
broadcom = Broadcom wl.o driver
ipw = Intel ipw2100/2200 driver
wired = wpa_supplicant wired Ethernet driver
```

You'll probably want to call wpa_supplicant during the boot process, so that you don't have to call it manually each time you log in. Of course, the way to do this will vary based on your Linux distribution and your wireless card.

With a MiniPCI wireless card in Ubuntu Linux, the easiest boot setup is to modify the /etc/network/interfaces file by adding these lines:

```
up wpa_supplicant -iath0 -c/etc/wpa_supplicant.conf -wB
down killall wpa_supplicant
```

The -w command-line option is used when calling wpa_supplicant at startup. It forces WPA negotiation to wait if the wireless interface is not started yet.

On a Fedora Core system with a MiniPCI card, you'll need to modify two files. First, add this code to the /etc/sysconfig/network-scripts/ifup-wireless file:

```
wpa_supplicant -iath0 -c/etc/wpa_supplicant.conf -Bw
```

Then, add the following line to /etc/sysconfig/network-scripts/ifup-wireless:

```
killall wpa_supplicant
```

If that file doesn't exist, create it and make sure it is executable:

```
echo "killall wpa_supplicant" > /etc/sysconfig/network-scripts/ifup-wireless
chmod +x /etc/sysconfig/network-scripts/ifup-wireless
```

Lastly, for any system in which you are using a PCMCIA wireless card, you can add the wpa_supplicant startup to the /etc/pcmcia scripts. Make the following three changes to your files.

1. Any of your network schemes in /etc/pcmcia.wireless.opts should include the following:

   ```
   MODE="Managed"
   WPA="y"
   ```

2. Add this code to the end of the start action handler in /etc/pcmcia/wireless:

   ```
   if [ "$WPA" = "y" -a -x /usr/local/bin/wpa_supplicant ]; then
       /usr/local/bin/wpa_supplicant -Bw -c/etc/wpa_supplicant.conf \
   ```

```
        -i$DEVICE
    fi
```

3. Finally, add this code to the end of the stop action handler in */etc/pcmcia/wireless*:

```
if [ "$WPA" = "y" -a -x /usr/local/bin/wpa_supplicant ]; then
    killall wpa_supplicant
fi
```

With these changes, the PCMCIA card manager daemon will start *wpa_supplicant* when a card is plugged in. Since *cardmgr* loads at boot time, *wpa_supplicant* will then wait until the card is configured with a static IP or gets a DHCP address before negotiating keys with the access point.

Running wpa_cli

wpa_supplicant is fairly flexible, because you can configure the *wpa_supplicant.conf* file with multiple ESSIDs and authentication types, for any network you need. In its basic form, it does require that passwords be entered in the file, which can be a security risk.

wpa_cli is a client frontend program included with the wpa_supplicant package, with which it interacts. It can query status, change configuration, and request interactive user input.

To use *wpa_cli* as a non-root user in interactive mode, you need to configure *wpa_supplicant* by adding extra lines to the beginning of */etc/wpa_supplicant.conf*. For this to work correctly, your user must be a member of the group listed:

```
ctrl_interface=/var/run/wpa_supplicant
ctrl_interface_group=someusergroup
```

You can run *wpa_cli* as a command-line or interactive utility. The same commands are available in each mode, but there are features available in the interactive mode that the command-line mode does not share. Enter interactive mode by calling wpa_cli with no parameters.

One useful feature of interactive mode is the ability of *wpa_cli* to relay requests for authentication from *wpa_supplicant*. For example, if */etc/wpa_supplicant.conf* has a listed username and certificate locations for EAP-TLS, but no password entry, *wpa_supplicant* will pass an authentication request to *wpa_cli*. The user, running *wpa_cli* in interactive mode, can respond like this:

```
CTRL-REQ-PASSWORD-1:Password needed for SSID MyWork
> password 1 myworkpassword
```

wpa_cli will give you a lot of information about your WPA connections. You can force reassociation, change your identity, list available WPA networks, and a lot more. Here's a full list of available commands:

```
status = get current WPA/EAPOL/EAP status
mib = get MIB variables (dot1x, dot11)
help = show this usage help
interface [ifname] = show interfaces/select interface
level <debug level> = change debug level
license = show full wpa_cli license
logoff = IEEE 802.1X EAPOL state machine logoff
logon = IEEE 802.1X EAPOL state machine logon
set = set variables (shows list of variables when run without arguments)
pmksa = show PMKSA cache
reassociate = force reassociation
reconfigure = force wpa_supplicant to re-read its configuration file
preauthenticate <BSSID> = force preauthentication
identity <network id> <identity> = configure identity for an SSID
password <network id> <password> = configure password for an SSID
pin <network id> <pin> = configure pin for an SSID
otp <network id> <password> = configure one-time-password for an SSID
bssid <network id> <BSSID> = set preferred BSSID for an SSID
list_networks = list configured networks
terminate = terminate wpa_supplicant
quit = exit wpa_cli
```

WPA is a vastly improved method of securing your wireless networks. It is widely available in just about any consumer or enterprise-grade Wi-Fi equipment, so there is no reason to keep exposing your personal or company data to possible intrusion. If you have wireless networks that are still using WEP, you don't really have any protection at all.

HACK #43 Control Wireless Access by MAC

Restrict your wireless client access using a hardware address set in FreeRADIUS.

Sometimes, you don't want just anybody using your wireless access point (AP). Most APs available now feature hardware-address–based (MAC) access control. With this feature enabled, only wireless devices with MAC addresses that you specify will be allowed to associate with the AP.

It's important to note here that MAC access control is not foolproof. It can be defeated by someone who is using a wireless scanning program such as Kismet **[Hack #29]**. Once an attacker has a valid MAC address, it is trivial to spoof that address and gain access to your network. You need to consider using a wireless encryption protocol such as WPA on all of your access points in addition to any access control that you choose to enable.

Many APs allow you to store a list of allowed MAC addresses in the AP itself. This is good enough if you have a small, infrequently changing set of allowed clients. The downside is that in order to change the list in the AP, it's usually necessary to use some special configuration utility and reset the AP (thus kicking all of the current users off) in order for the changes to take effect. The AP itself also usually has a limit on the number of access control entries that it can store.

There is a way around this problem, though: some APs, including the Apple AirPort line and the Linksys WAP54G, have the ability to query a RADIUS server for the access control information. This has several advantages, the most obvious being that changing the access control list means (at worst) restarting the RADIUS server. Nobody currently using the AP is kicked off when you change the access control list. The second advantage is that you can have a much larger set of allowed clients than can be easily managed on the AP itself.

There is also one disadvantage: using a RADIUS server for access control means that it has to be up in order for *anyone* to use the access point. All of the APs I've tested *fail closed*; that is, when they can't contact the RADIUS server, nobody gets in.

If you've decided that RADIUS-based access control is for you, it's time to set it up. The examples here assume an Apple AirPort AP and a FreeRADIUS server running on a Linux or Unix system on the same network. FreeRADIUS source code can be found at *http://www.freeradius.org*, and it is available as a package for most Linux and BSD distributions.

FreeRADIUS Configuration

First, let's get the RADIUS server set up. FreeRADIUS is so flexible that it would really take a whole book to cover it. Thankfully, you need only the tiniest subset of its functionality for this hack.

Whether you've installed from a vendor-supplied package or built from source, there will be a directory that holds the configuration files. On our example system, it's */etc/raddb*. Hopefully, your out-of-the-box configuration is amenable to just modifying the files mentioned in this hack. The distribution configuration files are full of helpful comments as well; they're probably the most accessible parts of the FreeRADIUS documentation set.

The first order of business is to allow the AP to talk to the RADIUS server. This setup happens in the */etc/raddb/clients.conf* file. On my network, my AP is 10.1.1.253; its stanza in *clients.conf* looks like this:

```
client 10.1.1.253 {
    secret = letmein
```

```
    shortname = travellingcircus
}
```

The shortname field is optional; I use it to keep track of which AP is which in the *clients.conf* file. Standard shell-style (#) comments are also supported, so you could keep track that way as well.

Now, it's time to set up your access control lists of user MAC addresses. These entries go in the */etc/raddb/users* file. There's a decision you need to make here. There are two different MAC address formats to choose from: the Lucent/Agere format or the Cisco format. Apple's Airport Admin Utility calls these Default and Alternate, respectively; don't worry if you can't remember the differences, because the configuration pane has a helpful explanation for each.

The Default (Lucent/Agere) format has the address formatted as *xxxxxx-xxxxxx* for the user name, and the password is the shared secret that you used in */etc/raddb/clients.conf*. The Airport card in my PowerBook has a MAC address of 00:30:65:24:E6:63, so the Default-format entry for it in the users file looks like this:

```
003065 24e663 Auth-Type := Local, User-Password == "letmein"
```

It's important that the hex digits of the MAC address be in lowercase. The Default format has the advantage of being slightly more flexible; if you have multiple APs with different shared secrets, you can use that to restrict who can associate with the different APs. On the other hand, if you don't want that degree of access control but still want your APs to have different shared secrets, the Default format can make adding new users slightly more painful.

The Alternate (Cisco) format is a little simpler. Both the address and the password are simply the MAC address, all in lowercase, with no delimiters. My PowerBook's Alternate format entry in */etc/raddb/users* looks like this:

```
00306524e663 Auth-Type := Local, User-Password == "00306524e663"
```

Now that the files are all set up, it's time to see if the configuration is correct enough to allow the server to start. FreeRADIUS has excellent (and copious) debugging output. Most problems can be located by reading the debug output carefully.

Initially, start radiusd with the -X flag to get a non-forking single server instance with debug output on stderr (your terminal). If all goes well, you'll see output at the bottom:

```
Listening on authentication *:1812
Listening on accounting *:1813
Ready to process requests.
```

If you don't see that Ready to process requests line, or if you get a prompt back, make sure you used the -X flag, and carefully read the debug output starting from the bottom up.

Access Point Configuration

Assuming that your RADIUS server started up, it's time to configure your AP. These examples configure an Apple AirPort Express using Apple's AirPort Admin Utility. If you have a different model AirPort, don't worry; the interface is the same. And if you have a different kind of AP, they will all need the same information to function with RADIUS.

Start the AirPort Admin Utility and select your AP from the list. Supply the admin password and you should see a panel-like interface with tab buttons along the top. Select the Access Control tab and you should see a screen that looks something like Figure 3-5.

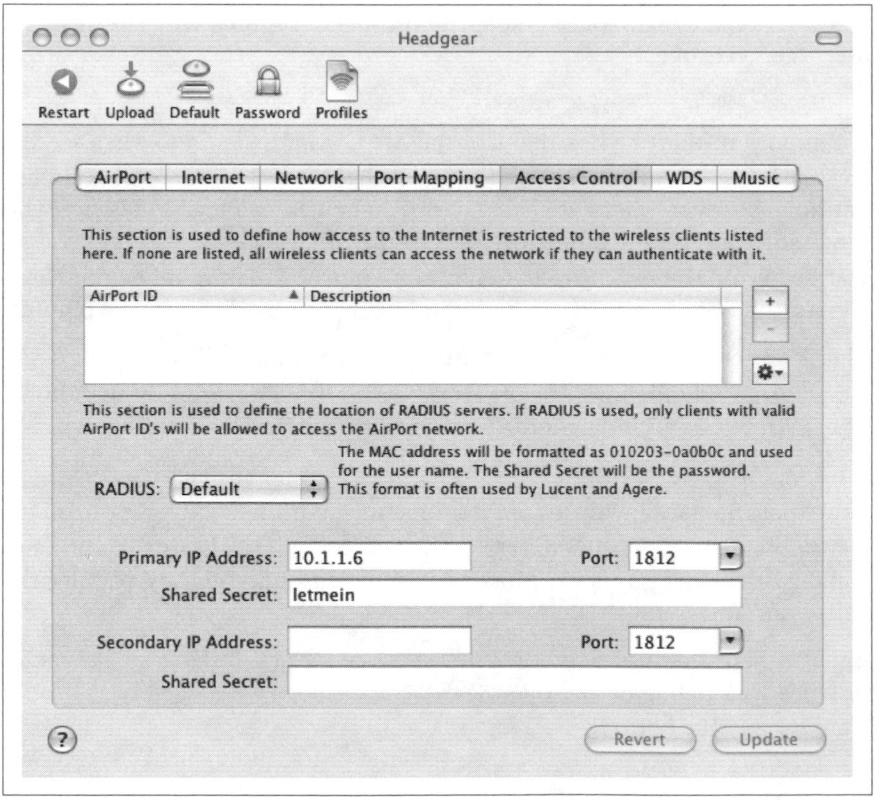

Figure 3-5. Access Control tab

There are four pieces of information you need to specify: the query format to use, the IP address of your RADIUS server, the port it's listening on, and the shared secret. The shared secret should match what you put in to the */etc/ raddb/clients.conf* file. The port number to use is the one that *radiusd* reported as its authentication port when you saw the debug output. The Primary IP Address is the IP address of the system running *radiusd*. The address format you pick is up to you. As shown in Figure 3-6, the data that you need to enter is the same for both.

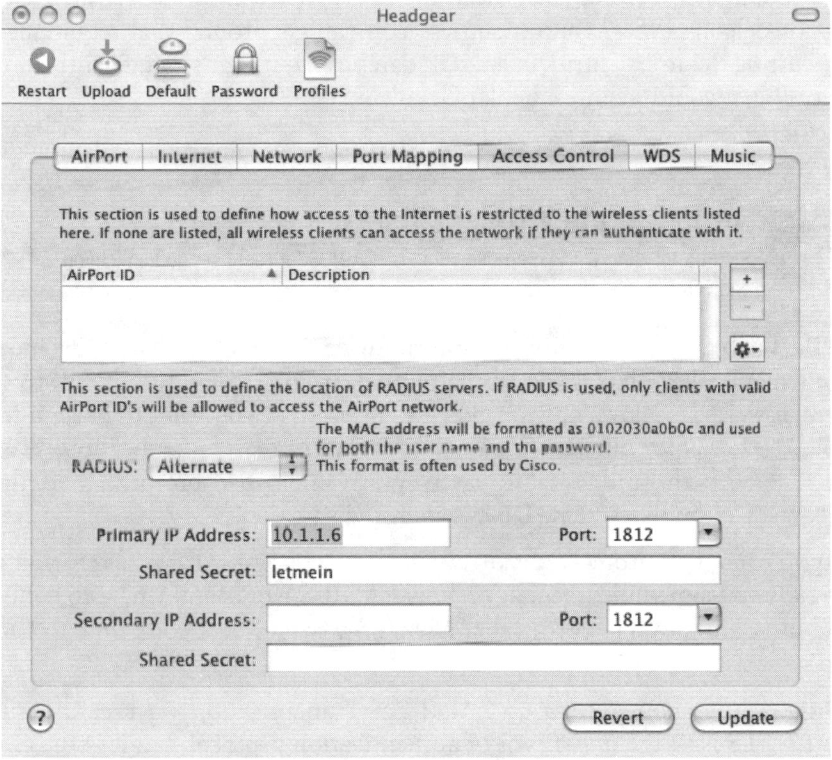

Figure 3-6. A full Access Control configuration

Click the Update button, wait for your AP to reboot, and then try to associate with it. The RADIUS server should keep you well apprised of the packets that it's receiving and sending. Here's some output from a successful association. As you can see from the following below, I'm currently using the Alternate format:

```
rad_recv: Access-Request packet from host 10.1.1.253:1812, id=28, length=70
        User-Password = "00306524e663"
        User-Name = "00306524e663"
        NAS-Identifier = "10.1.1.253"
        NAS-IP-Address = 10.1.1.253
```

This is a dump of the incoming RADIUS authentication packet. The NAS-Identifier comes from the AP, and the NAS-IP-Address is the AP's IP address. You could use this in your user file to further restrict access if you desired.

If you've gotten this far, the hard part is over. Now, arrange for your *radiusd* to start at system bootup, start it without the -X flag, and Bob's your uncle!

As I mentioned before, you'll need to restart the RADIUS server after adding or deleting access control entries. You can get around that requirement by storing the users entries in an SQL database, but that's significantly more effort, and would require a book of its own.

—*Cloyce Spradling*

H A C K   Authenticate Wireless Users
#44 Step up to using WPA Enterprise with FreeRADIUS for real user authentication and wireless security.

WPA is a big step up from WEP, security-wise. WPA's Pre-Shared Key mode (called WPA Personal, if you have an Apple AirPort) is handy and easy to set up. However, it allows only one key for all users. If you want to have different passwords for different users, or if you want real authentication, you'll need to use the full 802.11x-based WPA Enterprise protocol, and that means that you'll need a RADIUS server.

If you came here from "Control Wireless Access by MAC" [Hack #43], you've already got some fundamentals on how RADIUS works and where to configure it. If you haven't yet read that hack, now would be a good time to back up.

This hack is about setting up EAP/TTLS authentication via FreeRADIUS. EAP/TTLS isn't the only flavor of authentication protocol, but it is the easiest to set up and has the lowest per-client overhead. EAP/TLS is also good, but it requires each client to have its own certificate. EAP/PEAP is comparable to EAP/TTLS and is more commonly found in large enterprise networks.

FreeRADIUS is available at *http://www.freeradius.org* and is also available as a package in most flavors of Linux and BSD. Solaris and Mac OS X users will want to compile from source.

FreeRADIUS Configuration

As in "Control Wireless Access by MAC" [Hack #43], our example system configuration for FreeRADIUS is located in */etc/raddb*. Again, the first requirement is to allow your access point to talk to the RADIUS server. This setup happens in the */etc/raddb/clients.conf* file. Our sample configuration looks like this:

```
client 10.1.1.253 {
    secret = letmein
    shortname = travellingcircus
}
```

You'll also need an SSL certificate for the server. If you have a central place on the system for all of your various server certificates, you can place it there. If not, I recommend putting the certificate and private key in */etc/ raddb/certs*. If you don't already have a certificate, you can use the *certs.sh* script in the FreeRADIUS distribution to help you generate one.

Both the private key and the certificate should be in PEM format and can even be in the same file. The permissions on the private key are important; only the RADIUS server should be able to read it. If you run your RADIUS server as a non-root user (you should), just make sure that the RADIUS user owns the file and that its permissions are set to 400.

The */etc/raddb/eap.conf* file that comes with the FreeRADIUS distribution might require only a little customization, or you can use the *minimal* version shown here. Either way, you'll need to set the location of the private key file and the certificate file. This configuration happens in the tls section, which should be inside the eap section:

```
eap {
    default_eap_type = md5
    timer_expire      = 60
    ignore_unknown_eap_types = no
    cisco_accounting_username_bug = no
    md5 {
    }

    tls {
        private_key_password = blah
        private_key_file = ${raddbdir}/certs/radius.pem
        certificate_file = ${raddbdir}/certs/radius.pem
        CA_file = ${raddbdir}/certs/cacert.pem
        dh_file = ${raddbdir}/certs/dh
        random_file = ${raddbdir}/certs/random
    }

    ttls {
        default_eap_type = md5
        copy_request_to_tunnel = yes
        use_tunneled_reply = yes
    }
```

```
        peap {
            copy_request_to_tunnel = yes
            use_tunneled_reply = yes
            default_eap_type = md5
        }

    }
```

The key pieces here you need to modify are here:

```
private_key_file = ${raddbdir}/certs/radius.pem
certificate_file = ${raddbdir}/certs/radius.pem
```

If your private key has a password, you can set that also:

```
private_key_password = blah
```

Since that's pretty sensitive information, it should be protected in the same way as the private key file—that is, owned by the RADIUS user and chmod 400.

You'll also need to have a pointer to your Certificate Authority's certificate, which you can set like this:

```
CA_file = ${raddbdir}/certs/cacert.pem
```

Lastly, in the TTLS section, make sure that both of these lines are set to yes:

```
copy_request_to_tunnel = yes
use_tunneled_reply = yes
```

Otherwise, all of the attributes that the base station sends will not be available for use by the authentication module. In a basic setup, these settings might not be necessary. As you'll see later, the AP sends quite a lot of extra information that you can use to fine-tune permissions regarding who can access your network using which AP.

The only other configuration file that needs to be changed is */etc/raddb/ radiusd.conf*. In the modules section, make sure that the files module points to your users file:

```
files {
        usersfile = ${confdir}/users
        compat = no
}
```

Next, make sure to include *eap.conf*:

```
$INCLUDE ${confdir}/eap.conf
```

The authorize module should list both files and eap:

```
authorize {
        files
        eap
}
```

And finally, the authenticate module should list eap:

```
authenticate {
        eap
}
```

That's it for setting up the configuration files. Now, you'll need to set up a user. This part isn't any different than setting up any other RADIUS user. At a minimum, you need to list a user password (User-Password) and an authentication type (Auth-Type). The Auth-Type should always be Local.

An entry in the users file looks like this:

```
cloyce  Auth-Type := Local, User-Password == "sushi"
```

This says that for user cloyce, the Auth-Type is Local and the password *must* be sushi; otherwise, the access request will be denied.

Now that the files are all set up, it's time to start radiusd with the -X flag to get debugging output. If all goes well, you'll see output at the bottom:

```
Listening on authentication *:1812
Listening on accounting *:1813
Ready to process requests.
```

Access Point Configuration

Assuming that your RADIUS server started up, it's time to configure your AP. This section covers an Apple AirPort configuration, using the AirPort Admin Utility, as shown in Figure 3-7.

Click the Change Wireless Security… button and change the pull-down item at the top to WPA Enterprise. When that's done, the panel should change and have entries for a primary and secondary RADIUS server, as shown in Figure 3-8.

 Note that WPA Enterprise is not compatible with using RADIUS for MAC address–based access control, [Hack #43]. It's no loss, because WPA Enterprise provides for much finer-grained access control as well as authentication and encryption.

You must specify three pieces of information on this panel: the IP address of your RADIUS server, the port it's listening on, and the shared secret. The shared secret should match what you put in to the */etc/raddb/clients.conf* file. The port number to use is the one that *radiusd* reported as its authentication port when you started in debug mode.

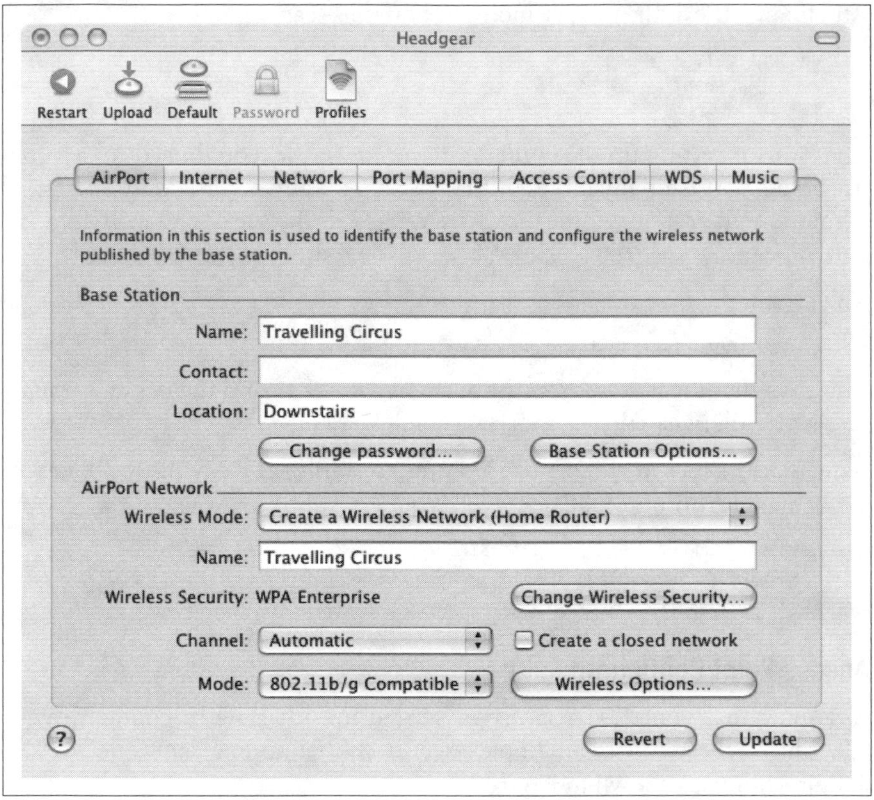

Figure 3-7. AirPort Admin Utility

Hit the Update button, wait for your AP to reboot, and then try to associate with it. Your client should prompt you for authentication of your username and password.

Here's some output from an access request that shows the attributes that the AirPort Express sends along with the username and password:

```
rlm_eap_ttls: Session established.  Proceeding to decode tunneled
attributes.
  TTLS: Got tunneled request
        User-Name = "cloyce"
        User-Password = "sushi"
        FreeRADIUS-Proxied-To = 127.0.0.1
  TTLS: Sending tunneled request
        User-Name = "cloyce"
        User-Password = "sushi"
        FreeRADIUS-Proxied-To = 127.0.0.1
        Framed-MTU = 1466
        NAS-IP-Address = 172.16.1.1
        NAS-Identifier = "Travelling Circus"
```

```
        Service-Type = Framed-User
        NAS-Port = 255
        NAS-Port-Type = Ethernet
        NAS-Port-Id = "wl0"
        Called-Station-Id = "00-11-24-03-45-77"
        Calling-Station-Id = "00-30-65-24-e6-63"
        Connect-Info = "CONNECT Ethernet 54Mbps Half duplex"
Processing the authorize section of radiusd.conf
```

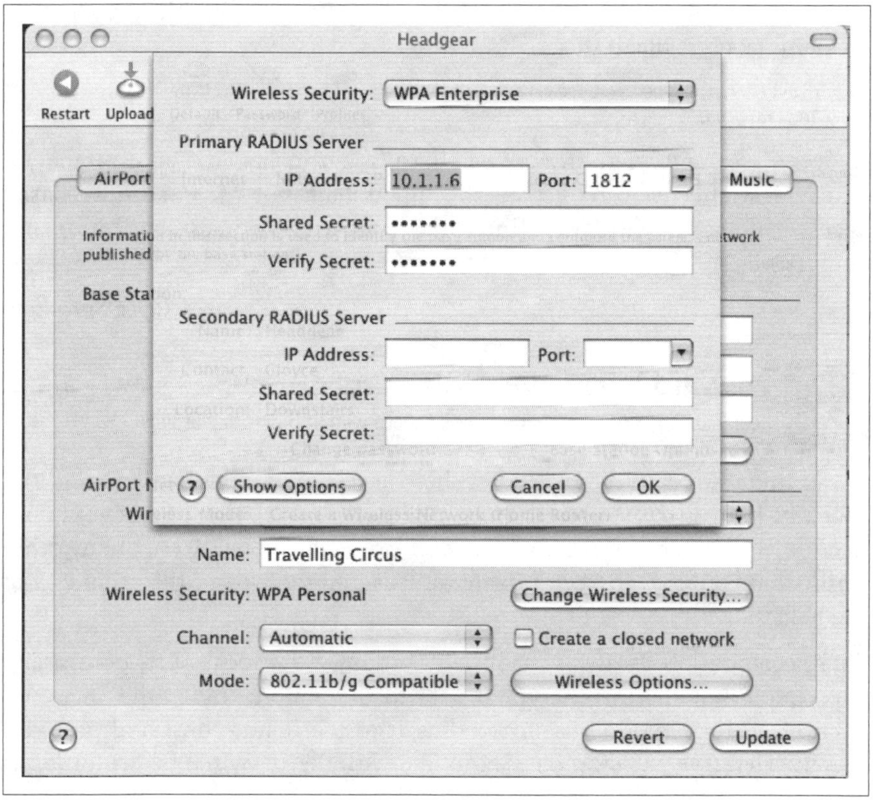

Figure 3-8. WPA Enterprise with RADIUS

The AirPort Extreme sends similar attributes; if you don't have an AirPort base station, just generate a request through your access point and see what it sends to the RADIUS server. This particular snippet is from deep within the request. If you read the comments in *eap.conf*, you'll have seen that EAP/ TTLS request is actually wrapped four times: RADIUS inside of EAP, inside of TLS, inside of Diameter, and inside of EAP. The attributes are printed each time the RADIUS server undoes another layer of wrapping. Look at the last instance to see exactly what's available to use for access control.

You can see my User-Name (cloyce) and my User-Password (sushi). Those are the only attributes that I supplied. Look at all the other stuff that the AP has added! Some of it isn't very useful, such as Framed-MTU, Service-Type, and NAS-Port. Other things, such as NAS-Identifier (the SNMP name you've assigned to the AP), Called-Station-Id (the MAC address of the AP's wireless interface), and Calling-Station-Id (the MAC address of the wireless device that I'm using to connect) can be useful. For example, if I want to make sure that I can use this AP only from my PowerBook, I just change my entry in the users file to this:

```
cloyce  Auth-Type := Local, User-Password == "sushi", Calling-Station-Id ==
"00-30-65-24-e6-63"
```

If every user entry requires a match to a particular Calling-Station-Id, you've just effectively replicated the functionality of MAC address–based access control, but with WPA Enterprise, you've also got authentication and encryption.

—Cloyce Spradling

HACK #45 Forward Ports over SSH

Keep network traffic to arbitrary ports secure with SSH port forwarding.

In addition to providing remote shell access and command execution, OpenSSH can also forward arbitrary TCP ports to the other end of your connection. This can be extremely handy for protecting email, web, or any other traffic that you need to keep private (at least, all the way to the other end of the SSH tunnel).

SSH accomplishes local forwarding by binding to a local port, performing encryption, sending the encrypted data to the remote end of the SSH connection, then decrypting it and sending it to the remote host and port you specify. Here, we will start an SSH tunnel with the -L switch (short for *local*) and use it to tunnel POP traffic on port 110:

```
# ssh -f -N -L110:mailhost:110 -l user mailhost
```

Naturally, substitute *user* with your username and *mailhost* with your mail server's name or IP address. Note that you will have to be root on your machine for this example, since you'll be binding to a privileged port (110, the POP port). You should also disable any locally running POP daemon (look in */etc/inetd.conf*) or it will get in the way.

Now, to encrypt all of your POP traffic, configure your mail client to connect to *localhost* port 110. It will happily talk to *mailhost* as if it were connected directly, except that the entire conversation will be encrypted.

The -f flag forks SSH into the background, and -N tells it not to actually run a command on the remote end, but just do the forwarding. If your SSH server supports it, try the -C switch to turn on compression. This can significantly improve the time it takes to download your email.

You can specify as many -L lines as you like when establishing the connection. To also forward outbound email traffic, try this:

```
# ssh -f -N -L110:mailhost:110 -L25:mailhost:25 -l user mailhost
```

Set your outbound email host to *localhost*, and your email traffic will be encrypted as far as *mailhost*. This generally is useful only if the email is bound for an internal host, or if you can't trust your local network connection (as is the case with most wireless networks). Obviously, once your email leaves *mailhost*, it will be transmitted in the clear, unless you've encrypted the message with a tool such as PGP or GPG.

If you're already logged into a remote host with SSH and need to forward a port quickly, try this:

1. Press Enter.
2. Type ~C.
3. You should be at an ssh> prompt. Enter the -L line as you would from the command line:

```
rob@catlin:~$
~C
(it doesn't echo)
ssh> -L8080:localhost:80

Forwarding port.
```

Your current shell then forwards local port 8080 to *catlin*'s port 80.

You can also allow other (remote) clients to connect to your forwarded port with the -g switch. If you're logged into a remote gateway that serves as a NAT for a private network, enter a command like this:

```
$ ssh -f -g -N -L8000:localhost:80 10.42.4.6
```

This command forwards all connections from the gateway's port 8000 to internal host 10.42.4.6's port 80. If the gateway has a live Internet address, anyone from the Net is allowed to connect to the web server on 10.42.4.6 as if it were running on port 8000 of the gateway.

Although SSH also has functionality for acting as a SOCKS 4 proxy with the -D switch [Hack #46], it just isn't well suited for routing all network traffic to the other end of a tunnel. You can use a real encapsulating tunnel such as *vtun* [Hack #47] in conjunction with SSH to forward everything.

See Also

- `man ssh`

- *SSH, The Secure Shell: The Definitive Guide* (*http://www.oreilly.com/catalog/sshtdg/*) by Daniel J. Barrett and Richard Silverman (O'Reilly)

HACK
#46   **Proxy Web Traffic over SSH**

Protect your web traffic using the basic VPN functionality built into SSH itself.

In the search for the perfect way to secure their wireless networks, many people overlook one of the most useful features of SSH: the -D switch. This simple little switch is buried within the SSH manpage, toward the bottom, and is described like this:

> Specifies a local "dynamic" application-level port forwarding. This works by allocating a socket to listen to port on the local side, and whenever a connection is made to this port, the connection is forwarded over the secure channel, and the application protocol is then used to determine where to connect to from the remote machine. Currently the SOCKS 4 protocol is supported, and SSH will act as a SOCKS 4 server. Only root can forward privileged ports. Dynamic port forwardings can also be specified in the configuration file.

This turns out to be an insanely useful feature if you have software that is capable of using a SOCKS 4 proxy—such as all modern web browsers, for instance. It effectively gives you an instant encrypted proxy server to any machine that you can SSH to. It does this without the need for further software, either on your laptop or on the remote server.

Just as with SSH port forwarding [Hack #45], the -D switch binds to the specified local port and encrypts any traffic to that port, sends it down the tunnel, and decrypts it on the other side. For example, to set up a SOCKS 4 proxy from local port 8080 to *remote* from your wireless laptop, type the following:

```
$ ssh -D 8080 remote ip
```

That's all there is to it. Now you simply specify localhost:8080 as the SOCKS 4 proxy in your application, and all connections made by that application will be sent down the encrypted tunnel. For example, to set your SOCKS proxy in Firefox, go to Preferences → General → Connection Settings, as shown in Figure 3-9.

Select "Manual proxy configuration," and type in localhost as the SOCKS host. Enter the port number (8080) that you passed to the -D switch, and be sure to check the SOCKS 4 button.

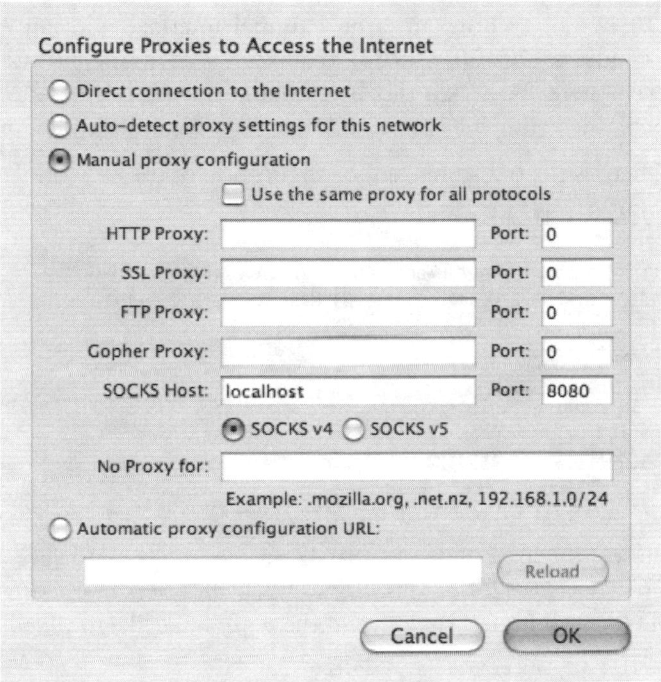

Figure 3-9. Proxy settings in Firefox

Click OK, and you're finished. All of the traffic that Firefox generates is now encrypted and appears to originate from the remote machine that you logged into with SSH. Anyone listening to your wireless traffic now sees a large volume of encrypted SSH traffic, but your actual data is well protected.

SOCKS 5 support is planned for an upcoming version of SSH, which will also make tunneled DNS resolution possible. This is particularly exciting for Mac OS X users, as there is support in the OS for SOCKS 5 proxies. Once SSH supports SOCKS 5, every native Mac OS X application will automatically be able to take advantage of encrypting SSH SOCKS proxies.

HACK
#47

Securely Connect Two Networks

Connect two networks together using vtun and a single SSH connection.

vtun is a user space tunnel server, allowing entire networks to be tunneled to each other using the *tun* universal tunnel kernel driver. Using an encrypted tunnel such as *vtun* allows roaming wireless clients to secure all of their IP traffic using strong encryption. It currently runs under Linux, BSD, and Mac OS X. These examples assume that you are using Linux.

The procedure described in this hack will allow a host with a private IP address (10.42.4.6) to bring up a new tunnel interface with an externally-routed IP address (208.201.239.33) that works as if the private network weren't even there. You'll do this by bringing up the tunnel, dropping the default route, then adding a new default route via the other end of the tunnel.

To begin, here is the (pre-tunneled) configuration of the network:

```
root@client:~# ifconfig eth2

eth2 Link encap:Ethernet HWaddr 00:02:2D:2A:27:EA
inet addr:10.42.3.2 Bcast:10.42.3.63 Mask:255.255.255.192
[snip]
root@client:~# route

Kernel IP routing table
Destination Gateway Genmask Flags Metric Ref Use Iface
10.42.3.0 * 255.255.255.192 U 0 0 0 eth2
loopback * 255.0.0.0 U 0 0 0 lo
default 10.42.3.1 0.0.0.0 UG 0 0 0 eth2
```

As you can see, the local network is 10.42.3.0/26, the IP is 10.42.3.2, and the default gateway is 10.42.3.1. This gateway provides network address translation (NAT) to the Internet. Here's what the path looks like to *yahoo.com*:

```
root@client:~# traceroute -n yahoo.com

traceroute to yahoo.com (64.58.79.230), 30 hops max, 40 byte packets
1 10.42.3.1 2.848 ms 2.304 ms 2.915 ms
2 209.204.179.1 16.654 ms 16.052 ms 19.224 ms
3 208.201.224.194 20.112 ms 20.863 ms 18.238 ms
4 208.201.224.5 213.466 ms 338.259 ms 357.7 ms
5 206.24.221.217 20.743 ms 23.504 ms 24.192 ms
6 206.24.210.62 22.379 ms 30.948 ms 54.475 ms
7 206.24.226.104 94.263 ms 94.192 ms 91.825 ms
8 206.24.238.61 97.107 ms 91.005 ms 91.133 ms
9 206.24.238.26 95.443 ms 98.846 ms 100.055 ms
10 216.109.66.7 92.133 ms 97.419 ms 94.22 ms
11 216.33.98.19 99.491 ms 94.661 ms 100.002 ms
12 216.35.210.126 97.945 ms 93.608 ms 95.347 ms
13 64.58.77.41 98.607 ms 99.588 ms 97.816 ms
```

vtun Setup

This example will connect to a tunnel server on the Internet at 208.201.239. 5. It has two spare live IP addresses (208.201.239.32 and 208.201.239.33) to be used for tunneling. I'll refer to that machine as the *server* and our local machine as the *client*.

Now, let's get the tunnel running. To begin, load the *tun* driver on both machines:

```
# modprobe tun
```

It is worth noting that the *tun* driver will sometimes fail if the kernel version on the server and client don't match. For best results, use a recent kernel, and the same version (e.g., 2.6.11) on both machines.

On the server machine, save this file to */usr/local/etc/vtund.conf*:

```
options {
port 5000;
ifconfig /sbin/ifconfig;
route /sbin/route;
syslog auth;
}

default {
compress no;
speed 0;
}

home {
type tun;
proto tcp;
stat yes;
keepalive yes;

pass sHHH; # Password is REQUIRED.

up {
ifconfig "%% 208.201.239.32 pointopoint 208.201.239.33";

program /sbin/arp "-Ds 208.201.239.33 %% pub";
program /sbin/arp "-Ds 208.201.239.33 eth0 pub";

route "add -net 10.42.0.0/16 gw 208.201.239.33";
};

down {
program /sbin/arp "-d 208.201.239.33 -i %%";
program /sbin/arp "-d 208.201.239.33 -i eth0";

route "del -net 10.42.0.0/16 gw 208.201.239.33";
};
}
```

Then launch the *vtund* server:

```
root@server:~# vtund -s
```

Now you'll need a *vtund.conf* file for the client side. Save this file as */usr/local/etc/vtund.conf* on the client side:

```
options {
port 5000;
ifconfig /sbin/ifconfig;
route /sbin/route;
}
```

```
default {
compress no;
speed 0;
}

home {
type tun;
proto tcp;
keepalive yes;

pass sHHH; # Password is REQUIRED.

up {
ifconfig "%% 208.201.239.33 pointopoint 208.201.239.32 arp";

route "add 208.201.239.5 gw 10.42.3.1";
route "del default";
route "add default gw 208.201.239.32";

};

down {
route "del default";
route "del 208.201.239.5 gw 10.42.3.1";
route "add default gw 10.42.3.1";
};
}
```

Finally, run this command on the client:

```
root@client:~# vtund -p home server
```

Presto! You now not only have a tunnel between *client* and *server*, but also have added a new default route via the other end of the tunnel. Take a look at what happens when we traceroute to *yahoo.com* with the tunnel in place:

```
root@client:~# traceroute -n yahoo.com

traceroute to yahoo.com (64.58.79.230), 30 hops max, 40 byte packets
1 208.201.239.32 24.368 ms 28.019 ms 19.114 ms
2 208.201.239.1 21.677 ms 22.644 ms 23.489 ms
3 208.201.224.194 20.41 ms 22.997 ms 23.788 ms
4 208.201.224.5 26.496 ms 23.8 ms 25.752 ms
5 206.24.221.217 26.174 ms 28.077 ms 26.344 ms
6 206.24.210.62 26.484 ms 27.851 ms 25.015 ms
7 206.24.226.103 104.22 ms 114.278 ms 108.575 ms
8 206.24.238.57 99.978 ms 99.028 ms 100.976 ms
9 206.24.238.26 103.749 ms 101.416 ms 101.09 ms
10 216.109.66.132 102.426 ms 104.222 ms 98.675 ms
11 216.33.98.19 99.985 ms 99.618 ms 103.827 ms
12 216.35.210.126 104.075 ms 103.247 ms 106.398 ms
13 64.58.77.41 107.219 ms 106.285 ms 101.169 ms
```

This means that any server processes running on *client* are now fully available to the Internet, at IP address 208.201.239.33. This has happened all without making a single change (e.g., port forwarding) on the gateway 10. 42.3.1.

Here's what the new tunnel interface looks like on the client:

```
root@client:~# ifconfig tun0

tun0 Link encap:Point-to-Point Protocol
inet addr:208.201.239.33 P-t-P:208.201.239.32 Mask:255.255.255.255
UP POINTOPOINT RUNNING MULTICAST MTU:1500 Metric:1
RX packets:39 errors:0 dropped:0 overruns:0 frame:0
TX packets:39 errors:0 dropped:0 overruns:0 carrier:0
collisions:0 txqueuelen:10
RX bytes:2220 (2.1 Kb) TX bytes:1560 (1.5 Kb)
```

And here's the updated routing table (note that we still need to keep a host route to the tunnel server's IP address via our old default gateway; otherwise, the tunnel traffic couldn't get out):

```
root@client:~# route

Kernel IP routing table
Destination Gateway Genmask Flags Metric Ref Use Iface
208.201.239.5 10.42.3.1 255.255.255.255 UGH 0 0 0 eth2
208.201.239.32 * 255.255.255.255 UH 0 0 0 tun0
10.42.3.0 * 255.255.255.192 U 0 0 0 eth2
10.42.4.0 * 255.255.255.192 U 0 0 0 eth0
loopback * 255.0.0.0 U 0 0 0 lo
default 208.201.239.32 0.0.0.0 UG 0 0 0 tun0
```

To bring down the tunnel, simply kill the vtund process on *client*. This restores all network settings back to their original state.

vtun with SSH

This method works fine, if you trust *vtun* to use strong encryption and to be free from remote exploits. Personally, I don't think you can be too paranoid when it comes to machines directly connected to the Internet. To use *vtun* over SSH (and therefore rely on the strong authentication and encryption that SSH provides), simply forward port 5000 on *client* to the same port on *server*. Give this a try:

```
root@client:~# ssh -f -N -c blowfish -C -L5000:localhost:5000 server
root@client:~# vtund -p home localhost
```

In order to discourage connections to *vtund* on port 5000 of the server, add an *iptables* rule to drop connections from the outside world:

```
root@server:~# iptables -A INPUT -t filter -i eth0 -p tcp --dport 5000 -j \
DROP
```

This allows local connections to get through (since they use loopback) and therefore requires an SSH tunnel to *server* before accepting a connection.

As you can see, this can be an extremely handy tool to have around. In addition to giving live IP addresses to machines behind a NAT, you can effectively connect any two networks together if you can obtain a single SSH connection between them (originating from either direction).

Tips and Tricks

While that should be enough information to get *vtund* up and running on your system, here are a couple of additional points to keep in mind.

- The session name (home in the preceding example) must match on the client *and* the server sides, or you'll get an ambiguous "server disconnected" message.

- The same goes for the password field in the *vtund.conf* file on both sides. It must be present *and* match on both sides, or the connection won't work.

- If you're having trouble connecting, make sure you're using the same kernel version on both sides, and that the server is up and running (try telnet server 5000 from the client side to verify that the server is happy).

- Try the direct method first, then get SSH working once you are happy with your *vtund.conf* settings.

If you're still having trouble, check */etc/syslog.conf* to see where your auth facility messages are going, and watch that log on both the client and server when trying to connect. It can be tricky getting *vtun* running the first time, but once it is properly configured, it works like a charm.

If your head is swimming from this *vtund.conf* configuration, or if you're feeling lazy and don't want to figure out what to change when setting up your own client's *vtund.conf* file, take a look at the automatic *vtund.conf* generator [Hack #48].

HACK #48   Generate a Tunnel Configuration Automatically

Generate a vtund.conf on the fly to match changing network conditions.

If you're trying to connect two networks securely with *vtun* [Hack #47] and have got a headache from trying to edit the configuration files, the script described in this Hack will help you generate a working *vtund.conf* for the client side automatically.

If you haven't read that hack (or if you've never used *vtun*), go back and read it before attempting to grok this bit of Perl. Essentially, it attempts to take the guesswork out of changing the routing table around on the client side by autodetecting the default gateway, and building the *vtund.conf* accordingly.

To configure the script, take a look at the Configuration section. The first line of $Config contains the addresses, port, and secret that were used in the *vtun* hack. The second is there simply as an example of how to add more.

To run the script, either call it as vtundconf home, or set $TunnelName to the one you want to use. Better yet, make symlinks to the script like this:

```
# ln -s vtundconf home
# ln -s vtundconf tunnel2
```

Then, generate the appropriate *vtund.conf* by calling the symlink directly:

```
# vtundconf home > /usr/local/etc/vtund.conf
```

The Code

Save this file as *vtundconf*, and run it each time you use a new wireless network to generate an appropriate *vtund.conf* for you on the fly:

```
#!/usr/bin/perl -w

# vtund wrapper in need of a better name.
#
# (c)2002 Schuyler Erle & Rob Flickenger
#
################ CONFIGURATION

# If TunnelName is blank, the wrapper will look at @ARGV or $0.
#
# Config is TunnelName, LocalIP, RemoteIP, TunnelHost, TunnelPort, Secret
#
my $TunnelName = "";
my $Config     = q{
   home    208.201.239.33 208.201.239.32 208.201.239.5  5000   sHHH
   tunnel2 10.0.1.100      10.0.1.1       192.168.1.4      6001 foobar
};

################ MAIN PROGRAM BEGINS HERE

use POSIX 'tmpnam';
use IO::File;
use File::Basename;
use strict;

# Where to find things...
#
$ENV{PATH}  = "/bin:/usr/bin:/usr/local/bin:/sbin:/usr/sbin:/usr/local/
[RETURN]
```

```
      sbin";
      my $IP_Match = '((?:\d{1,3}\.){3}\d{1,3})';          # match xxx.xxx.xxx.xxx
      my $Ifconfig = "ifconfig -a";
      my $Netstat = "netstat -rn";
      my $Vtund   = "/bin/echo";
      my $Debug   = 1;

      # Load the template from the data section.
      #
      my $template = join( "", );

      # Open a temp file -- adapted from Perl Cookbook, 1st Ed., sec. 7.5.
      #
      my ( $file, $name ) = ("", "");
      $name = tmpnam( )
        until $file = IO::File->new( $name, O_RDWR|O_CREAT|O_EXCL );
      END { unlink( $name ) or warn "Can't remove temporary file $name!\n"; }

      # If no TunnelName is specified, use the first thing on the command line,
      # or if there isn't one, the basename of the script.
      # This allows users to symlink different tunnel names to the same script.
      #
      $TunnelName ||= shift(@ARGV) || basename($0);
      die "Can't determine tunnel config to use!\n" unless $TunnelName;

      # Parse config.
      #
      my ($LocalIP, $RemoteIP, $TunnelHost, $TunnelPort, $Secret);
      for (split(/\r*\n+/, $Config)) {
        my ($conf, @vars) = grep( $_ ne "", split( /\s+/ ));
        next if not $conf or $conf =~ /^\s*#/o; # skip blank lines, comments
        if ($conf eq $TunnelName) {
          ($LocalIP, $RemoteIP, $TunnelHost, $TunnelPort, $Secret) = @vars;
          last;
        }
      }

      die "Can't determine configuration for TunnelName '$TunnelName'!\n"
        unless $RemoteIP and $TunnelHost and $TunnelPort;

      # Find the default gateway.
      #
      my ( $GatewayIP, $ExternalDevice );

      for (qx{ $Netstat }) {
        # In both Linux and BSD, the gateway is the next thing on the line,
        # and the interface is the last.
        #
        if ( /^(?:0.0.0.0|default)\s+(\S+)\s+.*?(\S+)\s*$/o ) {
          $GatewayIP = $1;
          $ExternalDevice = $2;
          last;
        }
      }
```

```perl
die "Can't determine default gateway!\n" unless $GatewayIP and
$ExternalDevice;

# Figure out the LocalIP and LocalNetwork.
#
my ( $LocalNetwork );
my ( $iface, $addr, $up, $network, $mask ) = "";

sub compute_netmask {
  ($addr, $mask) = @_;
  # We have to mask $addr with $mask because linux /sbin/route
  # complains if the network address doesn't match the netmask.
  #
  my @ip = split( /\./, $addr );
  my @mask = split( /\./, $mask );
  $ip[$_] = ($ip[$_] + 0) & ($mask[$_] + 0) for (0..$#ip);
  $addr = join(".", @ip);
  return $addr;
}

for (qx{ $Ifconfig }) {
  last unless defined $_;

  # If we got a new device, stash the previous one (if any).
  if ( /^([^\s:]+)/o ) {
    if ( $iface eq $ExternalDevice and $network and $up ) {
      $LocalNetwork = $network;
      last;
    }
    $iface = $1;
    $up = 0;
  ]

  # Get the network mask for the current interface.
  if ( /addr:$IP_Match.*?mask:$IP_Match/io ) {
    # Linux style ifconfig.
    compute_netmask($1, $2);
    $network = "$addr netmask $mask";
  } elsif ( /inet $IP_Match.*?mask 0x([a-f0-9]{8})/io ) {
    # BSD style ifconfig.
    ($addr, $mask) = ($1, $2);
    $mask = join(".", map( hex $_, $mask =~ /(..)/gs ));
    compute_netmask($addr, $mask);
    $network = "$addr/$mask";
  }

  # Ignore interfaces that are loopback devices or aren't up.
  $iface = "" if /\bLOOPBACK\b/o;
  $up++    if /\bUP\b/o;
}

die "Can't determine local IP address!\n" unless $LocalIP and $LocalNetwork;
```

```
# Set OS dependent variables.
#
my ( $GW, $NET, $PTP );
if ( $^O eq "linux" ) {
  $GW = "gw"; $PTP = "pointopoint"; $NET = "-net";
} else {
  $GW = $PTP = $NET = "";
}

# Parse the config template.
#
$template =~ s/(\$\w+)/$1/gee;

# Write the temp file and execute vtund.
#
if ($Debug) {
  print $template;
} else {
  print $file $template;
  close $file;
  system("$Vtund $name");
}

__DATA__

options {
  port $TunnelPort;
  ifconfig /sbin/ifconfig;
  route /sbin/route;
}

default {
  compress no;
  speed 0;
}

# 'mytunnel' should really be `basename $0` or some such
# for automagic config selection
$TunnelName {
  type tun;
  proto tcp;
  keepalive yes;

  pass $Secret;

  up {
   ifconfig "%% $LocalIP $PTP $RemoteIP arp";
   route "add $TunnelHost $GW $GatewayIP";
   route "delete default";
   route "add default $GW $RemoteIP";
   route "add $NET $LocalNetwork $GW $GatewayIP";
  };
```

```
    down {
     ifconfig "%% down";
     route "delete default";
     route "delete $TunnelHost $GW $GatewayIP";
     route "delete $NET $LocalNetwork";
     route "add default $GW $GatewayIP";
    };
}
```

You might be wondering why anyone would go to all of the trouble to make a script to generate a *vtund.conf* in the first place. Once you get the settings right, you'll never have to change them, right?

Well, usually that is the case. But consider the case of a Linux laptop that uses many different networks in the course of the day (say, a DSL line at home, Ethernet at work, and maybe a wireless connection at the local coffee shop). By running the *vtundconf* script once at each location, you will have a working configuration instantly, even if your IP and gateway are assigned by DHCP. This makes it easy to get up and running quickly with a live, routable IP address, regardless of the local network topology.

HACK #49 Poll Wireless Clients

Here's a quick and dirty method for determining who is on your local subnet.

This is a simple, quick hack, but it's useful in many circumstances. Suppose you are associated with a wireless network and are curious about who else is also using the network. You could fire up a network sniffer such as Ethereal [Hack #31] or *tcpdump* [Hack #33], or manually scan for associated clients using *nmap* [Hack #50], although that might be construed as antisocial. You're not so much interested in what people are doing, just how many people are online.

It is simple to find clients on your local network using the ubiquitous *ping* utility. Simply ping the broadcast address of your network and see who responds.

address by running *ifconfig* like so:

```
et HWaddr 00:40:63:C0:AA:4B
 Bcast:10.15.6.255 Mask:255.255.255.0
G MULTICAST MTU:1500 Metric:1
  errors:0 dropped:33 overruns:0 frame:0
  errors:1118 dropped:0 overruns:0 carrier:0
ielen:100
  (2930.8 Mb) TX bytes:1301320438 (1241.0 Mb)
 ldress:0xe800
```

There it is: the Bcast address. This is the broadcast address for your local subnet, which every machine is listening to. In Mac OS X and BSD, it is simply listed as the broadcast address:

```
$ ifconfig en1

en1: flags=8863<UP,BROADCAST,SMART,RUNNING,SIMPLEX,MULTICAST> mtu 1500
      inet6 fe80::230:65ff:fe03:e78a%en1 prefixlen 64 scopeid 0x5
      inet 10.15.6.49 netmask 0xffffff00 broadcast 10.15.6.255
      ether 00:30:65:03:e7:8a
      media: autoselect status: active
      supported media: autoselect
```

Most (but not all) machines will respond to a ping sent to this address. But simply running *ping* won't always leave enough time for the clients to respond between echo requests. Run *ping* with a long wait time (say, 60 seconds) between requests, and be sure to send at least one ping:

```
$ ping -c3 -i60 10.15.6.255

PING 10.15.6.255 (10.15.6.255): 56 octets data
64 octets from 10.15.6.1: icmp_seq=0 ttl=255 time=0.3 ms
64 octets from 10.15.6.72: icmp_seq=0 ttl=64 time=0.4 ms (DUP!)
64 octets from 10.15.6.61: icmp_seq=0 ttl=64 time=0.7 ms (DUP!)
64 octets from 10.15.6.65: icmp_seq=0 ttl=64 time=0.9 ms (DUP!)
64 octets from 10.15.6.64: icmp_seq=0 ttl=64 time=1.7 ms (DUP!)
64 octets from 10.15.6.66: icmp_seq=0 ttl=64 time=2.0 ms (DUP!)
64 octets from 10.15.6.69: icmp_seq=0 ttl=64 time=10.9 ms (DUP!)
64 octets from 10.15.6.68: icmp_seq=0 ttl=64 time=38.0 ms (DUP!)
^C
--- 10.15.6.255 ping statistics ---
1 packets transmitted, 1 packets received, +7 duplicates, 0% packet loss
round-trip min/avg/max = 0.3/6.9/38.0 ms
```

After duplicates (those suffixed with DUP!) stop arriving, press Ctrl-C to kill the running process, or wait 60 seconds for another try. This gives you a quick, rough idea of how many machines are connected to the local subnet.

Note that not all machines answer to broadcast ping requests, and some block ICMP traffic, which is *ping*'s protocol. Still, in terms of ease, speed, and ubiquity, you can't beat the results of the broadcast ping.

If you are curious about what kinds of wireless cards people are using, you might try looking up their serial numbers online [Hack #39].

HACK #50 Interrogate the Network

When you absolutely need to know everything you can about a network or host, nmap can help.

The network monitoring tools discussed so far all achieve their goals by passively listening to traffic on the network. You can often get better results by actually asking machines directly for information rather than waiting for them to divulge it on their own. To find out more information about a particular machine (or an entire network of machines), you need a good active scanning utility. One of the most advanced and widely used network scanners is *nmap*. It is available at *http://www.insecure.org/nmap*, and is best summarized by the description on the web site:

> *nmap* uses raw IP packets in novel ways to determine what hosts are available on the network, what services (ports) they are offering, what operating system (and OS version) they are running, what type of packet filters/firewalls are in use, and dozens of other characteristics.

The most common use for *nmap* is to scan the TCP ports on a machine to determine which services are available. If run as root, it can also use advanced TCP fingerprinting techniques to make an educated guess about the OS of the target machine:

```
# nmap -O 10.15.6.1


Starting nmap V. 3.75 ( www.insecure.org/nmap/ )
Interesting ports on florian.rob.swn (10.15.6.1):
(The 1590 ports scanned but not shown below are in state: closed)
Port       State      Service
22/tcp     open       ssh
53/tcp     open       domain
80/tcp     open       http
179/tcp    open       bgp
443/tcp    open       https
2601/tcp   filtered   zebra
```

also detect filtered TCP ports in addition to ports that accept connections. There is no guarantee that these services are actually in use, but since there is a firewall running, it's probably a good guess that at least some of them are active. Ports 10000 and 10005 are actually part of a home-grown monitoring system I'm using, as described in "Graph Your Wireless Performance" [Hack #38].

If you are curious about a particular user on your wireless network, *nmap* can tell you a good deal about the system they are running. Aside from scanning the ports of a single host, *nmap* can also scan entire networks. To fingerprint all of the machines on the local network, try something like this:

```
# nmap -sS -O 10.15.6.0/24
```

The /24 is *Classless Inter-Domain Routing* (CIDR) notation for the network mask, specifying that all IPs from 10.15.6.0 to 10.15.6.255 should be scanned. If the machine being scanned is running a good intrusion detection system (such as Snort; see *http://www.snort.org*), it might determine that a scan is in progress and take countermeasures. To try to work around this possibility, *nmap* provides a number of alternative scanning methods that can be very difficult to detect. The -sS switch tells *nmap* to use a stealth SYN scan rather than use a standard TCP connect. The scanning tool versus intrusion detection tool arms race has been going on ever since there have been such tools, and will likely continue for quite some time.

You can use *nmap* to help track down miscreants abusing your network or simply to take a poll of what your wireless users are running. It should be frequently used to probe your own machines to determine whether unexpected services suddenly crop up, or whether your firewall is properly configured. However you use it, *nmap* will provide valuable insight into the machines present on your wireless network.

HACK #51   Track Wireless Users

Automatically keep a database of MAC address to IP address mappings.

MAC address filters on access points are easily circumvented using commonly available tools. If your APs are bridged to the Ethernet segment [Hack #64], there are a couple of utilities you can use to look for people spoofing their MAC addresses. One such tool is *arpwatch*, available from *http://www-nrg.ee.lbl.gov/nrg.html*.

arpwatch runs as a daemon on any machine and keeps track of the MAC address/IP address pairs as ARP replies pass through the network. When it notices something out of the ordinary, it logs the activity to syslog and sends an email to the address of your choice. Aside from looking for suspicious activity, this also gives you a nice log of every new user on your wireless network. This can be fun to watch over time, particularly if you are running an open wireless network.

After you unpack the *arpwatch* archive, take a look at *addresses.h*. This is where the email address is set, so be sure to update it before you compile *arpwatch*. Set WATCHER to whatever you like. The default is root, which sends it to root at the machine that is running arpwatch.

You should be able to build and install the binaries with the usual commands:

```
/arpwatch-2.1a11# ./configure; make; make install
```

Unfortunately, this doesn't install all of the necessary pieces. In particular, *arpwatch* expects /usr/local/arpwatch to exist by default and to contain the *arp.dat* database file. It also looks in this directory for an Ethernet OUI to manufacturer a list to give more informative information about the machines it sees.

Check out "Find Radio Manufacturers by MAC" [Hack #39] for more details about the OUI portion of MAC addresses.

Create the necessary directory and files with the following commands:

```
/arpwatch-2.1a11# mkdir /usr/local/arpwatch
/arpwatch-2.1a11# cp ethercodes.dat /usr/local/arpwatch
/arpwatch-2.1a11# touch /usr/local/arpwatch/arp.dat
```

Finally, if you have sufficient space, you should install the manpages as well:

```
/arpwatch-2.1a11# cp *.8 /usr/local/man/man8
```

Now you can start *arpwatch* as a daemon. Use the -i switch to specify the interface you would like to watch:

```
# arpwatch -i eth0
```

If it doesn't seem to be running, it will log any problems to syslog.

```
ethernet address: 0:30:65:03:e7:8a
  ethernet vendor: APPLE COMPUTER, INC.
        timestamp: Monday, June 23, 2003 14:16:51 -0700
```

You will be notified by email whenever a new client is detected, when an already logged MAC address is seen in use with a new IP address, and when the MAC address associated with a particular IP changes. There are a number of legitimate reasons why IP-to-MAC address mappings might change, particularly if you are running a busy network with an insufficient number of available DHCP leases.

Regardless of the cause, *arpwatch* keeps a nice historical log of the traffic it sees, which can be valuable when tracking down potential miscreants. Since *arpwatch* logs to *syslog* as well as email, you can easily generate reports or graphs by processing these logs whenever you like.

While *arpwatch* faithfully logs everything it sees, it doesn't actually take any corrective action on its own. If you need an automated method for reacting to suspicious ARP or other activity on your network, take a look at Snort (*http://www.snort.org*).

## CHAPTER FOUR

Hardware Hacks
Hacks 52–62

Market forces have brought conventional wireless hardware down to unbelievably low prices in a very short time. At the time of this writing, the average 802.11g access point or wireless router costs less than $60, and prices continue to drop. These inexpensive devices are making it easier than ever for the average person to quickly set up their very own wireless network.

But what can you do with wireless hardware once you bring it home? As it turns out, quite a lot. You can replace the antennas and wireless cards to increase wireless transmission power, and build your own access point with off-the-shelf radio cards and hardware. In this chapter, you'll find all these hacks, as well as a number of hacks involving other types of wireless hardware.

HACK #52 Add an External Antenna
Improve the range of your laptop with an add-on antenna.

Possibly the most frequently asked question at any wireless user's group is "How can I make it go farther?" The single most effective means for increasing your range is to add antenna gain. Most people think of adding an exter-

Not all wireless cards accept external antennas. Some have removable antennas, allowing removal of the little plastic lump, and will accommodate two external antennas using pigtail adapters [Appendix A]. Others have no internal antenna at all and work only with an external antenna.

Here's an incomplete list of PCMCIA wireless cards that accept external antennas:

- Lucent/Orinoco/Proxim Gold or Silver 802.11b
- Senao/Engenius NL2511-EXT2 802.11b
- Cisco Aironet 350 802.11b
- Proxim Orinoco 11b/g 802.11g
- Buffalo AirStation 802.11g
- Wistron NeWeb CB9-GP 802.11a/b/g

Adding an external antenna to your laptop has two important effects. First, external antennas have much higher gain than the tiny dipole antennas contained in most wireless cards. Second, and possibly even more important, an external antenna brings the signal away from the desktop and the body of the computer, giving it more visibility, and making it easier to adjust the antenna to find the best possible signal.

While adding a proper external antenna will almost definitely increase your range, not all antennas are especially convenient. Here are three popular antennas that are quite small and unobtrusive.

Patch Antennas

HyperLink Technologies sells a 3.5" square, 8dBi patch antenna. It is small enough to Velcro to the back of a laptop, but it offers surprisingly high gain for the size (and price). It sells for $30 and is offered with a variety of connectors for different models of PCMCIA cards. You can find it online at *http://www.hyperlinktech.com/web/re09p.php*. A *patch* antenna is a directional antenna, with horizontal and vertical beam widths of 30 degrees.

Popsicle Omni Antennas

If you use a Lucent/Orinoco/Avaya/Proxim card (or a derivative, such as the AirPort), then you might have seen the Orinoco Range Extender. It is way overpriced, selling for about $65. It looks like a rectangular white popsicle stick with a heavy rubber base and long feed line, and is advertised as a 5dBi *omnidirectional* antenna. The Range Extender is available from *http://www.proxim.com/products/all/orinoco/client/rea/index.html*.

You can find a nearly identical version from HyperLink Technologies (*http://www.hyperlinktech.com/web/re05t.php*), which is much more reasonably priced at $15. As with the patch antenna, your main advantage is the ability to purchase the antenna with appropriate connectors for a variety of PCM-CIA cards.

If you need more gain, one of our antenna designs [Hack #83] works quite well with the popsicle stick antennas. The base is nice for sticking the antenna on a nearby table or shelf, but best of all, it is easily detached from the antenna. The stick on its own is portable and, like the patch, is well suited for a slab of Velcro on the back of your laptop LCD. Some antenna hackers have cracked it open, trimmed and resoldered the feed line, and glued it back together again to make the perfect length of wire for their laptop size (and cut down on unnecessary cable loss).

Rubber Ducky Antennas

Finally, if cost is an issue, you might consider recycling a discarded *rubber ducky* antenna from a WAP11, WET11, Cisco 350, or other access point. These are small, rugged black omnis or dipoles that offer 3 to 5 dBi gain. Some antennas even sport right-angle elbows.

A simple adapter or pigtail will let you use these low-gain antennas with your laptop, which is certainly better than leaving them to collect dust in a drawer. Pick a pigtail with as much flexible feed line as you need, and connect it to your laptop card. As always, be sure to check on the type of connectors you need for both ends of the pigtail (both the laptop card and the antenna will have unusual connectors). When in doubt, see Appendix B, or check the manufacturer's specs online.

HACK #53 Do-It-Yourself Access Point Hardware

Use one of these popular embedded PC boxes as a building block for your access point project.

point of view, as well as for reliability and ease of troubleshooting. While your dusty old 486 might be just taking up space, brand new embedded machines are coming down in price. These are tiny, fanless machines that are designed to run on DC power and boot from cheap compact flash RAM. This means no moving parts, simple ventilation requirements, and potentially very long uptimes.

Not all embedded solutions are necessarily cost effective. One notorious example is the PC/104 hardware used in industrial embedded applications. Although it offers relatively low performance, this hardware has a reputation for robustness and ease of programming, as well as the standard PC/ 104 *stackable* bus. But even its extreme popularity in the industrial world hasn't done much to bring down its price, relative to what is available in the general-purpose computing world.

Whatever hardware platform you choose, be sure that it meets your needs. When choosing a piece of hardware, you should remember to consider the number and type of radio and network interfaces, cooling and power requirements, size, RAM and CPU available, and of course, cost. Here are a number of solutions that DIY networks have found to bring a high performance-to-price ratio:

Linksys WRT54G (http://www.linksys.com)
> This might be the ultimate hackable embedded system. Linksys has released this wireless router in a number of flavors including the WAP54G access point, and the GS series with more onboard RAM and faster processors. Inside is a Broadcom CPU and radio, and out of the box it runs a custom 2.4 Linux kernel. You can pick up new WRT54G units online for around $50. There are also models from Asus, Buffalo, and Netgear with nearly identical internals. You can do a lot of hacking with the WRT54G, including running custom Linux images [Hack #67] and setting up mesh networking [Hack #68].

> Figure 4-1 shows a WRT54G Version 1.0 that has been taken apart. The operating system was corrupted while being hacked, and the box would not boot. A serial port has been soldered on to get a console and interrupt the boot process.

Soekris (http://www.soekris.com)
> Affectionately known as the "little green box," Soekris boards (shown in Figure 4-2) are a popular choice among do-it-yourself networkers. They are manufactured by Soekris Engineering in Santa Cruz, California. There are a number of Soekris models that work well as access points, with and without PCMCIA. All Soekris boards will boot from Compact Flash or the network via PXE. Most come standard with multiple

Figure 4-1 Slightly modified Linksys WRT54G

Ethernet interfaces, a mini-PCI slot, hardware watchdog, serial console, and various processor speeds. They are all fanless boards and use a DC power supply.

One popular model is the tiny Soekris net4826. It provides one Ethernet port, two mini PCI slots, USB, a 266 MHz Geode processor, 128 MB RAM, 64MB of integrated flash memory, and can be powered via Power over Ethernet. Most Soekris motherboards sell for $150 to $200.

Unfortunately, although the green metal Soekris case might be unique, it isn't watertight. If you are looking for a weatherproof Soekris kit com-

Figure 4-2. The Soekris net4826 motherboard

two Mini-PCI slots. The RouterBOARD 200 series is similar, and also includes PCMCIA support. Mikrotik also makes a commercial operating system that requires various licenses depending on functionality, but their boards will happily run Linux or BSD. WRAP boards cost around $175, while the RouterBOARD 200 series runs anywhere from $300 to $500. Mikrotik seems to be moving away from the DIY approach, and now offers a full line of rather expensive networking solutions.

PC Engines has its headquarters in Switzerland, while MikroTik is located in Latvia. Where they are available, these boards work quite well as wireless routers.

Via-based computers (http://www.via.com.tw)

There are a number of Via-based computers on the market. They are generally marked as desktop PCs, although small, fanless cases that take a DC power supply are becoming commonplace. As they are intended to be used as general purpose PCs, they typically have 500 MHz or better Via processors, on-board NICs, an IDE interface, USB, and a PCI slot. Even better is the MII series of motherboards, which include a CompactFlash reader as well as a Cardbus/PC card slot.

If you are looking for a fanless solution, be sure to get the 600 MHz version, because the 800 MHz and faster Via boards require a processor fan. A Via MII-6000E fanless motherboard (shown in Figure 4-3) without case, RAM, or storage, costs around $170 at the time of this writing.

Figure 4-3. A Via EPIA MII fanless motherboard

for my node on SeattleWireless). Fujitsu still makes the Stylistic series, although new machines are quite expensive (on par with modern laptops). The older 1000s or 1200s can frequently be found on the surplus market for less than $100.

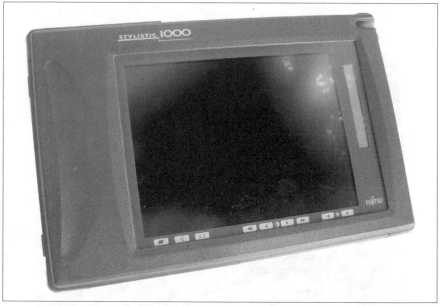

Figure 4-4. Fujitsu Stylistic 1000

Running your own custom access point can be considerably more challenging than the plug-and-play devices you can buy in consumer electronic stores, but building such devices can be much more rewarding as well. Bringing the power and flexibility of Linux or BSD to the access point itself can lead to all sorts of interesting possibilities that just can't be accomplished with most over-the-counter access points. For details on how to get your own Linux-powered access point set up, see "Build Your Own Access Point with Linux" [Hack #63].

HACK **Boot from a Compact Flash Hard Drive**
#54   Make your own tiny hard drive with no moving parts and low power consumption.

One challenge when building your own embedded wireless device is finding enough storage for the operating system and any data you need to keep track of. While 2.5" laptop hard drives probably have the highest ratio of storage space to physical space, they introduce a couple of challenges for an embedded system. A hard drive is a mechanical device, with fairly strict environmental operating conditions (for both temperature and humidity). They generate noise, draw a fair amount of power, and above all, are quite fragile. In other words, you probably wouldn't want to consider leaving one in a relatively unprotected plastic box on your roof through the winter or summer.

A popular alternative to traditional hard drives is to use flash RAM instead. Flash memory uses only a tiny fraction of the power that a hard drive uses, and it can operate over a much wider range of environmental conditions. It is tiny, lightweight, and noiseless. It can be rewritten many thousands of times, and can even be dropped on the floor without fear of loss of data. While it isn't nearly as cost effective in terms of price per bit, the popularity of digital cameras has driven flash memory prices down remarkably. If your application can fit in 32 MB to 2 GB of space, then flash storage is a viable alternative to 2.5" hard drives.

Many types of flash media can be used as a standard IDE device by using a simple converter, shown in Figure 1-5. One device I particularly like to use is the CFADPT-CS from Mesa Electronics. Their memory devices are available online at http://www.mesanet.com/diskcardinfo.html. It can be used on a standard IDE chain or with the SFF IDE found in laptops and embedded devices. As the SFF IDE bus provides power on the data cable (standard IDE doesn't), you'll need to connect a spare floppy power connector to the adapter when using it with standard IDE.

Once a CompactFlash card is inserted into the IDE adapter and attached to your computer, no further configuration is necessary. CF drives require no special drivers, and appear to be standard IDE devices to the host computer. Partition and format them as you would any other IDE device. Once an OS is installed, you can even boot from them.

Mesa also carries hard-to-find SFF IDE ribbon cable with connectors installed for a reasonable price—just ask. A number of suppliers carry CF-to-IDE adapters, and the going rate is about $20. While SmartMedia and Memory Stick adapters are also available, CF-to-IDE tends to be the cheapest way to go.

At the time of this writing, 512 MB compact flash cards are available for under $40, 256 MB cards are available for around $25, and 128 MB cards are going for an unbelievable price of under $20. These are ideal for running a micro distribution, such as Pebble [Hack #70] or m0n0wall [Hack #71]. Note that while you won't need one of these for use with the Soekris [Hack #53] as it boots from CF directly, these adapters will allow any computer with an IDE interface to eliminate its most unreliable component: the hard drive.

HACK #55 Increase the Range of a PowerBook

Radio waves don't penetrate metal well, but that shouldn't keep your PowerBook from getting online.

Apple's PowerBook is arguably one of the most aesthetically pleasing laptops on the market. Its wide-screen display is particularly striking, and like the rest of Apple's entire line, it can accommodate a built-in AirPort card. Unfortunately, while the choice of titanium or aluminum for an outer shell might make the PowerBook pleasing to the eye and touch, it wreaks havoc with wireless.

The all-metal case acts as an effective Faraday cage, blocking radio signals from anywhere but the tiny plastic antenna ports on either side of the keyboard. To make matters worse, the antenna ports coincide with the exact position that most people rest their hands when not typing. When this happens, it's all too common for connectivity to drop altogether as the client radio desperately tries to find a path to the access point (AP).

Apple made a stab at solving the problem with the latest PowerBooks, which have an aluminum skin instead of titanium. The properties of aluminum are such that the interference decreased, but did not go away. Some users report increased coverage simply by making sure that the antenna connector is firmly seated in the AirPort card, as it can sometimes become dislodged slightly after leaving the factory. But even with a perfectly operating card and antenna, PowerBooks routinely see about half of the range of the cheaper plastic iBooks, which have a much more visible internal antenna.

Fortunately, there is hope. Since the PowerBooks have a PCMCIA slot, it is perfectly possible to add another wireless card and use it instead of the built-in AirPort. The biggest drawback to this approach is that Apple's nicely integrated wireless tools work only with the internal AirPort card, so you will have to get used to using other means to control your wireless connection. But the two- to four-fold increase in range can be well worth the effort.

The WirelessDriver project lives on SourceForge at *http://wirelessdriver. sourceforge.net*. At the time of this writing, it is confirmed to support more than 40 different wireless cards under Mac OS X, and probably supports many more. It works with Prism-based cards as well as Hermes and Aironet cards. The software is available in a disk image installer, so no compilation is needed.

One popular add-on card is the EnGenius/Senao series, particularly the 2511. It puts out 200mW and is a particularly sensitive radio. It comes in two versions, with and without an internal amplifier. If you use the 2511 CD+EXT2, you need an external antenna, such as an 8dBi patch [Hack #52], as it has no internal antenna of its own. A good choice for a card with an internal antenna and an antenna connector is the Lucent/Orinoco/Proxim Silver or Gold card. Like the internal AirPort card, it puts out only 30mW, but is fairly sensitive, and quite inexpensive, averaging about $30 at this point.

Remember that the best thing you can do to improve the range of any wireless device is to make its antenna as visible as possible to the access point you are trying to communicate with. While an add-on card might not be as convenient as the built-in AirPort card, anything is better than hiding your antenna behind a suit of armor.

**HACK
#56**

Send Power over Your Ethernet

Power your access point with

travels well over CAT5 cable; a 2.4 GHz signal doesn't do as well over antenna cabling. Also, Ethernet cabling is much cheaper than antenna cable such as LMR400. This hack demonstrates how to build a simple PoE module pair.

In June 2003, the IEEE ratified the 802.3af standard for Power over Ethernet, which has spurred the release of standards-compliant PoE products. 802.3af defines two types of power source equipment: *end-span* and *mid-span* devices. An end-span device is an Ethernet switch with embedded PoE technology. These switches deliver data and power over the same wiring pairs: 1/2 and 3/6.

We're going to build a pair of mid-span devices, which in the 802.3af specification can be placed between a legacy switch and the device to be powered. A mid-span device has an RJ-45 data input and a power input, and it sends the data on pairs 1/2 and 3/6, while sending power on the unused 4/5 and 7/8 pairs.

Step by Step

If you have a device such as a VoIP phone or a Soekris PC that will accept Power over Ethernet without a secondary adapter, you will only need to build the power injector in steps 1–3.

 Don't try this unless you have some knowledge of electricity. 12v isn't going to kill you, but you might cause serious damage to your access point and other equipment.

1. Solder wires to the DC Male Power Plug. Solder one pair (two wires twisted together) to the inner-contact connection. These will be the positive power wires. Solder another pair to the outer-contact connection. Notice that there are three connectors on this DC male power plug. One is for the center pin, one is for the outer surface, and one goes to the plug housing. You do not need to solder anything to the plug-housing connector. Figure 4-6 shows what it should look like when finished.

2. Drill a hole in your two-port mount housing. Mount the male DC plug in the housing, as shown in Figure 4-7.

Figure 4-6. The completed power plug

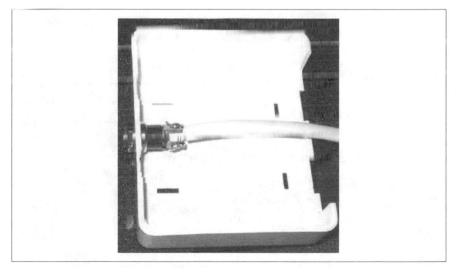

Figure 4-7. The DC plug mounted in the housing

3. Connect the wires in your two-port jack as foll...

4. Wire the one port wall mount jack as follows:

Output plug		Input jack		DC plug
Pin 1	<->	Pin 1		
Pin 2	<->	Pin 2		
Pin 3	<->	Pin 3		
		Pin 4	<->	DC Positive Wire 1 → Center Connector
		Pin 5	<->	DC Positive Wire 2 → Center Connector
Pin 6	<->	Pin 6		
		Pin 7	<->	DC Negative Wire 1 → Outer Connector
		Pin 8	<->	DC Negative Wire 2 → Outer Connector

5. Plug in and test. Figure 4-8 shows the completed modules.

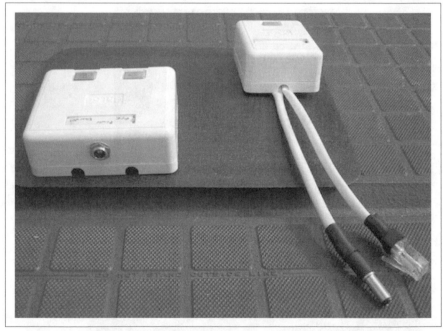

Figure 4-8. The completed PoE modules

Resistance Is Futile

The DC resistance of CAT5 is about 3 ohms per 100 feet per conductor, so a 250-foot cable has at least 7 ohms resistance. Most of the time, an AP draws much less than 0.8A, so you would still be above 6V at the AP. In fact, the access points typically use linear regulators to drop the voltage down to 5V on their insides, so as long as you're giving them something better than 6V at the terminals, they're likely to work.

There is a good calculator online at *http://www.gweep.net/~sfoskett/tech/ poecalc.html* that calculates the voltage drop for a given length of CAT5. Use it to estimate how much power you need to provide at one end of your cable run in order to power your access point.

—*Terry Schmidt*

HACK #57 The NoCat Night Light

Put your AP where everyone can see it: on the ceiling.

Back in May 2003, some friends and I were hanging out at a really good coffee shop in Sebastopol, CA. This particular coffee shop is housed in an old wooden train station building, with high ceilings, old-style hanging industrial lamps, and even a couple old trains still on the tracks, serving as small businesses.

Unfortunately, there's no wireless available at this shop. There was, once upon a time, back when the O'Reilly offices were located across the street. But that was ages ago, and even then the signal wasn't all that it could have been. As we sat around drinking our high-octane beverages, we got to talking about the best way to provide coverage in such a huge space. The room we were in was a common room, open at all hours (the front entrance is huge, and doesn't even have a door.) While you could put an access point in one of the enclosed shops in the building, coverage in the open area would likely be spotty at best. You would want the AP to be located high up off the ground, where everyone could see it.

Almost simultaneously, we all looked up and noticed the lamps hanging from the wooden rafters. What if you could house an AP in a package the size of a large light bulb and install it in an existing light socket? This seemed like a good idea, but how would you get network access to it without running CAT5 to the socket? Easy: Powerline Ethernet.

With the recent release of the Siemens' SpeedStream series of tiny

Figure 4-9. The tiny SpeedStream Powerline AP

One of our first concerns was practical rather than technical. Obviously, if you're going to replace a light bulb with an access point, the room will likely get darker. That is, unless the AP can also provide light as well. After fooling with a couple of lighting ideas, we finally soldered some copper romex onto a fluorescent bulb as a prototype. The romex is rigid enough to hold the lamp steady, and easy to solder. The fluorescent bulb would obviously be dimmer than a 300-Watt spot lamp, but it would be better than nothing. And as a flourescent runs much cooler, it probably wouldn't turn the guts of the access point to liquid. This solved the light issue well enough for the moment, but how could we connect the whole thing to a standard light bulb socket?

One trip to the hardware store later, we had a variety of Edison plugs, sockets, and adapters. We settled on a simple extender type of device, with a female socket on one side and a male plug on the other. Again, the contacts were copper, making it easy to solder on more romex, as shown in Figure 4-10. We had the basic design together, but what could we possibly use for housing?

Tupperware, of course. Adam painted the inside of a Tupperware bowl white, and the entire device just managed to squeeze inside. We first attempted to take the SpeedStream unit apart to save space, but it's already tightly packed inside; much of the unit is occupied by a large transformer. Besides, keeping the original enclosure made us all feel a bit more relaxed about plugging the thing in. The Edison plug poked through the bottom of the bowl, where we simply screwed on another connector to keep it tightly attached.

Figure 4-10. The AP, Edison connector, and bulb connected with romex

So, with all of the technical considerations accounted for, all that was left was the all-important marketing phase of the project. Some electrical tape and one vinyl sticker later, the NoCat Night Light was born! See it in all of its glory in Figure 4-11.

But how well would it actually work? Wouldn't the fluorescent throw off all sorts of noise that would interfere with the AP? We certainly thought so. Unfortunately, we didn't have a machine handy with which to do real throughput testing, but DSL Reports (*http://www.dslreports.com/stest*) showed a very respectable 2 Mbps or so. This was well above the rated capacity of the cable modem network we were using, so we were definitely satisfied with the results.

Figure 4-11. The completed "light bulb"

would be a good idea to insulate the bare contacts and find a better way of ventilating the fluorescent bulb (or replacing it altogether with an LED array). Build it at your own risk, but by all means have fun while doing it.

The Night Light Cabal:

—*Rob Flickenger (Design)*
—*Adam Flaherty (Construction)*
—*Jim Rosenbaum (Funding)*
—*Nate Boblitt and Roger Weeks (Idea Rats)*

HACK #58 Upgrade the Linksys WET11

Significantly increase the range, sensitivity, and functionality of your WET11.

The Linksys WET11 (*http://www.linksys.com/products/product.asp?prid=432*) is one of the most inexpensive Ethernet client bridge products on the market. It works with virtually any Ethernet device, and doesn't require any special drivers to configure. Many people use the WET11 to connect devices that otherwise can't accommodate a radio with their wireless network. For example, they are ideal for connecting to networked appliances such as the PlayStation 2 or Xbox to avoid having to run Ethernet cable to your television.

Linksys has manufactured the WET11 for several years. Its popularity can be gauged by looking at the Linksys web page and noting how many other 802.11b-only devices are still being sold (hint: not many). It has a big brother called the WET54G, but it is expensive and is not hacked as easily as the WET11.

As with all embedded hardware devices (particularly those manufactured by Linksys), it is a good idea to keep up on firmware updates. Updated firmware usually resolves most flaky behavior and occasionally even gives you a couple of new features. Previous firmware updates have fixed problems with DHCP.

The WET11 even has a crossover switch for the Ethernet side, making it simple to install, regardless of whether you are using a straight-through or crossover cable. Its tiny size and simplicity make it an ideal component for any situation where you need to get an Ethernet device to act as a client to an access point.

A WET11 can also be used to get entire networks online when used in conjunction with inexpensive firewalls like the Linksys BEFSR41. Simply connect the WET11 to the WAN port on the firewall, and every device plugged into it can share the WET11's wireless connection. People have had mixed results when using the WET11 directly bridged to a hub or switch, due to the implementation of the tiny device's MAC address handling.

But these features aren't nearly enough for wireless hackers. Here are a couple of nifty hacks for this piece of hardware.

Add an Antenna

The WET11 can easily accommodate an external antenna. Simply unscrew the small *rubber ducky* antenna and replace it with an RP-SMA pigtail [Appendix B] and an omni antenna of your choice. This alone significantly improves the range of the WET11 and, when using a directional antenna, can help reject noise and cause less interference f

(or EnGenius) 2511 Plus EXT 2 is an ideal card, as it even uses the same internal antenna connector, making the upgrade easy. Before you proceed, upgrade the replacement card with the latest firmware. Details on upgrading Prism 2 firmware can be found at *http://linux.junsun.net/intersil-prism*.

Unplug the Ethernet and power from the WET11. Remove the rubber feet from the bottom of the WET11 and open the case. Carefully unplug the antenna connector, unscrew the card from the brass stand-offs, and remove the internal card. Unfortunately, you won't be able to reuse the standoff screws, as the replacement card has a slightly different physical packaging.

Plug in the new card, and reconnect the antenna cable to it. If the PCMCIA card is oriented with the antenna connectors toward the right (and the Senao/EnGenius label is facing you), you want to use the connector on the top. This is the same side that was connected to the original card.

Finally, reassemble the case and power it up. You should now be enjoying the benefits of a much more sensitive radio and a full 200mW of power. Figure 4-12 shows an open WET11 with a Senao 200mw radio card and pigtail.

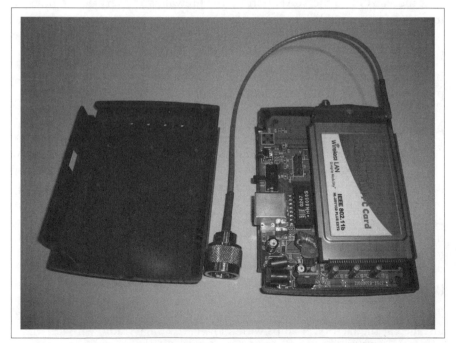

Figure 4-12. A 200mw WET11 bridge

Use a Battery Pack

The WET11 is expecting a 5V DC power source. A number of people have reported success using the WET11 with a battery pack in the field. Using four NiMH batteries in a series (at approximately 1.2V each) yields a 4.8V battery, which seems to work fine for several hours with the WET11. The WET11 can accept voltages a bit higher than 5 volts (some say as high as 12V), so you could even theoretically use four Alkaline batteries (4 × 1.5V – 6V). If you make your own battery pack, be sure to observe the proper polarity! Also note that operating time will likely be significantly shorter if you transmit a lot and use the 200mW card as described previously.

An external battery pack can be handy for generating a signal source when doing a site survey, or for hiding a signal source in a game of wireless hide-and-seek. There is a detailed discussion, with photos, online from a Belgian site at *http://reseaucitoyen.be/?SourcePortable* (be warned; the entire site is in French). With the size and ubiquity of the WET11, it's no wonder that so many people are hacking on it.

Scan for Wireless Networks Automatically

#59
Build yourself a motorized scanner that shows you all wireless networks in 360 degrees.

If you've done any number of wireless surveys, you know that one of the most time-consuming parts of the survey is moving the antenna. This is especially true if you are working with highly directional antennas. Sometimes, you might not have another person with you to move the antenna and take signal measurements.

The Automatic WLAN Scanner (AWS) is designed to help with these problems. It will perform a 360-degree scan for wireless networks and then give you the SSID, signal strength, noise, and best antenna position for all discovered networks.

- Reverse-SMA microwave connector
- Screws
- Hot glue gun
- Stepping motor
- Cantenna [Hack #86]
- Orinoco 802.11b wireless card
- Antenna cable & pigtail
- SMC800 Stepping motor steering card
- Ball bearings
- Worm drive
- Cog-wheel or toothed wheel

Construction

You could build the cantenna by following the instructions in "Pirouette Can Waveguide" [Hack #86]. However, I've made a modification to the design, as shown in Figure 4-13. I disassembled an omni antenna with a magnetic base. At the top of the magnetic base is a female Reverse SMA [Appendix A]) connector. Therefore, I constructed the cantenna with a male Reverse SMA connector, so that the cantenna easily screws onto the magnetic base.

Figure 4-13. Cantenna with magnetic base

Once you have completed the cantenna, the next step is to build the base, which will house the motor, worm gear, cog-wheel, and ball bearings to drive the cantenna. Figure 4-14 shows an overview of the assembled base, turned upside down. I used a hard drive frame from an ATX computer case, but you could cut your own sheet metal as well.

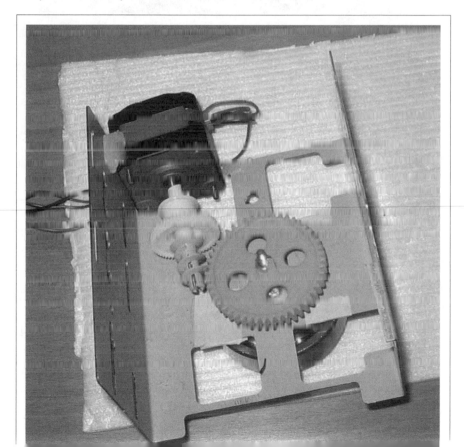

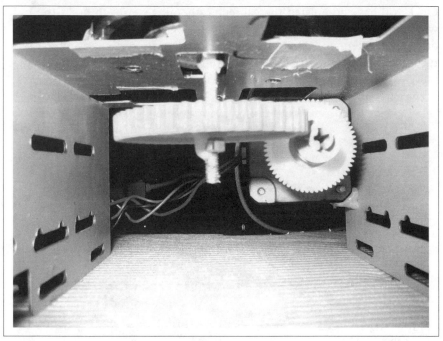

Figure 4-15. Close-up view of cog-wheel mounting

you don't lose the location. Next, use the hot glue gun to hold the motor in place on the metal hard disk frame.

With the base constructed, you can now turn it over, as shown in Figure 4-16. The ball bearing will rotate under command of the stepper motor and worm drive, and the magnetic base of the antenna will hold the can firmly in place while the motor turns.

I chose to house the SMC800 card in a small metal tin, which gives the card protection when the lid is closed. One end of the tin is cut out to allow connection of the parallel cable to the SMC800. In the other end of the tin, I punched a small hole for the power cables. The three power cables from one side of the ATX power cable were ran through the tin and connected to the SMC800 card pins that drive the external motor, and the other side of the connector was wired directly to the motor.

Power is supplied to the SMC800 card using an external AC/DC adapter. Prior to the installation of the card in the red tin, I made a third hole to allow insertion of the power adapter to the card. Figure 4-17 shows the power and data connections to the card.

Figure 4-16. The base ready for antenna mounting

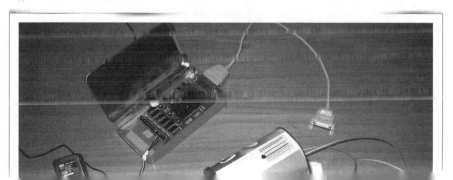

The hardware construction of the AWS is complete at this point. For my finished unit, shown in Figure 4-18, I spray-painted the tin and the cantenna and enclosed the base in waterproof vinyl. Lastly, I sealed the area between the ball bearing and the vinyl with hot glue.

Figure 4-18. The finished AWS hardware

Software

The SMC800 is an old card that has only DOS drivers available. Since my project relies on NetStumbler [Hack #24] to discover the wireless networks, I had to write new Windows XP drivers for the SMC800. These drivers, along with the other software I wrote for the project, are all available on my web site at *http://aws.netzfund.de*.

The second necessary piece of software is a Visual Basic script, which runs under NetStumbler and reads out the necessary wireless data.

The third piece is the AWS control software, which uses the new driver for the SMC800 to control the card over the parallel interface. Using the software, you can set your own scan speed, depending on your requirements. You can also start and stop the scan, and then go to a specific stepping position on the motor.

The AWS software receives input from the Visual Basic script running with NetStumbler, and shows the data as it is received. Figure 4-19 shows the AWS software up and running.

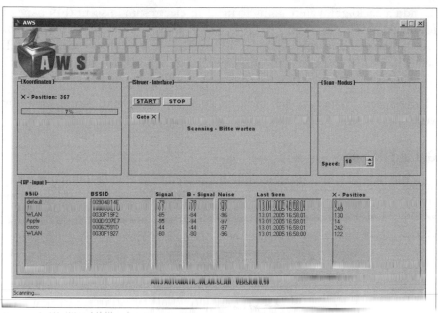

Figure 4-14. The AWS software in action

Hacking the Hack

The next feature that I plan for AWS is a position-locating system, so that AWS will steer the antenna in real time to follow a moving wireless source. Obviously, one limitation of the AWS as built is that it is capable of scanning only on a single flat plane. In order to scan above or below the horizon, you will need a variable mount for the cantenna.

—*Marcel Bilal*

Backlight Your Zipit

#60 Add a backlight to this tiny wireless communicator, so you can use it in the

To add a backlight, you're going to need an electro-luminiscent (EL) panel. I found a suitable piece of EL panel for this hack at Miller Engineering (*http://www.microstru.com*). Secondly, you'll need a driver chip to make the EL panel work. I found a chip already mounted to a tiny board from Jelu (*http://www.jelu.se/shop/product_info.php?cPath=1_29&products_id=33*).

Here's a step-by-step account of how I added the backlight. No, I won't buy you a new Zipit if you break yours while attempting this.

Getting It Open

Flip the little guy over. Unscrew the battery cover and yank the battery. Pry up the tiny rubber feet to reveal four Phillips-head screws, as shown in Figure 4-20.

Figure 4-20. Carefully opening the Zipit

Remove them. The entire bottom should come off easily. On my unit, the sticker covering the battery area was stuck to the CPU, so you might have to gently pry that up with a screwdriver. Be careful as you pull the bottom off, because the speaker is attached to a recess in the bottom with gummy glue. Pry up the speaker and completely remove the bottom shell.

Be careful not to lose the power button cover. Take it off and put it where you put the case screws (and don't lose those either).

Removing the Mainboard

You'll need a soldering iron for this step. First, apply heat to the antenna connector cable and remove it from the board. Next, lift the white part of the plastic LCD panel connector (it should swing away from the board) and gently remove the brown ribbon cable.

Put the mainboard and keyboard membrane aside. You can remove the rubber keyboard too if you like.

Opening the LCD

Open the Zipit lid, and remove the teeny rubber discs on the inside of the hinge. Remove the exposed Phillips head screws.

Leave the Zipit open and flip it back over, as shown in Figure 4-21.

Figure 4-21. The open Zipit case

Don't use a metal screwdriver; if you do, you'll leave nasty marks on the edge of the case. You have to pull pretty hard to unsnap the case, and directional pressure doesn't really help. Just yank the thing and it'll pop open.

Also, be careful when prying this apart not to lose the lid latch and spring. You can probably live without them, but if you want to keep them, now is your chance not to let them fly across the room or fall behind the workbench.

Removing the LCD Reflector

If all went well, you should see the white backing of the LCD panel, as well as more brown ribbon cable and the lid antenna, as shown in Figure 4-22. The white backing is held to the LCD with a sort of thick rubber cement. You need to peel this backing off and replace it with EL panel. The cement will stick to the LCD.

Figure 4-22. White LCD panel backing

Pick at a corner of the backing with a razor blade (or a fingernail). Try to peel off the backing all in one piece, pulling firmly away from the LCD. Keep in mind that the LCD is made of glass and is very, very fragile. You also don't want to touch the gummy cement with your fingers or any tools, since any marks you make in it will be visible when you install the backlight.

When the backing has been removed, it should look something like Figure 4-23.

Figure 4-23. LCD panel backing removed

Preparing and Installing the EL Panel

You should now be able to estimate how much EL panel you will need to cover the LCD. Trim yourself a nice piece using a pair of scissors. It should overlap the LCD panel on three sides by a couple of millimeters. On the side nearest the antenna, leave one set of leads and trim off the rest, as shown in Figure 4-24.

Once you have trimmed the panel, place it gently on the LCD. I installed mine sort of like you install a piece of linoleum floor. You want to avoid air bubbles, so start in the middle and gently press the panel out towards the edges. Try to push any air bubbles all the way to the edge. If you trap a bubble, start over by pulling the panel all the way back off. This is easier than stripping the backing, since the panel is made of plastic. Remember, that's delicate glass you're pushing on, so don't press too hard.

Wiring

Solder a couple of wires to the leads on the EL panel, similar to Figure 4-25. I used ribbon wire salvaged from an old floppy disk cable. It should be at least eight or nine inches long, preferably stranded, and as thin as you can find (recycled CAT5 cable is way too thick). Remember that plastic will melt if you're not careful with your soldering, so be quick.

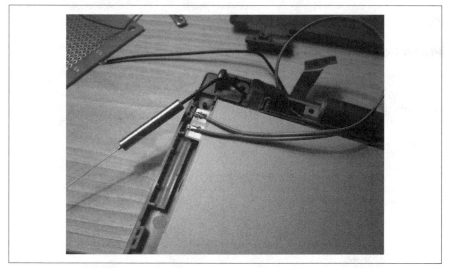

Figure 4-25. Soldering carefully

Run this wire the same way the antenna wire is run. Cover the exposed leads on the EL panel with a piece of electrical tape.

Flip the Zipit back over, and put the mainboard back in place. Feed the antenna cable and the two wires through the hole closest to the LCD panel connector.

Now comes the fun part: soldering the leads to the mainboard, as shown in Figure 4-26. Attach one wire each to the plus and minus poles on the battery connector. Solder a third wire to the corner pin on RP4, on the R108 side closest to C116.

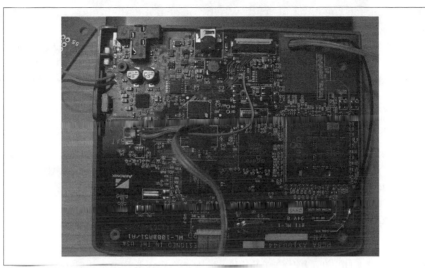

Figure 4-26. Soldering the leads even more carefully

Figure 4-27 shows a detail with the proper pin labeled EN.

Finally, reattach the antenna lead. When you're done, it should look like the unit shown in Figure 4-26. If your soldering iron isn't fine enough to solder the third wire, don't panic. This pin is pulled high when the LCD panel is active, so once we figure out power management on the board, this wire will turn the backlight on and off when the lid is closed. Of course, we haven't figured out power management as of this writing, so the backlight stays on all the time anyway under Linux. If you're running the Zipit messaging client, the backlight works beautifully and turns off to save battery time.

If you can't get this wire attached without destroying the board, just connect that wire directly to power and the backlight will stay lit all the time. It's not ideal, but it's better than nothing.

The Driver Board

Now, solder in the EL panel driver board. The driver board from Jelu is based on the Supertex HV857MG driver (it's pretty much a nice little implementation of the reference design). I've noticed that this chip isn't designed to drive a panel as big as the one for our Zipit, so it ends up being a mellow blue instead of bright white. If you change the chip to an HV826 or HV830, it should be much brighter. I'll likely give that a try at some point. Figure 4-28 shows the finished unclosed case with a close-up of the driver board.

Figure 4-28. Jelu EL driver board

Connect LA and LB to your EL panel (it doesn't matter which is which), and connect GND to minus, VDD to plus, and EN to the remaining wire. At this point, you probably will want to connect the battery and power up the Zipit to be sure that everything works as expected. Don't touch the driver board while it's on, unless you are partial to electric shocks for fun.

If all went well, completely cover the driver board in electrical tape and carefully reassemble the Zipit. There's plenty of room for the driver board in the channel next to the battery compartment.

Congratulations! You can now use your Zipit in lighting other than direct bright sunlight!

Hacking the Hack

Removal is the reverse of installation.

I'm definitely going to try a different EL driver chip to get the brightness up a bit. But the Jelu model should get you going. These things are really neat; you typically need a big, whiney transformer to drive EL, but these driver chips are small, quiet, and efficient. A tiny driver board combined with a light that you can cut with scissors to any shape should make it easy to add a backlight to just about any transparent LCD display.

HACK #61 Unwire Your Pistol Mouse

Why be stuck with a short cable when you can use Bluetooth in your pistol mouse instead?

The PistolMouse FPS by MonsterGecko (*http://www.monstergecko.com/ products.html*) is a great way to play first-person shooters. However, when you're at a LAN party and you want to wave the thing around after fragging your friends, you are rudely reminded of the short USB cord handing from the front of the unit.

By taking the main board out of a largus AMBATIIC Bl...... d Mini M

Figure 4-29. The PistolMouse FPS and Targus Bluetooth Mini Mouse

- 22 +/- 2 gauge stranded wire
- Heat shrink tubing for above wire
- Solder
- Liquid Solder Flux
- Desoldering tape or desoldering tool
- 2 AA Battery Holder from Radio Shack (catalog # 270-408)
- Philips screwdriver set
- Hex screwdriver set
- Soldering iron
- Multimeter for checking continuity
- Dremel tool or similar

Next, if you haven't already, test out both the PistolMouse and the Targus mouse to make sure they both function properly with the system where you plan to use them.

Disassembly

If you have any questions during the project process, check my Flickr photoset at *http://www.flickr.com/photos/_boseis/494023*, which contains 21 pictures of the process (I obviously couldn't include them all in this hack).

Disassemble the MiniMouse by removing the two small mouse feet stickers near the rear of the mouse. This will expose two screws. Remove these. Open the mouse and remove the battery cover. Then, remove the blue frame from the mouse, which is latched toward the front of the mouse with clips, as shown in Figure 4-30.

the LED on the back of the main board, because this is usually too large to keep in the finished device.

Disassemble the PistolMouse FPS with the Phillips screwdriver on the bottom and using a hex screwdriver on the sides. You will have to remove the red plastic grip (attached just with friction on the left side of the gun) to get to the hex screws. There are a total of 11 hex and 6 Phillips screws to remove from the PistolMouse. Be careful to keep track of any parts if they fly out during this step.

Remove the main board from the PistolMouse FPS and detach any wires and place to the side. You will need this for reference only, if at all. Figure 4-31 shows the MiniMouse board (on the right) and the much simpler Pistol-Mouse board (on the left).

Figure 4-31. Main boards from each mouse

Wiring

There are four sensors on the MiniMouse main board, which are highlighted in Figure 4-32. The left, right, and scroll wheel buttons, as well as the scroll wheel sensor, must all be removed. Remove these with any method you are comfortable with: either desoldering tape or a desoldering suction device. For your own reference, take note of the orientation of the scroll wheel sensor.

Figure 4-32. The four sensors that need to be removed

Now you will extend the wires from the original PistolMouse FPS to the

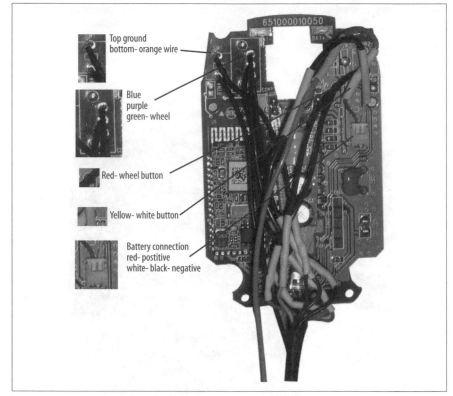

Top ground
bottom- orange wire

Blue
purple
green- wheel

Red- wheel button

Yellow- white button

Battery connection
red- postitive
white- black- negative

651000010050

Figure 4-33. Extending the wires from the PistolMouse

Please double-check the ground connections on your mouse before proceeding using the multimeter and the two connections for each button, in case Targus has changed the MiniMouse main board:

- The left mouse button is wired, so the front solder point is going to the brown wire (which is ground) and the rear is going to the orange wire.

- The scroll sensor uses the three solder points to the right of and between the sensor mounting points. From front to rear, use the blue, purple, then green wires.

- The wheel button uses the front solder point; the rear is ground and already connected via the left button.

- The right button uses the rear solder point, the front being the ground here.

Now, add an extension of wire to the AA battery holder, as shown in Figure 4-34. This will need to go from the top of the gun all the way to the bottom front. Attach the power plug to this extension so that it can plug into the MiniMouse main board.

Figure 4-34. Wiring the AA battery holder

Testing and Debugging

Put AA batteries in the holder and turn on the PistolMouse. As with Mini-Mouse in its original form, you might have to click the buttons a couple times to make sure the unit is on and working. Click or manually press the switches on the PistolMouse and verify that they are working on your system. At this point, you should have a disassembled working unit, like the one shown in Figure 4-35.

Figure 4-35. Disassembled PistolMouse with new components

Cutting

You'll need to make room in the plastic of the PistolMouse FPS for the new larger main board. Use a dremel or similar tool to remove the fins in the black plastic where the board sits. You will also have to remove red clear plastic material from the bottom. In the end, the board should sit gently on the red plastic with the lens optic in place. The optic from the original board and the new one were exactly the same in my experience, so you can use this to assist in positioning the board in place. The extra wires you now have on the board will press it down in actual use. Figure 4-36 shows the bottom of the PistolMouse with the new board and the modifications I made.

You will also have to cut two small holes in the red plastic, as shown in Figure 4-37. One will be for the on/off switch. I did this in order to be able to use the switch from the original mouse, but I still have to use a paper clip to flip the switch. Do this carefully.

For the connect switch, you will have to carefully figure out where it is under the red plastic, then drill a hole so the connect button can be installed. I used a few layers of electrical tape to make the hole walls taller so the button wouldn't come loose. Use incremental sizes of drill bits until the hole allows the button to be pushed and return to its place, but still tight enough that it won't come loose during use.

Figure 4-36. Modifications to the bottom case of the PistolMouse

Reassembly

Once everything is working properly, it's time to reassemble the unit. Begin by putting fresh high-quality AA batteries in the holder, because they are not easy to replace. Then, put the holder above the scroll wheel in the cavity above the trigger. Run the wires for all the buttons and batteries down the front of the gun, so they don't interfere with any other buttons or screw holes. Then, screw together the two halves and replace the rubber grip.

Put a piece of tape over the wires as they exit out of the top of the gun into the bottom, and make them run along the center channel on the bottom of the black plastic. Then, align the main board and optic on the red plastic and attach the bottom plate. Screw this on and everything should be together. Turn on the unit and test and debug further if needed. Often, you'll need multiple attempts to run the wires smoothly and reassemble the bottom piece. Figure 4-38 shows the finished reassembled unit.

Figure 4-38. The finished Bluetooth PistolMouse FPS

Use

Use the new mouse as you would any Bluetooth device. It should work on both Macs and PCs that have Bluetooth. It should perform similar to the original PistolMouse FPS, since they both are 800dpi devices.

Do not remove or fail to put back in place the orange tip to
the gun, because this signifies it as a toy weapon. If it is
removed, there might be civil penalties, as well as a danger to
yourself if you use the device in public.

Enjoy your new wireless Pistol Mouse, and play safe.

—*Bryan Hurley*

HACK #62 Mobilize Your WRT54G with the WiFiCar

Why keep your wireless router in one place when you can give it wheels?

I've always thought that remote-controlled toy cars offer a great platform
for other uses. For a while now, I've been thinking about how to put a
small-form-factor PC motherboard on an RC car, but that would require
quite a large car. When I stumbled upon OpenWRT [Hack #61], I realized that
the WRT54G provided wireless, processing, and general-purpose I/O interface capabilities in one small package! With a wireless router mounted on a
WiFi controllable car, you can patch holes in your wireless coverage,
drive the car from any Internet terminal in the world, or a variety of other
things that I couldn't think of right away. But I knew it would be cool. So I
set off to mobilize my WRT54G.

There are two separate hacks that need to be done here: the software for the
router, which will accept TCP connections and output the proper values to
the GPIO pins, and the hardware, which will take those GPIO outputs and
use that data to drive the car. Let's start with the software.

The Software

OpenWRT is a minimal Linux distribution for the Linksys WRT54G. The
router still works as a router, which I think is impressive, while allowing you
to tinker with things such as adding an SD card and so on.

was working. I also tested the GPIO tool from the LED System Load Monitor to see that it also worked well on my router.

Then, I merged these two programs. My program modified the TCP server to send the output to my subroutine, which determines which byte was sent. If the byte is an ASCII digit, corresponding to values 49–57 (zero is excluded), the program will set the GPIO pins so the car drives in the direction of that digit on a telephone keypad. Receiving a 1 makes the car drive forward-left, 2 is forward, 3 is forward-right, 4 is left, 5 is stop, 6 is right, 7 is back-left, 8 is back, and 9 is back-right. It took a while, but I eventually got that to work.

The complete C program follows.

> You can get a copy of the source code from my web site at
> *http://yasha.okshtein.net/wrt54g*. The compiled code is also
> available there if you don't want to play with cross-compilation yourself. But it's more fun that way!

```c
/* fpont 1/00 */
/* pont.net    */

#include <sys/types.h>
#include <sys/socket.h>
#include <netinet/in.h>
#include <arpa/inet.h>
#include <netdb.h>
#include <stdio.h>
#include <unistd.h> /* close */
#include <fcntl.h>


#define SUCCESS 0
#define ERROR   1

#define END_LINE 0x0
#define SERVER_PORT 1500
#define MAX_MSG 100

#define FORWARD 7
#define REVERSE 5
#define RIGHT 4
#define LEFT 3

int debug=0;

/* function readline */
int read_line( );
```

```
void enable(unsigned int pinset);
void disable(unsigned int pinset);

int poll(int pin);
void processMsg(char *msg);

int main (int argc, char *argv[]) {

  int sd, newSd, cliLen;

  struct sockaddr_in cliAddr, servAddr;
  char line[MAX_MSG];


  /* create socket */
  sd = socket(AF_INET, SOCK_STREAM, 0);
   if(sd<0) {
    perror("cannot open socket ");
    return ERROR;
  }

  /* bind server port */
  servAddr.sin_family = AF_INET;
  servAddr.sin_addr.s_addr = htonl(INADDR_ANY);
  servAddr.sin_port = htons(SERVER_PORT);

  if(bind(sd, (struct sockaddr *) &servAddr, sizeof(servAddr))<0) {
    perror("cannot bind port ");
    return ERROR;
  }

  listen(sd,5);

  while(1) {

    printf("%s: waiting for data on port TCP %u\n",argv[0],SERVER_PORT);

    cliLen = sizeof(cliAddr);
    newSd = accept(sd, (struct sockaddr *) &cliAddr, &cliLen);
```

```
        /* init line */
        processMsg(line);
        memset(line,0x0,MAX_MSG);

    } /* while(read_line) */

  } /* while (1) */

}


/* WARNING WARNING WARNING WARNING WARNING WARNING WARNING       */
/* this function is experimental.. I don't know yet if it works  */
/* correctly or not. Use Steven's readline() function to have    */
/* something robust.                                             */
/* WARNING WARNING WARNING WARNING WARNING WARNING WARNING        */

/* rcv_line is my function readline(). Data is read from the socket when */
/* needed, but not byte after bytes. All the received data is read.      */
/* This means only one call to recv(), instead of one call for          */
/* each received byte.                                                   */
/* You can set END_CHAR to whatever means endofline for you. (0x0A is \n)*/
/* read_lin returns the number of bytes returned in line_to_return       */
int read_line(int newSd, char *line_to_return) {

  static int rcv_ptr=0;
  static char rcv_msg[MAX_MSG];
  static int n;
  int offset;

  offset=0;

  while(1) {
    if(rcv_ptr==0) {
      /* read data from socket */
      memset(rcv_msg,0x0,MAX_MSG); /* init buffer */
      n = recv(newSd, rcv_msg, MAX_MSG, 0); /* wait for data */
      if (n<0) {
    perror(" cannot receive data ");
    return ERROR;
      } else if (n==0) {
    printf(" connection closed by client\n");
    close(newSd);
    return ERROR;
      }
    }

    /* if new data read on socket */
    /* OR */
    /* if another line is still in buffer */

    /* copy line into 'line_to_return' */
    while(*(rcv_msg+rcv_ptr)!=END_LINE && rcv_ptr<n) {
      memcpy(line_to_return+offset,rcv_msg+rcv_ptr,1);
```

```
        offset++;
        rcv_ptr++;
      }

      /* end of line + end of buffer => return line */
      if(rcv_ptr==n-1) {
        /* set last byte to END_LINE */
        *(line_to_return+offset)=END_LINE;
        rcv_ptr=0;
        return ++offset;
      }

      /* end of line but still some data in buffer => return line */
      if(rcv_ptr <n-1) {
        /* set last byte to END_LINE */
        *(line_to_return+offset)=END_LINE;
        rcv_ptr++;
        return ++offset;
      }

      /* end of buffer but line is not ended => */
      /* wait for more data to arrive on socket */
      if(rcv_ptr == n) {
        rcv_ptr = 0;
      }

  } /* while */
}

void enable(unsigned int pinset) {

  unsigned int gpio;

  unsigned int pin=1<<pinset;

  if (debug==1)
    printf("trying to enable pin.\n");

  int gpioouten=open("/dev/gpio/outen",O_RDWR);
```

```
   if (debug==1)
     printf("enabled pin\n");

   close(gpioout);
   close(gpioouten);

   if (debug==1)
     printf("closed gpioout and gpioouten\n");

}

void disable(unsigned int pinset) {

   unsigned int gpio;

   unsigned int pin=1<<pinset;

   if (debug==1)
/*     printf("entered disable pin %s\n",pin); */
     printf("entered disable pin\n");

   int gpioouten=open("/dev/gpio/outen",O_RDWR);
   int gpioout=open("/dev/gpio/out",O_RDWR);

   if (debug==1)
     printf("read gpioout and gpioouten\n");

   read(gpioouten, &gpio, sizeof(gpio));
   gpio |= pin;
   write(gpioouten, &gpio, sizeof(gpio));

   if (debug==1)
     printf("set pin as output\n");

   read(gpioout, &gpio, sizeof(gpio));
   gpio&=~pin;
   write(gpioout, &gpio, sizeof(gpio));

   if (debug==1)
     printf("disabled pin\n");

   close(gpioout);
   close(gpioouten);

   if (debug==1)
     printf("closed gpioout and gpioouten\n");

}

int poll(int pin) {

}
```

```
void processMsg(char *msg) {
/*
  if (debug==1)
    printf("gotmsg to processMsg\n");
  disable(FORWARD);
  if (debug==1)
    printf("returned from disable\n");

  int x;
  for (x=0;x<1000;x++) { }
  if (debug==1)
    printf("finished for loop\n");
  enable(FORWARD);
  if (debug==1)
    printf("finished enable pin\n");
*/

  if (debug==1)
    printf("entered processMsg\n");

  printf("dir should be: %i \n", *msg);

  int dir;
  dir = *msg-48;

  if (debug==1)
    printf("got drivedir\n");

  switch (dir) {
    case 1 :
      printf("*drive forward-left\n");
      enable(FORWARD); disable(REVERSE);
      enable(LEFT); disable(RIGHT);
      break;
    case 2 :
      printf("*drive forward\n");
      enable(FORWARD); disable(REVERSE);
      disable(LEFT); disable(RIGHT);
```

```
        disable(LEFT); disable(RIGHT);
        break;
      case 6 :
        printf("*steer right\n");
        disable(FORWARD); disable(REVERSE);
        enable(RIGHT); disable(LEFT);
        break;
      case 7 :
        printf("*drive reverse-left\n");
        enable(REVERSE); disable(FORWARD);
        enable(LEFT); disable(RIGHT);
        break;
      case 8 :
        printf("*drive reverse\n");
        enable(REVERSE); disable(FORWARD);
        disable(LEFT); disable(RIGHT);
        break;
      case 9 :
        printf("*drive reverse-right\n");
        enable(REVERSE); disable(FORWARD);
        enable(RIGHT); disable(LEFT);
        break;
      default :
        printf("?! invalid message! must be digit 1-9 !?\n");
  }

  if (debug==1)
    printf("finished processMsg\n");

}
```

To avoid typing numbers into an SSH connection, I wrote a small Visual Basic program to simplify sending data to the car. It uses the arrow keys on your keyboard to determine which data to send. I had trouble sending a null character from VB, but it works now. I tried porting it to eMbedded Visual Basic so that it runs from my PDA, but it, too, has trouble sending null characters. Once I get it to work, recall Q in James Bond, *Tomorrow Never Dies*: "Just push your finger gently across the pad to drive the car...."

So, that's the software component. The hardware proved every bit as challenging for an intermediate hacker like me. But if you're careful, you can avoid the mistakes that I made and save a few bucks.

The Hardware

Our remote-control victim car is a Chevy Avalanche, shown in Figure 4-39, that I picked up for about $10 at the local Radio Shack. Its retail price is about $30; this one was cheap because it was a display model with no remote. Since the whole point of this hack is to replace the remote with Wi-Fi, it was an even better deal!

Figure 4-39. The Chevy Avalanche, post-operation

The router's GPIO pins can source only a few milliamps, but the drive motors of the car want up to two Amperes (amps) or more. To convert between the low-power outputs of the router and the high-power needs of the car, Bell Laboratories invented the transistor in 1947 to do exactly that.

However, a transistor can provide only high-voltage (known as *logic high*) or low-voltage (known as *logic low*), but not both. The motors will need one

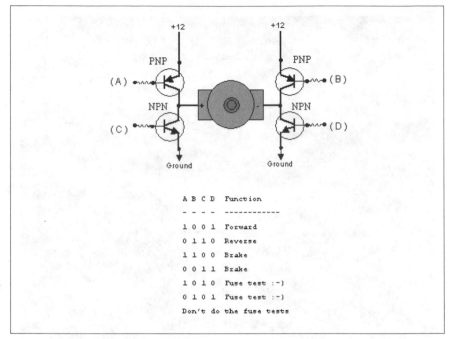

Figure 4-40. Schematic for the driver

www.acroname.com/robotics/parts/R6-754410.html. Fortunately, I ordered three.

Using a small proto-board and five-volt regulator model 7805 (*http://tinyurl. com/wqbv*) from Radio Shack, I put together a small driver board. It had 10 wires coming out of it: two power wires connected directly to the drive battery, and four small wires connected to a telephone connector that plugged into the router (so the router wasn't soldered to the car).

The drive motors, however, were soldered directly to the board, providing the last four wires that came into the board. The first time I powered it up, I was sure to test all the connections, because I felt something bad would happen. It did; I made sure that the power wires were indeed the power wires, but I forgot to check the polarity! The chip went up in smoke, leaving charred remains. Undaunted, I rebuilt the circuit with one of the other chips that I ordered and, finally, the driver board worked. Figure 4-41 shows the finished driver board installed inside the Chevy.

I taped the router to the bare base of the car to test it out; it worked! It looked ugly, but after connecting to the car's access point, using an SSH client to start the RC car server program rcServ, and loading my VB client, the

Figure 1-11. Installed driver board

car moved! I could have finished there, but I decided to see if it could work with the Chevy Avalanche cover on, just for looks.

A friend of mine, Manny, decided to take it upon himself to do this part. Using a dremel, he cut holes in the side of the case for the legs of the router, and also two holes up front for the antennas. Although I had placed that the car would work up to a hundred feet without the antennas, he decided to put the holes in, anyway. Given that it was his first time using the tool, results were as expected: the case still has to be stretched to fit the router, and even so it scratches the sides, as well as the antennas.

Figure 4-42. The finished WiFiCar

also working on a bigger version using a 1/6th scale Hummer. But this is, to my knowledge, the first self-controlled wireless router.

 For more details on the car, including a video of it actually moving under Wi-Fi control, check out the project web site at *http://yasha.okshtein.net/wrt54g*.

—*Yasha Okshtein*

## CHAPTER FIVE

Software Hacks
Hacks 63–82

One of the joys of wireless hacking is that it encompasses both the hardware and software worlds. If you're not comfortable with soldering irons, but you can hack Perl or C, many great things are waiting for you to hack. Software hacks permeate the wireless world, from alternate drivers to replacement firmware.

This chapter covers a wide range of subjects, from advertising services over your wireless, to using captive portals, to building your own access point using Linux or BSD.

HACK #63 Build Your Own Access Point with Linux

Run your own access point with off-the-shelf radio cards and open source drivers.

Commercial access points have multiple functions. Not only do they have 802.11a/b/g radios, but they also function as the master of any client radio that connects to the AP in Infrastructure mode. Access points broadcast beacon frames, which advertise the ESSID of the access point. Once a client associates, the access point manages all radio communications following

Hardware Choices

What you choose to build your access point really depends on how and where you want to use it:

Mobile

If you have a notebook, isn't that a perfect platform to always have with you as an access point? You have several options: connect your laptop to an Ethernet drop if one is available, use WDS [Hack #69] to redistribute an existing wireless signal, or even uplink via a data-capable mobile phone as your backhaul [Hack #4].

Portable/outdoor

There are a number of manufacturers of small form factor PC hardware that either are designed specifically with wireless use in mind or have all the features that you need to build an access point. "Do-It-Yourself Access Point Hardware" [Hack #53] covers some of these boards.

Existing hardware

Just about any PC hardware you can think of will make a capable access point. Intel architecture is not even a limiting factor here. One of the wireless routing nodes built for the West Sonoma County Internet Cooperative (*http://www.wscicc.org*) in Sonoma County, California, was a beige Macintosh G3/266 desktop machine. It ran Yellow Dog Linux and had two PCI-PCMCIA converters housing two Agere Orinoco Silver 802.11b radio cards. An odd choice, you might think, but it functioned as a wireless router for over a year.

Radio Cards and Antennas

Three radio chipsets and associated drivers are capable of running in Master mode under Linux, which allows the driver to assume functions in software that a commercial access point performs with custom hardware and firmware:

- Prism 2/2.5/3 802.11b radio cards with the HostAP driver
- Atheros 802.11a/b/g radio cards with the Madwifi driver
- Prism54 802.11b/g radio cards with the Prism54 driver

It can be maddeningly difficult to determine just what chipset your particular radio card uses; this book dedicates an entire hack to this subject. If you don't yet have a wireless card and are planning an access point project, read through "Find Radio Manufacturers by MAC" [Hack #39] first, do some research, and make sure you're buying the right card.

External antennas are covered in a whole series of hacks in this book, from the infamous Pringles can [Hack #85] to determining the gain of your home-built antenna [Hack #92]. If you're planning deployment of either a single AP for outdoor point-to-point use or multiple APs to cover a large building, you'll need external antennas specific to your project. See Appendix B for a complete tutorial on external antennas, cables, and connectors that you'll need to be familiar with.

Prism54 Cards

Prism54 cards are a third option for your access point. However, there is an issue with the cards currently being sold that makes it difficult to recommend them. The Prism54 chipset is available in a SoftMAC format, which is analogous to the Atheros cards; much or all of the radio is controlled entirely from software.

This has necessitated a complete rewrite of the Prism54 Linux driver. At the time of this writing, the driver does not support SoftMAC cards, and these are the only cards available on the market.

You can consult *http://www.prism54.org/supported_cards.php* for updates to the list of supported cards, and more information on the SoftMAC issue.

Software Requirements

This hack uses Linux as its base operating system. Again, depending on your host hardware, you have a number of choices. Small board PCs with limited amounts of memory will need custom distributions such as Pebble [Hack #70] or, if you're familiar with BSD, m0n0wall [Hack #71]. If you're using a notebook PC, just about any distribution you want would be appropriate, because they all support the wireless card drivers described later in this section. The examples in this hack use Ubuntu and Fedora Core distributions

HostAP

The author and maintainer of the HostAP driver is Jouni Malinen, and his web site for HostAP is located at *http://hostap.epitest.fi*. In addition to the HostAP driver, he is also the author of the *hostapd* daemon and *wpa_supplicant* [Hack #42]. If you run into problems with any of his projects, mailing lists hosted at the site can be a great deal of help. There is also anonymous CVS access for anyone who wants to run bleeding-edge code.

There are a couple of ways to get the source code for HostAP. Both options require you to compile from source.

Ubuntu package install. Ubuntu users can use apt-get to install the hostapsource package from the universe repository. In order to do this, you'll need to configure *apt*. Edit */etc/apt/sources.list* and uncomment the following lines:

```
deb http://us.archive.ubuntu.com/ubuntu hoary universe
deb-src http://us.archive.ubuntu.com/ubuntu hoary universe
deb http://security.ubuntu.com/ubuntu hoary-security universe
deb-src http://security.ubuntu.com/ubuntu hoary-security universe
```

The universe repository contains packages that are not developed or supported by the Ubuntu release crew. This is where you'll find the hostapsource package.

> The default kernel image installed by Ubuntu on Intel platforms appears to be the i386 architecture build. This kernel does not come with CONFIG_NET_RADIO enabled. However, all of the other available Ubuntu kernels do have this option enabled by default. This example uses the *2.6.10-5-686* kernel image.

You'll also need to get the Linux-headers package that matches the kernel version you are currently running. A quick way to determine your kernel version is to execute the uname command:

```
$uname -a
Linux hostname 2.6.10-5-686 #1 Tue Apr 5 12:12:40 UTC 2005 i686 GNU/Linux
```

To update your *apt* index, issue the following command:

```
sudo apt-get update
```

Once *apt* has finished updating the indexes, go ahead and install the packages:

```
sudo apt-get install hostap-source hostap-utils linux-headers-2.6.10-5-686
```

Lastly, you'll need to create some symbolic links so that compilation of kernel modules doesn't fail to find the necessary headers:

```
cd /lib/modules/2.6.10-5-686
ln -s /usr/src/linux-headers-2.6.10-5-686 source
ln -s /usr/src/linux-headers-2.6.10-5-686 build
ln -s /usr/src/linux-headers-2.6.10-5-686 /usr/src/linux
```

The hostap-source package will be placed in */usr/src/hostap-source.tar.bz2*. Unpack the file, change to the newly created directory, and build the modules:

```
tar xjvf hostap-source.tar.bz2
cd modules/hostap-source
sudo make
sudo make install
```

Once the modules are built and installed, you can load the modules:

```
sudo depmod -ae
sudo modprobe hostap
```

Insert your Prism 2/2.5/3 PC Card, or shut the system down and install your Prism 2.5/3 PCI card, and skip ahead to the "Configuring Your AP" section.

Compiling from source. Fedora Core users should download the source code package directly from *http://hostap.epitest.fi*. The compilation test for this hack, on a stock Fedora Core 3 system, was painless.

```
tar xzvf hostap-driver-0.3.7.tar.gz
cd hostap-driver-0.3.7
sudo make
sudo make install
```

The make install took care of running depmod, so all that was left was to execute the following command and insert the Prism 2 PC card:

```
sudo modprobe hostap
```

Madwifi

hardware. In other countries, regulations would allow governmental enforcement to be taken out against the hardware manufacturer for allowing invalid radio modes.

The solution to this problem was for Atheros to allow the development of a Hardware Abstraction Layer (HAL) by Sam Lefler. The HAL is in binary form and sits between the driver and the hardware to enforce valid FCC operating modes. This is viewed by some in the open source community as a *black sheep* project, one that pollutes the licensing of the Linux kernel by introducing code for which there is no available source.

That argument aside, the Multiband Atheros Driver for WiFi (Madwifi) was for quite some time the only available driver for Linux or BSD. It is still the only driver for Linux that allows the use of Master mode with Atheros radio cards. BSD users have the option of using the ath(4) driver, which has been developed by some of the same people responsible for Madwifi.

Until fairly recently, no package installs were available for Madwifi. That has changed, however, and more than one recent distribution now includes the Madwifi driver by default. The following sections show how to add the driver if your Ubuntu install did not include the right package, as well as how to compile from source.

Ubuntu package install. Installations of Ubuntu 4 and the recent 5.04 release both include packages titled *linux-restricted-modules*, which are described as "non-free Linux modules" for various architectures. If an Atheros-based Wi-Fi card was present in your machine during Ubuntu installation, this package should have been installed. It contains the Madwifi driver, along with other drivers that are not fully compliant with the Gnu Public License (GPL).

If you don't have this package, you can get it from the Ubuntu install CD or by modifying your */etc/apt/sources.list* to add the universe repository as described previously in the "HostAP" section. Once you have updated *apt*, locate the correct package for your architecture:

```
apt-cache search linux-restricted-modules
```

This will return a list of all possible architectures for which the package is available. In our case, we are using the 686 kernel, so we need to install the appropriate package:

```
apt-get install linux-restricted-modules-2.6.10-5-686
```

After installation you can reboot, or execute these three commands as root to load the necessary modules:

```
modprobe wlan
modprobe ath_hal
modprobe ath_pci
```

Compiling from source. Compilation of the driver is not complicated, but since the driver is a work in progress the developers have not yet put out a production release. You'll have to get the source code via a Subversion checkout, which is a simple one-line exercise:

```
svn checkout http://svn.madwifi.org/trunk madwifi-ng
```

This checks out the most current preview edition of the code, and drops it all in a folder titled *madwifi-ng* in the root of where you executed the svn command. You should be able to change to the *madwifi-ng* folder and just type make. For the most up-to-date information on Madwifi code releases, check with *http://madwifi.org/ wiki/UserDocs/GettingMadwifi*.

However, we ran into a snag here with our Fedora Core 3 installation. The make failed with an error, because it could not find the uudecode command. The binary HAL file is included in the source code as a uuencoded file. For some reason, our Fedora Core 3 default install didn't include the *sharutils* package, containing uudecode, so we used yum to install it and then compile.

```
yum install sharutils
make
make install
```

Now, you can reboot or execute the modprobe commands listed earlier to activate the driver modules.

Configuring Your AP

Now that you've got the radio card and the driver, it's time to have them start acting like an access point. The manual method for this is simple, using the Linux Wireless Tools:

```
iwconfig ath0 essid "Example" mode Master channel 6 rate Auto
```

This sets up your wireless card in *Master* mode, broadcasting the SSID of Example, on channel 6 using any wireless speed rate. This is easy to verify; just boot up any other machine you have with a wireless card and scan for

If you're setting up a permanent access point rather than something temporary on your laptop, you won't want to have to manually configure the radio
each time the system loses power or reboots. Traditionally, the accepted
method for configuring wireless card radio parameters was in the */etc/
pcmcia/wireless.opts* file. However, this works for PCMCIA-based radio
cards only, and you have to also configure */etc/pcmcia/network.opts* or
another file somewhere else to assign TCP/IP parameters to the card.

Fortunately, current Linux distributions have other methods of configuring
wireless cards that allow for all necessary parameters in a single file. Ubuntu
and Debian users should modify the entry in the */etc/network/interfaces* configuration file. Here's example with a static IP address:

```
iface ath0 inet static
    network 192.168.1.0
    broadcast 192.168.1.255
    address 192.168.1.200
    netmask 255.255.255.0
    gateway 192.168.1.1
    wireless_mode master
    wireless_essid Example
    wireless_channel 6
    wireless_rate Auto
auto ath0
```

Fedora Core and Red Hat users will need to dig another level deeper and
edit the correct file in */etc/sysconfig/network-scripts*. There will be an *ifcfg* file
that corresponds to your wireless card driver. In our case, with a Prism II
card, the file was *ifcfg-wlan0*. Again, here's an example with a static IP
address:

```
DEVICE=wlan0
ONBOOT=yes
BOOTPROTO=static
NETMASK=255.255.255.0
IPADDR=192.168.1.200
GATEWAY=192.168.1.1
TYPE=WIRELESS
ESSID=Example
CHANNEL=6
MODE=Master
RATE=Auto
```

There's one further caveat when using the PCMCIA Host AP driver: some
machines (notably, the Stylistic 1000 **[Hack #53]**) have a problem loading the
Host AP driver with some Prism II cards. The symptom is that the card is
detected on insert but mysteriously fails to initialize, reporting an obscure
error to the effect of "GetNextTuple: No more items." If you are having

trouble with the driver, try adding this line to your */etc/pcmcia/hostap_cs. conf* (replacing any existing module "hostap_cs" line):

```
module "hostap_cs" opts "ignore_cis_vcc=1"
```

Normally, the driver attempts to verify that one entry on the card's acceptable voltage table matches the voltage reported by your PCMCIA slot. In some cases, this voltage can be incorrectly reported, causing the driver to fail to initialize. This option causes the driver to ignore the reported voltage and load anyway.

Hacking the Hack

This is all you need to do to bring up a simple access point on your Linux machine. There are much more elaborate tweaks available that allow you to bridge your wireless and wired networks [Hack #64], bridge two access points together [Hack #69], and bridge a firewall [Hack #65].

Bridge Your Linux AP

#64

Make a simple Ethernet bridge with Host AP and one other network interface.

"Build Your Own Access Point with Linux" [Hack #63] covers all the basics of building your own Linux-based access point. Since, by default, each network interface in Linux must be part of a different subnet, you'll have to enable IP routing, and possibly Network Address Translation (NAT), if you want to make full use of your new access point.

However, what if you want your wireless clients to be on the same IP subnet as your access point? This hack shows how to do that by enabling wireless-to-wired bridging.

Bridge Setup

Bridging is straightforward to implement, and support for bridging has been

In our example, we want to bridge a Prism card running HostAP (*wlan0*) with the first Ethernet device (*eth0*). Execute these commands from the local machine console:

```
ifconfig eth0 0.0.0.0
ifconfig wlan0 0.0.0.0
brctl addbr br0
brctl addif br0 eth0
brctl addif br0 wlan0
ifconfig br0 192.168.3.2 netmask 255.255.255.0
route add default gw 192.168.3.1
```

When you first create the bridge device, it takes a moment or two for the bridge to "learn" the layout of your network. It can take several seconds for traffic to begin to pass through the bridge when first brought up, so don't panic if you don't immediately see traffic.

If you have only one bridge on your network, you can also safely turn off Spanning Tree:

```
brctl stp br0 off
```

This prevents the bridging code from needlessly sending 802.1d negotiation traffic to nonexistent bridges. You can see the configuration of your bridge at any time by using brctl show:

```
brctl show
```

```
bridge name     bridge id              STP enabled     interfaces
br0             8000.00026f018574      no              eth0
                                                       wlan0
```

If you are interested in which MACs have been found on the bridge interfaces, use brctl showmacs <interface>:

```
brctl showmacs br0
```

```
port no mac addr             is local?       ageing timer
   2    00:02:6f:01:aa:ff    yes                0.00
   1    00:03:93:6c:11:99    no               135.69
   2    00:30:65:03:00:aa    no                 0.08
   1    00:40:63:c0:aa:bb    no                 0.16
   1    00:a0:24:ab:cd:ef    yes                0.00
```

Generally, bridges are *set and forget* devices. Once configured, your bridge maintains itself, barring a huge amount of traffic or untoward miscreants fiddling with it. Be sure to read the documentation available at *http://bridge.sourceforge.net*, as well as the documents listed at the end of this hack.

Caveats

Not all network devices allow bridging. Specifically, some radio cards (notably, the Lucent/Orinoco/Avaya/Proxim Gold and Silver cards) prohibit Ethernet bridging in the radio firmware. If you need to bridge, we highly recommend upgrading these cards to a Prism II card or Atheros card. These cards not only allow bridging, but the drivers supporting them are also much more powerful.

Also keep in mind that, as easy as a simple bridge is to configure, it isn't the most secure device on the planet. If you have any interest in controlling the packets that flow across your bridge (and you should), you will want to implement some firewalling on your bridge. But unfortunately, standard *netfilter* commands don't work with bridges under Linux 2.4. Be sure to read "Protect Your Bridge with a Firewall" [Hack #65] if you need more control over your bridge.

See Also

• "Protect Your Bridge with a Firewall" [Hack #65]

• The Linux Bridge STP HOWTO (*http://www.linux.org/docs/ldp/howto/ BRIDGE-STP-HOWTO/*)

• The Linux Bridge and Firewall mini HOWTO (*http://www.tldp.org/ HOWTO/mini/Bridge+Firewall.html*)

Protect Your Bridge with a Firewall
HACK #65

Maintain control over your Layer 2 bridge with iptables and ebtables.

As shown in "Bridge Your Linux AP" [Hack #64], creating a Linux Ethernet-to-wireless bridge is straightforward. While this allows for easy integration with your existing network, it isn't always the best decision from a security point of view. Rather than simply connect two networks together at Layer 2, wouldn't it be nice to be able to pick and choose which packets flow from

compile. So, this hack concentrates on Ubuntu Linux. However, ebtables should work with any 2.6 kernel.

Bridge-nf is part of the 2.6 kernel, so all you need to do is add the user-space binary package:

```
sudo apt-get install ebtables
```

With the binary installed, you can now manipulate the firewall exactly as you would expect using *iptables*. You can also use *ebtables* to do all sorts of interesting things at the MAC layer. For example, to ignore all traffic from a given IP that doesn't match a known MAC address, you could try this:

```
ebtables -A FORWARD -p IPv4 --ip-src 10.15.6.10 -s ! 00:30:65:FF:AA:BB -j
DROP
```

This prevents other users from *camping* on known IP addresses. While it won't help much with MAC spoofing attacks, this will help keep average users from stepping on other people's IP addresses. You can also use it in reverse to lock a MAC address into a particular IP:

```
ebtables -A FORWARD -p IPv4 --ip-src ! 10.15.6.10 -s 00:30:65:FF:AA:BB -j
DROP
```

This will prohibit the machine with the specified MAC address from using any IP but 10.15.6.10.

These are just a couple of examples of the power and flexibility of *ebtables*. You can also do all sorts of other neat things, such as MAC redirection and NAT, or filter on protocol types. (Need to drop all IPv6 traffic? No problem!) For more information, check out the *ebtables* web site as well as man ebtables.

HACK #66 Filter MAC with HostAP and Madwifi

Filter MAC addresses before they associate with your Linux-powered access point.

While you can certainly perform MAC filtering at the link layer using iptables or ebtables [Hack #65], it is far safer to let the HostAP or Madwifi drivers [Hack #63] do it for you. This not only blocks traffic that is destined for your network, but also prevents casual snoopers from even associating with your access point.

Both drivers are configured to do MAC filtering through the *iwpriv* command. The most useful way to filter MAC address is to make a list of wireless devices that you wish to allow, and then deny all others:

```
iwpriv wlan0 addmac 00:30:65:23:17:05
iwpriv wlan0 addmac 00:40:96:aa:99:fd
```

```
iwpriv wlan0 maccmd 1
iwpriv wlan0 maccmd 4
```

The addmac directive adds a MAC address to the internal table. You can add as many MAC addresses as you like to the table by issuing more addmac commands. You then need to tell Host AP what to do with the table you've built. The maccmd 1 command tells Host AP to use the table as an *allowed* list, and to deny all other MAC addresses from associating. Finally, the maccmd 4 command boots off all associated clients, forcing them to reassociate.

Sometimes, you need to ban only a troublemaker or two, rather than set an explicit policy of permitted devices. If you need to ban a couple of specific MAC address but allow all others, try this:

```
iwpriv wlan0 addmac 00:30:65:fa:ca:de
iwpriv wlan0 maccmd 2
iwpriv wlan0 kickmac 00:30:65:fa:ca:de
```

As before, you can use addmac as many times as you like. The maccmd 2 command sets the policy to *deny*, and kickmac boots the specified MAC immediately, if it happens to be associated. This is probably nicer than booting everybody and making them re-associate just to ban one troublemaker. Incidentally, if you'd like to remove MAC filtering altogether, execute maccmd 0.

If you make a mistake typing in a MAC address, you can use the delmac command just as you would addmac, and it (predictably) deletes the given MAC address from the table. Should you ever need to flush the current MAC table entirely but keep the current policy, use this command:

```
iwpriv wlan0 maccmd 3
```

Finally, if you are running HostAP, you can view the running MAC table by viewing the appropriate data in */proc*:

```
cat /proc/net/hostap/wlan0/ap_control
```

The *iwpriv* program manipulates the running wireless driver, but doesn't preserve settings across reboots. Once you're happy with your MAC filter-

Upgrade Your Wireless Router

#67 Run a Linux distribution or other custom code on many models of wireless routers.

The release of the Linksys WRT54G wireless router back in 2003 was kind of a watershed moment for wireless hackers and Linux hackers alike. It was quickly determined that the WRT54G was running a Linux kernel. Source code for the unit was demanded (and eventually released), hacks were found to pass arbitrary commands to the unit, and an entire community slowly emerged around modifications to the Linksys firmware. In addition, complete Linux kernel distributions have become available, allowing all sorts of functionality that Linksys (probably) never imagined.

There are now wireless routers on the market from Linksys, Netgear, Asus, Buffalo, Belkin, Motorola, and Siemens. All of these routers use chipsets from Broadcom. Some use Broadcom radios as well, while others use Prism or Atheros radios. A pretty complete list of these devices can be found at *http://openwrt.org/TableOfHardware*.

This hack covers the Linksys-based alternate firmware for these wireless routers, and shows how to install a complete Linux distribution, as well as some of the cool things that will let you do.

When Linksys finally released the modified Linux kernel and utilities they had included with the WRT54G, and made the code available as required by the General Public License (GPL), it became possible for software developers around the world to start modifying this code to suit their purposes. Code for all Linksys products that use Linux internally is available at *http://www.linksys.com/support/gpl.asp*.

We don't have the space to cover all of the alternate firmware available for Linksys and other Broadcom-based wireless routers. Two good places to go for information on other firmware, as well as to find updated releases, are *http://linksysinfo.org* and *http://www.wrt54g.com*.

> Linksys and other manufacturers do not support third-party firmware. It's unclear if loading nonsupported firmware voids your warranty, but you should be aware that the process is not perfect. There is a possibility of corrupting the flash in your router and making it an expensive paperweight.
>
> You can take out some insurance by enabling the NVRAM boot_wait setting, which instructs the router to wait for a few seconds prior to loading firmware and instead expect a TFTP image load over the network. See the "OpenWRT" section for details on enabling boot_wait.

Sveasoft Firmware

One of the first modified versions of the Linksys firmware came from a Swedish company, Sveasoft. They have continued to improve their product and now have two different offerings. Their stable tested code is released to the public with source code, free of charge, as required by the GPL. Newer code under development and access to their support forums are available for a $20 yearly subscription fee.

Early in the development process, access to the development code and the forums was freely available, and the conversion from a free to a paid service met with a lot of resistance from the community. One result of this is that there are now several forks of the Sveasoft firmware, by different developers, and over time these forks have developed different feature sets. You can find many of these forked firmware images on the web sites mentioned in the previous section.

At the time of this writing, the freely available Sveasoft firmware is known as *Alchemy*. We obtained our copy from *http://linksysinfo.org*. Converting your wireless router to the Alchemy firmware is fairly trivial and follows the same process for installing upgraded Linksys firmware.

Use a web browser to load the Linksys administrative web pages. The default IP address for a Linksys router is 192.168.1.1. Login with the user name and password you set. (You did change the default password from *admin*, didn't you!) Choose Administration → Firmware Upgrade, as shown in Figure 5-1.

Click Browse and locate the unzipped firmware file *Alchemy-V1.0.bin*. Select Upgrade to begin the firmware upload and upgrade. Do not interrupt this process! Upon completion, the router will reboot and load the new firmware.

 Though you can perform a firmware upgrade over a wireless

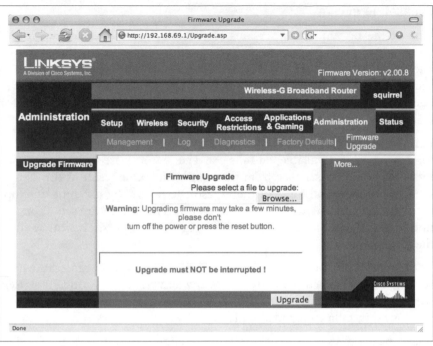

Figure 5-1. WRT54G firmware upgrade

As shown in Figure 5-2, you can set the maximum uplink and downlink speeds for your WAN or LAN/Wireless connections. Once enabled, you can set QoS service priorities for protocols such as SSH, VoIP, and many others. This means that you can set the service priority for VoIP to High to ensure no other traffic takes priority. You can also set priorities for specific netmasks, MAC addresses, or the four Ethernet ports on the WRT54G.

Among the other features the Sveasoft firmware gives you are the ability to do OSPF routing, enable communication between access points using the Wireless Distribution System [Hack #69], run a SSH client and server, and finally, enable a Client Mode that allows you to connect to other access points.

OpenWRT

OpenWRT is the antithesis of all the Linksys-based firmware projects. It is a minimal Linux distribution with basic command-line tools and support for adding functionality via a package manager. While not practical for basic home use, OpenWRT is a powerful option for anyone who wants to have specific features enabled on their wireless router.

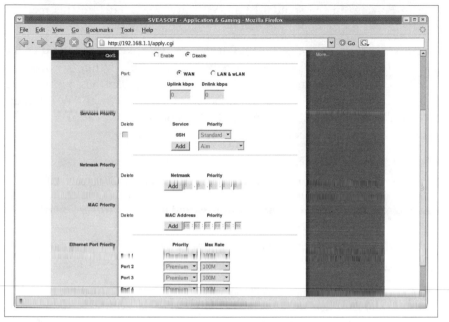

Figure 5-2. QoS settings

The project is under heavy development. As of this writing, the stable release has been removed from the web site, and the experimental code is available at *http://openwrt.org/downloads/experimental/bin*. The original OpenWRT code booted using a small partition in RAM, then created a secondary partition for loading the full firmware. The experimental release offers a second option of a single *jffs2* (Journaling Flash File System) partition, which makes operations of the distribution much more simple.

In order to install the experimental release of OpenWRT you'll need to get the right version for your wireless router hardware. There are specific versions for WRT54G and WRT54GS hardware, as well as Motorola routers,

bug in *Ping.asp* in the standard Linksys firmware. Details on this method can be found at *http://openwrt.org/OpenWrtDocs/Installing*.

The *jffs2* versions of the OpenWRT firmware will take several minutes for the first bootup and will reboot before becoming usable. While booting, the DMZ LED will be lit and will turn off once the firmware has booted. The firmware configures the network interfaces, using DHCP for the WAN interface, and sets up a basic NAT/firewall. Once booted, you can telnet to the router using the last LAN IP address it was configured for.

As the documentation says:

> Why no telnet password? Telnet is an insecure protocol with no encryption, we try to make a point of this insecurity by not enabling a password. If you're in an environment that requires password protection we suggest using the *dropbear* ssh server.

Setting up the *dropbear* SSH server is as simple as setting the root password:

```
# passwd foo
```

Once a password has been set, the telnet daemon is disabled, *sshd* is enabled, and you can now use any SSH client to access your router. You now have a complete, albeit small, Linux distribution running. What can you do with it?

The first thing you should do is see what packages come installed by default, using the *ipkg* package manager:

```
ipkg list_installed
```

Anyone who's used apt-get in Debian or Ubuntu distributions will be familiar with the syntax of *ipkg*. You'll want to update the list of available packages, and then you can list them:

```
ipkg update
ipkg list
```

Hacking the Hack

Your options are really unlimited at this point, especially if you've loaded OpenWRT. This is a complete Linux distribution, and short of running things like a window manager, just about anything is possible. There are packages available to run a web server, FreeRADIUS for authentication, IPSec VPN software, and at least two different captive portal packages: NoCatSplash [Hack #75] and WiFiDog (*http://old.ilesansfil.org/wiki/WiFiDog*). For even more fun with OpenWRT, you can set up true mesh networking [Hack #68] using the OLSR mesh networking protocol.

Set Up an OLSR Mesh Network

HACK #68

Always wondered about mesh networking, but afraid to try? The lads at Freifunk have made it easy for all of us.

The Freifunk Firmware (FFF) is a friendly repackaging of the OpenWRT embedded Linux [Hack #67] for the Linksys WRT54G and some other wireless routers. It offers a nice web admin interface that is easily customizable with your own templates and opens SSH, not Telnet, by default.

Most interestingly, the FFF allows you to easily enable Freifunk's implementation of OLSR *mesh networking*. If your node can get a signal from another OLSR node, appropriately configured, they will agree to carry traffic for each other and for other nodes on the mesh. If one node has a connection to the Internet, Net traffic will go through it transparently. This makes it easy to purchase a lot of bandwidth collectively, and then distribute it throughout a wide cloud of meshed nodes.

Getting the Firmware

To download the Freifunk Firmware, visit *http://ff-firmware.sourceforge.net*, or go straight to Sven-Ola's (the maintainer) package directory: *http://styx. commando.de/sven-ola/ipkg*.

You want the file labeled *g/openwrt-freifunk-language-version number.bin*, with your language of choice (*en*, *de*, etc.) and the latest version number. If your WRT is a 54GS or GS, look for the appropriate directory

> But if you're thinking about buying a WRT for this hack, a plain G is all you need.

Uploading the Firmware

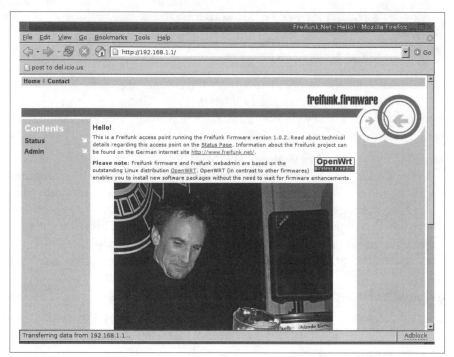

Figure 5-3. Freifunk Firmware web admin GUI

You must make sure to assign a different, non-conflicting IP address to each of the routers that you're going to mesh. By default, each new Linksys WRT comes configured as 192.168.1.1. Many people prefer to allocate a chunk of the 10.*.*.* space instead. It should be noted that both of these IP address ranges follow the Internet RFC 1918, which defines *private* IP addresses that are not routable on the Internet.

In the Admin → Wireless menu, you can pick an IP range and address for your new node. Set the ESSID here as well, and to enable OLSR meshing, put the WRT into Ad-hoc Mode and save the new settings. After changing the IP address, you can restart the WRT either via the web admin GUI or simply by powercycling the device, and the changes should take effect. If you're changing the default IP address, you should powercycle the box anyway. Figure 5-4 shows the settings on the test mesh.

The Admin → WAN screen lets you set your connection to the outside world. If one of the nodes in your mesh has a connection to the Internet, all the others will route through it. Plug an Ethernet cable into the back of the node that's going to act as an Internet gateway, and set it via the WAN screen either to a static IP address or to obtain an IP address via DHCP.

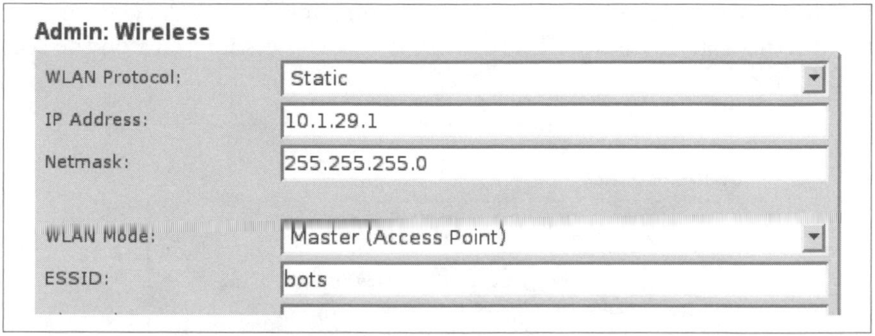

Admin: Wireless

WLAN Protocol:	Static
IP Address:	10.1.29.1
Netmask:	255.255.255.0
WLAN Mode:	Master (Access Point)
ESSID:	bots

Figure 5-4. Configuring the Admin → Wireless screen

The Freifunk Firmware will mesh via OLSR out of the box, once you've configured your OLSR settings as described previously. The Admin → OLSR screen lets you limit the nodes that can connect to this network. Up to a limit, though, the more mesh nodes, the merrier. One option you should set here is OLSR DHCP. This indicates an IP address range that the node will offer, via DHCP, to non-OLSR devices that try to connect to it. It's optional, but in the interests of open connectivity, enable it on each node in your mesh. Make sure the DHCP IP range is different from the range you're using for your main mesh network, though.

Rinse and Repeat

Now, take a second WRT. It's best to unplug the first one, in case you accidentally associate with it, or talk to it through an Ethernet cable instead. Go through the same process.

In the Admin → Wireless dialog, set the IP of this node to be a different address in the same range (in the examples, I used 10.1.29.1 and 10.1.29.2). Set the ESSID to the same as the first WRT, because all the nodes in your mesh should have the same ESSID. Make sure the WRT is set to Ad-hoc Mode. Fix the OLSR DHCP settings as discussed previously.

Figure 5-5 shows the Status/Routes display on a mesh node. As you can see, the Internet gateway is 10.1.50.1, which is the wireless interface on the second router.

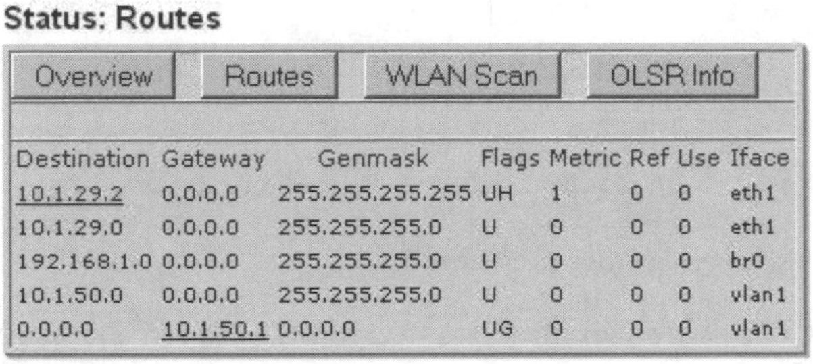

Status: Routes

Overview	Routes	WLAN Scan	OLSR Info

Destination	Gateway	Genmask	Flags	Metric	Ref	Use	Iface
10.1.29.2	0.0.0.0	255.255.255.255	UH	1	0	0	eth1
10.1.29.0	0.0.0.0	255.255.255.0	U	0	0	0	eth1
192.168.1.0	0.0.0.0	255.255.255.0	U	0	0	0	br0
10.1.50.0	0.0.0.0	255.255.255.0	U	0	0	0	vlan1
0.0.0.0	10.1.50.1	0.0.0.0	UG	0	0	0	vlan1

Figure 5-5. Node with Internet gateway showing OLSR routes

Adding new nodes to the mesh and watching them discover each other is lovely to see!

Troubleshooting the Firmware Upload

If your WRT is in a state where it won't appear to boot properly, it might give you some indications of trouble. For example, it might be hanging while the DMZ light shines constantly. Try putting the firmware into *failsafe* mode; power on the router, and then, just as the DMZ light starts to flash, hold down the Reset button on the back of the WRT with a small implement, such as a pen tip, for a few seconds.

This should cause the WRT to boot into failsafe mode, which should enable you to upload new firmware and connect to the device via Telnet. You should also be able to flash a new firmware to the device, using an Ethernet cable, your laptop, and a TFTP client such as *atftp*. When the WRT boots up, it waits for a three-second window in which it can expect to have a new firmware flashed onto it.

Here's a sample conversation between *atftp* and a WRT:

```
jo@frot:~$ atftp
tftp> connect 192.168.1.1
tftp> mode octet
tftp> timeout 1
tftp> trace
tftp> put openwrt-g-freifunk-1.0.2-en.bin
...
[ lots of activity ensues ]
```

It might be that you have installed an OpenWRT-based firmware without an admin GUI and it boots immediately, without waiting for three seconds while the DMZ light flashes. The NVRAM, the writeable permanent memory of the WRT, needs to be told to boot_wait for a new firmware image via TFTP:

```
frot:/home/jo# telnet 192.168.1.1
[login screen exchanged; type in admin username and password.]
@OpenWrt:/# nvram set boot_wait=on
@OpenWrt:/# nvram commit
```

Next time you reboot, you should see the WRT waiting for a few seconds before the DMZ light starts to flash.

See Also

- freifunk.net (*http://www.freifunk.net*; in German)
- OpenWRT (*http://www.openwrt.org*)
- What A Mesh (*http://www.what-a-mesh.net*)

—Jo Walsh

HACK
#69

Extend Your Wireless Network with WDS

Use the Wireless Distribution System to have multiple access points communicate wirelessly.

There are many reasons you might want to use this hack: your house is too large for a single access point to cover and you don't want to run Ethernet cable in your walls, you want to provide wireless access in a location that has power but no connection to the network backbone, or any situation in which you would like to have a wireless signal but can't or don't have the necessary network infrastructure.

Wireless Distribution System (WDS) is a layer 2 standard originally defined in the revised IEEE 802.11 specification from 1999. WDS enabled

One final caveat: WDS is not part of the Wi-Fi Alliance testing and certification program, so vendors are free to implement it however they choose. If you're considering using WDS, you might want to spec out access points from the same manufacturer. It's worth noting that if you are okay with 802. 11b only, HostAP-based access points on Linux hardware are capable of speaking WDS to many other brands of access points.

WDS Requirements

In order to take advantage of WDS, your access point hardware must support it. Fortunately, a lot of consumer-grade wireless hardware now comes with WDS support built in. Access points from Linksys, Apple, Buffalo, and NetGear all are capable of participating in a WDS network.

On the homebrew side, any machine running the HostAP driver with a Prism II radio can create or join a WDS network. Atheros card users with the Madwifi driver will need to get the preview release of the Madwifi-ng driver code. Details can be found on the Madwifi Wiki (*http://madwifi.org/ UserDocs/WDSBridge*). "Build Your Own Access Point with Linux" [Hack #63] provides details on building both of these drivers.

Lastly, if you've installed alternate firmware or a complete Linux distribution on your wireless router such as a Linksys WRT54G [Hack #67], a Netgear wgt634u, or an Intel ipx42x-based device like the Linksys WRV54G, you'll also be able to set up a WDS connection.

This hack sets up two Linksys WRT54G units with the Sveasoft Alchemy firmware to use WDS. It then takes two Linux machines running HostAP and shows how to automatically find and provision WDS links between HostAP devices.

Linksys Alchemy Setup

Setting up WDS on a Linksys WRT54G is dead simple, using the Sveasoft Alchemy custom firmware [Hack #67]. Make sure that you're connected via wireless or Ethernet to the private LAN side of the Linksys. Navigate to the administrative web pages, which on the default configuration is 192.168.1.1. Enter the username and password when prompted, and then choose Wireless → Basic Settings, as shown in Figure 5-6.

Here, you'll need to choose the wireless channel that your WDS bridge will use. WDS requires that all participating access points use the same channel. Using the same SSID is not required. In fact, you should use a different SSID for each AP and choose a name based on the access point's physical location.

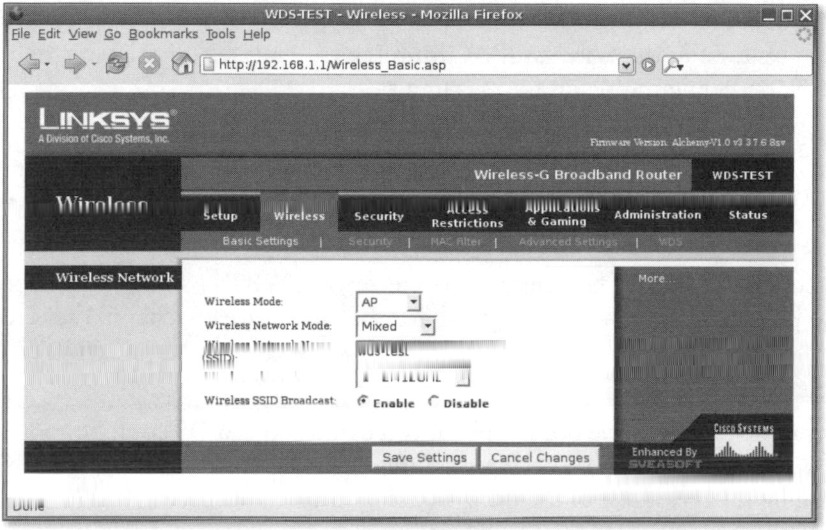

Figure 5-6. WRT54G basic wireless settings

Next, choose Wireless → WDS in the tab navigation, as shown in Figure 5-7.

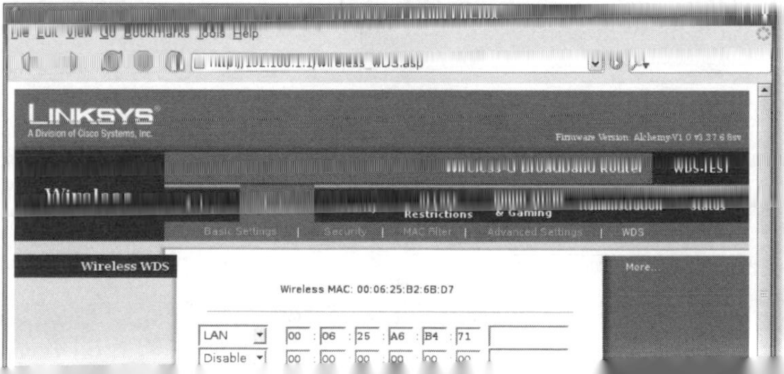

You'll need to do this on both Linksys units, because you will need the Wireless MAC shown at the top of the screen to correctly configure WDS on each unit. Enter the Wireless MAC from Linksys unit #2 into the first line of the WDS configuration on Linksys unit #1.

This completes a simple WDS configuration. All that is required is the Wireless MAC from the second Linksys unit, which we have entered into the first line of the WDS configuration. Lastly, choose a LAN configuration in the first drop-down of the menu.

To complete the WDS setup, go to the second WRT54G unit, and repeat the previous steps. Make sure you have the same wireless channel selected, and in the WDS section, enter the Wireless MAC from the first WRT54G unit.

Once the changes have been applied, you can test the WDS configuration by associating with one of the Linksys units, getting an IP address, and then pinging the IP address of the other Linksys unit.

The Alchemy firmware also supports an advanced configuration, which allows you to assign an IP subnet to the WDS interface. This is handy if you want to keep the WDS addresses of the Linksys units private or unpublished. As shown in Figure 5-8, you can set up your units with a private subnet that is only capable of having two devices on it, so you have turned the bridged WDS network into a point-to-point IP network.

HostAP Setup

If you've built and are using the HostAP driver [Hack #63] for Prism II 802.11b cards, you already know it has many great features. You might not realize that it is capable of WDS or that it has a neat trick or two available that makes setting up WDS a snap.

When you compiled the HostAP utilities, one of the included tools is *prism2_param*. If you took the default configuration, it should have been installed in */usr/sbin*. This is a powerful tool for setting (and potentially breaking) all sorts of parameters in your Prism II card.

> This bears repeating: *prism2_param* is a wrapper around the very powerful *iwpriv* command. You can do some seriously funky things to your Prism II firmware with this utility, so be very careful when using it. If your card starts acting strangely, you may need to reboot or unload and reload HostAP.

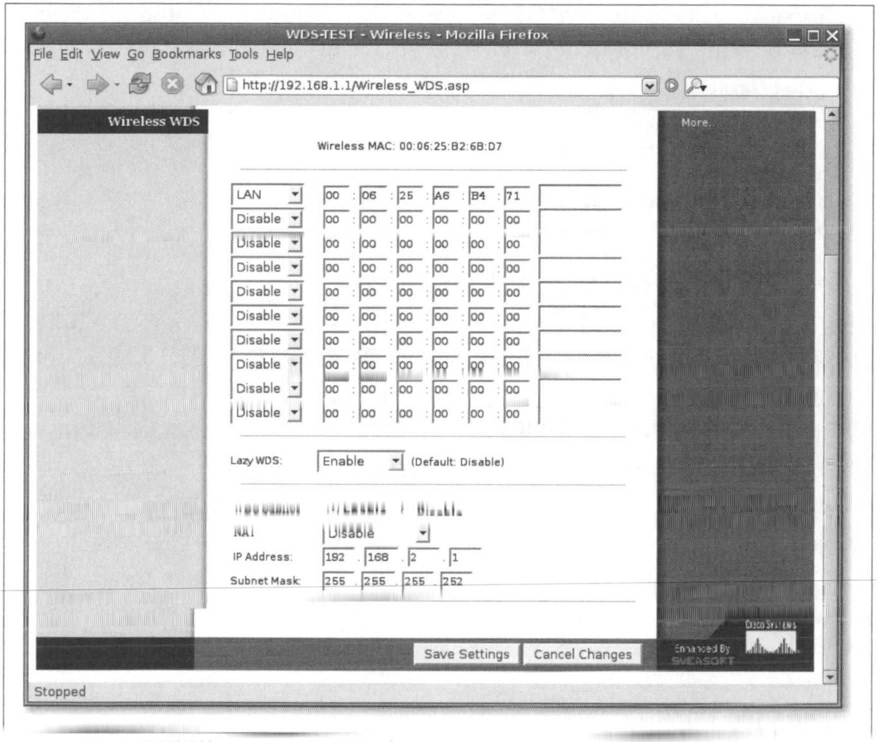

Figure 5-8. WRT54G separate WDS subnet

You can set your Prism II card to automatically detect other Prism II cards in WDS mode and create WDS links on the fly. This requires three commands:

```
prism2_param wlan0 wds_type 4
prism2_param wlan0 autom_ap_wds 1
prism2_param wlan0 other_ap_policy 1
```

The first commands makes the card use standards-compliant WDS framing, the second command is the kicker that tells HostAP to automatically establish WDS links, and the third command tells HostAP to...

utils package. Once you've taken care of that, you can execute these commands to create and bring up a wireless bridge using the WDS:

```
brctl addbr br0
brctl addif br0 wlan0
brctl addif br0 wlan0wds0
ifconfig wlan0 0.0.0.0
ifconfig wlan0wds0 0.0.0.0
ifconfig wlan0 up
ifconfig wlan0wds0 up
ifconfig br0 192.168.2.1 netmask 255.255.255.0
```

This creates a bridge, adds the wlan0 and wlan0wds0 interfaces to the bridge, brings up those interfaces, and assigns an IP address of 192.168.2.1 to the bridge. Now, execute these commands on the second HostAP machine, making sure to alter the last line:

```
ifconfig br0 192.168.2.2 netmask 255.255.255.0
```

You'll want to wait 30 seconds or so for the bridges and WDS to come up on each side; then, you should be able to ping across the bridge. The bridge code needs this time to learn MAC addresses on either side of the bridge to prevent bridging deadlocks. Your WDS network is now live; you can associate with either AP and WDS will take care of the rest.

Hacking the Hack

There a number of things you can do to extend your WDS network. For example, you can add up to five other access points, but bear in mind that your performance will decrease each time you add a new AP to WDS. For better performance, you could set up three machines in a WDS network, and set up another three in another location that has wired access. You can also implement WDS on the Linksys WRT54G using the OpenWRT linux distribution [Hack #67].

HACK
#70   **Pebble**

Use this tiny Debian-based Linux distribution for your own custom wireless access point.

Terry Schmidt of NYCwireless has done terrific work in getting together a stripped down Linux distribution specifically tailored for wireless access points in general, and for the Soekris [Hack #53] platform in particular. This distribution is called Pebble and is freely available at *http://www.nycwireless. net/pebble*. It aims to balance functionality with size, weighing in at about 47 MB.

Because it is based on Debian, customizing the installed software is straight-forward. Unlike some other *very* tiny distributions, it uses standard libraries and binaries. This significantly simplifies upgrades, and it means that custom packages don't have to be built from source and linked to custom, stripped-down libraries. The distribution includes:

- Based on Debian GNU/Linux 3.0r1 (Woody)
- Linux Kernel 2.4.26 with Crypto modules
- HostAP 0.1.3 stable including utils and hostapd
- Madwifi CVS version from 4/2004
- bridge-tools
- djbdns caching DNS server
- NoCatAuth running as non-root user, post 0.81 nightly
- openSSH server 3.4p1
  openSSL 0.9.6c patched
- pcmcia-cs
- PPP and PPPoE
- Zebra 0.92a-5

There are also a number of shell niceties, including *wget*, *elvis*, *tcpdump*, *Perl*, and even *lynx*. It runs well on every Soekris model and will spawn a serial console on those machines (or any machine that has a serial port available). It runs on virtually any 486 class machine (or better) with at least 32 MB RAM. If you don't need all of the functionality provided in the standard distribution, you can easily strip out the components you don't need, to fit it into an even smaller space. For example, eliminating Perl, NoCatAuth, *djbdns*, and a couple of nonessential shell utilities will easily let Pebble fit on a 32 MB flash card (although since 128 MB flash cards are now selling for $15, perhaps this is a waste of effort).

If you have about 50 MB of storage available, you might also look at and

channels, and received signal / noise of all networks that are in range of your kit. This lets you troubleshoot network interference problems at a glance.

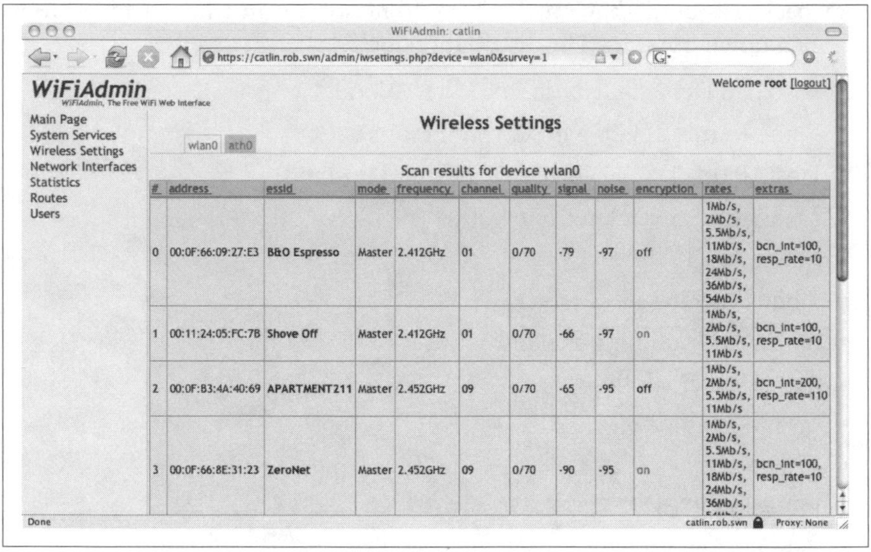

Figure 5-9. Detailed wireless survey information

When using a radio as a point-to-multipoint master or standard Access Point, Metrix Pebble also provides statistics about the number of connected clients, including MAC address and amount of data sent and received, as shown in Figure 5-10. Not only does this allow you to instantly identify potential network abusers, but the graphs help to forecast network capacity and plan for upgrades.

If you are running from flash memory [Hack #54], one of the most useful features in Pebble is that it mounts the bootable medium read only, and creates a RAM disk for its temporary files. This means that once it is configured, the flash is never written to, which considerably extends the lifetime of your flash.

HACK #71 Wall Off Your Wireless

Build a tiny wireless firewall using a wide range of PC hardware and a BSD firewall.

If you've decided that small form factor PCs are for you, and have invested in such a motherboard [Hack #53] with the intentions of making your own access point, you're in the right hack. You certainly have other options for an operating system. Pebble [Hack #70] is a good example of a small Linux distribution designed for wireless applications. However, it has a couple

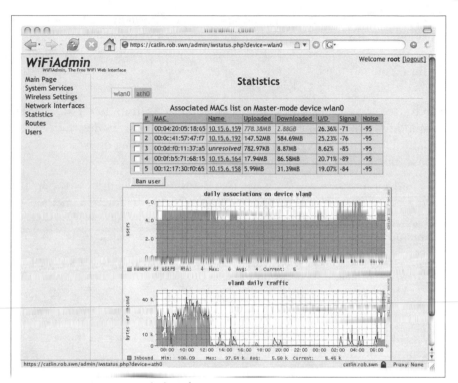

Figure 5-10. Stats on your wireless client connections

negative factors: it hasn't been updated in over a year and configuration requires a pretty good knowledge of Linux daemons and how they like to be configured (with text files).

m0n0wall is an extremely tiny distribution of FreeBSD 4 that initially was designed as a tiny firewall, capable of running in a very small footprint. It has maintained those capabilities, weighing in at a surprisingly tiny 4.43MB for the image that runs on the Soekris net4521 hardware **[Hack #53]**. In addi-

To get the Soekris hardware up and functioning with m0n0wall, you'll need a Compact Flash (CF) card at least 8MB in size, and some method of writing to that CF card from another working computer. There are a few ways to do this. You can use a CF to IDE adapter [Hack #54], a PC Card adapter that holds the CF card, or a USB CF reader.

You'll need to get your card reader or adapter hooked up to a Linux, BSD, or Windows box. Download the correct image for your hardware from the m0n0wall web site onto your chosen machine. Depending on which OS you choose, the methods for writing will be different.

BSD and Linux users will both use a *gzip* utility to decompress the image during the writing process. However, each OS has a different method of naming inserted rewritable media, so you will need to run *dmesg* from the command line to determine exactly the name of the device assigned to your CF card.

To write the image, BSD users should execute the following command:

```
gzcat net45xx-xxx.img | dd of=/dev/rad[n] bs=16k
```

Your CF card will be assigned a device name of something like */dev/rad3*. Make sure the command you execute has exactly the name of the device as determined from the output of dmesg.

Linux users will need to execute this command:

```
gunzip -c net45xx-xxx.img | dd of=/dev/hdX bs=16k
```

Again, you'll need to use the output of *dmesg* to determine what device name to use. If you have a USB CF reader, chances are good that your device will be loaded using a SCSI emulation device such as */dev/sda0*.

Users of both operating systems should ignore the error regarding "trailing garbage." This occurs because the software image is written with a digital signature.

Windows users need a special program that will write images directly to the media without the Windows disk system getting in the way. Physdiskwrite is just such a program, available from the m0n0wall web site at *http://www. m0n0.ch/wall/physdiskwrite.php*.

After inserting the CF on your Windows system, you can either call Physdiskwrite from a command window or drag the icon of the image file over the executable program icon. Figure 5-11 shows a screenshot of the completed process. Note specifically that you will have to choose the correct physical drive! Choosing badly will overwrite another mounted physical disk on your system, and this could be very bad for you and your Windows install.

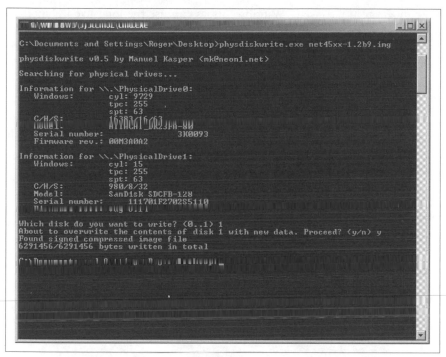

Figure 5-11. Output from Physdiskwrite

Congratulations! You've got m0n0wall written to your boot media. Unplug the CF card from your host system, insert it into the Soekris, and power up your new firewall with all of the network interfaces unplugged.

Configuration

Practically all of the m0n0wall configuration can be done from the web interface, but before that's possible you need to get the network interfaces configured. Since the Soekris is a headless (no display) device, you will need to connect to the serial port with a terminal program and

To connect to the console, Windows users can use the long-lived Hyperter-
minal program, found in Accessories → Communications. Linux and BSD
users should investigate *minicom* or *ckermit*. Whatever your terminal program, set your communication parameters for `19200,8,N,1`.

The reason for this slightly unusual configuration is that, by default, the
Soekris motherboards come set with a default console speed of 19200 bps.
m0n0wall will function only with a 9600 bps speed, so you will have to
change the Soekris defaults. Immediately after power-up, the Soekris will
display a status screen. Press Ctrl-P to enter the ROM monitor mode. Enter
the following commands:

```
set conspeed=9600
reboot
```

You'll now need to disconnect your terminal session, change the terminal
speed to 9600 bps, and reconnect.

If you're successful, FreeBSD will boot, and then m0n0wall will present you
with a menu, as shown in Figure 5-12.

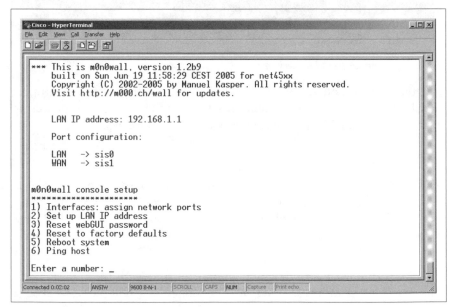

Figure 5-12. m0n0wall console configuration

The first three options in this menu are important:

1) Interfaces: assign network ports

   Allows you to determine which interface on your Soekris will be
   assigned to LAN, WAN, and OPT ports of the firewall. OPT is a special
   port also referred to in other firewalls as a DMZ.

2) *Set up LAN IP address*

Lets you change the default LAN IP address from 192.168.1.1 to some other address of your choosing.

3) *Reset webGUI password*

Resets the web interface password if for some reason you have forgotten it.

Once you have your network interfaces configured the way you want them, m0n0wall will want to reboot the system. When the reboot is complete, you will be able to access the firewall using the LAN IP address. m0n0wall runs a DHCP server by default on the LAN, so you should be able to set your client computer for DHCP, obtain a lease, and point a web browser at *http://192.168.1.1*. If you changed the LAN IP address in the previous setup, alter this URL accordingly.

Using m0n0wall

For having such a small footprint, this operating system is positively packed with features. The webGUI configuration, shown in Figure 5-13, breaks these features down into sections, easily accessible from the navigation on the left side of the browser. When you first connect to the webGUI, you'll be prompted for a username (admin) and password (mono).

First, click on General Setup and change the admin password. If your system is going to see a lot of public traffic, it's not a bad idea to alter the admin username to something else as well. Another security feature worth turning on is the HTTPS protocol for the webGUI, so all management traffic is encrypted. You can even alter the HTTPS port to a nonstandard one if you are really paranoid. (You *are* really paranoid about security, aren't you?) Lastly, you should set a hostname, your DNS servers, and an NTP server if you want to keep accurate time on your firewall.

Next you'll want to set up the WAN interface. If you've set up any wireless

Figure 5-13. WebGUI configuration

quickly, click on the tab for Magic Shaper Wizard. This will let you set your downstream and upstream speeds for shaping. You can also set P2P traffic to the lowest priority, and share bandwidth evenly across all LAN users. After you apply the wizard's changes, you can go back and look at the other traffic shaper settings to get an idea of how to configure your own advanced shaping.

By default, m0n0wall sets itself up as a DNS forwarder and advertises its LAN address as the DNS server for all DHCP clients. This reduces DNS traffic on your WAN. You also have the option of enabling dynamic DNS through one of the online services that offer it, or setting up m0n0wall to talk to a RFC2136 compliant DNS server like BIND. You can configure all of these options from the Dynamic DNS menu.

If you've already looked at captive portals such as NoCatAuth **[Hack #74]** or WiFiDog, you'll be pleased to find that m0n0wall includes its own configurable captive portal, listed under the Services menu.

There are too many captive portal features to cover here, but some of the most important ones include:

- Setting idle and hard timeout in minutes for clients
- Enabling authentication for clients via local users or RADIUS
- HTTPS logins for clients
- Custom HTML portal and error pages

m0n0wall also supports several kinds of VPN connections. Under the VPN menu, you can enable support for IPSec, PPTP, and OpenVPN.

The system Status menu has a number of pages you can use to monitor your system performance. The Interfaces page gives you In/Out packets and errors, the Traffic graph shows you utilization of your interfaces if you have the Adobe SVG plug in installed, and supported wireless cards using the wi driver show detailed connection information in the Wireless page.

If you want even more detailed information on system operation, the Diagnostics menu lets you view system logs, DHCP leases, IPSec connection details, as well as lets you backup and restore the system, reset to factory defaults, and reboot the system.

For the size and the price, you can't really beat m0n0wall for features on a small form factor PC.

HACK #72 Run Your Mac as an Access Point

Use a Mac OS X machine with an AirPort card as a true access point.

Mac OS 9 had a handy AirPort feature called *Software Base Station*. It allowed any Mac with an AirPort card and an Ethernet (or dialup) connection to act like a hardware access point, sharing its Internet connection over the wireless. The early versions of Mac OS X were noticeably lacking this handy feature, but it has been restored in Versions 10.2 and later.

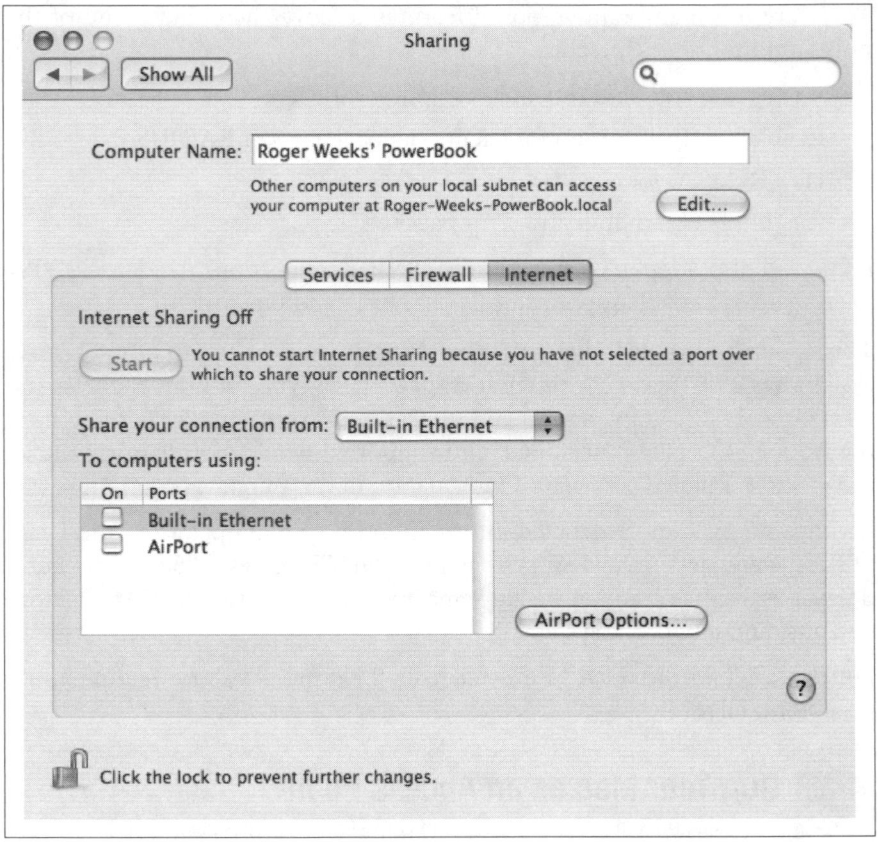

Figure 5-14. Sharing System Preferences

AirPort Options… button, and you should see a drop-down menu like the one shown in Figure 5-15.

Specify a network name and channel, and turn on WEP if you need it. Click OK, and then click the Start button. Close the control panel, and your Air-Port icon should change to include an arrow, as shown in Figure 5-16. This means that your AirPort is now operating as a real access point.

To turn off sharing and return to normal AirPort operations, go back to the Sharing control panel, select the Internet tab, and click the Stop button. As long as you have Internet sharing enabled, anyone in range of your Mac will see it as a normal access point, and can access the Internet just as if it were a hardware access point.

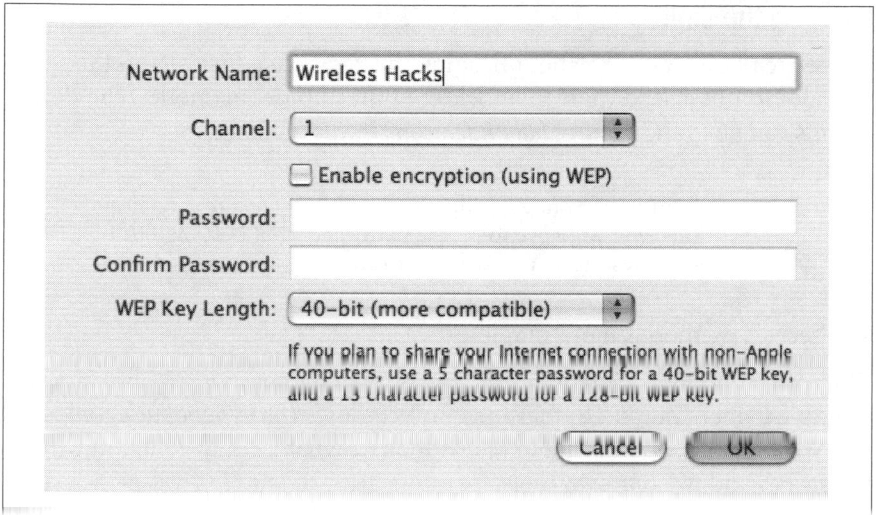

Network Name:	Wireless Hacks
Channel:	1
	☐ Enable encryption (using WEP)
Password:	
Confirm Password:	
WEP Key Length:	40-bit (more compatible)

If you plan to share your Internet connection with non-Apple
computers, use a 5 character password for a 40-bit WEP key,
and a 13 character password for a 128-bit WEP key.

(Cancel)   (OK)

Figure 5-15. AirPort Wireless Options

Figure 5-16. Access point engaged

Run Linux on the Zipit Wireless Messenger

Get the most out of your $100 handheld.

The Zipit Wireless Messenger is a Wi-Fi–enabled instant messaging (IM) device aimed at teens and sold at retail outlets. The Zipit requires a wireless Internet connection and an IM account on AIM, MSN, or Yahoo! Messenger. Since it uses Wi-Fi, it requires no contract or mobile phone carrier. Contrasted with the other handheld messengers out there, this is a pretty good deal with a $100 list price.

Flashing the Zipit

There are two ways to go about flashing the Zipit. The first method requires the addition of a serial port to knock the unit into debug mode. The details on this can be found at *http://aibohack.com/zipit/serial.htm*.

 If you brick your Zipit doing any of the software modifications, you will have to do the hardware serial port modification to restore it. You've been warned.

The second method is more simple.

The software-only hack requires the use of another computer. AiboHack has a simple loader (*ZRS.EXE*) that runs on Windows (*http://aibohack.com/zipit/reflash.htm*), but we're going to take a look at what's really going on behind the scenes and use our own tools.

Becoming the man in the middle. For the Zipit to work as advertised, it must be connected to the Internet, contact its IM providers, and occasionally grab an updated version of firmware. It's this last step that makes everything possible. The first thing the Zipit does after finding a wireless network is to determine if it's on the Internet.

To do this, it first performs an HTTP HEAD request to *http://zipitwireless.com*. Yes, if their site ever goes down, all stock Zipits will die! Then, it contacts the autoupdate server at *http://zipitwireless.net/~zippy/somerandomnumber.txt*. If the text file returns a version number that is higher than its current version, it fetches a new *.bin* file and auto updates the device.

Since we're not interested in getting updates from the official mother ship, we will need to divert all of this action to our own machine. The best way to do this is if you are running your own DNS nameserver using BIND. You can set your local DNS server to be authoritative for the *http://www.zipitwireless.net* domain, allowing you to redirect all queries on your network to a web server of your choice. The examples that follow assume that your web server is powered by Apache.

Setting up the DNS. Go into your *etc/named.conf* and add the following lines:

```
zone "zipitwireless.com" {
        type master;
        file "/etc/bind/zipitwireless.com";
};
zone "zipitwireless.net" {
        type master;
        file "/etc/bind/zipitwireless.net";
};
```

You'll need some zone files too. Add the following lines to */etc/bind/zipitwireless.com*:

```
$ORIGIN .
$TTL 3600       ; 1 hour
zipitwireless.com               IN SOA  ns0.ugp.org. root.ugp.org. (
                                2004040420
                                3600       ; refresh (1 hour)
                                300        ; retry (5 minutes)
                                604800     ; expire (1 week)
                                3600       ; minimum (1 hour)
                                )
                IN      NS      n1gw.seattlewireless.net.
                IN      A       216.254.21.186
$ORIGIN zipitwireless.com.
www             IN      A       10.15.3.230
```

And add these lines to */etc/bind/zipitwireless.net*:

```
$ORIGIN .
$TTL 3600       ; 1 hour
zipitwireless.net               IN SOA  ns0.ugp.org. root.ugp.org. (
                                2004040420
                                3600       ; refresh (1 hour)
                                300        ; retry (5 minutes)
                                604800     ; expire (1 week)
                                3600       ; minimum (1 hour)
                                )
                IN      NS      n1gw.seattlewireless.net.
                IN      A       216.254.21.186
$ORIGIN zipitwireless.net.
www             IN      A       10.15.3.230
```

Setting up the web server. Now that we've got the Zipit pointing to our web server, we need to have some files for it to fetch. Grab the AiboHack BURN3 image from *http://www.aibohack.com/zipit/zipit_parts_burn3.zip*. BURN3 is a filesystem image used for bootstrapping the OS. It comes with limited functionality, as well as zflash, which is used for the next step.

zflash OpenZipit over NFS

Now that the box is bootstrapped, it's time to make it useful. OpenZipit is a bundle of OS and applications that comes with *dropbear* (SSH), *weechat*, and some small audio applications. There are several distributions out there for the Zipit, but this is the oldest stable distribution and is a great starting point with lots of features.

OpenZipit is available in the File Section of the Zipit Wireless Yahoo Group *http://groups.yahoo.com/group/zipitwireless/* and is maintained by Ken McGuire (cynfab). You will need to have a NFS (Version 3) server to hold your images.

NFS setup. NFS setup is fairly straightforward and can be set up on a wide variety of operating systems including Linux, BSD, and Solaris. In Linux, create an */etc/exports* file with the following line:

```
/nfs            *(rw,async)
```

You'll need to start the NFS server. RedHat users can do this with `service nfsd start`; Debian and Ubuntu users can use `/etc/init.d/nfsd start`.

Grab the OpenZipit packages from the Yahoo Group and put *zflash*, *loader. bin*, *zimage.dat* and *ramdisk.gz* in your */nfs* directory. *zflash* will need to be set as an executable:

```
chmod +x zflash
```

zflash. On the Zipit, you will need to type these commands after logging in by typing root at the login prompt. Substitute the IP address of your NFS server for the one in the example:

```
udhcpc
mount -t nfs -o nolock -o tcp -o intr 10.15.3.230:/nfs /mnt
cd /mnt
./zflash loader.bin zmage.dat ramdisk.gz
```

Type Yes at the prompt from *zflash*, and reboot when it tells you it's finished.

Customizing Your Image

Compiling Busybox apps isn't a task for the weak-at-heart, but setting up your configuration files, using some simple scripts and adding an application or two to OpenZipit is a good way to save your thumbs and give you a lot more bang for your C-note.

On your NFS host machine, mount the *ramdisk.gz* as a loopback device:

```
gunzip ramdisk.gz
mount -t loop ramdisk /mnt
```

Now, you can start editing your new filesystem. Once you're done, you will have to recompress the image:

```
umount /mnt
gzip -9 ramdisk
```

Lastly, you'll have to re-run *zflash* from the Zipit:

```
udhcpc
mount -t nfs -o nolock -o tcp -o intr 10.15.3.230:/nfs /mnt
cd /mnt
./zflash loader.bin zmage.dat ramdisk.gz
```

Modify the default settings. OpenZipit doesn't have a password for root, and since it is read-only, *passwd* isn't going to do you much good. Either copy your encrypted password over from another machine or generate a CRYPT password to put in */mnt/etc/shadow*. You can easily generate a CRYPT password using the JPRR CRYPT Password Generator (*http://jpirr.mnis.ad.jp/crypt_gen_web.html*).

There is no good reason that I can possibly think of to leave *telnetd* running so kill it:

```
rm /mnt/etc/init.d/S45/telnetd
```

There are already SSH host keys on the box, but if you care at all about security you will want to make your own:

```
ssh-keygen -t rsa -f /mnt/etc/dropbear/ssh_rsa_host_key
ssh-keygen -t dsa -f /mnt/etc/ssh_dss_host_key
mv /mnt/etc/init.d/dropbear /mnt/etc/init.d/S45dropbear
```

Change */mnt/etc/init.d/S45dropbear* to convert your SSH keys rather than generate them:

```
# Check for the Dropbear DSS key
if [ ! -f /etc/dropbear/dropbear_dss_host_key ] ; then
        echo Converting DSS Key...
```

Add useful scripts. It's always a good idea to write a script to get you back to your development environment with some sane defaults so you don't have to type in the NFS commands each time. My dev box is a Corel Netwinder, but typing in the hostname or IP address just takes too long, so I put this script in */mnt/usr/bin/nw*:

```
iwconfig eth0 essid swn-nodeone
ifconfig eth0 10.15.3.243 netmask 255.255.255.0 broadcast 10.15.1.255
route add default gw 10.15.3.1
rdate -s 10.15.3.230
mount -t nfs -o nolock -o intr 10.15.3.230:/nfs /mnt
```

You'll also want to alias some common hosts that you ssh to often, add your personal SSH keys and so on. I've found that due to the limited space on the Zipit, any large-footprint applications such as mail, RSS readers, and web browsers do best on remote machines. *ash* executes *.profile* on login, not *.bash_profile*, so make all of your aliases there. If you feel like cleaning up, remove all the *.bash* files in */mnt/root*.

Here's an alias that gives you a nice list of open access points:

```
echo "alias s='iwlist eth0 scanning|grep -B1 key:off|grep ESSID|cut \
-d\\\" -f2'" >> /mnt/root/.profile
```

You might also add a little script that attaches you to an open AP:

```
echo iwconfig eth0 essid \$1 \;udhcpc > /mnt/usr/bin/c & chmod +x \
/mnt/usr/bin/c
```

Get some tunes going. The audio card in the Zipit can't play anything above 64k without some skipping, and there isn't a lot of room for your MP3 collection, but it streams 56k Internet radio stations like a champ. You need to load the modules for the audio driver. Make a new file */mnt/etc/init.d/ S99local* and include the following lines:

```
insmod ep7212_audiodma
insmod wm8751l
insmod zipitaudio
```

Set up your mixer:

```
echo mix='aumix -d /dev/zipm -I' >> /mnt/root/.profile
```

The *freebase* application can play local files or streams. I like Groove Salad (Soma FM), so I always add this alias:

```
echo alias gs='freebase http://somafm-sc.streamguys.com:8066' >> \
/mnt/root/.profile
```

Hacking the Hack

So, now you have a pocketable Linux machine and some experience in customizing your images. You have rudimentary open AP scanning, so you're only a couple of keystrokes away from getting on the Internet at any given time. You have secure communications with Internet hosts over SSH, and you've got streaming Groove Salad.

What else can you do? Make it a remote control for iTunes? Control robots remotely? Those ideas and more are being discussed in the ZipitWireless Yahoo Group every day. You can also check out [Hack #60] to add a backlight to the screen.

What do you want to do with your Zipit? Once you figure that out, all that's left is to make it happen.

See Also

- Zipit Wireless Yahoo Group (*http://groups.yahoo.com/group/zipitwireless*)
- Remote control your Aibo (*http://aibohack.com/zipit/aibo.htm*)
- Zipit-controlled iTunes (*http://www.smassey.com/embedded.html*)

Capture Wireless Users with NoCatAuth

#74

Provide cryptographically sound access control using only a web browser.

NoCatAuth is an open source implementation of a *captive portal*. The idea behind a captive portal is fairly straightforward. When a user behind a captive portal attempts to browse to any web page, she is redirected to a page with a login prompt as well as information about the wireless network they are connected to. If the gateway consults with a central authority to determine the identity of the connected wireless user, once satisfied, it then relaxes its firewall rules accordingly. Until the user logs in, no other net-

throttling and firewall rules, and times out old logins after a user-specified time limit. The software is freely available and released under the GPL. You can find the source code at *http://nocat.net*. NoCatAuth runs best on Linux, because it is designed to work with the *iptables* firewall.

NoCatAuth is designed so that trust is ultimately preserved: the gateways and end users need trust only the Auth system, which is secured with a registered SSL certificate. Passwords are never given to the wireless gateway (thus protecting the users from *bad guy* node owners), and gateway rules are modified only by a cryptographically signed message from the Auth system (protecting the gateway from users or upstream sites trying to spoof the Auth system).

There are three possible classes of wireless user in NoCatAuth: Public Class, Co-op Class, and Owner Class:

Public Class
> This kind of user would be someone who knows nothing about the local wireless network, and simply is looking for access to the Internet. This class is granted very little bandwidth, and users are restricted in what services they can access by the use of firewall rules. The Public Class user is given the opportunity to learn more about who is providing the wireless service and how they can get in touch with the local owner (and ultimately get more access). They do not have personal logins, but must still authenticate by manually skipping the login process.

Co-op Class
> This class consists of users with prearranged login information. The rules for membership should be determined by the wireless node owner and are configured in the central Auth system database. This class is typically granted much greater bandwidth and access to ports, as users can now be held accountable for their own actions.

Owner Class
> This is much the same as the Co-op Class, but it is reserved for the owner of a given node and anyone else to whom they want to grant access. The Owner Class pre-empts traffic from all other classes and has free use of all network resources.

Figure 5-17 shows the typical connection process.

A roaming user associates with the access point and is immediately issued a DHCP lease by the router. All access beyond contacting the Authentication Service is denied by default using *iptables*. When the user tries to browse the Web, she is immediately redirected to the gateway service, which then redirects her to the Auth system's SSL login page (after appending a random

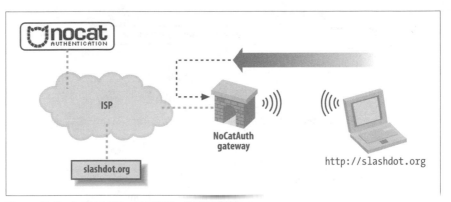

Figure 5-17. Web traffic captured by the gateway

token and some other information to the URL line). This process is completely transparent to the user, as shown in Figure 5-18.

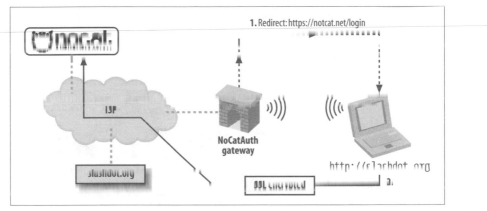

Figure 5-18. Redirection to an SSL-encrypted page on the Authentication Server

The user is then presented with three choices: log in with their prearranged

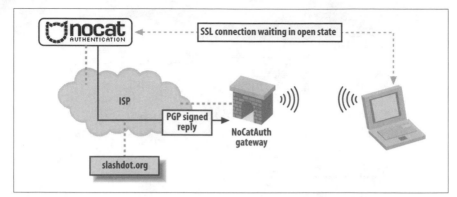

Figure 5-19. Credentials passed to the Authentication Service, which then notifies the gateway

Now, if all has gone well for the user, the wireless gateway modifies its firewall rules to grant further access and redirects the user back to the site to which they were originally trying to browse, as shown in Figure 5-20.

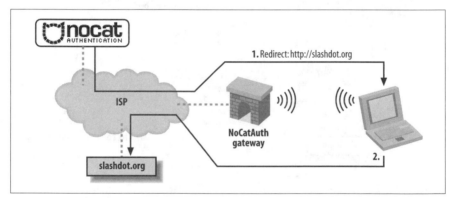

Figure 5-20. Redirection to the original web site

In order to keep the connection open to the Auth system, a small window is opened on the client side (via JavaScript) that refreshes the login page every few minutes. Once the user moves out of range or quits his browser, the connection is reset and requires another manual login.

The requirements on the gateway side are minimal. NoCatAuth was designed to run under Linux 2.4, on a 486 with 16MB of RAM. The Authentication Service is designed to be administered by a group that maintains its user database in whatever way they see fit. It can easily be configured to provide Members Only access, so rather than use a graded, class-based mechanism, users are either granted full access or none at all.

The NoCatAuth system is a mature project that is not receiving active development, but there are a number of other features of the software. Passive mode now allows operation without the connect-back phase (to allow installation behind a NAT firewall). There are also many additional back-end authentication methods, including PAM, RADIUS, TACACS+, and even IMAP. The gateways can be configured to throttle inbound and outbound traffic to a specified rate, as well as filter ports, protocols, services, and anything else that *iptables* can track. If you use the Pebble distribution [Hack #70], it comes with the NoCat gateway preconfigured.

There are a number of other captive portals available for you to experiment with. NoCatSplash [Hack #75] is a tiny implementation of NoCatAuth designed to run on embedded devices. WiFiDog (*http://dd.llesunsfil.org/wiki/WiFiDog*) and m0n0wall [Hack #71] can also run on small devices and have a number of other interesting features.

Capture Wireless Users on a Small Scale

If you need a simple "splash screen" for your wireless users, try this simple captive portal.

Perl is too heavy of a requirement for some gateway hardware, making it impractical to use NoCatAuth [Hack #74]. Fortunately, there is a captive portal you can use as an alternative.

If you are only looking for a "click here to continue" sort of splash page (without the full authentication mechanism), you might be interested in NoCatSplash, a port of NoCatAuth that is rewritten entirely in C and is under active development. Its requirements are quite small, but it supports only simple open mode portal functionality. The current version works under Linux, and portability to BSD and other systems is planned for the near future.

Owners of a Linksys WRT54G or similar hardware that is capable of run

This installs *splashd* to */usr/local/sbin*, and puts the *nocat.conf* configuration file in */usr/local/etc*. Edit the *nocat.conf* file to your tastes, making sure to set the ExternalDevice, InternalDevice, LocalNetwork, and DNSAddr options to fit your network layout. See the comments in the configuration file for details.

Start the portal by running *splashd* as root:

```
# /usr/local/sbin/splashd &
```

NoCatSplash uses the same firewall scripts as NoCatAuth to do the actual *iptables* firewall manipulation. It installs these scripts to */usr/local/libexec/nocat*, making it simple to customize your firewall rules if you need to. With *splashd* running, any users whose traffic originates on the InternalDevice will be captured and shown the splash page defined in *nocat.conf*. The default HTML files for the splash page are kept in */usr/local/share/nocat/htdocs*, but you can keep them wherever you like by setting the DocumentRoot option in *nocat.conf*.

While NoCatSplash might not be as feature rich as NoCatAuth, its requirements are simple. It can be ideal for situations where you simply want to give people an idea of whose network they are using, especially if the capabilities of your wireless gateway are limited.

HACK #76 Build an Online Community in Your Offline Neighborhood

Allow people in a café or other public Wi-Fi place to share information locally, apart from the global Web.

Wi-Fi is great for standard web and email access away from home. But take a closer look. That little router holds a world of opportunity that most people never consider.

Wi-Fi can:

- Connect people in a neighborhood, through web services tied intimately to a place.

- Offer an open venue for sharing digital information *locally,* which is a very different thing from publishing on the global Web (think: a chat with a regular at the local pub versus an interview with *The New York Times*).

- Provide a useful platform for location-based services that doesn't require participation by (or permission from) cellular carriers or Internet service providers.

You can work all this Wi-Fi mojo without forcing users to install any new hardware or software, and without requiring your favorite café owner (or other hotspot operator) to buy and maintain a server.

PlaceSite

Inspired by Sean Savage's research of Wi-Fi cafés at Intel Research Seattle in 2004, we (along with Jon Snydal) made PlaceSite our final Masters project at UC Berkeley. Marti Hearst at Berkeley's School of Information Management & Systems was our project advisor.

In May 2005, we launched an embryonic PlaceSite service in a Berkeley café, as shown in Figure 5-21. For a month, we studied how people used it and what they thought of it.

We think we're on to something.

The software for both components is still under heavy development, and much of this information will change, but the following description applies to the PlaceSite codebase as of July 2005. As we wrote this, we were preparing the code for release. As you read this, the code might be available for download. Please visit *http://www.placesite.com* for the latest.

The server. We wrote the first version of the PlaceSite server code in JSP. The server requires the following code base:

- Tomcat 5.0.28 (*http://jakarta.apache.org/site/downloads/downloads_ tomcat-5.cgi*) or later
- The latest stable release of MySQL 4.1 or greater (*http://dev.mysql.com/ downloads/mysql/4.1.html*)

The node. The PlaceSite node is a Linksys WRT54G router (available off the shelf for about US$50 as of July 2005) whose firmware has been replaced by the PlaceSite node software, which includes:

A specific version of OpenWRT [Hack #67]
A Linux distribution designed for the WRT54G. The code is download-able at *http://www.ilesansfil.org/tiki-list_file_gallery.php?galleryId=3*.

This is *not* the standard OpenWRT release. The WiFiDog project provides a specialized OpenWRT firmware image that must be used in order for WiFiDog, and PlaceSite, to function.

WiFiDog
Open source captive portal software designed to let hotspot owners create splash pages, password prompts, and so on that appear when users hit their hotspots. The WiFiDog package can be found at *http://old. ilesansfil.org/dist/WiFiDog*.

Our modifications
They're under heavy development, but once they're stable, we'll make them available at *http://placesite.com*.

PlaceSite in Action

The modified router and server deliver location-specific content to every Wi-Fi client within range of that place's PlaceSite router.

When someone fires up a laptop in the place, starts a session, and opens a browser, the router informs the server of that person's presence. The server sends that place's current PlaceSite home page to the router, which transmits it to the person's browser. It's the first web page the person sees at the start of her session.

Figure 5-22 shows what this person might see in her browser.

a lack of activity). Figure 5-23 shows an example of how to reveal or hide information in a profile.

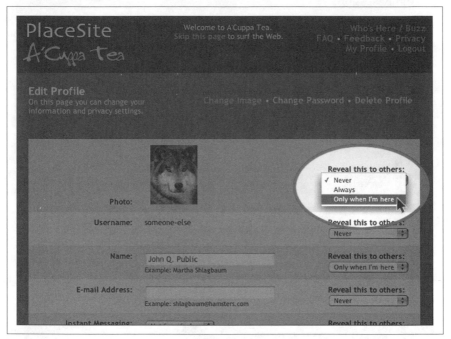

Figure 5-23. "Reveal" settings for personal information

Note that, in addition to user authentication (username/password login), the system provides *place authentication*: it serves up a node's content to *everyone* within range of that node's Wi-Fi router, and it serves that content *only* to those people. Currently, this authentication is performed via IP address, user token, and HTTP header validation. We are in the process of implementing a certificate-based authentication scheme. The router's contribution of simple place and presence data infuses traditional web services with powerful new benefits.

The real magic happens when many PlaceSite nodes talk to a single server, or to a federated group of servers that share live user and presence data. This forms a *network* of PlaceSite places and a *platform* that developers anywhere can build new location-based services on top of. Users can share their accounts across places, eliminating the need to reregister in each new place.

> See *http://www.placesite.com* for the latest on how this fits in with federated identity systems.

Views and communication between places become possible. Traditional web services (social networking/dating applications, mapping applications, local content providers, etc.) can hook into the platform's location and proximity data to dramatically boost the fun and usefulness of their offerings.

Setting Up Your Own PlaceSite

Follow the instructions from "Upgrade Your Wireless Router" [Hack #67] to install the OpenWRT firmware obtained from the WiFiDog project page. Once you have your firmware up and running, select the latest stable version of WiFiDog and install it via *ipkg*:

```
ipkg install http://old.ilesansfil.org/dist/WiFiDog/WiFiDog_1.1.1_mipsel.ipk
```

Once WiFiDog is installed, change the GatewayID option and setup an appropriate AuthServer section in the WiFiDog configuration file, */etc/wifidog.conf*:

```
GatewayID PlaceSite

AuthServer {
    Hostname yourserver.com
    HTTPPort 8080
    Path /path/to/PlaceSite/
}
```

To get the PlaceSite server set up, please see *http://www.placesite.com* for details. Since the public release of the code is imminent, any instructions we'd give you here are going to be out of date.

Running the Hack

Make sure that Tomcat and MySQL are running on the server and fire up WiFiDog on the node:

```
wifidog-init start
```

If it fails to talk to the PlaceSite AuthServer, check the values in your */etc/ wifidog.conf* file. Any other troubleshooting is beyond the scope of this hack, so consult the documentation for the relevant application.

Hacking the Hack

Now, open up your network to your community and use PlaceSite to get to know your neighbors. There's no limit to the ways you can customize your PlaceSite and remix it with other web services and with people, places, and things. Dig in.

At the time of this writing, we have three critical requests:

Keep the nodes connected
> The more nodes that are linked together, the more useful the network will be for everyone. We strongly encourage you to link any nodes that you create into the wider network. Please visit *http://www.placesite.com* for the latest on how to accomplish this.

Respect users' privacy
> While there's no such thing as complete privacy or security, we strive to never reveal data provided at one of our PlaceSite nodes beyond that place (either in other places or to other services or organizations)—until the user who owns the data specifically requests that it be shared in such a way. You're free to do what you wish, but we strongly recommend that you also follow this policy. If you choose not to, please don't use the PlaceSite name and branding with your services.

Check in at placesite.com
> I know, we're starting to sound like broken records. But by the time you read this, there are sure to be all sorts of new goodies and capabilities available so swing by and see what's cooking.

> —*Sean Savage and Damon McCormick*

HACK
#77   Manage Multiple AirPort Base Stations

Managing one AirPort Base Station is easy enough, but managing multiple stations can be an exercise in repetition. But it doesn't have to be.

Managing an AirPort Base Station is easy enough using the AirPort Admin Utility (*/Applications/Utilities*). In fact, one of the strong selling points of the AirPort Base Station over other wireless access points is the ease of use of the configuration tools compared to the web configuration interfaces found on the others. But there is a feature of the AirPort Admin Utility that you might not be aware of: the ability to save and load configurations.

At first glance, the ability to save and reload an AirPort Base Station's configuration might seem superfluous. After all, once the base station is configured, what's the point? Well, there's at least three that we can think of:

- Having a backup of your configuration is never a bad idea. If you have a simple configuration using just DHCP and no access control, losing your configuration is not a big loss. But if you've spent quite a bit of time adding lots of AirPort IDs (née MAC addresses) into the access control settings, you'll want to preserve that work somewhere.

- It allows you to have multiple configurations, which is handy for when you travel with your base station. For example, you could save your home configuration before you leave, then tweak the base station to work with whatever hotel or conference-room networks you encounter, and then reload your home configuration when you return.

- If you have multiple base stations, having one configuration that you can upload to all of them, making small tweaks as necessary, can be a godsend compared to manually making sure that all of their settings are correct.

To save your configuration, open your base station in AirPort Admin Utility and go to File → Save a Copy As. This saves a file with the extension *.baseconfig*. Once you have a configuration file, you can open it with AirPort Admin Utility, modify it, and then save it again.

To upload a configuration to a base station, completely replacing its current configuration, go to the File → Import and select the *baseconfig* file to use.

A Power Tool for Configuration Management

As nice as it is to be able to store and modify *.baseconfig* files for individual base stations, it's not the greatest solution for network administrators who need to take care of multiple base stations, especially when they need to update a particular setting across all of their base stations at once. In April

Figure 5-24. Airport Management Utility in action

network, you can select the base stations and make a change to a single line, as shown in Figure 5-25.

AirPort Management Utility will take care of updating the value on all of the base stations simultaneously.

Tweaking Placement of Base Stations

Another task that falls to administrators of wireless networks is the placement of base stations to best serve the machines for the network. Quite frankly, the signal strength meter on the menu bar leaves quite a bit to be desired as a tool to help get the best signal possible. Luckily, we now have the AirPort Client Monitor, another tool that comes as part of the AirPort Management Tools package. This tool not only reports signal strength much more accurately than the menu bar meter, but it also reports the noise on the connection, as well as the bandwidth available, as shown in Figure 5-26.

By using the AirPort Client Monitor, you can gather information about any computer and position it for best network performance. This tool fails, however, when you need to balance the position of a base station against

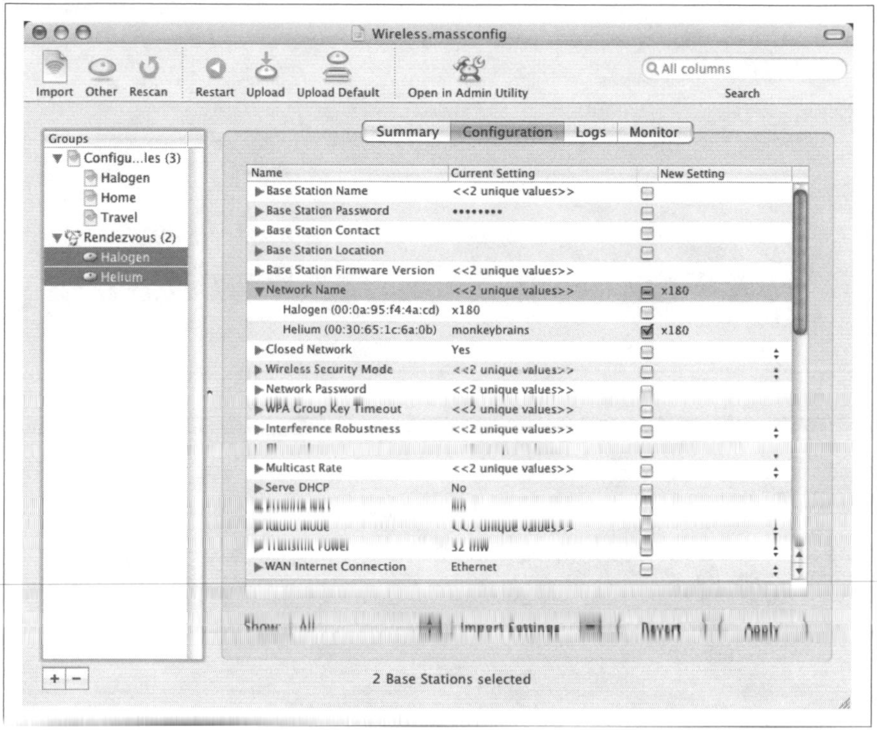

Figure 5-25. Editing values for multiple base stations

multiple machines. Sure, you could run back and forth between Macs and see their signal strengths one at a time as you make adjustments. But that would be the proverbial pain in the rear, not to mention a major threat to the color of your shoes.

Never fear; your soles are safe. Simply fire up AirPort Management Utility, select a base station, and click on the Monitor tab. This produces a chart of the signal strengths of all of the computers that are using that base station,

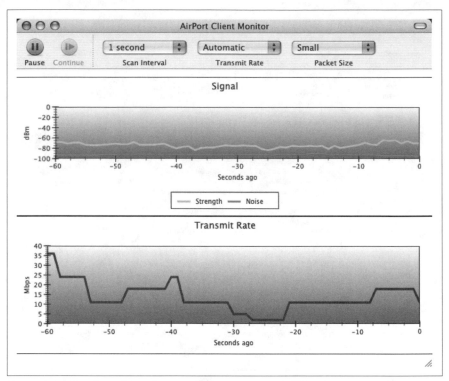

Figure 5-26. Tracking the performance of an AirPort connection

Advertise Bonjour Services in Linux
HACK #78

Use the Howl toolkit to publish services to Bonjour clients from your Linux box.

If you've already built your own access point [Hack #63], if you have a Windows, Linux, or BSD machine that you use as a server, or if you just want to share your streaming MP3 collection from your laptop, this hack is for you.

Background

Back in September 1999, the Internet Engineering Task Force (IETF) chartered a Zeroconf Working Group. Their purpose was to develop IP protocols for simple network usage similar to what AppleTalk had historically provided on proprietary Apple networks. Based on their work, there are now specifications for several items classified under Zero Configuration Networking:

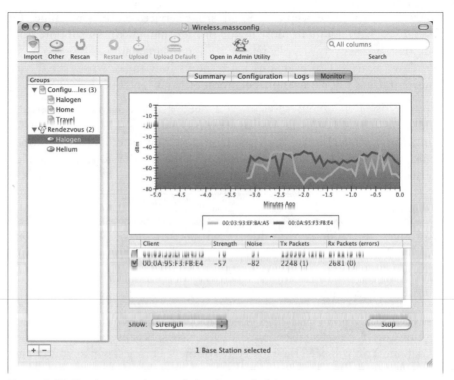

Figure 5-27. Tracking signal strength for clients of a base station

IPv4 Link-Local Addressing

If you've ever seen your computer attempt to get an IP address via DHCP, fail, and assign itself an IP address like 169.254.100.1, you have seen this specification in action. It allows a network device to assign itself a unique address on an ad hoc basis.

Multicast DNS

This allows translation between DNS names and IP addresses on the

Mac OS X users have been able to advertise services on their machines for several years. In addition, most major printer manufacturers support Bonjour device discovery. Apple released an implementation of Bonjour for Windows as well. However, this hack shows how to advertise any service you want using a Bonjour implementation on your Linux box.

To advertise Rendezvous services, you need a Multicast DNS advertiser. Apple has released a Posix implementation, which is adequate, but fairly limited in features. Instead, we're going to use Howl, a cross-platform open source Zeroconf implementation written by the friendly folks at Porchdog Software.

Using Howl

Download the source code for Howl at *http://www.porchdogsoft.com/ products/howl*. This hack won't compile Howl, since both of our example operating systems offer packages of the software.

Ubuntu users can install the necessary packages like so:

```
sudo apt-get install howl-utils mdnsresponder libhowl-dev
```

Fedora Core 3 (or later) users have it even easier, because Howl is included by default. You will need the Howl development libraries, which you can get using yum:

```
yum install howl-devel
```

> Mac OS X users can download the source code for Howl and compile it. You'll need to have the Xcode tools installed. Installation instructions can be found at *http://www. porchdogsoft.com/products/howl/InstallUnix.html*. Alternatively, Howl packages can be installed using Fink, available from *http://fink.sourceforge.net*. For a graphical method of advertising any service on OS X, see "Advertise Any Service with Bonjour in Mac OS X" **[Hack #79]**.

The configuration for howl is located in */etc/howl/mDNSResponder.conf* on Fedora Core, and */etc/mdnsresponder/mDNSResponder.conf* in Ubuntu. The sample *.conf* file has a couple commented out lines that show the parameters required:

```
[Name] [Service type] [Domain] [Port] [Text]
```

The first argument, *Name*, is the name of the service that users will see advertised. The name should be a descriptive name and should be enclosed in double quotes if there are any spaces.

The Service type field is a little tricky. It takes the following form, where *service* is a well-known IANA service name (i.e., something out of */etc/ services*, such as http) and *transport* is the actual transport (such as _tcp. or _udp.):

```
_service._transport.
```

The *Domain* argument in all of our examples will be local. (with the trailing dot). The *Port* argument is simply the port number of the service, and the optional *Text* field supplies additional information to the application receiving the advertisements (more on this later).

For example, here's how to advertise your local HTTP server:

```
example _http._tcp. local. 80
```

This creates an *example.local* address that resolves to your machine's IP address via Multicast DNS. It is an HTTP service, running on TCP port 80. This is fine, if you want to advertise the root of your web server, but what if you need to go to a particular URL? For example, to get to a wiki, you need to go to *http://example.local/wiki*, not just *http://example.local/*. This is where the optional text field at the end comes in. Web browsers will accept a path-argument in this field that gets appended to the URL line:

```
example _http._tcp. local. 80 "path /wiki"
```

Incidentally, if you're using VirtualHosts in Apache, you'll have to tell Apache to respond to the name you're advertising (*example.local* in the previous example). This is done easily with the ServerAlias directive from within your <VirtualHost> stanza:

```
ServerName example.too.com
ServerAlias example.local
```

You'll want to use *mDNSresponder.conf* for any services that you want Howl to advertise on startup. Howl also has included a binary that allows you to add published ser

HACK
#79

Advertise Any Service with Bonjour in Mac OS X

Use these two methods in Mac OS X to advertise any services you like.

While you can certainly use Howl [Hack #78] to advertise arbitrary Bonjour services from the command line, Mac OS X has a number of Aqua apps that will also do this for you. This hack presents two of the best available options.

Network Beacon

One good example is a freeware app called Network Beacon, available at *http://www.chaoticsoftware.com/ProductPages/NetworkBeacon.html*. It incorporates all of the functionality of Howl's mDNSPublish inside a simple, well-organized interface (Figure 5-28).

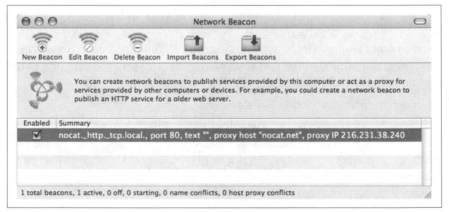

Figure 5-28. Network Beacon's main screen

Turning beacons on and off is as simple as clicking a checkbox. You can add as many beacons as you like, to whatever service, protocol, and port you need. It even allows you to advertise services that aren't local to your machine or network, as shown in Figure 5-28.

In this example, we're advertising the NoCat web site as the local Multicast DNS name *nocat.local*. This causes any Bonjour-enabled browsers on the local wireless network (such as Safari or Camino) to see a service called NoCat, which directs them to the IP address shown. As with Howl, you can change the URL that the user lands on by changing the Path= line in the Text Record box.

You can advertise any service you like by supplying the appropriate Service Type and Port Number. For example, to advertise an iTunes DAAP share, use _daap._tcp. as the Service Type, and 3689 as the port number. The little triangle button to the right of these fields provides a drop-down menu of common services and ports.

To make Network Beacon run whenever you are using your machine, simply add it to your Login Items in System Preferences. If you are interested in advertising Bonjour services, I highly recommend trying out this nifty free application.

mod_bonjour

Another quick and easy method for advertising web pages with Bonjour is to use mod_bonjour, part of the Apache installation on every Mac OS X box. Installations of Mac OS X prior to 10.4 will instead have a mod_rendezvous module. Add an entry like this to your */private/etc/httpd/httpd.conf* file:

```
<IfModule mod_bonjour.c>
    RegisterResource "Music on Example" "/Music/"
</IfModule>
```

This registers a path with the given description for your local machine. Restart Apache by clicking Stop and then Start under System Preferences → Sharing → Personal Web Sharing. Unfortunately, mod_bonjour doesn't support proxy like the previous method does, but it makes publishing local paths easy, without any additional software.

HACK #80 Redirect "Brought to you by" Bonjour Ads

Spam your fellow Bonjour users with sponsored links.

"Advertise Bonjour Services in Linux" [Hack #78] shows how simple it is to advertise arbitrary services using Bonjour. This makes it easy to provide easy reference links to every user on your wireless network.

> You may use this hack only for the forces of Good.

Wouldn't it be nice to give those users a public service announcement en route to their destination, to let them know who was kind enough to provide the link? You could even give them more information about yourself or the network you provide before they head out to the Internet. This is easily achieved with a simple application of Apache magic.

In the *httpd.conf* on your web server, create a new VirtualHost entry like this:

```
<VirtualHost *>
   ServerName adserver.local
   DocumentRoot /home/example/ads/
</VirtualHost>
```

You can, of course, call the server anything you want and put the DocumentRoot wherever is convenient. Restart your Apache for the change to take effect. Just be sure that the ServerName ends in .local.

Now create as many HTML files in DocumentRoot as you like, using this as a template:

```
<html>
<head>
    <meta http-equiv="Refresh" content="5;http://freenetworks.org" />
</head>
<body>

<h1>This Bonjour link brought to you by: me!</h1>

Redirecting you automatically in five seconds...
</body>
</html>
```

The URL at the end of the Refresh line will be the users' final destination, and the number at the beginning specifies the number of seconds to wait before redirecting. The body of the HTML can contain whatever message you want the users to see before the redirect takes effect.

Finally, advertise *adserver.local* (or whatever you used in your VirtualHost entry) as a proxy service using one of the methods described in "Advertise Bonjour Services in Linux" **[Hack #78]** or "Advertise Any Service with Bonjour in Mac OS X" **[Hack #79]**. In the text field of the Bonjour advertisement, specify the HTML file you just created. This example saves the HTML code to */home/example/ads/freenetworks.html* and specifies path=/freenetworks.html as the text field.

Now, users who share my wireless network see a Bonjour advertisement called FreeNetworks and are presented with the previous HTML when they browse to the site. Five seconds later, they are redirected automatically to the real *http://freenetworks.org* and are left to go about their merry way. This sort of service is ideal for permanent services on public access wireless nodes, to give users an idea of who is providing Internet access.

Use a Windows-Only Wireless Card in Linux

HACK #81

Take advantage of Windows NDIS drivers using WLAN DriverLoader or NdisWrapper.

Open source software is just that: open. There's no law requiring software or hardware manufacturers to ensure compatibility with operating systems. In the case of some wireless card manufacturers, this is exactly what has happened. Wireless cards are released, with accompanying drivers for Windows, and that's it. The companies, for various reasons, are not interested in allowing their cards to run under Linux, and do not release any information on their cards.

Unfortunately, some of these manufacturers are rather large, and one in particular—Broadcom—accounts for a significant percentage of the 802.11g wireless cards being sold on the market. What is the dedicated Linux user to do?

There are a couple of options, both of which use the Windows binary drivers that come with a wireless card and load them under Linux. As with the Madwifi driver for Atheros cards [Hack #83], neither of these options is fully open source, since you are using the binary closed-source Windows driver.

WLAN DriverLoader

WLAN DriverLoader (available from *http://www.linuxant.com/driverloader*) is a compatibility wrapper program from a company called Linuxant. It allows the use of Windows NDIS (Network Driver Interface Specification) wireless network drivers in Linux.

You can get packages and the source code, but Linuxant has also provided a downloadable script that you can run to automates the installation. To work properly, you'll need to have existing Internet access for the script to download pieces it needs.

The script is named *dldrinstall.run* and you can execute it as follows:

```
sh dldrinstall.run
```

When the script runs, a web browser opens, and you'll be prompted for the root username and password for your machine. This is required, because you're installing kernel-level drivers. The script will determine what kind of system you're running on and present a couple options for packages that can be installed.

The package will download and install. Once the installation is complete, you'll be prompted to send your browser to a different local URL to configure DriverLoader, as shown in Figure 5-29.

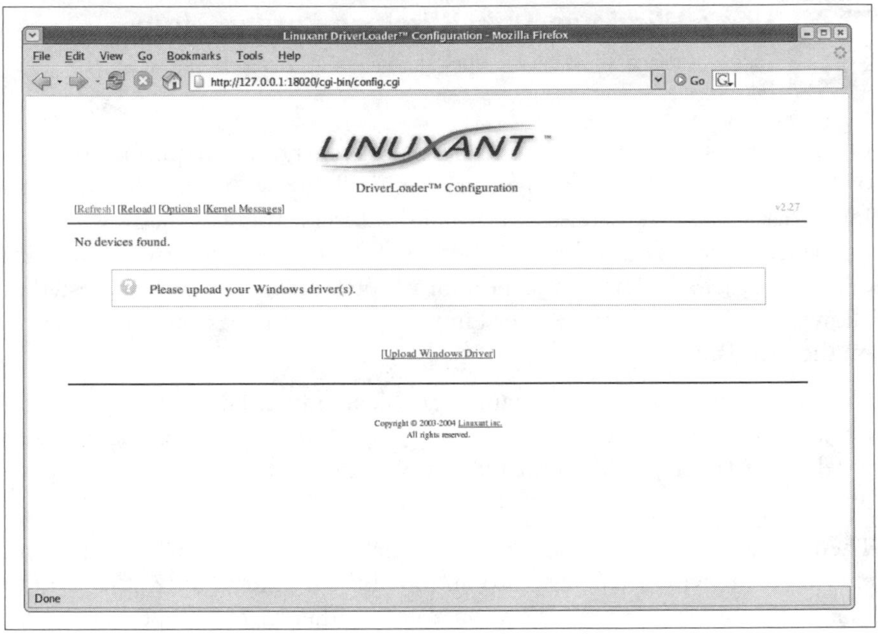

Figure 5-29. DriverLoader main configuration screen

At this point, you'll need the Windows driver for your wireless card. You can get these from the install disk that came with your card, or download them from the vendor. Linuxant also keeps a web page with lists of commonly used wireless cards and links directly to their driver downloads at *http://www.linuxant.com/driverloader/drivers.php*.

The pieces you'll need from the Windows driver package will be an INF and a SYS file. In our case, we were using an Atheros-based Linksys wireless card, so the required files were *net5211.inf* and *ar5211.sys*. Filenames and location of driver files will obviously vary for each vendor and card.

After you have uploaded both required files, the DriverLoader web page will show you a status screen that lists installed drivers and any hardware that matches the drivers. Assuming you have your card inserted or installed, you'll see a screen similar to Figure 5-30.

DriverLoader is commercial software and requires a license. You can get a 30-day trial license key from their web site, to ensure that the software works correctly for you and your card. Once you've verified that it works, a permanent license, keyed to the MAC address of your wireless card, costs $20. You can obtain either a trial or permanent license at *https://www. linuxant.com/store*.

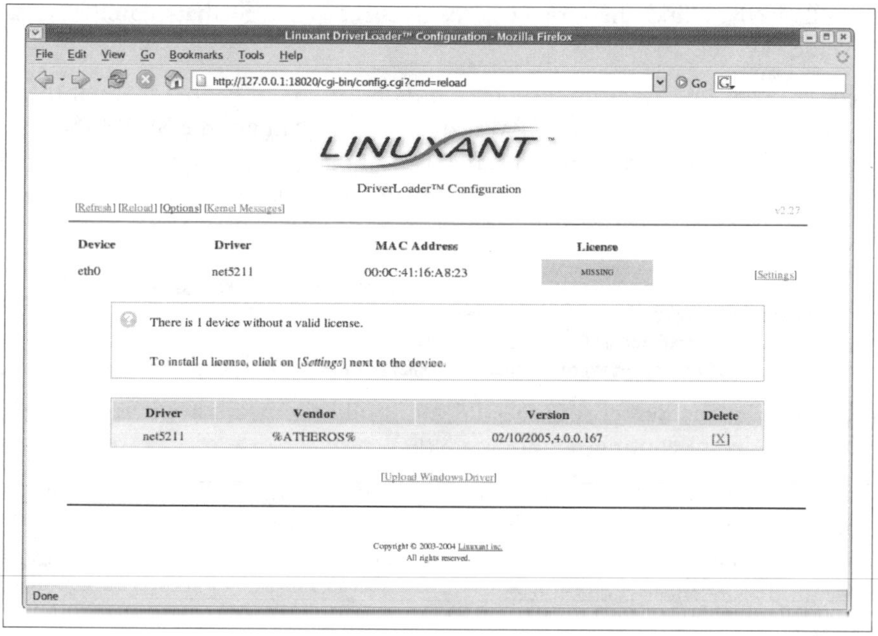

Figure 5-30. Windows drivers loaded correctly

Now that you have entered a valid license key, you should have an active wireless interface. In our case, we had removed a MiniPCI Ethernet card from our system and installed a MiniPCI wireless card. This caused Driver-Loader to bring up the wireless card as *eth0*, since there were no other active network interfaces. Users installing on Fedora Core may have to manually create an */etc/sysconfig/ifcfg-eth0* file to bring up the interface on boot, since the original file for the MiniPCI ethernet card will be removed after a reboot.

An added advantage of using DriverLoader is support for WPA capabilities in the Windows drivers. To take advantage of this support, you'll need additional WPA supplicant software [Hack #42].

NdisWrapper

NdisWrapper is an open-source project hosted at SourceForge, which has essentially the same features and goals as Linux DriverLoader. There are no license fees, but there is also no technical support department. You'll have to do some heavy lifting to get it working, but it does work well.

The first thing to do is to make sure that you have the source for your Linux kernel. Debian and Ubuntu users can find the correct kernel source with the following command:

```
apt-cache search kernel-source
```

You'll need to find the correct kernel-source package that matches your installed kernel.

Fedora users have to jump through a little hoop. As of Fedora Core 3, there is no longer a kernel-source RPM available. You can get the SRPM (Source RPM) from the Fedora Core 3 install CD, but chances are it won't match the current kernel you're running, because of kernel updates.

Instead, execute the following commands:

```
sudo rpm -Uvh ftp://mirrors.kernel.org/fedora/core/updates/3/SRPMS/kernel-
`uname -r`.src.rpm
cd /usr/src/redhat/SPECS
sudo rpmbuild -bp -target=`uname -m` kernel-2.6.spec
```

This will get the kernel source RPM and build the necessary kernel source files you need to continue compiling NdisWrapper.

Now that you have the kernel sources, you'll need the NdisWrapper source code, which you can download from *http://ndiswrapper.sourceforge.net*. Extract the compressed file, change to the newly created *ndiswrapper* directory, and issue these commands:

```
make distclean
sudo make
sudo make install
```

This will compile and install the NdisWrapper kernel modules and user utilities.

According to the developers, you might or might not have good luck with the Windows drivers that came with your wireless card. Instead, they suggest that you first check *http://ndiswrapper.sourceforge.net/phpwiki/index. php/List?* for an updated list of known working cards and the correct drivers.

Once you've identified your card and downloaded the driver, or have decided to experiment with your own card and driver that isn't listed, you'll need to find the INF and SYS files in the driver directory. Again, we're using an Atheros-based Linksys card, so we're looking for *net5211.inf* and *ar5211.sys*.

Make sure the INF and SYS files are in one directory, and then execute the following as root:

```
ndiswrapper -i filename.inf
```

This will copy necessary files to */etc/ndiswrapper* and set up configuration files for your wireless card. At this point, if you don't have your wireless card inserted or installed, go ahead and do it. You can now check the status of the drivers:

```
ndiswrapper -l
```

If all is well, you'll see output like this:

```
Installed ndis drivers:
net5211 driver present, hardware present
```

Finally, you'll need to manually load the kernel module:

modprobe ndiswrapper

To verify that the module loaded successfully, execute the dmesg command. You should see output at the end like this:

```
ndiswrapper: driver net5211 loaded
wlan0: ndiswrapper ethernet device 0a:43:32:6a:33:01
```

If you don't see the second line, chances are the driver has not successfully loaded. Check to see if there is more diagnostic information.

You can now configure the card using the Wireless Tools:

iwconfig wlan0 essid Example mode Managed

At this point, there are a couple of things you'll want to do in order for your card to be recognized at boot. Add a line of ndiswrapper to the */etc/modules* file, and then execute this command:

ndiswrapper -m

Depending on your distribution, you'll also want to make sure there is TCP/IP configuration for your wireless interface. Debian and Ubuntu users should edit */etc/network/interfaces*, RedHat and Fedora users will need to create or edit */etc/sysconfig/network-scripts/ifcfg-interface*.

Final Thoughts

Both of these programs require quite a bit of configuration and fiddling. However, for using certain brands of wireless cards with Linux, they are your only options. If you want technical support and don't mind forking over the $20 for a license, DriverLoader is probably your better choice. NdisWrapper works well but does take a little more knowledge up front.

HACK #82 Use Your Orinoco Card with Hermes AP

Enable BSS master mode on Hermes-based radios.

Hermes-based radio cards (such as the tremendously popular but confusingly named Lucent/Orinoco/Avaya/Proxim Silver and Gold cards) are notoriously difficult to operate in BSS **[Hack #63]** master mode. By design, the cards themselves are actually not able to provide BSS master services on their own.

You might find this surprising, since they are the radio card embedded in the original AirPort AP, as well as the RG1000, RG1100, AP1000, and many others. Before these cards can operate as a BSS master, they need additional firmware uploaded to the card. This *tertiary firmware* is uploaded to the card's RAM, and is lost if the card loses power. To make matters even more difficult, the firmware in question is licensed software, and can't legally be distributed by anyone but the manufacturer.

The ingenious Hermes AP project, located at *http://hunz.org/hermesap.html*, addresses both of these tricky issues. It consists of a set of modified drivers, a utility for uploading the tertiary firmware, and a simple script that downloads the firmware from Proxim's public FTP server. Hermes AP isn't trivial to get running, but can be the perfect piece of software if you absolutely need a host-based Orinoco AP.

To get Hermes AP running, you need a 2.4-series kernel (2.6 kernels will *not* work with this hack) with Dev FS enabled. This allows the kernel to manage the */dev* directory, dynamically creating device files for every physical device that the kernel supports. You'll need to compile your own kernel with Dev FS enabled. If you haven't compiled a kernel before, you might want to skip this hack.

Run a make menuconfig, and select "Code maturity level options" → "Prompt for development and/or incomplete code/drivers." Now, go back to the main menu, and under "File systems," enable "/dev file system support," as well as "Automatically mount at boot." When running Dev FS, it's also a good idea to disable "/dev/pts file system support."

Before you recompile your kernel, copy all of the source code under the *drivers/* directory from Hermes AP over top of the existing drivers in the kernel (right over top of the files in *linux/drivers/net/wireless/*). Now, build your kernel and modules as you normally would, and reboot.

Your Orinoco card should come up as usual with the new driver, but won't support BSS master mode yet. First, cd to the Hermes AP source directory. To download a copy of the tertiary firmware from Proxim's site, run the *hfwget.sh* script in the *firmware/* directory. Next, build the hfwload utility by running make in the *hfw/* directory. This utility uploads the tertiary firmware to your card. Copy the utility and the card firmware somewhere handy (I keep mine in */usr/local/hermesap*) and run a command like this at boot time, before the interface comes up:

```
cd /usr/local/hermesap; ./hfwload eth1 T1085800.hfw
```

Note that the card must not be configured as up when you load the firmware; if it is already up, an ifconfig eth1 down will bring it down for you. If all goes well, an iwconfig should show that eth1 is in Master mode! You can now configure the radio with an ESSID, WEP keys, and any other features as you normally would.

For an 802.11b access point, we prefer HostAP and a Senao/EnGenius card, or Madwifi and an Atheros card [Hack #63] to Hermes AP. The radio cards are more powerful and sensitive, the drivers are under active development, and they have many more features. But if you are stuck with an Orinoco flavor radio card, Hermes AP might be just the code you need.

Do-It-Yourself Antennas
Hacks 83–93

The price of wireless networking hardware has fallen dramatically in a very short time. Wireless adapters now come standard with many computers, and off-the-shelf access points are commonplace, making it easy for just about anyone to set up an off-the-shelf wireless network. However, the prices of antennas and related components have also fallen sharply as high demand and extreme competition have driven the industry to an increasingly high-volume, low-margin business.

These lower prices have enabled do-it-yourselfers to experiment and find out just how little it takes to build a working network. There is something almost magical about radio networking. Tales of war driving (and even war walking) aside, just imagine that today in many cities around the world, dozens of invisible networks exist on any given street corner. As you sit at a cafe eating your lunch, you might be completely unaware of the dozens of people simultaneously using the environment around you to communicate with people around the world. I believe that it is largely this mysterious, intangible aspect of unseen global communications that draws people to embark on their own antenna projects. The deeply rewarding feeling of making something useful out of virtually nothing is worth much more than saving a few dollars on an off-the-shelf network component.

When comparing antenna designs, there are a number of important factors to keep in mind. The first antenna property that people usually refer to is *gain*. The gain of an antenna is a measurement of how well it radiates in the direction you intend it to, measured in decibels. This measurement is actually the antenna's performance as compared to an imaginary invention called an *isotropic radiator* (this is the *i* in dBi).

Imagine an infinitely small light suspended in the vacuum of space. It radiates light equally in all directions, and by definition has no gain in any direction. Now, take this light and place it in the head of a flashlight. Without increasing the brightness of the bulb, you can turn the head of the flashlight to focus its beam in a particular direction. This is gain. By directing the energy in a particular direction, you both make the light cover a smaller area and appear to be brighter in the area it does cover. The higher the gain, the tighter and brighter the beam appears to be. Also note that antenna gain is *reciprocal*, meaning that it works for both transmission and reception. Adding an antenna to either end of a radio link will help performance for both ends of the link.

Another important property to keep in mind when designing or purchasing an antenna is that it must be tuned to the frequency for which you are using it. An antenna that is well matched to the radio it is connected to is said to have a low *standing wave ratio* (SWR). The SWR of an antenna is measured using an SWR meter or reflectometer. It is a measurement of how much energy actually leaves the antenna versus how much energy is reflected back at the radio from the antenna itself. At (legal) 802.11-power levels, a badly mismatched antenna with a high SWR simply results in poor performance. At higher power levels, a mismatched SWR can actually damage your radio or amplifier. As you'll see in the antenna designs in this chapter, the antenna is tuned by manipulating a number of factors, including the size of various active components, and their relative distance away from reflective components.

One property of antennas that is frequently overlooked by beginners is their *front-to-back* (F/B) ratio. This is a measurement of how much energy radiates in the expected direction (at the center of the strongest beam) versus the average amount of energy radiated in the opposite direction. A high F/B ratio means that most of the energy goes in the direction that the antenna is pointed. A low F/B ratio means that more energy is lost in the reverse direction, potentially causing unwanted interference with nearby devices. This is particularly important if you are using two or more antennas adjacent to each other, pointed in different directions. A higher F/B means that it is less likely that adjacent antennas will interfere with each other.

Finally, one last important property of antennas to keep in mind is their *polarization*. Briefly, this refers to the orientation of the electrical and magnetic parts of the radio wave as they leave the antenna. Polarization is discussed in greater detail in "Take Advantage of Antenna Polarization" [Hack #100]. There is also a comparison of the various general types of antennas and their typical uses in Appendix B.

The hacks in this chapter describe a number of inexpensive, highly effective antenna designs that you might find useful for your own wireless networking project.

> Federal Communications Commission (FCC) regulations govern the use of wireless antennas, largely to make sure they don't interfere with communications systems of emegency vehicles and keep people from inadvertently disrupting their neighbors' electronics systems. The FCC web site (*http://www.fcc.gov*) provides a search tool to help you find relevant information on the new FCC regulations, which allow for high-gain certification of the types of antennas covered in this chapter.

H A C K   Make a Deep Dish Cylindrical Parabolic Reflector
#83   This simple design provides high gain without pigtails or modifying your AP.

We needed a parabolic reflector to focus coverage. This design can reduce signal from some areas while enhancing signal in other areas. The reflector was designed to be installed in outdoor enclosures with WAP-11 access points, but it is becoming quite popular with people building indoor LANs, as well as with people building short point-to-point links. This design offers high performance and easy construction: scissors, tape, cardboard, tin foil, and 20 minutes, and you are in business. The completed project is shown in Figure 6-1.

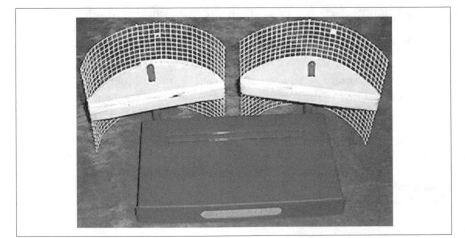

Figure 6-1. Reflector installs without any pigtails

This antenna is so easy to make, tune, and install, and it performs so well, that you should try one before electing to purchase a commercial antenna. One benefit is that you can cheaply check to see whether you are purchasing enough commercial antenna gain to make the link you want.

Here are some advantages over other antennas:

- No pigtail [Appendix B] required
- No modification to AP (no voiding of warranty)
- No matching (SWR) problems
- No purchased parts
- Trivially easy construction
- Very low probability of error
- As good as or better performance than the Pringles can antenna [Hack #85]
- Superior front-to-back/front-to-rear ratio
- Improves wireless LAN privacy
- Reduces interference

This design can easily complete links up to one kilometer by sitting two WAP-11s in windows at each end of a link with clean line of sight. The 6-inch version of the antenna gives you about 10 to 12 dB of gain over the stock antenna. With a WAP11, this equates to approximately 27 to 33 dB of *Effective Isotropically Radiated Power* (EIRP). This means you wind up with an apparent power in the favored direction between 500 mW and 2 watts.

Of course, that gain has to come from somewhere. It comes from the back side of the reflector, so power that is normally transmitted in that direction is *bounced* forward. That feature of this antenna can be used to enhance the privacy of your wireless network, which was my reason for designing it in the first place. The rest is just gravy (but it is real and rather tasty gravy). Figure 6-2 shows the approximate radiation pattern of a 9-inch reflector.

To build this reflector, you can use the sample template in Figure 6-3 or download the original reflector template from *http://www.freeantennas.com/ projects/template/parabolic.pdf*. The drawing can be scaled using a copy machine to make a dish of any reasonable size. The gain computations for various sizes of the dish are also provided on the web site, as well as rough graphs showing beam width and gain/frequency. This reflector is frequency independent, meaning it works with any wireless gear, on any band.

The square drawn on the diagram will help you to ensure that your scaling does not corrupt the aspect ratio of the template. In other words, if the square is still square after you enlarge or reduce the template, you still have a good template.

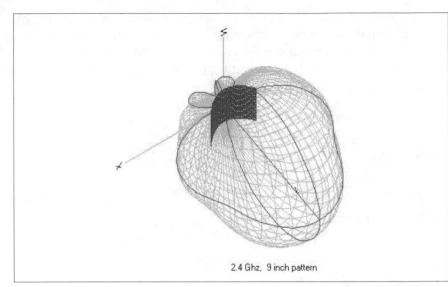

2.4 Ghz, 9 inch pattern

Figure 6-2. Approximate radiation pattern for a 9" reflector

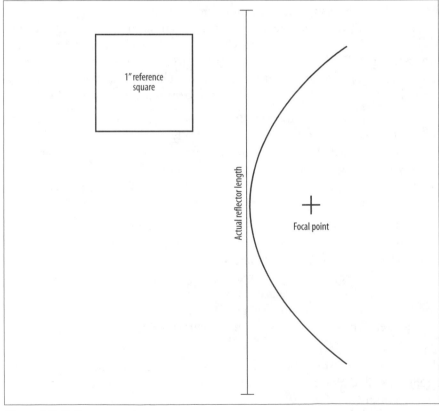

1" reference square

Actual reflector length

Focal point

Figure 6-3. Reflector template

Focal length varies proportionally with the size of the dish, so the focal point is also shown in the drawings. Positioning of the feed point (focal point) is the most critical aspect of a deep dish parabolic. Errors of 1/4" or more are unacceptable at these frequencies. It might help to fiddle with the positioning, as small irregularities (~1/4" or greater) will move the focal point slightly. If the dipole is not in the focal point, you will lose gain. Parabolic reflectors also lose gain if your finished reflector varies much from the correct curve.

The reflector is designed to be fed by a dipole, which is why it is not circular. A dipole is long and cylindrical, while the focal point on a circular dish is circular. The focal point on this design is a cylinder. Many access points (such as the WAP-11) use one or more dipoles as their antenna. This reflector is the optimal shape for such an antenna. Some units, such as the WET-11, do *not* use dipoles as their antenna. You can download a modified template for the WET-11 at *http://www.freeantennas.com/projects/template/index.html*.

The reflector should be made from a piece of square material to shape the curve. If you need to reduce height for packaging reasons, a shorter antenna will work but will lose roughly 3 dB for each halving of reflector height. It is also important to try to get the dipole lined up in the center of the reflector.

Front-to-back ratio is a measurement of how well a directional antenna rejects interference from directions other than the desired direction. The front-to-back ratio with this antenna depends upon the size of the wire mesh you use to make the antenna. Finer mesh yields only slightly better gain but yields much better front-to-back ratio. Modeling shows the F/B ratio to be better than ~25 dB if you use 1/4" or smaller mesh. My calculated gain figures presume the reflector is 55 percent efficient. If you use a solid sheet of aluminum or copper as your reflector, your gain figures may be a little bit higher than these. The radiation pattern is narrower in the vertical plane than the horizontal plane.

People have made good reflectors from Pringles cans, large tin cans, wire screen, aluminum sheet, and tin roofing material. Any flat metal surface or screen, such as tinfoil taped to cardboard, will work. You can build one of these in less than a half an hour using an old shoebox and a roll of tin foil.

—Michael Erskine

HACK #84 Spider Omni Antenna

The spider omni is possibly the smallest and simplest omnidirectional antenna design around.

This is one of the simplest and smallest homemade antenna designs we've seen for 2.4 GHz. It isn't much larger than a standard N connector—

because that is exactly what it is made of. It has been dubbed the *spider omni*, because it looks a bit like a crazed spider crawling up your antenna feed, as shown in Figure 6-4. Technically, it is a ground plane antenna, but practically speaking, it acts like a vertically polarized 3 dB omni.

Figure 6-4. The spider omni

The spider is simple to construct, if you have a good soldering iron and some basic tools. You need a standard N connector and about a foot or so of solid copper 12-2 romex (common 12-gauge electrical wiring). You'll also need a good vice to hold onto the pieces as you solder them, as well as a pair of needle-nose pliers, some good solder, and a bottle of flux.

First, cut five pieces of bare copper romex, each about 3 cm long. Straighten out each piece as best as you can. Using needle nose pliers, make a small 180-degree bend on one end of four of the pieces. Now, tin the bent tip of each piece, as well as one end of the remaining straight piece. This will make your soldering job much easier later.

> If you don't know what *tinning* is, you might want to get the help of a friend who has experience with soldering. To *tin* means to cover the end of a piece of wire with solder before actually soldering it to your project. This helps the solder to flow better, and ultimately makes a better bond between the metal surfaces.

Next, solder the straight piece to the gold cup on your N connector [Appendix B]. Don't use too much solder; there should be just enough to fill the cup without overflowing. Prepare to solder the four legs directly onto the N connector's chassis. You need to use a lot of heat, and liquid flux will help the solder to flow better and bond to the body of the connector. I found it easiest to clamp the straight piece of wire, rather than the threaded bottom of the N connector. This helps to keep the heat from dissipating into your vise while you solder to the chassis.

Take your time, and don't use too much solder on the legs. When you are finished, let the whole thing cool for several minutes, as the chassis will be quite hot.

Now, trim all of the leads to about 20 mm past the edge of the housing. Trim the center lead to about 20 mm past the end of the gold cup. Bend the four radials connected to the housing down at a slight angle. Physically mounting the omni is straightforward if you use heavy feed line, such as LMR 400. Mount the antenna with the center lead pointing up.

The spider omni doesn't provide a tremendous amount of gain, about 3 dB or so, as far as we can tell from informal tests, but it does work quite well for what it is. Higher gain antennas are certainly possible [Hack #89], but they tend to be more complicated and much larger. For many applications, you just can't beat the size and cost of this tiny little antenna.

HACK #85 Pringles Can Waveguide

Here's how to make the infamous Pringles cantenna.

At the Portland Summit in June 2001, Andrew Clapp presented a novel yagi antenna design (*http://www.aeonic.com/~clapp/wireless*). It used a bolt, metal tubing, washers, and PVC tubing to make an inexpensive *shotgun* yagi, either 18" or 36" long. While his antenna shows between 12 and 15 dBi gain (which is impressive for such a simple design), it's also quite large. When we returned from Portland, some members of our local group realized that, if we were careful, we could fit a full wavelength inside of a Pringles can (see Figure 6-5). This would show a reduced total gain, but it would also make the entire antenna much more compact.

This now infamous hack takes about an hour to construct. Table 6-1 shows a list of the parts you need to get started.

Figure 6-5. The complete Pringles can antenna

Table 6-1. Part list for a Pringles can waveguide

Part	Approximate cost
All-thread, 5 5/8" long, 1/8" OD	$1.00
Two nylon lock nuts	$0.10
Five 1" washers, 1/8" ID	$0.10
6" aluminum tubing, 1/4" ID	$0.75
A connector to match your radio pigtail or antenna cable (we used a female N connector)	$3.00
One 1/2" piece of 12-gauge solid copper wire (we used ground wire from house electrical wiring)	Negligible
A tall Pringles can (any flavor, Ridges are optional)	$1.50
Scrap plastic disc, 3" across (for example, another Pringles can lid)	Negligible
Total:	$6.45

Of course, buying in bulk helps a lot. You probably won't be able to find a 6" piece of all-thread; buy the standard size (usually one or two feet) and a 10-pack of washers and nuts while you're at it. Then you'll have more than enough parts to make two antennas, all for about $10.

You'll also need the following tools:

- Ruler
- Scissors
- Pipe cutter (or hacksaw or dremel tool, in a pinch)

- Heavy-duty cutters (or dremel again, to cut the all-thread)
- Something sharp to pierce the plastic (such as an awl or a drill bit)
- Hot glue gun (unless you have a screw-down type connector)
- Soldering iron

Front Collector Construction

Mark and cut four pieces of tubing, about 1.2" (1 15/64"). Where did I get this number? First figure out the wavelength at the bottom of the frequency range we're using (2.412 GHz, or Channel One). This will be the longest that the pipe should be:

```
W = 3.0 * 10^8 * (1 / 2.412) * 10^-9
W = (3.0 / 2.412) * 10^-1
W = 0.124 meters
W = 4.88 inches
```

We'll be cutting the pipe to quarter wavelength, so:

```
1/4 W = 4.88 / 4
1/4 W = 1.22"
```

Now, figure out what the shortest range we'll ever use is (2.462 GHz, or channel 11 in the United States):

```
W = 3.0 * 10^8 * (1 / 2.462) * 10^-9
W = (3.0 / 2.462) * 10^-1
W = 0.122 meters
W = 4.80 inches
1/4 W = 1.20"
```

Practically speaking, what's the difference between the shortest pipe and the longest pipe length? The answer is about 0.02" or less than 1/32". That's probably about the size of the pipe cutter blade you're using. So, just shoot for 1.2" and you'll get it close enough.

Cut the all-thread to exactly 5 5/8". The washers we used are about 1/16" thick, so that should leave just enough room for the pipe, washers, and nuts.

Pierce a hole in the center of the Pringles can lid big enough for the all-thread to pass through. Now is probably a good time to start eating Pringles.

 We found it better for all concerned to just toss the things; "Salt & Vinegar" Pringles are almost caustic after the first 15 or so. Heed the recommended serving size!

Cut a 3" plastic disc, just big enough to fit snugly inside the can. We found that another Pringles lid, with the outer ridge trimmed off, works just fine. Poke a hole in the center of it, and slip it over one of the lengths of pipe.

Now, assemble the pipe. You might have to use a file or dremel tool to shave the tips of the thread, if you have trouble getting the nuts on. The pipe is a sandwich that goes on the all-thread like this:

Nut → Lid → Washer → Pipe → Washer → Pipe → Washer → Pipe-with-Plastic → Washer → Pipe → Washer → Nut

You can see the collector assembly clearly in Figure 6-5. Tighten down the nuts to be snug, but don't overtighten (I bent the tubing on our first try; aluminum bends *very* easily). Just get it snug. Congratulations; you now you have the front collector.

Preparing the Can

By now, you should have eaten (or tossed) the actual chips. Wipe out the can, and measure 3 3/8" up from the bottom of the can. Cut a hole just big enough for the connector to pass through. We found through trial and error that this seems to be the *sweet spot* of the can. On our Pringles "Salt & Vinegar" can, the N connector sat directly between "Sodium" and "Protein."

Element Construction

Straighten the heavy copper wire and solder it to the connector. When inside the can, the wire should be just below its midpoint (ours turned out to be about 1 1/16"). You lose a few dB by going longer, so cut it just shy of the middle of the can.

We were in a hurry, so we used hot glue to hold the connector in place on our first antenna. If you have a connector that uses a nut and washer, and you're really careful about cutting the hole, these work very well (and aren't nearly as messy as hot glue). Just remember that you're screwing into cardboard when you connect your pigtail. It's easy to forget and accidentally tear the wall of the can.

Now, insert the collector assembly into the can and close the lid. The inside end of the pipe should *not* touch the copper element; it should be just forward of it. If it touches, your all-thread is probably too long.

How can you estimate gain without access to high-end radio analysis gear? Using the Link Test software that comes with the Orinoco Silver cards, you can see the signal and noise readings (in dB) of a received signal, as well as your test partner's reception of your signal. As I happen to live 0.6 mile (with clean line of sight) from O'Reilly headquarters, we had a fairly controlled test bed to experiment with. We shot at the omni on the roof and used the access point at O'Reilly as our link test partner.

To estimate antenna performance, we started by connecting commercial antennas of known gain and taking readings. Then, we connected our test antennas and compared the results. We had the following at our disposal:

- Two 10 dBi, 180-degree sector panel antennas
- One 11 dBi, 120-degree sector panel antenna
- One 24 dBi parabolic dish
- The Pringles can antenna

Table 6-2 shows the average received signal and noise readings from each, in approximately the same physical position.

Table 6-2. Average received signal and noise readings

Antenna	Signal	Noise
10dBi A	-83db	-92db
10dBi B	-83db	-92db
11dBi	-82db	-95db
24dBi	-67db	-102db
Pringles can	-81db	-98db

The test partner (AP side) signal results were virtually the same. Interestingly, even at only 0.6 mile, we saw some thermal fade effect; as the evening turned into night, we saw about a 3 dB gain across the board.

It had been a particularly hot day: almost 100 degrees. I don't know what the relative humidity was, but it felt fairly dry.

Yagis and dishes are much more directional than sectors and omnis. This bore out in the numbers, as the perceived noise level was consistently lower with the more directional antennas. This can help a lot on long-distance shots, as not only will your perceived signal be greater, but the competing noise will also seem to be less. More directional antennas also help keep noise down for your neighbors trying to share the spectrum as well. Be a good neighbor and use the most directional antennas that will work for your application (yes, noise is everybody's problem).

The Pringles can seemed to have large side lobes that extend about 45 degrees from the center of the can. Don't point the can directly at where you're trying to go; instead, aim slightly to the left or the right. We also found that elevating the antenna helped a bit as well. When aiming the antenna, hold it behind the connector, and *slowly* sweep from left to right, with the Link Test program running. When you get the maximum signal, slowly raise the end of the can to see whether it makes a difference. Go slowly, changing only one variable at a time.

Remember that the can is polarized, so match the phase of the antenna you're talking to (for example, if shooting at an omni, be sure the element is on the bottom or the top of the can; otherwise, you won't be able to see it). See [Hack #100] for how you can use this effect to your advantage.

We were fortunate enough to have a member of our community group bring a return loss meter to one of our meetings, and were able to get some actual measurements of how much signal was returning to the radio. The results weren't as good as I had hoped, but they showed that the antenna was usable, particularly at lower frequencies. Most likely, failing to take into account the thickness of the washers made the entire front element a little too long. There isn't nearly enough power leaving the radio to cause damage due to high return loss, but it does point out that the antenna isn't as well-tuned as it could be.

For a simpler, higher-gain waveguide antenna, read "Pirouette Can Waveguide" [Hack #86].

The original article that this hack is based on is available online at *http://www.oreillynet.com/cs/weblog/view/wlg/448*.

HACK #86 Pirouette Can Waveguide
Build a simpler, higher-gain antenna-in-a-can.

Since the Pringles can story [Hack #85] was published, many have people said, "You know, that's not a bad design, but some friends and I found a better way to do it." One such person was Gregory Rehm. He took the Pringles can design, and another coffee can design, and pitted them against his own designs (including a 40 oz stew can) in a Wireless Cantenna Shoot-Out Battle Royale. His experimentation and excellent analysis is documented on his web site at *http://www.turnpoint.net/wireless/has.html*. It is entertaining to read (and in case you're too filled with suspense to wait until you can check his site, his stew can won by a mile).

As it turns out, it is much simpler to make a tin can waveguide antenna than to bother with cutting pipe and spacing washers apart on all-thread. He has an excellent how-to posted online at *http://www.turnpoint.net/wireless/cantennahowto.html*, complete with photos, diagrams, and formulae.

Another common can that approaches the ideal diameter for 2.4 GHz is the Pepperidge Farm Pirouette can (see Figure 6-6). It makes a much simpler, sturdier, and more efficient antenna than a Pringles antenna, and the best part is, you get to eat the cookies!

Figure 6-6. The Pirouette cantenna

Essentially, you are looking for a can that is about 3 1/2" in diameter. Make an N connector with a 1.2" intentional radiator (just as used in the Pringles Can Waveguide [Hack #85]), and attach it to the Pirouette can about 1.9" from its back surface.

Presto, you have an instant waveguide without cutting a single piece of pipe!

See Also

- *The ARRL Antenna Book*, by R. Dean Straw, Contributor
- *The ARRL Microwave Experimenter's Guide*, by Dana G. Reed, Editor

Primestar Dish with Waveguide Feed

HACK
#87

Use a cantenna waveguide in conjunction with a recycled satellite dish.

Primestar was purchased a few years ago by DirecTV, who phased out all the Primestar equipment. This means that the dishes have been trashed and are available for other uses such as the one I describe here. It is easy to turn a surplus Primestar dish into a highly directional antenna for 802.11b/g wireless networking. The resulting antenna has about 22 dB of gain and is fed with 50 ohm coaxial cable. LMR400 or 9913 low-loss cable should be used if the radio source is more than a few feet from the antenna. (See Appendix B for more details on cabling options.)

Figure 6-7 shows the Primestar dish in action.

Figure 6-7. Primestar dish on the roof

Construction

To build your own, you'll need the following parts and a couple of hours:

- A Primestar dish (you can use any old satellite dish, but if it is bigger than the Primestar, the gain will be higher)
- A juice can (about four inches in diameter and at least eight inches long)
- A chassis-mount N connector

After deciding on a place to mount your antenna, remove the apparatus at the feed position of the dish. Be sure to save the mounting hardware. Using a can opener, cut one end of the juice can out, drink the juice, and wash the can out. Solder a quarter wavelength (1.15") of wire onto the center conductor of the chassis-mount N connector.

Using a punch or whatever other tools you deem necessary, mount the N connector so that it is about 1.2" from the closed end of the juice can. It is also a good idea to put a drip hole at the lowest point of the can to ensure that water doesn't build up inside. After having one of these on my roof for a few months, it seemed to be a good idea to put a plastic lid on the open end of the can so that the inside doesn't rust. During the time mine has been up, it has rusted and I have lost a couple of dB of signal strength. These two details may be correlated.

Mount the juice can so that the opening is just at the focus of the dish. In my installation (see Figure 6-8), I didn't quite achieve this, but I only lost a dB or two by taking the easy route. I still have about 25 dB signal-to-noise ratio, so the loss wasn't important to me. The easy route is to mount the can as far back as you can along the mount, by punching two holes through the can and bolting it in. The perfectionist's method would be to find the best feed place (which I found to be just a little farther back) and use some PVC tubing to extend the mount so the feed is in the perfect position. In some installations, every dB will count, which should be taken into consideration.

Other Considerations

This antenna is very directional. You must have it aligned very carefully or you will lose a lot of signal. It also needs to be mounted securely, so the wind won't be able to rotate it even a few degrees.

This antenna is an offset fed dish, which means that the feed horn (the juice can) is not positioned as much in the way of an incoming signal, so it doesn't shadow the dish. This makes the aiming a bit tricky, because it actually looks like it is aimed down when it is aimed for the horizon (as you can see in Figure 6-7).

You can use the scale on the dish mount to determine the elevation it is aimed at. The dish isn't as directional in the up/down directions as it is side to side. This is fortunate, because without turning the mounting upside down, a standard mount will only get it a few degrees above the horizon. I sacrificed a dB of gain here by not turning it over, mostly because I mounted it on a vent pipe, and didn't want to put that kind of wind load on it. As already mentioned, I don't really need the extra signal either.

Figure 6-8. The inside of the feed can

Hacking in 802.11a

As if this hack weren't already hackish enough, this antenna is easily adapted for use with 802.11a gear at 5.8 GHz. Simply scale the dimensions on the feed can and the excitation antenna to 2.4 / 5 = 48% of the dimensions just mentioned. Remember that wavelength goes down as frequency increases, so antennas of equivalent gain at higher frequencies are actually smaller.

The original article that this hack is based on is available online at *http://www.wwc.edu/~frohro/Airport/Primestar/Primestar.html.*

—*Rob Frohne*

Primestar Dish with Biquad Feed
Make an even higher gain antenna out of a recycled Primestar dish.

The Primestar dishes [Hack #87] are high-gain, low-cost, parabolic reflectors with an offset feed. They have superior sidelobe performance when compared with a wire grid antenna, reducing the chance that somebody off of the axis of your link will be able to interfere with your signal.

However, the spacing between the feed slot and the feed mounting bar is small. It is about 55 mm, which is less than a half wavelength at 2.4 GHz. Failure to couple efficiently to the dish's wide aperture or to minimize radiation into the mounting bar results in poor gain and/or significant sidelobes.

The feed is oriented for vertical polarization, as shown in Figure 6-9. To make it horizontal, merely rotate the feed by 90 degrees. You will lose about 3 dB of gain when using the horizontal mode, as the biquad's radiation pattern is a better match for the dish's oblong shape when vertical polarization is used.

Figure 6-9. The biquad feed mounted on the dish

Construction of the Biquad

We used printed circuit (PC) board scraps for the 110×110 mm reflector, but it will be just as effective if made out of sheet brass or copper. Aluminum can be used if soldering of the rigid coax is not required at the feed point.

The reflector's *lips* are 30 mm high, and serve to reduce coupling into the mounting bar. Note that they are only required along the main edge axis of the reflector. The lips cut down radiation from the rear lobes of the biquad by about 6 dB. The best SWR is obtained when the biquad loop is about 15 mm above the ground plane, and the SWR may be adjusted by varying this distance.

A piece of 3/4-inch copper piping makes a tight fit with the mount supplied on the Primestar dish. The rigid 0.141-diameter coax is soldered to the ground plane to provide physical support for the structure. If the biquad element is constructed carefully, there will be no component of radiation along the axis of the coax, there will be no current induced into the coax outer conductor, and a balun is not needed.

To make the element, take a piece of 1.2 mm bare or enameled copper wire exactly 244 millimeters long. Bend it in half, and then make the bends at the halfway point on each leg (where the solder joints will be). Next, bend the four remaining right angles so that the element sides are rectangular and there is about a 1.5 mm gap for soldering to the feed. The widths of the two quad elements will be approximately 30.5 mm from wire center to wire center. Figure 6-10 shows the completed feed.

Figure 6-10. The completed feed

You can use a standard coax cable to connect at this point if you do not have rigid cable available, but you will have to figure out how to support the loop physically. The best SWR is obtained when the loop is about 15 mm above the ground plane and when the reflector is mounted about 10 mm in front of the Primestar's feed bracket.

That's all there is to it; you now have a dish with 27–31 dBi of gain and negligible sidelobe radiation (<40 dB). The beam width is about 4 degrees. Figure 6-11 shows a model of the BiQuad's radiation pattern.

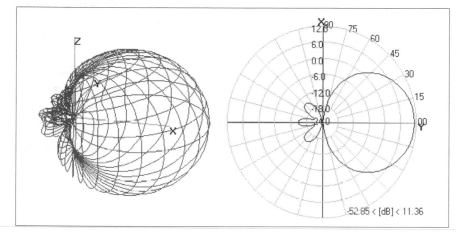

Figure 6-11. Approximate radiation pattern for the Biquad

Biquad Antenna for PCS Cellular Radio

Need a little bit more range for your PCS or GSM phone? You can make a Biquad for 1,900 MHz exactly the same as the preceding one, but you must start with a 304 mm long piece of wire, and fold it into eight arms that are approximately 39.5 and 38.5 mm long. The ground plane needs to be a little larger; use one about 160 mm (6.2 inches) square.

If you don't have a coaxial RF input jack on your cell phone, you can couple the signal into its existing antenna using a single quad as a matching stub. It's not perfect, but in practice it works well. Solder an alligator clip to either of the high voltage apex (39 mm from the feed) of a single 152 mm loop, and clip that to the antenna stub you are currently using. Now you can put 100 feet of coax between your phone and the antenna on your roof to operate even in fringe areas.

The original article upon which this hack is based is available online at *http://www.trevormarshall.com/biquad.htm*.

—Trevor Marshall

Cut a Cable Omni Antenna

#89   Make a high-gain omni out of bits of feed cable.

Most of the designs on the Web for a 2.4 GHz omni antenna seem to involve brass tubing and LMR-400 cable, none of which are readily available to me. I then found a coax-only design for 444 MHz that was based on the same designs. The only reasonable cable I could get my hands on was RG-213 from Maplin (*http://www.maplin.co.uk*). I thought I'd give it a try by scaling the 444 MHz design up to 2.4 GHz and using RG-213. In order to get about a 6 dB gain from the antenna, it needs 8 sectors, with a 1/4 wave section at the top and a fly lead with an N-connector at the bottom.

It should take about two to three hours to build an antenna using this design, but don't worry if it takes longer. You will get quicker, especially as you need to make the jig only once. Figure 6-12 shows the completed antenna.

Figure 6-12. The completed omni antenna

Each sector of the antenna needs to be 1/2 a wavelength long, multiplied by the velocity factor of the cable. The velocity factor of RG-213 is 0.66. If you decide to use a different cable (such as LMR-400), you need to get the velocity factor of that cable (which will be different), and recalculate all the dimensions:

```
                         V * C      0.66 * 299792458
    1/2 wavelength = ------    = ----------------  = 0.0405m  = 40.5mm
                         2 * F      2 * 2441000000

    V = Velocity Factor of RG213 = 0.66
    C = Speed of light = 299792458
    F = Frequency of Signal = 2441000000 (mid  point of 2.4Ghz range)
```

The 1/4 wave element is not adjusted by the velocity factor, as it is in the open, so it works out at just 31 mm long, giving a total antenna length of 355 mm + fly lead.

All of the parts needed to make this antenna are available cheaply from either Maplin or any DIY shop. You need the following:

1 meter RG-213U cable
> Available by the meter from Maplin. One meter is enough for two antennas. Buy more for whatever fly-lead length you want.

1 N connector
> Depending on what you want to connect the antenna to, use either male or female connectors, and inline or bulkhead. Remember that inline connectors need to fit 10 mm diameter RG-213 cable.

20 mm PVC conduit
> Available from any DIY store, the conduit should have a 20 mm inside diameter, and 22 mm outside.

22 mm pipe clips
> Depending on how you want to mount the antenna, pipe clips make mounting the antenna easy.

You also need the following standard tools:

- Millimeter ruler for measuring
- Junior hacksaw
- Stanley blade knife
- Pliers
- Standard soldering iron (you don't need a heavy duty one) and solder
- Scraps of wood to make a jig to aid soldering
- Bench or vise to hold the cable while you cut it

Cutting the Pieces

After much trial and error, I found that the neatest way to cut the cable is actually with a junior hacksaw. It gives a much cleaner finish than wire cutters. Each sector consists of a short length of RG-213 cable, with the central core sticking out each end.

When building the antenna, the exact length of each piece of RG-213 is not that important; it is the overall length of each sector that counts. I found that cutting the cable to 37 mm with 6 mm of core sticking out each end gets enough overlap to easily solder the segments together. If you allow 1 mm for the width of the hacksaw when cutting the sectors apart, it means you need 37 + 6 + 6 + 1 = 50 mm of cable for each sector. Making 8 sectors + 1/4 wave section comes to 420 mm of cable for the antenna + cable for the fly lead.

The best way to cut each sector is to make the cuts where each end of the sheathed section of the sector will be, before making the cut between each sector. Figure 6-13 displays the top three sections of the antenna, and the 1/4 wave section, showing the order that the cuts should be made.

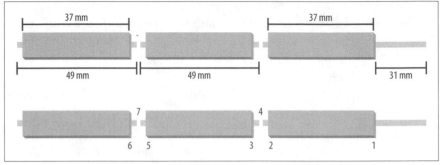

Figure 6-13. Segment lengths

The best way to make the cuts is to mark them out on the cable first. When sawing the cable, you'll find it has a tendency to deform and bend, so lightly sawing round the outside sheath first—but not cutting through—helps guide the actual cut. I use the junior hacksaw to gently saw round the cable sheath to make the mark for each section.

The first mark will be at 31 mm from the end of the cable, which is for the 1/4 wave section at the top. Once you make the mark, it is time to cut around the cable. You want to cut through the sheath and shielding, and just into the central insulation, but not into the central copper wires. You might need to practice a bit first, but you should be able to feel it as you cut through the shielding into the central insulation. By leaving plenty of sheathed section on either side of the cuts, the shielding stays in place when being cut.

Now with pliers, gently twist off 31 mm of sheath and shielding at the end of the cable. This should leave the central insulator exposed. Using the Stanley knife, score round through the central insulator (not too hard, or you will cut the central cable). Now twist off the insulation, as shown in Figure 6-14. You should be able to see the twist in the central cable through the insulation, which will show you which way to twist off the insulation, resulting in the central core twisting more tightly.

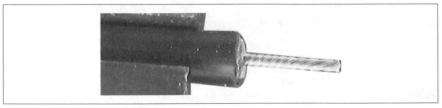

Figure 6-14. Exposing the center conductor

The next mark is 37 mm down (68 mm from end of the cable) and is the cut for the other end of the sheathed section of the top sector. The next mark is 13 mm down (this section consists of 6 mm core from each sector and 1 mm for the cut between sectors; 81 mm from the end) and is the top of the sheathed section of the second sector. The next mark is again 37 mm down, then 13 mm, then 37 mm, and so on, until you have each of the sheathed sections marked out.

You can now start making the cuts, remembering to cut only through the sheath and shielding, and just into the central insulation. First make the cut at 37 mm down, then make the next cut another 13 mm down. You might find that some of the shielding pulls out when you make this cut, as the 13 mm length of sheath cannot hold the shielding tight enough. Don't worry; it doesn't matter.

Now you are ready to cut off the top sector from the cable. Cut through the whole cable at the midpoint of the two cuts you just made; that is, about 43.5 mm from the end of the sheath, or 74.5 mm from the end of the cable (see position 4 in Figure 6-13). Just carefully saw the whole way through the cable. Now, you can pull off the sheath and shielding from each end.

Score around the insulation as you did before, being careful not to cut the central cable. Carry on, making cuts 37 mm down from the end of the sheath, and then 13 mm further down (50 mm from the end of the sheath). Then, cut through the cable in the middle of the two cuts. Another sector made. You need 8 sectors total. Make the same cuts as usual for the eighth sector, as it will make the top of the fly lead as well. Now that you have all 8 sectors, you need to check round the end of each sector to make sure that none of the shielding is touching the central cable, as odd strands can get left behind.

Next, you need to make a gentle V-shaped cut with the Stanley knife at each end of the sectors to expose the shielding, which is where the central core of the next sector will be soldered. Figure 6-15 shows an example V cut.

Figure 6-15. A gentle V cut

Make sure that the V cuts at each end of the sector line up; otherwise, when you come to solder the antenna together, the whole thing will be twisted all around. Once you have all eight sectors finished, it is time to put them together.

Building a Jig

If you do not have a handy helper to hold the sectors together, you will find it easier to make a small jig from scraps of wood to hold the sectors together as you solder them. The clamps on the right side of Figure 6-16 need to be no more than 30 mm long. The baseboard of the jig must extend to the right far enough to take the whole length of the completed antenna, as the baseboard will need to support the antenna during the soldering since the antenna is not rigid enough to support itself. Don't make the clamps too tight, because you need to be able to easily lift the cable out after it has been soldered.

Figure 6-16. A jig to hold your cable while soldering

When you are ready to solder the sectors together, take care that each sector is correctly spaced. The overall length of each sector needs to be 40.5 mm. Measure from one end of the shielding of the sector that you are adding to the same end on the next sector, and slide the sectors together/apart until the distance between them is 40.5 mm. Try to get it as accurate as you can, as it affects the direction the antenna transmits in if you get it wrong. There should be a small 3 mm gap between the sheaths of each sector. Figure 6-17 shows the details of a soldered sector.

Once you have soldered each sector together, lift the sector up, turn it over, and move it down the clamp to get ready for the next sector. This results in a nice, straight antenna. When soldering, remember to heat both the shielding and core so that the solder runs smoothly and fixes them together.

Figure 6-17. A soldered section of cable

Once complete, test the cable with either a lightbulb and battery or a multi-meter. The center of the fly lead should form a circuit to the 1/4 wave section, and to the shield of the fly lead to the shield of the top section. Now, test that there are no crossed connections by ensuring there is no circuit between the center of the fly lead and the shielding of the top sector, and there is no circuit between the 1/4 wave section and the shielding of the fly lead.

Fix the N connector of your choice onto the end of the fly lead. The type of connector you use depends on what you want to connect to. I use inline connectors, but you could use any connector you like. Slide the antenna into a length of conduit. It should be a snug fit, so you might need to gently ease it in. Find an old soft drink bottle top, and pop it on the top end of the antenna.

Voilà, you have one complete antenna! Securing the antenna in the conduit is best left until you are ready to mount it somewhere. You can cut 5 cm slots in the bottom of the conduit and use a jubilee clamp to grip the fly lead, drill a hole through the conduit and use a cable tie to hold the fly lead, use a bulkhead mount connector on a bottle cap and glue it to the bottom of the conduit, or glue the fly lead in place. It's up to you.

The original article on which this hack is based is available online at *http://wireless.gumph.org/articles/homemadeomni.html*.

Build a Slotted Waveguide Antenna

#90 Make a high-gain, horizontally polarized omni or unidirectional antenna that looks cool.

Unlike wideband antennas such as the Biquad [Hack #88], *slotted waveguides* are resonant antennas and have a relatively narrow operating frequency range. The designs described in this hack have an adequate bandwidth for any 802.11b/g wireless LAN, but they have been carefully designed and must be equally constructed with care.

The major attraction of a slotted waveguide design is its simplicity. Once you have built the first one, it is very simple to build many more. The gain varies little across the 2.4 GHz spectrum, dropping a little bit at the extreme ends. Figure 6-18 shows a finished 8-element directional.

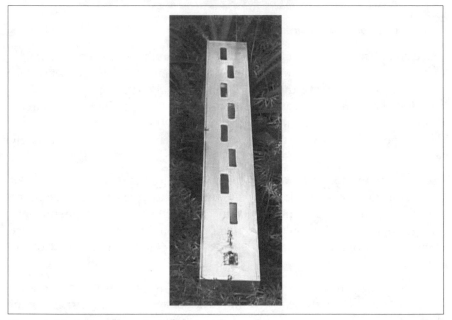

Figure 6-18. An 8-element slotted waveguide

How a Waveguide Antenna Works

A waveguide is a low-loss transmission line. It allows us to propagate signals to a number of smaller antennas (*slots*). The signal is coupled into the waveguide with a simple coaxial probe; as it travels along the guide, it traverses the slots. Each of these slots allows a little of the energy to radiate. The slots are in a linear array pattern, and the total of all the radiated signals adds up to a significant power gain over a small range of angles close to the horizon.

In other words, the waveguide antenna transmits almost all of its energy at the horizon, usually exactly where we want it to go. Its exceptional directivity in the elevation plane gives it quite a high-power gain. Additionally, unlike vertical colinear antennas, the slotted waveguide transmits its energy using *horizontal* polarization, which is the best type for distance transmission.

Unidirectional Waveguide Antennas

This hack describes two unidirectional designs. The first has 8 slots and is about 30 inches long. The second has 16 slots and is about 5 feet long. Simple to construct, the 8-slot has been provided as a good starting point for an antenna novice. I built my 8-slot prototype using only hand tools.

The 16-slot design has been made to radiate over a wider beamwidth by the addition of *wings* to each side of the guide, flush with the front (slotted) surface. It is, of necessity, higher Q, and the higher gain is obtained over a narrower bandwidth. The wings can be expanded aluminum or sheet metal and should extend 9.6 inches beyond the sides of the guide. They act as a ground plane for the slots. Do not change this dimension; it is two electrical wavelengths.

Omnidirectional Slotted Waveguide Antennas

The slotted waveguide has achieved most of its success when used in an omnidirectional role. It is the simplest way to get a real 15-dBi gain over 360 degrees of beamwidth.

Horizontal polarization [Hack #100] in a wide area network can often double the number of users that can interconnect without interference. When using horizontally polarized Biquads or patch antennas (provided that they have been tested for good cross-polarization performance) at the client site, these omnis will be 20 dB stronger than the signal from a similar vertical collinear. Conversely, vertically polarized receiver antennas prefer the vertically polarized colinear over the slotted waveguide by a similar amount. Transmission on an immediately adjacent channel (say, channels 5 or 7), normally not permissible because of interference, is now possible. So, a judicious intermingling of horizontally polarized clients can talk with a horizontal central station on the same or adjacent channels that other clients are using with vertical polarization.

To make the unidrectional antenna radiate over the entire 360 degrees of azimuth, a second set of slots is cut in the back face of the waveguide. When looking straight at the face of the waveguide, you will be able to see clearly through both slots.

Unfortunately, unless a lot of slots are used, the antenna becomes more like a bidirectional radiator, rather than an omnidirectional. This antenna was invented in the 1940s, and as our simulation and measurement technologies have become more accurate, it is apparent that the slotted waveguide designs we used in the past are far from optimum. The most common defect is a *tilt* in the radiation pattern at the extreme ends of the frequency range. This occurs when the wavelength of the signal traveling down the guide differs from the slot spacing.

My current favorite uses 32 slots to get 15 dBi of gain, radiated in a uniformly omnidirectional manner. The large number of slots makes it easier to dissipate the energy from the waveguide. As with the 16-slot unidirectional, two sets of wings (one set at each slot surface) are required to get equal radiation of energy over a full 360 degrees. Note that a higher Q is necessary to get all the slots illuminated evenly.

Note that the gain-versus-frequency curve peaks at 2,440 KHz, and it radiates well over all 14 possible 802.11b/g channels.

Highly Directional Slotted Waveguide Antennas

Sometimes, it is useful to have a highly directional antenna. For example, when installing a point-to-point link between two buildings, it is not desirable to have a wide angle of coverage. Any interference from other 802.11b devices (or microwave ovens) that are in the radiation zone will affect your link integrity.

The ideal antenna for such a situation is a dish, such as Primestar's. When using a Biquad feed [Hack #88], it is possible to reject interference outside the dish's primary 5-degree cone by 30 dB or more.

But if a 16-slot waveguide antenna is turned to a horizontal position, parallel with the ground, it radiates vertical polarization. Its directivity in this plane is extremely good. So, if you don't have a dish handy, using a pair of these slotted waveguides, parallel to the ground, will work well.

Construction Details for the 8-Slot Unidirectional Antenna

The base extrusion for all of my slotted waveguides is 4"×2" O.D. rectangular aluminum tubing with approximately 1/8-inch thick walls. Inside dimensions are 3.756×1.756 inches (95.4 mm × 44.6 mm). These inside dimensions are critical, and must be within +/- 0.040 inches or +/-1mm if the antenna center frequency is to be +/- 1 channel. I cut the end inserts from a 5/16"×1 3/4" flat aluminum bar extrusion.

Waveguide antennas are fairly critical in their constructional dimensions, and are easiest to make with a CNC milling machine. I have computed these designs so that they would be easy to replicate; if you are plus or minus 1 mm, the design will work fine, but you must be careful. I used a jig, a hand operated DeWalt heavy duty cut-out tool, a 1/4-inch router bit, and lots of water to machine the slots. This worked fine (even if it was a little tedious). Really, folks—plus or minus 1 mm will not kill your antenna!

Coupling the Signal into the Waveguide

As mentioned previously, we are propagating the WLAN signal down a waveguide and then using it to excite a number of elemental radiators, or slots. The first task is to get the signal into the waveguide with a feed probe. First, obtain a suitable N connector. Take a piece of 20 mm × 40 mm copper or brass shim, and form it into the shape of a cone. Use Figure 6-19 as a template.

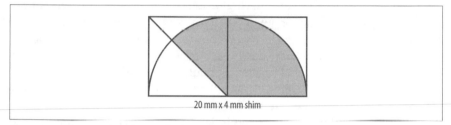

20 mm x 4 mm shim

Figure 6-19. A template for the feed cone

Solder it to the inner conductor of your Type N connector. Its length should be 20 mm, and its largest diameter should be about 15 mm. When soldered to the N connector, it should protrude exactly into the center of the waveguide and no further. Figure 6-20 illustrates the finished feed cone.

Figure 6-20. The completed feed cone

Both ends of the waveguide need to be terminated for RF. The easiest way I found to do this was to cut 3.75-inch pieces of 5/16" × 1.75" aluminum bar stock. I do not recommend that you make the end plugs sloppily, but good electrical contact is not required.

Remember not to have any screws protruding into the waveguide for more than 1/8 inch, especially the screws holding down the N connector. They will affect performance.

8+8 Slot Omnidirectional Antenna

The total length of air inside the 8+8 slot omnidirectional waveguide, from end to end, is 765 mm. Mount the N connector in the center of the widest side: 27.5 mm from one end (the *base*) of the airspace in the waveguide, and offset 10 mm from the center line of the face, in the direction as the offset of the first slot. The wavelength of the radiation passing down the waveguide is longer than a wavelength in free air (it is 161 mm in this design).

The first slot is centered 1.0 wavelength from the base, at a maximum of the H field in the waveguide. This length is 161 mm from the base of the airspace. It is the H component of the field that induces the energy into the slots and makes them radiate. Each slot is 59 mm long, and extends outwards from the centerline for a width of 17 mm. The waveguide excites each edge of the slot, depending on its position across the wide surface of the guide. If it straddled the exact center, each edge of the slot would be excited in antiphase (the waves cancel each other out), and there would be no radiation. So as we offset the edges of the slots, the more the offset, the greater the energy that is dissipated into each slot. The electrical length of each slot should be 59 mm. Do not allow too much kerf at the ends (it should be 2 mm radius max). I recommend finishing the cut with a 1/8-inch router bit (or a file). Or you might use the 1/8 bit in a CNC machine to cut the entire rectangular outline. Remember, even though these slots are arranged *vertically*, they radiate *horizontal* polarization.

For the 8+8 slot omnidirectional, slots 2 through 8 are centered at distances of 241, 322, 403, 483, 564, 644, and 724 mm from the base of the airspace, staggered across the centerline. It doesn't matter which direction the first one is cut, but they must alternate. The end plate should create a 765 mm airspace. Looking straight on at the front of the guide, you can see right through both the front and back slots.

8-Slot Unidirectional Antenna

The total length of air inside the 8-slot unidirectional, from end to end, is 760 mm. Mount the N connector in the center of the widest side, 25 mm from the base of the airspace in the waveguide. The wavelength of the radiation passing down the waveguide is 160 mm in this design. The first slot is centered 1.0 wavelength from the base, at a maximum of the H field in the waveguide. This length is 160 mm from the base of the airspace. Each slot is 58 mm long, and extends outwards from the centerline for a width of 20 mm.

The waveguide excites each edge of the slot depending on its position across the wide surface of the guide. If it straddled the exact center, each edge of the slot would be excited in antiphase and there would be no radiation. So, as we offset the edges of the slots; the more the offset, the greater the energy that is dissipated into each slot. The electrical length of each slot should be 59 mm. Do not allow too much kerf at the ends. Remember, even though these slots are arranged vertically, they radiate horizontal polarization.

Slots 2 through 8 are centered at distances of 240, 320, 400, 480, 560, 640, and 720 mm from the base of the airspace, staggered across the centerline. It doesn't matter which direction the first one is cut, but they must alternate. The end plate should be to create a 760 mm airspace.

Construction Details for 16- and 16+16-Slot Design

The correct wavelength for these designs is 161 mm. The gain for the 16-slot unidirectional is 15 dBi–17 dBi, verified on my test range, across the whole band. On the range, the 16 slotter gives slightly higher gain than my Hyperlink Technologies model 2419G Mesh Parabolic, which is *rated* at 19.1 dBi gain.

The slot width for the 16 slotter is 15 mm, and it is 12 mm for the 32 slotter; otherwise, the key dimensions are the same.

The original article upon which this hack is based is available online at *http://www.trevormarshall.com/waveguides.htm*.

—*Trevor Marshall*

The Passive Repeater

Use a passive device that requires no power to shoot around obstacles.

Everyone you know is getting wireless signals across 5, 10, 15, or even more miles per hop. You need to go only four miles, but there's a hill in the middle; it's not distance, it's the obstacle that's killing you. You know you could put a repeater station on the hill, but there's no power, and you can't afford the cost of a solar power system big enough to ride out a few cloudy days. What you need is a *passive repeater*.

Suppose the hill is right at the halfway point. Just to make sure you get a big enough signal, you buy two 24 dBi parabolic dishes, mount them on a 20-foot pole, and have lots of clearance in the now line-of-sight paths to the end stations. Both ends are also provided with 24 dBi dishes. You anticipate the joy of getting high speed down to your house for the first time, but when you turn your gear on, there's no signal to be seen. Argh! What went wrong?

Why a Passive Repeater Won't Work

Let's think about how our system is supposed to work. If we didn't have the obstacle in the middle of the path, our endpoint antennas would ensure that we had a strong signal over our four-mile path. Our signal from the originating end had to go only half the distance, so we know the signal at the two-mile point is four times bigger than it would be at four miles (due to the inverse square law [Hack #97]). Our thinking is that this signal in the cable is supposed to get launched from the second antenna and beam strongly to your house, since it has to go only a relatively easy two-mile hop.

Well, actually, the system is working just the way you thought. The reason you can't see a signal is that it's just too weak. First, let's predict how much signal we'd see if we had a clear four-mile path.

At 2.4 GHz, the free space path attenuation (loss) can be calculated like this:

    Loss (in dB) = 104.2 + 20 log d

where d is in miles (if you'd rather use kilometers, use 92.4 as the constant instead of 104.2, or substitute 32.4 if you prefer your distance in meters). With an algebraic (scientific) calculator, get the path loss for four miles by keying in:

    104.2 [plus key (+)] 20 [times key (x)] [log key] 4 [equals key (=)]

You'll see 116.24 in the display. For the terminally lazy (or those without a calculator), consult the precomputed lookup table [Hack #97] to find a rough estimate of loss for a given distance.

How much signal is available over our unobstructed four-mile path? Let's assume that we have 24 dBi antennas on each end and that our radios are in a box near each antenna. Let's allow a 3 dB loss for pigtails, connector attenuation, and transmission line (coax).

We use dBs for our ratios since it makes it easy to calculate total path gains and losses. Just add the dB for each element in the path, and the sum is the effective path:

    Coax + Antenna + Free Space Loss + Antenna + Coax
     -3   +   24   +   -116   +   24   +   -3 = -74

It looks like we'll get 74 dB less out of the connector at our receiver than we put in at the transmitter. That's about 25 million times smaller, so it's a good thing that our receivers can detect weak signals!

Now, let's put the hill back in place and put the passive repeater on top, coupling the antenna leads directly into each other with an appropriate *barrel* connector. To calculate our signal, we note that the distance is half, so we'll see 6 dB more signal over a two-mile path, which is -68 dB. (Do the calculation and you'll see for yourself.)

The calculation is simple, because we have the same antennas everywhere. When we connect our two antennas together on the hill, we just add the connector-to-connector loss for the two two-mile paths, and we get -136 dB less at the receiver than we put in at the transmitter when our passive repeater is in place.

If we have a 200 mW transmitter (23dBm) when we have the four-mile unobstructed path, we get -51 dBm for our receiver—a great signal, as we expected. But with the passive repeater in the middle of the obstructed path, we get only -113dB and, sorry to say, we won't get any bandwidth. Even the thermal noise of the antenna would exceed the tiny signal provided by our passive repeater. In fact, if the hill is about 500 feet high, diffraction over the top is likely to give us a path loss 35 or 45 dB worse than free space loss. So, the signal from the passive repeater is about 200 times smaller than what just falls over the hill.

An Example that Almost Works

So, have we proven that passive repeaters don't work? While it looks pretty bad, let's look at another example. Let's keep the four-mile distance, but say that we live just 500 feet from the ridge. We are still obstructed and can't get a direct signal, but let's do the calculation for a passive repeater on this ridge.

We don't have to recalculate the four-mile minus 500 feet path, since it's virtually the same as the full four-mile path, or -74 dB. Our second hop is now about 1/10 mile, so this hop gives us -84 dB. Adding up our components in this hop, we get -3 + 24 + -74 + 24 + -3 = -42 dB. Coupling our antennas together at the passive repeater, we add the two paths and get 74 + 42 - 116 dB. Our 23 dBm transmitter now gets us -93 dBm at the receiver end. Not a great signal, but we should be able to get 1 Mb/s connections through the passive repeater. Of course, you could argue that you should just put your radio on the peak and run 500 feet of cable, and that might be a reasonable alternative. The passive repeater is just barely working for us here.

A Working Example

However, there are situations where you can't just run a cable. Let's say that you live in the city, and across from you is a building 60 feet high. You can get permission to put antennas on the roof of the obstructing building, but there's no power there. You can't run a cable across the street, and you can't build a tower tall enough to get over the building. In this case, we have a 100-foot path from the passive repeater to your house (approximately .02 mile). Our free space loss for this path is -70 dB and the connector-toconnnector loss is -28 dB. Assuming that the originating station is still 4 miles away, our total connector-to-connector loss is 102 dB. Now our +23 dBm transmitter gets a respectable -79 dBm signal to the receiver. Yay! We can get our full 11 Mb/s speed and still have an 8 dB fade margin.

So, in certain circumstances, a passive repeater can give you great results. It works best when the two path lengths are vastly different. The absolute poorest result occurs when the obstruction is in the middle of the path. In this case, you have to use an active repeater to get the signal through.

—*Ron Wickersham*

HACK #92 Determine Your Antenna Gain

Figure out the approximate gain of your home brew antenna—without a spectrum analyzer.

After building one of the many antennas in this chapter, or perhaps designing one of your own, you will inevitably wonder just how much gain your antenna provides. While an ideal testing rig would include a spectrum analyzer and lab conditions, most people can't afford to bring such resources to bear on their little antenna project. Fortunately, informal gain tests are simple to perform, given some simple tools and a little patience.

Here is one method for estimating gain. While your results might not be as accurate as those provided by a "real" radio lab, it can give you a fair estimate of how well your equipment performs, for little cost.

Here's what you'll need:

- Two radio cards of the same manufacturer and firmware revision, as well as external antenna connectors (Lucent/Orinoco/Proxim cards or Prism II cards, such as the Senao/EnGenius models, work well)
- Two laptops
- The antenna to be tested
- Two antennas of known gain (preferably low gain and somewhat directional, like 8 dBi patch antennas)
- Two tripods, mounts, and pigtails for the above antennas
- A large, flat outdoor space free of obstacles
- A notebook
- A friend and a means of communicating with that friend (such as cell phones or FRS radios)

Connect an antenna to one of the cards and, using a program such as NetStumbler [Hack #24], run a simple site survey. Walk around the area a bit, and look for an unused (or lightly used) channel. Once you decide on a channel, quit NetStumbler and return to the other laptop. With the two laptops close to each other, set up an ad hoc network on that channel. Don't worry about your IP configuration; just set both machines to the same ESSID and channel. If you are using a Prism II card, you might prefer to use one laptop in HostAP mode [Hack #63] instead.

If you are using an Orinoco card on a Windows machine, open the Site Monitor utility in the client driver, on both machines. If you are running Linux, I recommend using Wavemon [Hack #30] on both machines. Both these tools update quickly and keep a history. Don't use a network scanner like NetStumbler, as it has been known to get confused when performing simple signal strength tests. Otherwise, open the client-monitoring tool that came with your card. While still close together, verify that the two laptops can monitor each other with no problems. It is much easier to debug configuration problems now than when you are far away from your friend later.

When you are satisfied that everything is working properly, you are ready to head out into the field. Set up the tripods and mounts about 300 feet or so apart. Be sure that your tripods are at least 5 feet high, to clear the 0.6 Fresnel zone. The Fresnel (pronounced "fray-NELL") zone refers to the shape of a wave as it leaves the antenna, expanding in a circular direction as it travels. The diagram at *http://www.ydi.com/deployinfo/ad-fresnel-zone.php* illustrates it well.

Using antennas of known gain on both sides, plug in your laptop and see what kind of signal you can find. With your friend keeping his end steady, slowly rotate your antenna until you achieve the highest possible gain between the two points. Now, lock down your side, and let your friend rotate his end until he achieves the highest gain. Work slowly, and keep in constant communication with your friend at the other end, until you agree on the best possible position for both antennas. Be sure that both of you take your hands off of the antenna before taking a reading.

Once you are satisfied that the antennas are well aligned, make a note of the received signal and noise from both sides. Let the entire rig rest a couple of minutes, and see if the signal fluctuates at all. If it does, you might be encountering unexpected noise on the band, so you might try a different channel.

When you are happy with your link, it is time to try out your new antenna. Without moving the other end, carefully replace one antenna with the antenna to be tested. Ideally, you should use the same pigtail and feed line to eliminate the possibility of variations in the cabling. While watching the signal strength meter, slowly rotate the antenna until the highest possible gain is achieved. Again, let the entire system rest for a moment or two. When the link looks stable, record the received signal and noise from both sides.

The difference between both readings, plus the gain of the antenna that was traded out, is the approximate gain of your home brew antenna. For example, suppose you first measured a signal of -56 dBm using an 8 dBi patch antenna. When you swapped it out for a circular waveguide, your signal strength jumped to -46 dBm. The difference between the readings (8 dBm) plus the gain of the known antenna (8 dBi) equals the approximate gain of the waveguide, which is approximately 16 dBi.

You can also compute the difference in noise readings to see an approximate estimation of how well the antenna rejects noise from the path. With noise, a lower signal is better. Remember that you are dealing with negative numbers, so a noise reading of -100dBm is actually *better* than -90dBm. Likewise, since you want *more* signal, a reading of -46 dBm is much better than -56 dBm.

One critical point that isn't measured in this sort of test is *Standing Wave Ratio* (SWR). This is a measurement of how much signal is being reflected back into your radio from the antenna, and tells whether your antenna is well matched to the frequency your radio is transmitting on. Unfortunately, determining the SWR of very low power cards at 2.4 GHz is typically measured with expensive equipment. Fortunately, as these radios put out only a few milliwatts, there is little chance that your radio will actually be damaged by a mismatched antenna. It just won't work very well. If you have some soldering skill and a bit of time, this DIY project is an interesting design for a home brew SWR meter: *http://home.wanadoo.nl/erwin.gijzen/wifiswr/*.

Once your antennas are aligned in a setup like this, you can test as many home brew designs as you like. Just be sure to keep the other end steady, and take everything one step at a time. Make a note of everything you observe as you go, and keep the number of variables to a minimum. While this method might not be as accurate as a spectrum analyzer, it is a very cost-effective way of getting an estimation of how your antenna design actually performs.

Build Cheap, Effective Roof Mounts

Install wireless gear on your roof without piercing it with mounting hardware.

If you intend to build a long distance wireless link, you will likely need to get your antennas up as high as they can comfortably go. For many people, adding a dedicated tower is out of the question (for aesthetic and local ordinance reasons), so the next logical place for gear is the rooftop.

Ideally, the equipment should be installed in such a way that it doesn't pierce the roof of the building, lest the rainy season come and bring expensive roof repair bills with it. If you are working with a flat roof, you may find it useful to build a small *sled* on which to mount your gear. Figure 6-21 shows a typical plywood sled with a 24 dBi dish mounted on it.

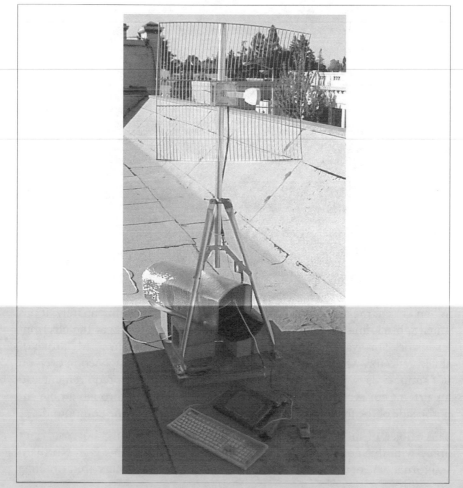

Figure 6-21. Simple plywood sled weighted with cinder blocks

It consists of a piece of plywood that is a few feet square around with sections of 2 4 screwed to it from above. This gets the wood slightly up and off of the roof's surface to allow rainwater to flow past as it normally would. The sled is weighed down with cinder blocks, and has an inexpensive aluminum tripod mount (found at Radio Shack) bolted to it. Figure 6-22 shows a detail of the *experimental* equipment housing.

Figure 6-22. A rubber mailbox, a cheap and effective solution

In this installation, cost was one of the primary concerns. The owner had a Stylistic 1000 that needed housing, and the cheapest deal we could find at the time was a rubberized mailbox (just a few dollars at the hardware store). When closed, the mailbox is practically water tight, but unfortunately, it has a matte black finish, which will soak up the sun and overheat the electronics inside. This was mitigated by wrapping the box in a cheap Mylar windshield reflector, which keeps the inside of the box surprisingly cool, even on hot summer days. Note that the Stylistic has no ventilation requirements, so an airtight box was an ideal choice. The cables were run through a hole cut in the side of the mailbox that was then filled in with silicone compound.

This choice of mounting hardware might sound ridiculous, but you can't argue with this node's uptime: over two years! Granted, this is in Northern California, where the winters are quite mild and the summers aren't boiling too hot. But then again, this node isn't running on a Compact Flash card, but instead uses an eight-year-old PCMCIA hard drive (found installed in the Stylistic when purchased from the local surplus electronics store). We originally installed it just to see how long such a setup would last and were pleasantly surprised at the results. The only downtime this node has suffered has been to upgrade the radio card.

The other end of the link isn't on a flat roof, so we couldn't use a sled. Fortunately, there was plenty of signal available at the pitched edge of the roof, allowing us to use a recycled DSS dish mount. You can see it in action in Figure 6-23.

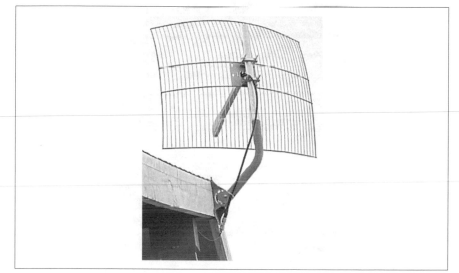

Figure 6-23. DSS dish mount and short length of pipe

By adding a short piece of pipe, the DSS dish mount was extended enough to accommodate a 24 dBi dish. The metal box beneath the eaves is a $10 metal sprinkler box with an Orinoco RG-1100 installed in it. By bolting directly to wooden studs, we avoided piercing the tar paper on the roof. The two white lines running to the box are Ethernet and power for the RG-1100.

The owner had a considerable amount of Ethernet cable on hand, and decided to run the data separate from power, rather than bother with power over Ethernet [Hack #56]. These cables were later tacked back and run under the eaves, and were virtually invisible from the ground.

Another approach is to avoid the use of plywood altogether and simply make a base out of wide wooden planks, as shown in Figure 6-24. These can be weighed down with sandbags or cinder blocks, and the pole steadied with guy wires if necessary. These materials can be easier to get up on a roof than a sheet of plywood and won't have as much potential wind load.

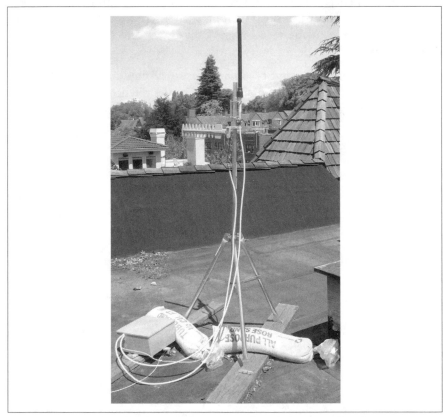

Figure 6-24. A simpler sled design using two boards and aluminum tripod

If you're curious about the white antenna feed line in the photo, yes, it is in fact Heliax. The omni and yagi terminate in a metal sprinkler box (screwed to one of the boards), which contains a Soekris net4511 **[Hack #53]**. The Soekris is fed Ethernet and power over a piece of outdoor CAT5, which enters the building through a skylight. The 12 dBi yagi feeds a link to another part of town a couple of miles away, and the 9 dBi omni provides local service.

Another popular choice for roof mounting is the metal chimney mount. This type of mount consists of metal bands that are tightened around an existing vertical structure, such as an unused chimney or metal pipe. This kind of mount requires no additional weight, and makes no actual contact with the roof surface. When using this style of mount, be sure to observe fire codes, and only attach equipment to surfaces that do not heat up.

Roof mounts don't necessarily need to be elaborate. Antennas for 2.4-GHz gear tend to be small and have little wind load, allowing you to get away with surprisingly little for structural support. Whenever working on roofs, remember to take your time, bring a friend, and work only in good weather when you have plenty of daylight. Building your own rooftop node can be very exciting, but remember that roofs can be dangerous places, no matter how many times you have been up on them.

## CHAPTER SEVEN

Wireless Network Design
Hacks 94–100

The stated average range of a piece of consumer 802.11b equipment is 300 to 1,500 feet. Of course, this estimate is what is printed on the side of the box, and the number is chosen to be somewhere between actual technical constraints and the marketing department's agenda—and should therefore be taken with the standard issue grain of salt. What the side of the box doesn't tell you is that radio range isn't something *built into* a product, but is in fact the same for all wireless devices: potentially infinite, but bounded by transmitter power, antenna gain, clean line of sight, and relative noise in the environment.

While the intended range might just be a couple hundred feet, wireless aficionados everywhere have proven that it is possible to use the 802.11 family of devices to build reliable data links of 10 miles or more. The hacks in this chapter expose some of the important details you need to keep in mind, as well as techniques you can use to make your wireless network projects possible.

HACK #94 Analyze Elevation Profiles for Better Long-Range Wireless Networking

A web application and a few digital elevation models can significantly ease the pain of building wireless networks in remote areas.

If you're trying to build wireless community networks out in the hills, like the NoCat Network has done in Sonoma County, California, the first thing you discover is that hills eat Wi-Fi signals for lunch. Wireless networking technologies such as 802.11b/g need line-of-sight to establish a connection, and any significant amount of intervening terrain, trees, or buildings between two points will quickly ruin your chances of setting up a long-distance, point-to-point wireless connection. In places where DSL and cable are unavailable, however, point-to-point community wireless links are often the only way that local residents can get high speed Internet connectivity, so there's a lot of motivation to find ways to work with the surrounding terrain.

Naturally, the first question a newbie asks when they show up at a community network meeting is, "Can I get on the network?" The answer is, inevitably, "That depends. Where do you live?" Armed with the GPS coordinates of the newbie's house, you can do a certain amount of terrain analysis using digital elevation models (DEMs) in commercial software such as TopoUSA [Hack #96] or free software such as GRASS (*http://grass.ibiblio.org*). The downside to this is that, if you have 50 would-be participants in a community network, the total number of possible links to evaluate is, apropos of nothing else, $50 \times 49 \div 2 = 1225$. That's a lot of work to do by hand!

NoCat Maps

We knew there had to be a better way. My ambition was to create a tool that would allow a community member to get their house on the NoCat Network with nothing more than a compass and a Wi-Fi card with a high-gain antenna. Rich Gibson demonstrated that, using GRASS, he could extract elevations from 10-meter resolution USGS DEMs along the line connecting two locations, and use that to plot a contour profile with Perl and the GD:: Graph module from CPAN (*http://www.cpan.org*).

If the elevation of the straight line in three dimensions between those two points is less than or equal to the elevation at any point along that line, it means there's a hill in the way, and a link probably won't be feasible. If the elevation of the line-of-sight is above ground elevation along the whole distance, a wireless connection might be possible (but see "The Caveats" later in this hack, for some exceptions).

We took the contour profiler from GRASS and combined it with a web-based network node database, so that any new locations would be automatically tested against all existing locations for link viability. Finally, we added a rudimentary address geocoder based on TIGER/Line data for users who didn't know their GPS coordinates already. The result was NoCat Maps, which now lives at *http://maps.nocat.net*.

Now, when people come to NoCat Network meetings and ask how they can get on the network, they're told to go to the web site and add themselves to the database. If they know their GPS coordinates, they can enter them there; otherwise, their address is looked up in the TIGER/Line database of Sonoma County. The application analyzes the elevation profile along the line-of-sight to every other possible node and then presents the user with a list of possible connections, as shown in Figure 7-1.

🐾nocat View Link		[Add your location!] [Show all nodes] [Contact]		
		[Status: Interested Desired Proved Link In Progress Active Inactive]		
Alembic	rjw (at) alembic (dot) com	Santa Rosa	ACTIVE	38.405564°N -122.718989°E
Greg S	gregs (at) nocat (dot) net	Graton	ACTIVE	38.436346°N -122.866591°E
Max S	max (at) nocat (dot) net		ACTIVE	38.378992°N -122.884796°E
Rich G	rich (at) nocat (dot) net	Sebastopol	ACTIVE	38.402338°N -122.828978°E
Rob F	rob (at) nocat (dot) net		ACTIVE	38.401127°N -122.825224°E
Victorian Tree Farm	victrees (at) nocat (dot) net	Sebastopol	ACTIVE	38.413096°N -122.843222°E
William Barrow	billyjan (at) juno (dot) com	Sebastopol	ACTIVE	38.411813°N -122.845303°E
WillieB	billyjan (at) juno (dot) com	Sebastopol	ACTIVE	38.411813°N -122.845303°E
Mill Station	schuyler (at) nocat (dot) net	Sebastopol	IN_PROGRESS	38.417213°N -122.871304°E
Nate B	nate (at) nocat (dot) net		IN_PROGRESS	38.378434°N -122.810872°E
Arthur R	arthurr (at) pogowave (dot) com	Graton	INTERESTED	38.431075°N -122.869339°E

Figure 7-1. Viewing likely point-to-point links at a glance

The listing of possible links comes sorted by *clearance*: approximately how much room a link has to spare, given the intervening terrain, ignoring Fresnel zones and other potential radio problems. Antennas are assumed to be at least 5 meters off the ground, so the maximum possible clearance is about 16 feet. A negative clearance indicates the presence of a hill at least that high in the way.

Additionally, since we know the latitude and longitude of both points, we can calculate the straight-line distance and true bearing for each possible link. This means that, if you know that there's a live antenna at a given node, and NoCat Maps suggests that a link might be possible, you can go outside with a Wi-Fi card and your own high-gain antenna and a compass and give it a shot before you ever show up at a meeting.

Rich's original contour profiler has been preserved, as well. If you click the View link next to any pair of nodes in the node listing, you get a detailed view of the prospective link, with a Google Map depicting the line-of-sight and a graph showing the elevation profile between them. Figure 7-2 shows a potentially successful link, while Figure 7-3 shows one doomed to failure.

This view offers some other features as well. First, likely lines-of-sight are listed at the bottom of the page. Second, clicking on the graph opens a full-page version of the same. Finally, the Google Map can be used to get a sense

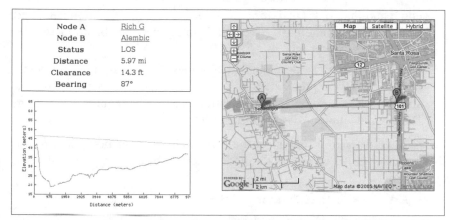

Figure 7-2. A possible point-to-point link

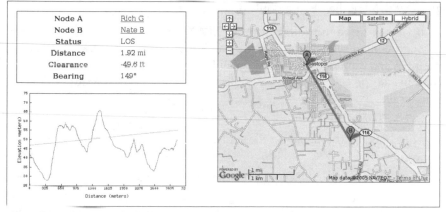

Figure 7-3. This is not the link you are looking for; move along

of what's in between points A and B, by zooming in and perhaps by switching the map to Satellite Mode. This will give you a much better idea of potential buildings and trees, which the line-of-sight data will not include.

Installing Your Own Profile Analyzer

If you don't happen to live in Sonoma County, you can set up a copy of NoCat Maps on your own web server. First, you'll need to install the requisite C libraries:

1. You'll need the GDAL library to read raster data from digital elevation models. You can get it from Debian or Ubuntu APT (apt-get install libgdal1) or from the *Mapping Hacks* GIS RPM archive at *http://mappinghacks.com/rpm*. You will probably also want the GDAL

command-line tools (gdal-bin) for preprocessing the elevation data, and also the Python bindings (python-gdal) in order to be able to merge elevation datasets later on.

2. You'll also want the development bindings for the GD image-processing library. GD is pretty standard with *NIX operating systems, so you shouldn't have too much trouble with this one. The requisite package in Debian and Ubuntu APT is called libgd2-dev.

Next, you'll want to install all of the Perl modules. Your best bet is to use the CPAN shell to get all of the code at once, by running the following command:

```
# perl -MCPAN -e 'install NoCat::Profile'
```

This command will go out to the Comprehensive Perl Archive Network (CPAN), download the Perl libraries for NoCat Maps, and then install them, along with all of their Perl module prerequisites.

If this is the first time you've run the CPAN shell, you might have to walk through configuring it first, but the configuration process takes only a few minutes and comes with mostly sensible defaults. The CPAN shell should then install the following Perl modules, which are listed here for completeness's sake:

Inline::C
: For building the actual profile analyzer.

Template
: The Template Toolkit, for generating HTML pages.

Geo::Coordinates::UTM
: For converting lat/long coordinates to UTM. This prerequisite may be removed at some point, since the GDAL library is capable of doing cartographic transformations, as well.

XMLRPC::Lite
: For looking up the lat/long of street addresses via *http://geocoder.us*.

DBI
: For storing nodes and links in a database.

GD::Graph
: Optional, for generating elevation graphs.

DBD::SQLite
: Optional, for using the SQLite standalone database.

Next, you'll need to get the source distribution of NoCat Maps, in order to install the other components. You can download the code from *http://maps. nocat.net*. The tarball will be called something like *NoCat-Profile-x.xx.tar. gz*. Untar it in a convenient place. If you chose not to install the libraries using the CPAN shell, you can build and install the NoCat Maps libraries as follows (assuming you have all the other prerequisites from the CPAN):

```
$ ./configure
$ make
# make install
```

Finally, copy the following directories to somewhere on the filesystem where your Apache web server can see them:

bin/
    Contains the actual profile analysis script

cgi-bin/
    Contains the CGI scripts that form the application UI

tt2/
    Contains the Template Toolkit templates for the web interface

Getting the Elevation Data

In the United States, you can obtain elevation data for your area from *http://seamless.usgs.gov*. You'll want to get the 1/3 arc-second National Elevation Data (NED), which comes at about 10m resolution. The data comes in a Zip file named with a long string of digits. Inside the Zip, the data is in ArcInfo Grid format, which you'll want to unpack and convert to GeoTIFF as follows, using the *gdalwarp* tool from GDAL:

```
$ unzip 01234567.zip
$ gdalwarp -t_srs "+proj=utm +zone=10" -co "TILED=YES" 01234567/01234567 \
elevation.tif
```

Universal Transverse Mercator (UTM) projection and is a useful cartographic projection for doing this type of geospatial analysis. You will need to find out what UTM zone you're in and fix the zone=10 portion above to match. Zone 10 is the west coast of the US, where this software was originally written. You can find a map of UTM zones at *http://www.dmap.co.uk/utmworld.html*.

Since the maximum download size from *http://www.seamless.usgs.gov* is about 60 MB, and your area of interest is of any significant size, you'll wind up having to download multiple files and merge them together as follows:

```
$ eg/gdal_merge.py -o merged.tif 01234567/01234567 0987654/0987654 ...
$ gdalwarp -t_srs "+proj=utm +zone=10" -co "TILED=YES" merged.tif \
elevation.tif
```

The *gdal_merge.py* script comes from the GDAL distribution but is also included with the NoCat Maps distribution for convenience. You will definitely need the Python bindings for GDAL installed in order for the data merging to work.

If you're outside the United States, you won't be able to use the USGS NED dataset, but you can get WRS2 tiles of NASA's Shuttle Radar Topography Mission (SRTM) data at 90m resolution from *http://www.landcover.org*. Since these tiles will already be in UTM format for your zone, you should simply tile them internally for efficient lookups:

```
$ gdal_translate -co "TILED=YES" p201r24.tif elevation.tif
```

If you have access to other, better elevation data sets, by all means use them, but do make sure they're in the UTM projection for your particular area. If they're not, use *gdalwarp* (as shown in the previous example) to convert them.

Now that you've created your elevation model, you'll want to copy it some place that your Apache web server can access it from.

Setting Up the Application

Having installed the code and assembled the elevation data, we're ready to configure the application. Create a new SQL database somewhere, and load the appropriate schema for your database server from the *eg/* directory in the distribution. You can use SQLite, a lightweight standalone database, but if you decide to do so, you'll need to install the *sqlite3* executable for your OS. You can get the source code for SQLite 3 from *http://www.sqlite.org*. Then, load the database schema as follows:

```
$ sqlite3 node.db < eg/nodedb.sqlite
$ chown apache node.db    (or whatever user your webserver runs as)
```

You'll want to put the node database somewhere convenient. Note that both the database file itself *and* the directory that contains the database file *must* be writable by your Apache server. Of course, if you want to use a *real* database, you can just as easily load the supplied MySQL schema or, with a bit of editing, use the same schema for PostgreSQL.

Next, install and configure Apache, if you haven't already. The configuration in your *httpd.conf* for the VirtualHost on which the profiler will run will probably look something like this:

```
<VirtualHost *>
    ServerName maps.nocat.net
    DocumentRoot /home/www/maps.nocat.net/docs
    ScriptAlias /cgi-bin/ /home/www/maps.nocat.net/src/cgi-bin/
    SetEnv MAP_CONF /home/www/maps.nocat.net/db/map.conf
</VirtualHost>
```

The SetEnv parameter in your *httpd.conf* tells the application where to find its configuration file. An example copy of this *map.conf* file can be found in the *eg/* directory in the distribution. Place a copy of it in the location you specified for the MAP_CONF environment variable in the previous step. If you don't specify a value for MAP_CONF, the CGI scripts default to looking for *map.conf* in the directory above the one they're running in.

Wherever you put your *map.conf* file, you will want to customize it accordingly, of course. Here's what the default *map.conf* configuration looks like:

```
Database        dbi:SQLite:/www/maps.nocat.net/node.db
DB_User         map
DB_Password     censored

Template_Path   /www/maps.nocat.net/src/tt2
Script_Path     /www/maps.nocat.net/src/bin

Elevation_File  sonoma_ned_utm.tif
Node_Height     5
Geocoder_URI    http://rpc.geocoder.us/service/xmlrpc

Contact_Email   maps@wscicc.org
GMaps_API_Key   [Add Your Google Maps API Key Here]
```

The Database parameter specifies the Perl DBI connect string for your database. The string is case sensitive and always starts with dbi:, followed by SQLite, mysql, or Pg for PostgreSQL. You might need to refer to the appropriate Perl DBD:: module documentation for details. The DB_User and DB_Password options are what you'd expect, and are unused if the database runs in SQLite. The Template_Path and Script_Path parameters should point to wherever you put the *tt2/* and *bin/* directories earlier.

The Elevation_File parameter should point to the GeoTIFF you made earlier, while the Node_Height parameter specifies how far above ground level (in meters) we assume antennas to be situated, on average. The default value is five meters. The Geocoder_URI parameter specifies the address of an XML-RPC service for looking up the coordinates of street addresses. The default behavior is to use the geocoder.us service, which is free for non-profit use, so you probably won't want to change this. See *http://www.geocoder.us* for more details.

The Contact_Email address is used in various places in the application's templates. Finally, the GMaps_API_Key parameter specifies your Google Maps API key, which you will need in order to be able to show Google Maps on your site. You can sign up for an API key at *http://www.google.com/apis/maps/ signup.html*, and cut and paste the long alphanumeric string into the *map. conf* file. Be sure not to leave a line break in the middle of the key.

Starting Your Elevation Profiler for the First Time

Now that everything's set up, visit the URL you configured in Apache for the service. Try the *add_node.cgi* script, and add a couple of new nodes. If all goes well, the elevation profile between the two nodes should be plotted when you add the second node, and you should be able to view the profile graph to verify that everything is working.

Unfortunately, much of the facility for editing and removing nodes themselves is absent from the UI itself, so keep your command-line database client handy. Much of this will be addressed in an upcoming release of the code.

The Caveats

What are the caveats of using such an application? First, the mapping data takes no account whatsoever of *ground clutter* (e.g., buildings, trees, and such). Realistically, it's difficult to do so, because these things change a bit from month to month and year to year. One approach, suggested by Jerritt Collord, might be to integrate the 30-meter resolution SRTM data, which could be compared against a matching DEM to infer the presence of ground clutter.

However, even correlating against SRTM data would suffer from the other general caveat of NoCat Maps, which is that the resolution of the DEMs isn't perfect for the task. Experience shows that 10 meters in one direction or another can easily be make-or-break for a wireless link, much less 30 meters. As a result, NoCat Maps rates some proven, working wireless links as being impossible, and rates some other links as possible which later turned out not to be. The practical upshot is that NoCat Maps is intended to provide a rule of thumb, a starting point for planning community networks, rather than a definitive resource. If a link looks marginal, it's often worth trying anyway!

Creating an application like NoCat Maps has become much easier in the last three years. For starters, you no longer need to create your own custom geocoder to get the latitude and longitude of a particular street address; instead, you can use *http://geocoder.us*. You can also lighten the load of the application quite a bit by using the Geo::GDAL Perl module from the CPAN to directly access DEM files, instead of having to integrate with GRASS.

There are plans afoot to improve NoCat Maps and to generalize the tool so that anyone can download and implement a NoCat Map database for their own community network. Stay tuned to *http://maps.nocat.net* for more details.

—Schuyler Erle

Build a Wireless Network for the Large House

#95

If you have a large home (or even a smaller one with outbuildings that you want to cover with your wireless network), building a wireless network that covers the whole thing is not impossible.

Large houses can be a problem for wireless networks. Apart from the issue of trying to remember which bedroom is yours, most consumer-grade wireless access points aren't powerful enough to provide wireless access over a home that's bigger than your typical split-level house. And you don't have to be a dot-com millionaire to have problems: if you have outbuildings or a large garden that you want covered by your wireless network, a single router probably won't cut it. Fortunately, it isn't difficult to extend the range of a wireless network to cover the entire house and garden.

There are three approaches to dealing with this problem: use hi-gain antennas that increase or direct the signal from your access point range [Hack #52], use Wireless Distribution System (WDS) to extend your wireless range [Hack #69], or use multiple access points. This hack shows how to use the third approach, providing multiple access points in different locations.

Two Antennas Are Better Than One

Let's take a typical example. Say you live in a large house or apartment that's spread over several floors, as shown in Figure 7-4. You've bought a wireless router or access point and tried it in several locations, surveying the signal strength around the house. The signal won't go between floors, because it can't penetrate the floor. If you put the router on one floor, you get no signal (or a signal too weak to use) on the next.

So, we are going to put the wireless router on one floor, and then run an Ethernet cable from the router up to the next floor and add an access point that provides wireless signal upstairs. Similarly, you might find that there is a *dead spot* in one room of a smaller house that you want to add wireless coverage to, and adding an access point can easily do this.

An *access point* is different from a *wireless router* in that it doesn't contain any of the code or equipment that connects your wireless network to your broadband Internet connection. Instead, it acts as an interface or bridge between a wired network and the wireless one. Most wireless equipment manufacturers sell them, and they are typically a bit cheaper than the wireless routers. It's a good idea to go with the same manufacturer as your wireless router: although these devices are designed to be compatible between manufacturers, using one manufacturer makes finding problems and tech support calls easier. You should also go with the same wireless standard as your router.

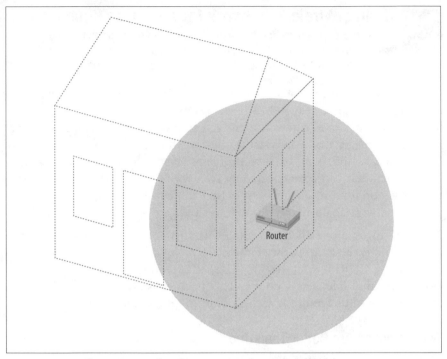

Figure 7-4. Wireless coverage that does not span the whole house

Next, you'll need to run an Ethernet cable from the wireless router to the access point. You can either buy a pre-made cable or make your own. There's a good guide to rolling your own at *http://www.groundcontrol.com/ galileo/ch5-ethernet.htm*. For this hack, you'll need a standard cable, not the crossover type. Either way, use a Category-5 cable that can support gigabit networking speeds. (Even if your network isn't that fast, it is easier to use a cable that supports it than running a new cable when you upgrade.)

> If you are making your own cable, don't put the connector on either end of the cable until you have the cable in place, because the bare cable is easier to run between floors. You should also avoid having the cable running parallel to electric cables if possible, because they can cause interference. If you want to make it look more professional, you can add wall jacks at either end. There's a good guide to how to do this (as well as how to run cables through walls and the like) at *http://www.homepcnetwork.com/wireintrof.htm*.

You'll also need to find a way to run the cable between the floors. If you have air conditioning or other pipes that run between floors, they provide a handy prebuilt route, and there's usually enough room to run a cable or two alongside them.

Plugging Into Wireless

Once you've run the cable, plug one end into one of the Ethernet ports of the wireless router and the other into the access point. To avoid interference, follow the manufacturer's instructions to configure the access point to run on a different channel than the wireless router. Select channels that are at least four numbers apart (say, channel 1 and channel 6). You should now have wireless coverage on both floors, as shown in Figure 7-5. Computers on the floor with the wireless router should connect to that, while those on the floor with the access point should connect to that instead.

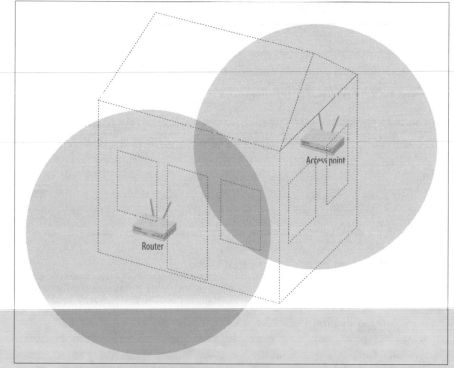

Figure 7-5. Wireless coverage for the whole house

You can use the same SSID for both networks if you want, but I generally recommend that you use a variation to avoid confusion. If, for instance, your network is called *HomeNet*, set the router to use the SSID of *HomeNet-first* and the access point to use *HomeNet-second*.

Hacking the Hack

You can also adapt this to provide coverage to outbuildings and outdoor areas. Instead of running the Ethernet cable between floors, run the cable to the outbuilding or a location that provides coverage to the area. If you need to run the cable outdoors, either bury it in conduit at least eight inches underground or use special hardened outdoor Ethernet cable running along a fence or between poles. Gel-filled direct burial Ethernet cable is also available, budget permitting. In any case, the maximum length you can run is around 100 meters. Any longer than that and you will need to add a switch or hub to the run, or look at using a wireless link [Hack #69].

—Richard Baguley

Establish Line of Sight

#96   Use these methods to quickly tell if a long-distance wireless shot is possible.

Wireless networks operate at microwave frequencies and, as such, work much better when the client's antenna can see the AP's antenna, with nothing but air between. Over short distances (within a few hundred feet), wireless networks can tolerate a few objects in the way. But as you try to push your signal further, having clean *line of sight* (LOS) is absolutely critical.

How can you tell if a given point has LOS to another point several miles away? The short answer is that, without actually having a look, you can't. If the far end is more than a couple miles away, it becomes difficult to tell, even with a high-powered telescope. But using the techniques in this hack, you can make an educated guess as to what is at least within the realm of possibility.

Using a GPS to Log Prospective LAT/LONG/ALT

When visiting a potential node site, it's a good idea to bring along a GPS unit. It can log not only the latitude and longitude, but also the altitude of the site. After collecting points, you can pull them into your topographical software and plot them. For example, the Topo! package from National Geographic (*http://maps.nationalgeographic.com/topo*) allows you to easily mark up a topographical map and analyze arbitrary points and routes. Draw routes between any two points to figure out how the land lies between them. This gives you an easy visual reference for a given shot, as shown in the cross section provided by Topo! in Figure 7-6.

Keep in mind that, although the Topo! software includes surveyed geological data, it won't have tree or building information. You can get a general

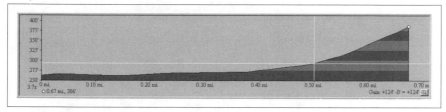

Figure 7-6. A cross-section "lay of the land" between two points

idea of how cluttered an area is, but you won't really know until you try the shot. Using the overhead view in conjunction with the cross section, you can not only weed out the obvious negatives (as shown in Figure 7-7), but also find potential workarounds.

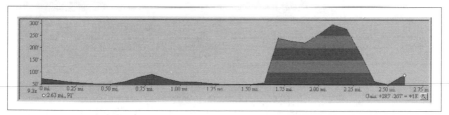

Figure 7-7. A long-distance nightmare with no chance of a decent shot

Using the overhead view to locate key repeater points can be fun. Find out where the good sites are, and try contacting the people at those points. More often than not, people are willing to work with local community groups to provide free access to the site.

Plotting the Points on a 3D Map

A couple software packages from DeLorme (Topo USA and 3-D Topo-Quads, available at *http://www.delorme.com*) have the ability to create 3D renderings of a topological region, complete with data markers and labels, as shown in Figure 7-8. While it's a cool feature and is rather compelling in presentations, it has limited practical value beyond helping to visualize the surrounding terrain.

Generally speaking, the more data points you collect, the more impressive your visual presentation will be.

Once your points are plotted on a map, you can very quickly determine which sites are worth developing. If you can't get direct line of sight to a place you'd like, take a look at the surrounding geography and see whether you can find another way. If you can't go through, you'll have to go over or around. Software topo maps can make finding the bank shots much easier.

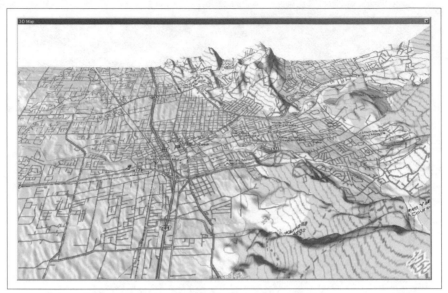

Figure 7-8. A 3D rendering of any topo region, complete with data points

Remember that these tools will show you the lay of the land but don't provide data on ground clutter, such as trees and buildings. The tools aren't perfect, but they can give you an idea of what you have to work with when building a large wireless network.

HACK #97 Calculate the Link Budget

Figure out whether a long-distance link is even possible before you buy any equipment.

How far will your link go? That's a very good question. It depends on all sorts of factors, including the power output and sensitivity of your card, quality of your cable, connectors and antenna, intervening clutter and noise, and even weather patterns on long distance links. While it's impossible to precisely take all of these variables into account, you can make a good estimate before buying any hardware. This hack describes a simple way to build an estimate, referred to as the *link budget*.

First, figure out how much loss the signal will incur in the space between the two sites. This is called the *path loss*. One common formula for estimating path loss at 2.4 GHz is:

$$L = 20 \log(d) + 20 \log(f) + 36.6$$

where L is the loss in dB, d is the distance in miles, and f is the frequency in Megahertz.

So, suppose you wanted to set up a five-mile link between two points, using channel 6 (2.437 GHz):

```
L = 20 log(5) + 20 log(2437) + 36.6
L = (20 * 0.69) + (20 * 3.38) + 36.6
L = 13.8 + 67.6 + 36.6
L = 118
```

At five miles, with no obstacles in between, you will lose 118 db of signal between the two points. Our link must tolerate that much loss (plus a bit extra to account for weather and miscellaneous interference) or it will be unreliable.

If you don't want to bother calculating path loss on your own, you can use Table 7-1 to get a rough estimate. This table was computed with the previous formula and rounded up.

Table 7-1. Approximate free space path loss at 2.412GHz

Distance (in miles)	Loss (in dB) @ 2.412GHz (ch. 1)
0.5	98
1	104
2	110
3	114
4	116
5	118
7	121
10	124
15	128
20	130
25	132
30	134

Now that you have the free space path loss, add up all of your gains (radio power + antennas + amplifier) and subtract your losses (cable length, connectors, lightning arrestors, and miscellaneous other losses). Be sure to only add the radio and amplifier power on one end of the link, but do include antenna gain from both sides of the link.

Let's assume you are using Senao 200mW Prism 2 cards (23 dBm) and no amplifiers, with a 12 dBi sector on one side, and a 15 dBi yagi on the other. We'll also assume you're using 1 meter of LMR 400 and a lightning arrestor on each side, allowing a 0.25 dB loss for each connector, and 1 dB for each pigtail. Since all of the units are in dB, we can use simple addition and subtraction:

```
Site A:
Radio - Pigtail - Arrestor - Connector - Cable - Connector + Antenna
 23   -   1    -  1.25   -    .25   -  .22  -    .25   +  12  = 32.03
Plus Site B:
 *    -   1    -  1.25   -    .25   -  .22  -    .25   +  15  = 12.03
Equals: 44.06 total gain
```

Now, subtract the path loss from that total:

```
44.06  - 118 = -73.94
```

There you have the perceived signal level at either end of the link: -73.94 dBm. But is it enough for communications? Look up the receiver sensitivity specs for the radio card to see how much signal it needs. You can look it up in the radio card manufacturer's documentation.

Consulting the documentation, it appears that the Senao card has a receive sensitivity of -89 dBm at 11 Mbps. As we are providing a signal of -73.94 dBm, we have a *fudge factor* of 15.06 dB (89 − 73.94 = 15.06). Theoretically, this link should usually work at 11 Mbps (in good weather), and should have no problem at all syncing at 5.5 Mbps. The radios should automatically sense when the link becomes unreliable, and re-sync at the fastest possible speed. Depending on your situation, you might want to consider locking the cards in at a lower speed to avoid any transient network problems if the cards have trouble re-syncing.

Typically, a margin of error of 20 dB or so is safe enough to account for normal intervening weather patterns. Using more powerful radios (such as the new 300 mW and 400 mW Atheros cards), more sensitive radios, or higher-gain antennas would help shore up this connection. Using higher-gain cards in conjunction with high-gain dishes makes it possible to extend your range well beyond 25 miles, but be sure to observe the FCC limits on power and gain.

Online tools such as Green Bay Professional Packet Radio's Wireless Network Link Analysis can give you a good ballpark estimate on what it will take to make your link possible. Check out their excellent resources at *http://my.athenet.net/~multiplx/cgi-bin/wireless.main.cgi*.

HACK #98 Align Antennas at Long Distances

By working methodically and communicating well, you can easily bring up wireless links several miles apart.

The farther apart your points are, the harder it is to aim your antennas. Make sure you have enough total gain to overcome the path loss, which you should have calculated by now [Hack #97]. At greater distances, getting the antennas pointed directly at each other can be quite tricky. Here is a list of techniques that might help you get your dishes pointed where they need to be:

- Use mobile phones or FRS/GMRS radios to maintain communications between the two points while you're aiming the antennas. It helps to have at least two people at each end; one to manipulate the antenna, and another to coordinate with the other end. FRS radios often work much better in areas where mobile phone coverage is spotty.

- Set up all of your network settings ahead of time, so there aren't any variables once you get to the remote site. Check all gear, ping each box, and even transfer a file or two to be sure that your equipment works at close range. You don't want to question it later if you have problems getting the link going.

- Use a tool like the Wavemon [Hack #30], or a good built-in client [Hack #23] to show the signal strength and noise readings in real time. This kind of tool is your best friend, short of an actual spectrum analyzer.

- Work on one end of the link at a time, slowly changing one variable at a time, until you see the maximum signal strength and lowest noise at each end of the link.

- If you have one handy (and your link budget permits it), first try an omni or sector antenna on one end of the link. Once you find the other end of the link, replace it with your dish or yagi and tune it in. Typically, the higher gain the antenna, the narrower the beam width, and therefore, the harder it is to aim.

- Sweep slowly, and don't be afraid to go beyond the best perceived signal. Most antennas have smaller side lobes that can appear as false positives. Keep moving until you find the main lobe. It should stand out significantly from the others, once you find it.

- Many times, particularly with offset dish antennas like the Primestar [Hack #87] and yagi antennas, the antenna appears to be aimed too low or far to the left or right of the other end of the link. This is normal. Don't worry about how it looks, worry about finding the greatest possible signal.

- Do *not* touch the antenna while taking a reading. Resting your hand on the antenna interferes with the radiation pattern, and can drain your signal quickly. Take your readings with all hands clear of the equipment.

- Don't forget to compare horizontal and vertical polarization. Try the antennas in both positions, and use the position that shows the lowest noise.

- Once your link is in place, consider using WPA to discourage others from attempting to connect to it. If you want to provide wireless access at either endpoint, set up another gateway specifically for client stations, preferably with caching services (such as caching DNS and a transparent web proxy, like Squid). This helps reduce the amount of traffic that goes over the long link, cuts down on network collisions, and generally makes more efficient use of the link.

It can take all day to properly align antennas at a great distance, but it can also be fun, with the right group of people. Just take your time, think about what you're doing, and be sure to leave time at the end of the day to celebrate!

HACK
#99 Slow Down to Speed Up

On a flaky link, talking slowly can actually speed up data transfers.

In wireless networking, the speed at which a radio can communicate with another depends on how much signal is available. To maintain communications as the available signal fades, the radios need to transmit data at a slower rate. Normally, the radios attempt to work out the available signal on their own and automatically select the fastest possible speed for communications. But in fringe areas with a barely adequate signal, packets might be needlessly lost while the radios continually renegotiate the link speed.

For example, suppose you have a long distance point-to-point link made of Orinoco radios. The received signal at each end varies between -83 and -80 dBm. The threshold for an Orinoco to flip from 11 Mbps to 5.5 Mbps is -82 dBm, so the radios spend at least part of their time negotiating the best speed. Operating on a borderline signal level like this leads to excessive retransmissions that can seriously degrade performance.

While you may think that simply upgrading to 802.11g will provide a faster connection than 802.11b, remember that you still need to provide enough power to be received on the other end. With too much distance or interference in the path, 802.11g will come to a crawl just as quickly as 802.11b. When in doubt, calculate the estimated path loss [Hack #97] and make sure you have enough gain to achieve the data rate you need.

If you can't add more antenna gain or reposition your equipment to achieve enough signal for your link, consider forcing your card to sync at a lower rate. This will mean fewer retries, and can be substantially faster than using a continually flip-flopping link. Each driver has its own method for setting the link speed. In Linux, set the link speed with *iwconfig*:

```
iwconfig eth0 rate 2M
```

This forces the radio to always sync at 2 Mbps, even if other speeds are available. You can also set a particular speed as a ceiling, and allow the card to automatically scale to any slower speed, but go no faster. For example, you might use this on the previous example link:

```
iwconfig eth0 rate 5.5M auto
```

Using the auto directive this way tells the driver to allow speeds up to 5.5 Mbps, and to run slower if necessary, but will never try to sync at anything faster. To restore the card to full auto scaling, just specify auto by itself:

```
iwconfig eth0 rate auto
```

Cards can generally reach much further at 1 Mbps than they can at 11 Mbps. There is a difference of 12 dB between the 1 Mbps and 11 Mbps ratings of the Orinoco card; that's four times the potential distance just by dropping the data rate! On a marginal link, it is usually worth sacrificing an attempt at speed to achieve a more efficient link. If you absolutely need to go faster, find a way to get more signal between the two points.

HACK 100   Take Advantage of Antenna Polarization

Use electromagnetic polarization to avoid noise from other antennas in the same spectrum.

One extremely important property of electromagnetic waves to consider is *polarization*. An electromagnetic wave is actually comprised of two simultaneous and inseparable fields: the electrical field and the magnetic field. These two fields are perpendicular to each other, and both are perpendicular to the direction in which the wave propagates.

An antenna must be oriented to match the polarization of the incoming energy; otherwise, it will receive only a small portion of it. Practically speaking, this means that antennas with matching polarization will see each other well, while antennas with opposite polarization will hardly see each other at all.

Both horizontally and vertically polarized antennas are common, but in some exotic antennas, circular (clockwise or counter-clockwise) polarization is possible. The polarization of the antenna on each end of a link must match, or the radios will have trouble talking to each other. Omnis and sectors are generally vertically polarized, although horizontally polarized variations do exist (see "Build a Slotted Waveguide Antenna" [Hack #90] for an example of a do-it-yourself horizontally polarized omni). Yagis and dishes can be mounted vertically or horizontally, depending on the application.

On a long distance point-to-point link, be sure to try both horizontal and vertical polarization to see which incurs the lowest noise. Simply try the link one way, and then rotate both dishes 90 degrees and try it again. You can tell the polarization of most antennas by the position of their driven element (the part connected to the center conductor of your antenna feed). The polarization of a dish is indicated by the position of the front element, not the rear reflector, so an oval dish that points *up and down* is probably mounted in horizontal polarization and therefore won't be able to talk very well to a vertically polarized omni. Sectors and other sealed antennas typically indicate their polarization on the back of the antenna.

You can use polarization to your advantage to use multiple radios on a single point-to-point link. For example, you can run two parallel links on the same channel, one with vertical and one with horizontal polarization. If separated by a few feet, two dishes can operate quite happily on the same channel without substantially interfering with each other, while providing twice the bandwidth using the same channel.

When setting up a point to point link, remember to try various positions to see how polarization interacts with the environment. Sometimes vertical polarization outperforms horizontal, sometimes not. Occasionally, rotating the antennas to somewhere in between horizontal and vertical yields the best performance. The environment between two points on a long distance shot is complicated, so it's impossible to know for certain which orientation will work best. You'll never know until you try it!

Wireless Standards

The mad rush to bring wireless products to market has left a slew of similar sounding yet often completely incompatible technologies and standards in its wake. 802.11b is the sequel to 802.11a, right? (Wrong.) If I just buy Wi-Fi, then everything will work together, right? (Unfortunately, no.) What is the difference between 802.11 a/b/g, 802.16, and 802.1x? How about GSM, GPRS, GMRS, and GPS? Where does Bluetooth fit into the picture?

802.11: The Mother of All IEEE Wireless Ethernet

The first wireless standard to be defined in the 802 wireless family was 802.11. It was approved by the IEEE in 1997, and defines three possible physical layers: Frequency Hopping Spread Spectrum (FHSS) at 2.4 GHz, Direct Sequence Spread Spectrum (DSSS) at 2.4 GHz, and Infrared. 802.11 could achieve data rates of 1 or 2 Mbps. 802.11 radios that use DSSS are interoperable with 802.11b and 802.11g radios at those speeds, while FHSS radios and Infrared obviously are not.

The original 802.11 devices are increasingly hard to come by, but can still be useful for point-to-point links with low bandwidth requirements.

Pros

- Very inexpensive (a few dollars or even free) when you can find them.
- DSSS cards are compatible with 802.11b/g.
- Infrared 802.11 cards (while rare) can offer interference-free wireless connections, particularly in noisy RF environments.
- Infrared also offers increased security due to significantly shorter range.

Cons

- No longer manufactured.
- Low data rate of 1 or 2 Mbps.
- FHSS radios are incompatible with everything else.

Recommendation

802.11 devices can still be useful, particularly if you find that you already have a few on hand. But the ever falling price of 802.11b and 802.11g gear makes the old 802.11 equipment less attractive each day. The FHSS and Infrared cards talk only to cards of the same era, so don't expect them to work outside of your own projects. Infrared requires an absolutely clean line of sight between devices and offers limited range, but it operates well away from the popular ISM and UNII bands. This means that it won't interfere with (or see interference from) other networking devices, which can be a huge advantage in some situations.

I probably wouldn't go out of my way to acquire 802.11 equipment, but you can still build a useful network if it's all you have to work with. They are probably best used for building point-to-point links, but might be better avoided altogether.

802.11a: The Betamax of the 802.11 Family

According to the specifications available from the IEEE (at *http://standards. ieee.org/getieee802/*), both 802.11a and 802.11b were ratified on September 16, 1999. Early on, 802.11a was widely touted as the "802.11b killer," as it not only provides significantly faster data rates (up to 54 Mbps raw, or about 27 Mbps actual data), but also operates in a completely different spectrum—the 5 GHz UNII band. It uses an encoding technique called Orthogonal Frequency Division Multiplexing (OFDM).

While the promises of higher speeds and freedom from interference with 2.4 GHz devices made 802.11a sound promising, it came to market much later than 802.11b. It also suffers from range problems: at the same power and gain, signals at 5 GHz appear to travel only half as far as signals at 2.4 GHz, presenting a real technical hurdle for designers and implementers. The rapid adoption of 802.11b and then 802.11g only made matters worse, since users of 802.11b gear didn't have a clear upgrade path to 802.11a (as the two are not compatible). As a result, 802.11a still isn't nearly as ubiquitous or inexpensive as 802.11g, although client cards and dual-band access points (which essentially incorporate two radios, or a single radio with a dual-band chipset) have come down in price.

Pros

- Very fast data rates: up to 54 Mbps (raw radio rate), with some vendors providing 108 Mbps or faster with proprietary extensions.
- Uses the much less cluttered (for now, in the United States) UNII band, at 5.8 GHz.

Cons

- As of this writing, 802.11a equipment is still more expensive on average than 802.11b/g.
- Most 802.11a client devices are add-on cards, and the technology is built into relatively few consumer devices (specifically laptops).
- 802.11a PCMCIA cards require a 32-bit CardBus slot, and won't work in older devices.
- Cards and APs with external antenna connectors are hard to find, making distance work difficult.
- Upgrading from 802.11b/g can be painful, as 5.8 GHz radiates very differently from 2.4 GHz, requiring a new site survey and likely more APs.
- Limited range compared to 802.11b/g, at the same power levels and gain.
- Internal 802.11a antennas tend to be quite directional, making them sometimes annoyingly sensitive to proper orientation for best results.

Recommendation

The Wi-Fi alliance (*http://www.weca.net*) tried to call 802.11a "Wi-Fi5," but the name never stuck. These devices are also sometimes confusingly labeled "Wi-Fi," just like the completely incompatible 802.11b/g. Be sure to look for the specification's real name (802.11a) when purchasing gear.

802.11a can be significantly faster than 802.11b, but achieves roughly the same throughput as 802.11g (27 Mbps for 802.11a, compared to 20-25 Mbps for 802.11g). 802.11a would be ideal for creating point-to-point links, if devices with external antenna connectors were more readily available. Many people tout OFDM's ability to cope with reflections caused by obstacles (called *multipath*) as a good reason to use 802.11a, but 802.11g uses the same encoding while achieving greater range at the same power and gain. Some consider the shorter range of 802.11a to be a security advantage, but this can lead to a false sense of security.

Keep in mind that the 54 Mbps data rate is the theoretical maximum, and frequently is only achieved when in very close proximity to the AP. The speed scales back sharply as your distance from the AP increases, and suffers dramatically when separated by a wall or other solid obstacle. It is a very good idea to perform a site survey complete with throughput testing to determine whether 802.11a is suitable for your intended location.

It is probably a bad idea to build an 802.11a-only network unless you are already committed to using only 802.11a gear. If you want to allow guests to use your network, it is a very good idea to at least incorporate a few dual-band APs (or perhaps a dedicated 802.11g AP), as guest users are more likely to bring 802.11b or 802.11g gear with them.

802.11b: The De Facto Standard

802.11b has been the de facto wireless networking standard of the last few years, and for good reason. It offers excellent range and respectable throughput. (While the radio can send frames at up to 11 Mbps, protocol overhead puts the data rate at 5 to 6 Mbps, which is about on par with 10baseT Ethernet.) It operates using DSSS at 2.4 GHz, and automatically selects the best data rate (either 1, 2, 5.5, or 11 Mbps), depending on available signal strength. Its greatest advantage at this point is its ubiquity: millions of 802.11b devices have shipped, and the cost of client and access point gear is not only phenomenally low, but also ships embedded in many laptop and handheld devices. Since it can move data at rates much faster than the average Internet connection, it is widely regarded as "good enough" for general use.

Pros

- Near universal ubiquity in standard consumer devices, add-on cards, and APs.
- Extreme popularity and pressure from 802.11a/g has led to massively discounted hardware. Cards less than $20 and APs less than $50 are common as of this writing.
- 802.11b "hot spots" are available at many coffee shops, restaurants, public parks, libraries, and airports, further increasing its popularity.
- With many people using and experimenting with it, 802.11b is arguably the most hackable (and customizable) wireless protocol on the planet.

Cons

- The 11 Mbps data rate of 802.11b will never get any faster, and is already surpassed by 802.11a and 802.11g.

- 802.11b's channel scheme allows only for three non-overlapping channels, making for considerable contention in the 2.4 GHz ISM band.

- Standard 802.11b security features have been revealed to be less than effective.

Recommendation

While it is impossible to forecast the fickle weather patterns of the consumer marketplace, it is very likely that 802.11b has at least a few years left in it. Millions of devices have shipped, making it the most popular wireless networking protocol on the planet. Ironically, it will probably get a life extension from its competitor 802.11g, as the newer 802.11g equipment will work with existing 802.11b access points. This makes upgrades less of an immediate issue, and if there's anything that network administrators hate, it's upgrading the critical network devices.

Considering that average home Internet speeds are still much slower than 802.11b, it is likely that 802.11b will be used as a mechanism for providing Internet access for some time yet. Backbone links and corporate networks may have an immediate need for the increased bandwidth of 802.11a and 802.11g, but for the average Internet user, 802.11b provides sufficient speed and a very simple mechanism for accessing networks. Even after five years of explosive growth, 802.11b continues to enjoy a lively general acceptance.

802.11g: Like 802.11b, only Faster

The 802.11g specification was ratified by the IEEE in 2003. 802.11g uses the OFDM encoding of 802.11a in the 2.4 GHz band, and also falls back to DSSS to maintain backwards compatibility with 802.11b radios. This means that raw speeds of 54 Mbps (20 to 25 Mbps data) are achievable in the 2.4 GHz band, all while keeping backwards compatibility with existing 802.11b gear. This is a very promising technology—so promising, in fact, that the lack of ratification didn't stop some manufacturers from shipping gear that used the draft standard, even before it was ratified. In addition, those same manufacturers continue to push the envelope with development of proprietary extensions to 802.11g that can double raw speeds to 108Mbps and faster.

Pros

- Very high data rates of up to 54 Mbps, and up to 108Mbps with proprietary vendor extensions.

- Backwards compatibility with the phenomenally popular 802.11b offers a simple upgrade path for existing users.

- 802.11g uses the same band as 802.11b, so existing antennas and feed lines can be reused.

Cons

- As it uses the 2.4 GHz ISM band, 802.11g will have to contend with many other devices, leading to more interference in crowded areas.

Recommendation

If you are building a network from scratch, strongly consider the benefits of 802.11g. It allows existing 802.11b users to continue to use the network, while providing a significant speed boost for 802.11g users. 802.11g is a massively popular technology, as it provides many of the advantages of 802.11a without significantly raising cost or breaking backwards compatibility. Since it offers many advantages with relatively few drawbacks, it is already the next massively ubiquitous wireless technology.

802.16: WiMAX Long Distance Wireless Infrastructure

Approved on December 6, 2001, 802.16 promises to be the answer to all of the shortcomings of long distance applications that people have encountered using 802.11 protocols. It should be pointed out that the 802.11 family was never intended to provide long distance, metropolitan-area coverage (although this book shows you some examples of people doing exactly that). The 802.16 specification is specifically designed for providing wireless infrastructure that will cover entire cities, with typical ranges measured in kilometers. It will use frequencies from 10 to 66 GHz to provide commercial quality services to stationary locations (i.e., buildings).

In January 2003, a new extension (802.16a) was ratified, which will operate in the 2 to 11 GHz range. This should help significantly with line-of-sight requirements of the extremely short waves of 10 to 66 GHz. Realistically, actual equipment that implements 802.16 is just now coming to market, and is priced well above the consumer-grade equipment of the 802.11 family.

Pros

- 802.16 is designed for long-range networking, likely providing ranges of 20 to 30 kilometers.
- Very high speed for fixed wireless, probably about 70 Mbps.

Cons

- Shorter wavelengths of 10 to 66 GHz are more susceptible to signal fade due to environmental conditions (such as rain).
- Many bands used by 802.16 and 802.16a are licensed spectrum.
- Standards-based equipment is only just available, and very expensive.

Recommendation

It will be interesting to see the 802.16 story as it evolves, but it's too early to tell how this technology will fare. 802.16 will certainly be a welcome technology for long distance point-to-multipoint applications, which are difficult to implement effectively using 802.11.

Bluetooth: Cable Replacement for Devices

While the 802.11 protocols were designed to replace the ubiquitous CAT5 networking cable, Bluetooth aims to replace all of the *other* cables connected to your computer (with the sad exception of the power cable). Operating as a frequency hopper in the 2.4 GHz ISM band, it shares the same spectrum as 802.11b/g and many other devices. It is designed to create a so-called "Personal Area Network" for devices like cell phones, digital cameras, PDAs, headsets, keyboards and mice, and of course, computers. While it is possible to use Bluetooth for an actual Internet connection, it seems to be better suited for low-bandwidth data and voice applications.

Pros

- Very low power requirements, making it ideal for small battery-powered devices such as handhelds, phones, and headsets.
- Simple interface and security model.
- Exceptional interoperability between devices.
- Built-in support for simultaneous data and voice traffic.

Cons

- Relatively low data throughput (about 720 Kbps maximum).
- Shares the 2.4 GHz band with many other devices, including 802.11b/g.
- Very limited range, by design.

Recommendation

Bluetooth uses an aggressive full-duplex frequency-hopping scheme (changing channels up to 1,600 times per second) to attempt to avoid noise in the 2.4 GHz band. While this may be good for Bluetooth, high power frequency-hopping devices can cause considerable interference for other devices using the band. Fortunately, most Bluetooth products operate only at 1 mW, keeping most interference limited to a very small area. Even when using Bluetooth alongside an 802.11b connection, the perceived interference turns out to be minimal, and most people don't even notice the difference with normal usage. If you are using 802.11a in the presence of Bluetooth devices, the two will not interfere with each other at all.

The 802.11 protocols and Bluetooth are complementary and solve very different problems. I show you some cool things you can do with Bluetooth in Chapter 2, and much of the rest of this book focuses on fun with 802.11.

900 MHz: Low Speed, Better Coverage

In the days before 802.11, a number of FCC Part 15 wireless networking products were competing in the marketplace. For example, Aironet, Inc. (before it was bought by Cisco) produced the Arlan networking series. The Arlan APs and bridges use 10baseT Ethernet, operate at 900 MHz, and have a data rate of 215 Kbps or 860 Kbps. They also made a number of complementary PCMCIA radio cards (the 655-900, 690-900, and PC1000, for example). These devices put out up to a whopping 1 Watt at 900 MHz. NCR had the WaveLAN 900 MHz line that included an ISA and PCMCIA card that would push 2 Mbps at 250 mW. While the data rate can't compare to modern wireless networking gear, the higher power and lower frequency of this equipment offers significant advantages.

As the frequency of a signal increases, the apparent range it can cover at the same power and gain decreases. For example, a 100 mW signal at 5.8 GHz appears to travel less than half the distance of a 100 mW signal at 2.4 GHz, which appears to travel less than half that of a 100mW signal at 900 MHz. There is no limit to how far a signal can actually go, but its ability to rise above the background noise and be detected at a usable level is bounded by its power, frequency, and antenna gain. So to put it simply, all other variables being equal, lower frequency signals travel further than higher frequency signals. You can make higher frequency signals appear to travel further, but to do so you need to increase the power, antenna gain, or both.

Another curious property of radio is that the requirement of having line of sight between the devices becomes more important at higher frequencies, but is less critical at lower frequencies. Higher frequencies don't fare so well when there are obstacles between the ends of the radio link (particularly in urban and indoor settings). This property, combined with the advantage of greater range, means that 900 MHz equipment can be used in a variety of situations where 802.11b/g or 802.11a don't fare as well. It can penetrate foliage, buildings, and other obstacles better than its 802.11 counterparts. Of course, the big trade-off is throughput.

Pros

- Higher power and superior range.
- Equipment doesn't compete with the increasingly crowded 2.4 GHz ISM band, but must still tolerate 900 MHz phones, video cameras, baby monitors, and other devices.

Cons

- Low data throughput, from serial speeds of 9,600 bps up to 2 Mbps or so.
- Very little vendor interoperability.
- With the advent of 802.11 networking, 900 MHz gear has increasingly limited availability and compatibility with newer operating systems.
- Equipment can be quite expensive compared to 802.11 gear.

Recommendation

A number of manufacturers offer serial or Ethernet to 900 MHz bridges. While Ethernet is generally preferable, the serial devices are perfectly capable of supporting a PPP connection between two sites. If you need to create a long distance point-to-point link (particularly where clean line of sight just isn't possible) and can cope with limited data rates, then this equipment might be right for your project. Expect the hardware to be difficult to locate and a bit more expensive than the typical consumer grade 802.11b equivalent.

CDPD, 1xRTT, and GPRS: Cellular Data Networks

When it comes to data rates, most people are in agreement that faster is better. But current communications technology always involves a trade-off between speed, power, and range. 54 Mbps may be great if you can get it, but can be difficult to maintain on a large scale. The 802.11 protocols compensate for increased range by scaling back the data rate, but these devices simply aren't designed to serve hundreds of people scattered over many miles.

There are times when any data to the Internet is better than none at all, no matter how slow it might be. For example, you might need to log in to a remote machine or send a quick email while traveling, when Wi-Fi or even wired network access just isn't available. Or maybe you want to have an alternate communications channel into a wireless node in a remote place (say, on a mountaintop or deep in the woods) where telephone lines aren't even available. For these situations, you might consider exploiting the biggest advantage of the commercial mobile data networks: their ubiquity.

Mobile networks maybe be slow and relatively expensive, but you can't beat their coverage compared to current Wi-Fi networks. They can give you an IP address just about anywhere, but be warned that most mobile data services are not cheap. Most charge by the byte, and all charge for airtime while you are using it.

The type of data service you can use depends on the underlying wireless technology. Obviously, before choosing a technology, determine the coverage area of the mobile network in the place you intend to use it. The three leading mobile data services are described next, in decreasing order of availability in the United States.

CDPD on TDMA

CDPD stands for *Cellular Digital Packet Data*. It works over the enormously popular *Time Division Multiple Access* (TDMA) mobile network, which is easily the most widely deployed mobile network in the United States. CDPD "modems" typically use a serial port or PCMCIA slot and offer speeds of up to 19.2 Kbps (real world is typically closer to 9,600 bps).

All of the TDMA operators are generally migrating to GSM, so it is probably unlikely that TDMA data services will ever be upgraded. In some areas, TDMA is being phased out altogether, making it difficult to obtain a CDPD account. But despite the relatively slow speed of CDPD, you can't beat its coverage. Virtually all of the populated regions of the United States are covered by TDMA.

1xRTT on CDMA

CDMA stands for *Code Division Multiple Access*: it is the second most popular mobile technology in the United States. The original CDMA data services offered speeds of 9600 bps to 14.4 Kbps. 1xRTT boasts speeds of up to 144 Kbps, but by many reports, real-world throughput is somewhere between 60 and 80 Kbps, occasionally bursting to 144 Kbps if you get lucky. If you think the 802.11 protocol names aren't confusing enough, you should really try following mobile phone technology. 1xRTT is also known in various circles as CDMA2000 Phase 1, or simply 95-C.

1xRTT is just the first phase of the CDMA2000 plan. A few communities are lucky to have the newer 1xEV-DO technology, which can theoretically achieve 2 Mbps from fixed locations over CDMA. This technology hasn't yet been widely deployed.

GPRS on GSM

GPRS stands for *General Packet Radio Service*, and is the data service available on *Global System for Mobile communications* (GSM) networks. The original GSM data services offered only 9,600 bps throughput, but GPRS allows real-world speeds of 20 to 30 Kbps. GPRS is a packet-based protocol, meaning that the GPRS radio transmits only when it actually has data to send. This can save on battery usage, and theoretically makes more efficient use of the network. A number of nifty gadgets such as the HipTop by Danger (*http://www.danger.com/*) use GPRS for connectivity.

Eventually, GPRS will be replaced by technologies like *Enhanced Data for Global Evolution* (EDGE—you have to ask yourself how they can use these acronyms with a straight face), which offers theoretical speeds of up to 384 Kbps over GSM. EDGE is still experimental, and hasn't yet been widely deployed. GSM coverage is increasing rapidly in the United States, but still isn't as ubiquitous as CDMA or TDMA. Much of the rest of the world has a more thoroughly deployed GSM network.

If you find that you need simple wireless connectivity beyond what you can hope to provide with 802.11 technologies, commercial data networks are a viable alternative. They don't come cheap, but can be perfect for many low-bandwidth applications.

FRS and GMRS: Super Walkie-Talkies

In the last couple of years, a number of manufacturers have come out with "high power" radios for general use, marketed as family or recreational communication devices and sold as impulse buy items at department stores.

They claim a couple of miles of range, operate on a chargeable battery pack or AA batteries, and most are surprisingly rugged and simple to use.

The two technologies behind these popular radios are *FRS* and *GMRS*. While sold in similar packaging and frequently sitting on shelves right next to each other, these two types of radios are quite different in capabilities and operating rules.

FRS

FRS stands for *Family Radio Service*, and was approved by the FCC for unlicensed use in 1996. It operates around 462 and 467 MHz, and is sometimes referred to as "UHF Citizens Band." It is *not* a Part 15 device like 802.11 radios, but is governed by FCC Part 95, *Personal Radio Services*. FRS radios share some channels with GMRS radios but are restricted to 500 mW maximum power. Manufacturers typically claim two miles as the maximum range of FRS radios. FRS radios come with fixed antennas, and cannot be legally modified to accommodate antennas or amplifiers.

FRS channels 1 through 7 overlap with GMRS and can be used to communicate with GMRS radios. If you need to talk only to other FRS radios, use channels 8 through 14 to avoid possible interference with low band GMRS users. See Table A-1 for the full list of FRS and GMRS frequencies.

Table A-1. FRS and GMRS frequencies

Lower frequency	Upper frequency	Purpose
462.550	467.550	GMRS "550"
462.5625	N/A	FRS channel 1, GMRS "5625"
462.575	467.575	GMRS "575"
462.5875	N/A	FRS channel 2, GMRS "5875"
462.600	467.600	GMRS "600"
462.6125	N/A	FRS channel 3, GMRS "6125"
462.625	467.625	GMRS "625"
462.6375	N/A	FRS channel 4, GMRS "6375"
462.650	467.650	GMRS "650"
462.6625	N/A	FRS channel 5, GMRS "6625"
462.675	467.675	GMRS "675"
462.6875	N/A	FRS channel 6, GMRS "6875"
462.700	467.700	GMRS "700"
462.7125	N/A	FRS channel 7, GMRS "7125"
462.725	467.725	GMRS "725"
467.5625	N/A	FRS channel 8

Lower frequency	Upper frequency	Purpose
467.5875	N/A	FRS channel 9
467.6125	N/A	FRS channel 10
467.6375	N/A	FRS channel 11
467.6625	N/A	FRS channel 12
467.6875	N/A	FRS channel 13
467.7125	N/A	FRS channel 14

GMRS

GMRS stands for *General Mobile Radio Service*, and is also known as "Class A Citizens Band." Its use is also covered by FCC Part 95, but requires a license to operate. As of this writing, a personal license costs $75 and can be obtained online at *http://wireless.fcc.gov/uls/*.

Handheld GMRS units can put out up to 5 Watts of power, although 4-Watt handhelds are more common. While fixed-base stations can use up to 15 Watts on most frequencies, they are restricted to 5 Watts when communicating on the FRS channels. Repeater stations are allowed and can transmit as high as 50 Watts. Both fixed-base stations and repeaters can only transmit on the lower "462" frequencies, while handhelds can operate on any GMRS frequency. Again, see Table A-1 for the full list of FRS and GMRS frequencies. GMRS gear can include removable antennas, making it simple to use a handheld with a car mount or stationary antenna. Combined with the ability to use repeaters, GMRS can be used to communicate over considerable distances.

Typically, handheld GMRS units use lower frequencies to communicate with each other when possible, and transmit on the upper frequencies (while listening 5 MHz lower) to talk to a repeater. This allows anyone listening on the "462" side to hear traffic both from handhelds as well as from anyone using the repeater. Always use the lower frequencies and the lowest power settings whenever possible to help avoid unnecessary interference with other GMRS users. Use repeaters only when you can't otherwise establish communications.

Extending Range

While higher power radios can help extend your range a little, the best method for increasing your range is to increase your altitude. UHF radios can reach significantly further when the antenna is high in the air, even with limited power. This is one reason why the Part 95 rules limit "small control stations" to antennas no more than 20 feet higher than the structure to which they are mounted. To make the best use of your FRS or GMRS radio, find high ground when transmitting. In some cases, this can push your available range out many, many miles. If you are using a GMRS radio, attaching it to a tall antenna can significantly improve your effective range.

While these radios are half duplex and allow only limited data transmissions, they are handy in a number of situations. For example, when fine tuning a long distance point-to-point 802.11 link, you may find them far more useful than mobile phones. Any time you are working far away from a city, particularly on hills and mountains, FRS and GMRS radios can work considerably better than a phone. But don't get any bright ideas about connecting a radio to a telephone patch; this is prohibited on both FRS and GMRS.

This writing is by no means authoritative on the labyrinthine FCC rulebook, but should give you an idea of what each technology is good for. If in doubt, see the rules for yourself online at *http://www.access.gpo.gov/nara/cfr/waisidx_00/47cfr95_00.html*. If you are looking for more information about FRS and GMRS, there is also a wealth of information available from the Personal Radio Steering Group at *http://www.provide.net/~prsg/rules.htm*.

802.1x: Port Security for Network Communications

The 802.1x protocol is actually not a wireless protocol at all. It describes a method for port authentication that can be applied to nearly any network connection, whether wired or wireless.

Just when you thought you knew every IEEE spec relating to wireless, suddenly 802.1x appeared on the scene. The full title of 802.1x is "802.1x: Port Based Network Access Control." Interestingly enough, 802.1x wasn't originally designed for use in wireless networks; it is a generic solution to the problem of port security. Imagine a college campus with thousands of Ethernet jacks scattered throughout libraries, classrooms, and computer labs. At any time, someone could bring their laptop on campus, sit down at an unoccupied jack, plug in, and instantly gain unlimited access to the campus network. If network abuse by the general public were common, it might be desirable to enforce a policy of port access control that permitted only students and faculty to use the network.

This is where 802.1x fits in. Before any network access (to Layer 2 or above) is permitted, the client (the *supplicant*, in 802.1x parlance) must authenticate itself. When first connected, the supplicant can only exchange data with a component called the *authenticator*. This in turn checks credentials with a central data source (the *Authentication Server*), typically a RADIUS server or other existing user database. If all goes well, the authenticator noti-fies the supplicant that access is granted (along with some other optional data) and the client can go about its merry way. The various encryption methods employed are not defined in particular, but an extensible frame-work for encryption is provided—the *Extensible Authentication Protocol* (EAP).

802.1x is widely regarded by the popular press as "the fix" for the problems of authentication in wireless networks. For example, the "other data" that is sent back to the supplicant could contain WEP keys that are dynamically assigned per session and are automatically renewed every so often, making most data collection attacks against WEP futile. Unfortunately, 802.1x has been found to be susceptible to certain session hijacking, denial of service, and man-in-the-middle attacks when used with wireless networks, making the use of 802.1x as the "ultimate" security tool a questionable proposition.

As of this writing, 802.1x drivers for Windows XP and 2000 are available, and many access points (notably Cisco and Proxim) support some flavor of 802.1x. There is also an open source 802.1x supplicant implementation project available at *http://www.open1x.org/*. It is possible to use the Host AP driver to provide authenticator services to a RADIUS server or other authen-tication server via the backend.

Unfortunately, the popular press tends to abbreviate 802.11a/b/g as 802.11x, which looks a lot like 802.1x—but don't be fooled. While it has an application in wireless networks, 802.1x actually has nothing to do with wireless networking. For a good discussion of 802.1x security methods and problems online, take a look at *http://www.sans.org/rr/wireless/802.11.php*.

WPA & 802.11i

The IEEE began work in 2001 on 802.11i, an amendment to the original 802.11 specifications. It was widely acknowledged that the original security standard of 802.11b, known as WEP (Wired Equivalent Privacy), was inade-quate and contained many security holes.

The original version of WPA was devised by the Wi-Fi Alliance in 2002 and was based on a draft version of the IEEE 802.11i protocol. WPA defined a subset of the draft 802.11i and was designed to be implemented on existing Wi-Fi hardware. WPA is an intermediate solution to improve the hopeless security quagmire of WEP while waiting for the full 802.11i standard to be ratified. WPA uses the Temporal Key Integrity Protocol (TKIP) to generate per-packet encryption keys, supports both external or preshared key authen-tication, and implements new key handshakes.

The IEEE working group approved the full 802.11i specifications in June 2004. The Wi-Fi Alliance has based their new WPA2 standard on the completed 802.11i. WPA2 supports the more robust AES encryption algorithms to replace TKIP. In addition, 802.11i mandates the use of 802.11x authentication. At the time of this writing, access points, wireless cards, and drivers that support WPA2 are just becoming available.

Pros

- WPA and WPA2 provide much improved forms of encryption and authentication.
- WPA is widely supported across Windows, Macintosh, Linux and BSD platforms.

Cons

- WPA2 requires AES encryption, which is very computationally intensive. Many older models of 802.11a/b/g cards and access points are not capable of supporting AES encryption.

Recommendation

If your cards and access points support WPA or WPA2, there is absolutely no reason not to go ahead and use it. You will have a robust form of encryption which is difficult, if not impossible, to hack. You'll also be able to leave behind WEP and its various security holes. The only reason to skip WPA2 is financial—if your cards and APs don't support AES encryption, you'll need to upgrade to get the full benefits of WPA2.

BSS Versus IBSS

802.11b/g defines two possible (and mutually exclusive) radio modes that stations can use to intercommunicate. Those modes are *BSS* and *IBSS*.

BSS stands for *Basic Service Set*. In this operating mode, one station (the *BSS master*, usually a piece of hardware called an *access point*) acts as a gateway between the wireless and a wired (likely Ethernet) backbone. Before gaining access to the wired network, wireless clients (also called *BSS clients*) must first establish communications with an access point within range. Once the AP has authenticated the wireless client, it allows packets to flow between the client and the attached wired network, either routing traffic at Layer 3, or acting as a true Layer 2 bridge. A related term, *Extended Service Set* (ESS), refers to a physical subnet that contains more than one access point (AP). In this sort of arrangement, the APs can communicate with each other to allow authenticated clients to "roam" between them, handing off IP information as the clients move about. Note that (as of this writing) there are no APs that allow roaming across networks separated by a router.

IBSS (*Independent Basic Service Set*) is frequently referred to as Ad-Hoc or Peer-to-Peer mode. In this mode, no hardware AP is required. Any network node that is within range of any other can communicate if both nodes agree on a few basic parameters. If one of those peers also has a wired connection to another network, it can provide access to that network.

Note that an 802.11b radio must be set to work in either BSS or IBSS mode, but cannot work in both simultaneously. Also, BSS Masters (that is, APs) cannot speak to each other over the air without using WDS or some other tricky mechanism.

Generally speaking, most 802.11b networks consist of one or more BSS Master devices (like a hardware access point, or a general-purpose computer running the Host AP driver [Hack #63]) and several BSS clients (laptops, handhelds, etc). Ad-Hoc networks, on the other hand, are handy for setting up a point-to-point connection between two fixed devices, or if a couple of laptops need to exchange files and there is no other wireless network present.

In the early days of 802.11b, many manufacturers implemented their own version of Ad-Hoc mode, sometimes referred to as Peer-to-Peer or Ad-Hoc Demo mode. Such devices could only communicate with each other and weren't compatible with true IBSS mode. Recent firmware updates have helped IBSS mode interoperability quite a bit, but not all cards can communicate with each other when speaking IBSS. Generally, any client device can talk to any access point regardless of the manufacturer, provided that both are certified to speak 802.11b/g.

Wireless Hardware Guide

Hacking on 802.11 devices can come with a corresponding confusion fac-tor. Why do you need a pigtail? Isn't that what little girls wear? What on earth is LMR cable? Why do I need it? What is a RP-TNC connector, and where would I find one?

This appendix attempts to answer these questions and more, by discussing a number of common wireless hardware parts that you will run across.

Microwave Cabling

Not all coaxial cable is appropriate for 2.4 GHz use. The same cable that delivers high quality video and audio to your TV is nearly useless for con-necting microwave antennas. Choosing the proper type and length of cable is just as important as choosing the right antenna for the job. A 12 dB sector antenna is useless if you lose 18 dB in the cable that connects it to the radio. While all cable introduces some loss as signal travels through it, some types of cable do better than others at 2.4 GHz.

LMR is a kind of coax cable made by Times Microwave, and is possibly the most popular type of cable used for extending 802.11b networks. LMR uses a braided outer shield and solid center conductor, and comes in various sizes.

Heliax is another kind of microwave cabling made by Andrew. It is made of a semi-rigid corrugated outer shell (a sort of flexible copper tubing), rather than the braided strands found in coax. The center conductor can either be solid or a corrugated tube inner conductor. It is designed to handle loads *much* greater than (legal) 802.11b installations, is very expensive, and can be difficult to work with. It is also extremely low loss. The foam dielectric type part numbers start with LDF.

Don't mess with *air dielectric* unless you enjoy the challenge of keeping your feed lines pressurized with nitrogen. Air dielectric cable at 802.11b power levels is like the proverbial elephant gun to kill the mosquito.

In addition to Times Microwave and Andrew's offerings, Belden also makes a very common piece of cable that works okay in the 2.4 GHz range. You'll frequently see references to "9913"; this is Belden 9913.

The properties of some common cables are provided in Table B-1. Generally speaking, the thicker and better built the cable, the lower the loss (and the higher the cost). Cable in excess of half an inch or so in thickness is difficult to work with, and it can be hard to find connectors for it. Whenever possible, order the specific length you need, with the proper connectors pre-installed, rather than try to cut and crimp it yourself. A commercial outlet will usually have the tools and experience needed to make a well-built cable. The best cable in the world won't help you if your connector isn't properly installed.

Table B-1. Attenuation, size, and approximate cost of microwave coax

Cable type	Diameter	Loss in db/100' at 2,500 MHz	Approximate price per foot
LMR-200	0.195"	16.9	$0.37
LMR-400	0.405"	6.8	$0.64
LMR-600	0.509"	4.4	$1.30
LMR-900	0.870"	3.0	$3.70
LMR-1200	1.200"	2.3	$5.50
Belden 9913	0.405"	8.2	$0.97
LDF1-50	0.250"	6.1	$1.66
LDF4-50A	0.500"	3.9	$3.91
LDF5-50A	0.875"	2.3	$2.27
LDF6-50	1.250"	1.7	$10.94
LDF7-50A	1.625"	1.4	$15.76

To sum up: use the best quality cable you can afford, at the shortest length possible. A couple of dB here and there really adds up when dealing with the very low power levels of 802.11b. If you want to put an antenna on the roof, you might look into weatherproof enclosures for your AP, and mount it as close to the antenna as possible. Then run your Ethernet cable as long as you need (up to 100 meters!).

Microwave Connector Reference

So you have the radio, an antenna, and a length of cable. How do you connect them together? You need to use connectors that work well in the 2.4 GHz range, fit the kind of cabling you're using, and mate with each other. Practically all common connectors have two halves, a male and a female (or a pin and a socket). A few of the more exotic types (such as the APC-7; see later in this section) are sexless, so any connector will match up with any other. Here are the most common connectors you are likely to encounter in the microwave bestiary.

The BNC (Bayonet Neill Concelman) connector, as shown in Figure B-1, is a small, cheap connector using a quick-connect half turn (the same connector found on 10base2 Ethernet). The BNC isn't well suited for 2.4 GHz use, but is mentioned here because, with the death of 10base2, the connectors are frequently sold for pennies per pound. Don't be tempted.

Figure B-1. BNC connector

The TNC (Figure B-2) is a threaded version of the BNC. The fine threads help eliminate leakage at microwave frequencies. TNCs work well all the way through 12 GHz, and are usually used with smaller (and higher-loss) cable.

An N (Neill) connector (Figure B-3) is a larger, threaded connector found on many commercial 2.4 GHz antennas. It is much larger than the TNC. It works very well on thicker cable (such as LMR-400) and operates well up to 10 GHz. The N is probably the most commonly encountered connector when dealing with 802.11b/g-compatible gear.

The connector commonly referred to as a "UHF" connector looks like a coarse-thread version of the N (Figure B-4). It is *not* usable for 2.4 GHz, but is sometimes confused with the N. According to the ARRL Microwave

Figure B-2. TNC connector

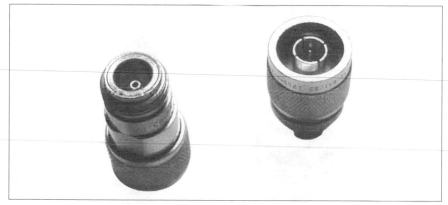

Figure B-3. N connector.

manual, it's a PL-259 (which mates with the SO-239 socket). It's not designed to work at microwave frequencies. Avoid this connector.

SMA (Sub-Miniature, variation A) connectors (Figure B-5) are very popular, small, threaded connectors that work great through 18 GHz. Their small size precludes using them with large, low-loss cable without using a pigtail.

The SMB (Figure B-6) is a quick-connect version of the SMC.

The SMC (Figure B-7) is a very small version of the SMA. It is designed to work well through 10 GHz, but accepts only very small cables.

The APC-7 (Amphenol Precision) connector, as shown in Figure B-8, is a 7mm sexless connector, usable through 18 GHz. It is a high grade connector manufactured by Amphenol, and is expensive, fairly rare, and very low loss.

Figure B-4. The so-called "UHF" connector

Figure B-5. SMA connector

Remember that each connector in the system introduces some loss. Avoid adapters and unnecessary connectors whenever possible. Also, commercially built cables tend to be of higher quality than cables you terminate yourself (unless you're really good and have the right tools). Whenever possible, try to buy a pre-made cable with the proper connectors already attached, at the shortest length you can stand. 802.11b gear doesn't put out much power, and every little bit helps extend your range and reliability. It's very easy to make a bad cable, and bad cables can cause no end of trouble.

When matching cables to your equipment, you may encounter connectors of reverse gender (sometimes called "reverse polarity," or male and female ends swapped with the same threads), reverse threading (lefthand instead of righthand thread), or even reverse gender reverse threading (both). For

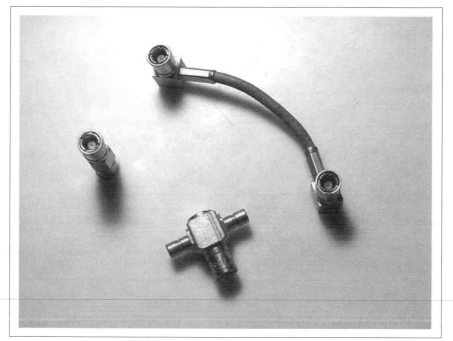

Figure B-6. SMB connector

Figure B-7. SMC connector (tiny!)

example, the popular WAP11 uses an RP-TNC. Make sure you know what you're getting before you order parts online!

Antenna Guide

The single most effective way to extend the range of your access point or client radio is to add an external antenna. Contrary to popular belief, antennas do *not* give you more signal than you started with (that's what amplifiers are for). They focus the available signal in a particular direction, much like

Figure B-8. APC-7, 7mm

what happens when you turn the focus head of a flashlight. It doesn't make the bulb any brighter, it just focuses what you have into a tighter space.

Focusing a flashlight gives you a brighter beam that covers a smaller total area, and likewise, more directional antennas give you a stronger perceived signal in a smaller area. All antennas are somewhat directional, and the measure of their directionality is referred to as *gain*. Typically, the higher the gain, the better the range (in the direction that the antenna radiates best in).

Another important characteristic of antennas is the phenomenon of polarization [Hack #100].

There are a few general types of antennas suitable for use at microwave frequencies. Each works well for its own application, and no single antenna works best for every application. When shopping for antennas, be sure to look at the actual radiation pattern of the antenna to be sure that it fits your needs.

Plan your goals ahead of time, and configure your network to meet those goals. The following sections describe the most common types of antennas, listed in rough order of increasing gain.

Omni

Omnidirectional antennas (or *omnis*) radiate outward in horizontal directions in a roughly equal manner. Imagine putting an enormous donut around the center pole of an omni: that's what the radiation pattern looks like. Omnis are good for covering a large area when you don't know which direction your clients might come from. The downside is that they also receive noise from every direction, and so typically aren't as efficient as more directional antennas.

As you can see in Figure B-9, they look like tall, thin poles (anywhere from a few inches to several feet long), and tend to be expensive.

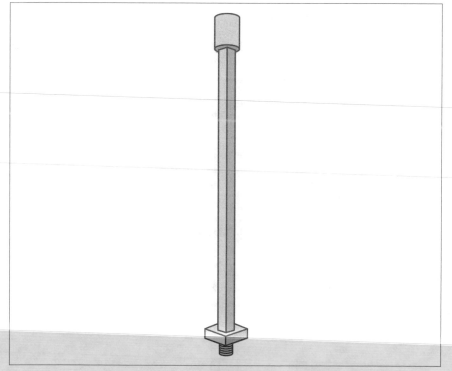

Figure B-9. An omni

The longer they are, the more elements they have (and usually the more gain and the higher the price). Small "rubber ducky" antennas ship standard with many access points, such as the Linksys WAP11 or the Cisco 350. Omni antennas are mounted vertically, like a Popsicle stick reaching skyward. They gain in the horizontal, at the expense of the vertical. This means that the worst place to be in relation to an omni is directly beneath (or above) it.

The vertical response improves dramatically as you move away from the antenna.

Sector (or Sectoral)

Sector antennas come in a variety of packages, from flattened omnis (tall, thin, and rectangular) to small flat squares or circles (Figure B-10). A close cousin of the sector is the *patch* antenna, which shares most of the same properties. Some are only a few inches across, and mount flat against a vertical wall or on a swivel mount. They can also be ceiling mounted to provide access to a single room, such as a meeting room, classroom, or tradeshow floor. As with omnis, cost is usually proportional to gain.

Figure B-10. A sector antenna, flat and thin

Picture an omni with a mirror behind it, and you'll have the radiation pattern of a sector antenna. Sectors radiate best in one direction, with a beam as wide as 180 degrees or as narrow as you like. They excel in point-to-multipoint applications, where several clients will be accessing the wireless network, all coming from the same general direction.

Yagi

As you can see in Figure B-11, a *yagi* looks something like an old television aerial. Some yagis are simply bare, like a flat Christmas tree, and are pointed vaguely in the direction of communications. Others are mounted in long horizontal PVC housings. They can work well in point-to-point or point-to-multipoint applications, and can usually achieve higher gain than sectors.

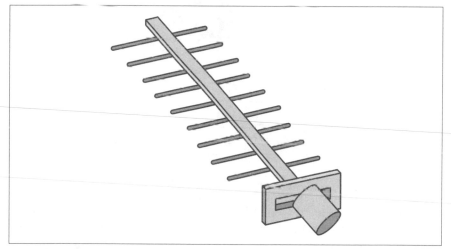

Figure B-11. A yagi

The typical beam width can vary from 15 degrees to as much as 60, depending on the type of yagi design. As with omnis, adding more elements means more gain, a longer antenna, and higher cost.

Waveguides and "Cantennas"

An increasingly popular antenna design is the waveguide. The so-called *cantennas* are simple antennas for home-brew designers to build, which offer very high gain for relatively little effort. Waveguides most closely resemble plumbing, in that they are boxes or cans with nothing in them but a tiny radiator. Figure B-12 shows an ambitious design, made from extruded and milled aluminum.

The Pringles can and coffee can antennas are examples of simple (but effective) home-brew cylindrical waveguide antennas. A rectangular waveguide can behave like a sector or an omni, depending on how it is constructed.

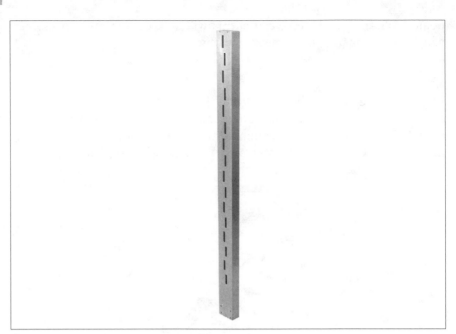

Figure B-12. A 16 dBi, horizontally polarized waveguide

Parabolic Dishes

In some ways, a dish is the opposite of an omni. Rather than try to cover a wide area, a dish focuses on a very tight space. Dishes typically have the highest gain and most directionality of any antenna. They are ideal for a point-to-point link, and nearly useless for anything else.

Figure B-13 shows a mesh antenna, although solid variations exist. Dishes come as small as 18" across or as big as you like (a 30-foot dish is possible, but probably not very convenient). A dish that can send an 802.11b/g signal more than 20 miles can be as small as a few feet across. In terms of gain for the buck, dishes are probably the cheapest type of antenna. Many people have been successful in converting old satellite and DSS dishes into 2.4 GHz dishes. Generally speaking, the difference between a mesh reflector and a solid reflector has little to do with gain, but is a consideration when mounting your dish, as solid dishes tend to pick up more load from the wind.

Putting It All Together

When trying to estimate what antennas will be required for a particular installation, I find it helpful to draw an overhead picture of the project site. Sketch out where you intend to install your equipment and where you expect your network clients to come from. Also include any obstacles (such

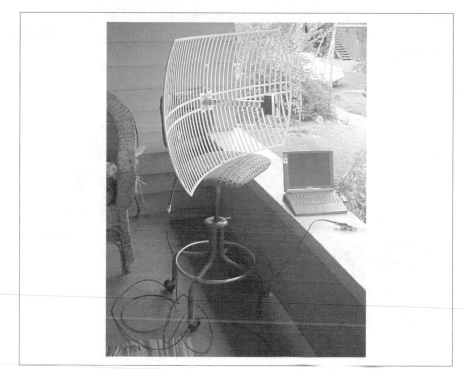

Figure B-13. A 24 dBi parabolic dish

as walls containing metal, or intervening buildings and trees on a long distance shot). This should help to determine your desired coverage area, as well as help suggest optimal placement of your access points and antennas.

For example, if you are trying to cover a large office with obstacles in the center (such as an elevator shaft or bathrooms), access points at opposite ends of the room with sector antennas pointed inward might make more sense than a single AP in the center with an omni. On a long distance shot, it might make more sense to go around an intervening tree or building by adding an extra hop, rather than trying to shoot through it with high gain dishes. Knowing the approximate radiation pattern and gain of your antennas ahead of time will help to focus your energy in the direction that you intend to use it, so you can design the most efficient network possible.

Pigtails

While some wireless equipment has no external antenna connector available at all, many devices ship with a tiny, non-standard port to accommodate an external antenna. Most antennas use a standard microwave connector, discussed above. Typically, to connect one to the other, you need a short length of cable with one of each sort of connector. This connector is commonly referred to as a *pigtail* adapter. A pigtail in all its glory is depicted in Figure B-14.

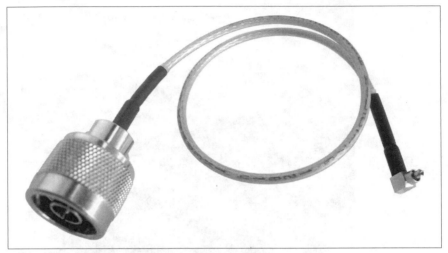

Figure B-14. Orinoco pigtail with an N male end

Pigtails are available from a number of sources. They typically sell for $10 to $20, depending on the length and type of cable, and what connectors you need on each end. Be sure that you know what sort of connector you need on the card side as well as on the antenna side. Most 802.11 manufacturers will also sell you a pigtail adapter for a phenomenally inflated price ($80 to $100 or more, for virtually the same piece of cable).

Pigtails have extremely high loss compared to a larger cable (such as LMR400), and usually use a cable such as LMR100 or LMR195. It is generally a good idea to keep your pigtail lengths as short as possible, and run larger, lower-loss cable for the bulk of your antenna run. Be sure to observe the type of connector, as well as the gender (male or female) that you need for either end. Adapters and gender changers can help in a pinch, but remember that excessive adapters will add unnecessary loss to your overall system.

The client card end of a pigtail is typically available in straight or right-angle versions. Both connectors have identical loss, but the best choice depends on the physical layout of your equipment. Most times, a right-angle connector is preferred, but depending on how your cable needs to run, a straight connector may work better. Also remember that the small end of the pigtail is very fragile, and will snap easily if pulled or forced into the connector. Use care when installing or removing pigtails, and whenever possible, tie off the cable to help eliminate cable stress on the connector. It is common to use a nylon zip tie to fasten the cable to the card itself, the chassis, or another stationary part.

When you are sure of the sort of pigtail you need for your application, consult the list of hardware vendors below.

802.11 Hardware Suppliers

Generally speaking, the typical consumer channels are great for obtaining radios, access points, and routers. But external antennas, adapters, pigtails, and cable can be harder to come by. On their quest for long-distance networking, many people find themselves dealing with general-purpose radio suppliers who have a great deal of knowledge about microwave gear, but very little experience with 802.11 devices.

Here is a list of popular suppliers for 802.11-related equipment. Among these vendors, you will find virtually everything you need for long-distance networking, from antennas and feed line to outdoor enclosures and weatherproofing supplies. Many of them will build cables to custom lengths with whatever connectors you require, for a reasonable fee. They offer a nice selection of various 802.11-specific equipment, as well as general-purpose radio gear. These vendors are listed for reference only, and shouldn't be interpreted as an endorsement by either myself or O'Reilly.

* Aeralix, Peabody, MA (*http://www.aerialix.com*)
* Antenna Systems and Supplies, Schaumburg, IL (*http://www. antennasystems.com*)
* Down East Microwave, Frenchtown, NJ (*http://www. downeastmicrowave.com*)
* ElectroComm, Denver, CO (*http://www.ecommwireless.com*)
* FAB Corp, Tampa Bay, FL (*http://www.fab-corp.com*)
* HD Communications, Ronkonkoma, NY (*http://www.hdcom.com*)
* Hyperlink Tech, Boca Raton, FL (*http://www.hyperlinktech.com*)
* Metrix, Seattle, WA (*http://metrix.net*)
* NetGate, Spokane, WA (*http://www.netgate.com*)
* NetNimble, Sacramento, CA (*http://www.netnimble.net*)
* Pasadena Networks, Pasadena, CA (*http://www.pasadena.net*)
* Superpass, Waterloo, Ontario, Canada (*http://www.superpass.com*)
* The RF Connection, Gaithersburg, MD (*http://www.therfc.com*)

With competition in the 802.11 market heating up, combined with the often confusing intricacies of wireless networking specifications, many vendors are realizing the importance of customer service. A good vendor should provide a great deal of information about their products online, and be willing to answer questions about your particular application.

Index

We'd like to hear your suggestions for improving our indexes. Send email to *index@oreilly.com*.

Colophon

Our look is the result of reader comments, our own experimentation, and feedback from distribution channels. Distinctive covers complement our distinctive approach to technical topics, breathing personality and life into potentially dry subjects.

The tool on the cover of *Wireless Hacks* is a wire cutter/pliers combo tool. It is typically used to cut or trim a piece of wire, and can bend it into an appropriate shape. In a pinch, it can also strip the insulation from heavy gauge wire, although a wire stripper is really the proper tool for that job. Its insulated handle provides a small measure of protection from electricity, but when using a wire cutter, be sure to first disconnect power from the wire you are cutting. Always wear eye protection when using a cutting device of any kind.

Philip Dangler was the production editor and proofreader for *Wireless Hacks*. Derek Di Matteo was the proofreader. Mary Brady and Colleen Gorman provided quality control. Ellen Troutman-Zaig wrote the index.

Ellie Volckhausen designed the cover of this book, based on a series design by Edie Freedman. The cover image is a photograph from the Stockbyte WorkTools CD. Linda Palo and Karen Montgomery produced the cover layout with QuarkXPress 4.1 using Adobe's Helvetica Neue and ITC Garamond fonts.

David Futato designed the interior layout. This book was converted by Keith Fahlgren to FrameMaker 5.5.6 with a format conversion tool created by Erik Ray, Jason McIntosh, Neil Walls, and Mike Sierra that uses Perl and XML technologies. The text font is Linotype Birka; the heading font is Adobe Helvetica Neue Condensed; and the code font is LucasFont's TheSans Mono Condensed. The illustrations that appear in the book were produced by Robert Romano and Jessamyn Read using Macromedia FreeHand MX and Adobe Photoshop CS. This colophon was written by Rob Flickenger.

Better than e-books

Buy *Wireless Hacks*, 2nd Edition, and access
the digital edition FREE on Safari for 45 days.

Go to www.oreilly.com/go/safarienabled
and type in coupon code AUJC-7NLL-LYIV-PWKE-79BJ

Search
thousands of
top tech books

Download
whole chapters

Cut and Paste
code examples

Find
answers fast

Search Safari! The premier electronic reference
library for programmers and IT professionals.